RESTORING THE PROMISE
OF AMERICAN LABOR LAW

Restoring the Promise

of American Labor Law

EDITED BY

SHELDON FRIEDMAN

RICHARD W. HURD

RUDOLPH A. OSWALD

RONALD L. SEEBER

ILR PRESS
ITHACA, NEW YORK

Library of Congress Cataloging-in-Publication Data

Restoring the promise of American labor law / Sheldon Friedman . . . [et al.],
editors
p.   cm.
Includes bibliographical references and index.
ISBN 0-87546-326-6 (acid-free paper)
1. Trade-unions—Law and legislation—United States.
2. Collective labor agreements—United States.   3. Labor laws and
legislation—United States.   I. Friedman, Sheldon.
KF3389.A2R47   1994
344.73'01—dc20
[347.3041]   94–539

Copies may be ordered through bookstores or directly from

ILR Press
School of Industrial and Labor Relations
Cornell University
Ithaca, NY 14853–3901

Printed on acid-free paper in the United States of America

5 4 3 2 1

In loving memory of my parents, Nat and Tillie.

—*Sheldon Friedman*

To Ellie, Alex, and Taylor for their humor, love, and companionship.

—*Richard Hurd*

To workers in their struggle for dignity and justice.

—*Rudolph Oswald*

For Ellen, Brent, Zach, and Keith.

—*Ronald Seeber*

Contents

Acknowledgments

This volume is the product of a conference jointly sponsored by the School of Industrial and Labor Relations at Cornell University and the Department of Economic Research at the AFL-CIO. A project such as this could not have been completed in such a timely manner at a high level of quality without the able assistance of a large number of individuals. The authors and anonymous referees all deserve thanks for completing their work in a speedy and devoted fashion. The discussants and the attendees at the conference, through their individual comments, have also contributed greatly to the quality of this volume.

Susan Barry and Janet Coco of the Economic Research Department at the AFL-CIO provided able assistance for the conference effort. This effort would not have proceeded so smoothly without their devoted work during the spring and summer of 1993. The editors and authors owe them an important and significant debt.

Before and after the conference, our efforts were directed to the timely publication of this book. We wished to get it into print as soon as possible so that it might contribute to the important debate on labor law reform, and this would not have been possible without the single-minded devotion of two individuals at Cornell University. Mike Belzer provided the editors with reviews and comments on all the papers. He also worked with many of the authors on revising their papers and made important suggestions to the contributors and to the editors. His advice could not have been replicated from any other source. Also deserving of praise is Theresa Woodhouse, without whose skills this manuscript might still lie in a pile of computer disks. We thank her and Mike for their contributions.

Finally, we acknowledge the important contributions of our colleagues and supporters at the ILR Press. Their tolerance for the quirks of the editors, the authors, and this project in general has been beyond the call of duty.

RESTORING THE PROMISE OF AMERICAN LABOR LAW

Introduction: The Context for the Reform of Labor Law

Sheldon Friedman, Richard W. Hurd,
Rudolph A. Oswald, and Ronald L. Seeber

The American system of collective bargaining is at a crossroads. Practitioners, academics, and policy makers are scrutinizing the U.S. method of workplace representation and the legal and institutional framework that undergird it and are questioning its capacity to protect workers' rights, to promote industrial peace, and to serve the economic interests of the United States. Some proponents of change focus on the failure of the system to deliver on the Wagner Act's fundamental promise that workers "shall have the right to self-organization, to form, join, or assist labor organizations, to bargain collectively through representatives of their own choosing, and to engage in other concerted activities for the purpose of collective bargaining or other mutual aid or protection." In the interests of increasing productivity and enhancing competitiveness, others propose modifying the framework for collective bargaining so as to promote labor-management collaboration more directly.

The time has come to raise public awareness about the seriousness of these problems and to initiate a wide-ranging national discussion that will lead to the formulation and implementation of badly needed reform. The last such national debate occurred in 1978, more than sixteen years ago, and ended in gridlock and inaction, despite the willingness of a substantial majority in the Congress to support modest but important changes. If anything, the same problems addressed in that debate are more pervasive now, and, in the meantime, new and significant issues have arisen.

It has become increasingly clear that the U.S. system of collective bargaining is no longer a realistic option for a large and growing proportion of American workers, and the situation will continue to worsen absent a major redirection of public policy. The decline in union density rates in this country is alarming to those who value and promote unionization. The extent to which this decline is due to management resistance and the failure of the law to promote collective bargaining is an important question that requires continued study and debate. Opinion polls reveal that for millions of nonunion American workers, workplace representation is an unfulfilled goal.

These and other concerns about the inadequacy of U.S. labor law motivated the Clinton Administration to create the Commission on the Future of Worker-Management Relations, chaired by John Dunlop and charged with examining the laws that govern and shape relations in America's workplaces. In the same spirit, the Department of Economic Research of the AFL-CIO and the School of Industrial and Labor Relations at Cornell University convened a conference on labor law reform in October 1993. Nearly forty papers and speeches advanced a variety of ways to correct the inadequacies in our system of union-management regulation.

This volume contains a selection of the papers from that conference, chosen to reflect the diversity of opinion and thought represented. While all of the views and policy recommendations expressed in the papers are not necessarily fully shared by the editors, the AFL-CIO, or Cornell, they are stimulating and provocative and deserve the widest possible discussion and debate. Our aim in producing this book is to stimulate public awareness about the need for fundamental reform of the legal and institutional underpinnings of the U.S. system of workplace representation and to offer proposals for the content of that reform.

All of the discussion that follows proceeds from the widely held view that collective bargaining between employers and the unions of their employees is a valuable institution worthy of promotion and dissemination. Of necessity, a well-functioning collective bargaining system requires a strong and independent labor movement. The clear preference of the editors and of the vast preponderance of the authors, therefore, is to find a means of strengthening the law so as to extend collective bargaining in the U.S. economy.

A few facts drawn from the papers highlight key concerns that were addressed at the conference. Dorothy Sue Cobble estimates that more than half of women workers are excluded from coverage under the National Labor Relations Act (NLRA). This reflects changes in both the economy and the employment relationship that have resulted in millions of American workers being stripped of the right granted under the act to choose independent workplace representation.

Kate L. Bronfenbrenner found that 75 percent of employers actively oppose unionization of their workforces. And nearly every antiunion device an employer uses, whether legal or illegal, has a measurable negative effect. Phil Comstock and Maier B. Fox, for instance, report that 36 percent of "no" voters in union representation elections explain their vote as a response to management pressure, and 86 percent of those mention fear of job loss specifically. This was perhaps the most consistent theme at the conference—the right of U.S. workers to organize and bargain collectively has become increasingly limited as a result of widespread employer practices, allowed by law and underregulated by the National Labor Relations Board (NLRB) and the courts.

Contrary to the concerns of some observers, researchers have found that the restrictions on company-dominated unions (Section 8(a)(2) of the Wagner Act) in no way limit labor-management cooperation. In fact, as James Rundle concludes, management violations of Section 8(a)(2) are nearly always associated with other antiunion activity. In 97 percent of the fifty-eight NLRB decisions involving 8(a)(2) violations since 1972, management either was found guilty of committing additional unfair labor practices or to have established the company union in direct response to a union organizing campaign.

Workers should not be denied the freedom to associate, to form and join organizations under their own control and of their own choosing, any more than African-Americans or other minorities should be denied their civil rights or women equal rights. Yet this basic right of U.S. workers has been in great peril in recent years. It is important that, through organizations of their own creation and control, workers deal with their employers as equals. Without such equality, society ultimately suffers.

The papers in the chapters that follow touch upon many subjects. We have attempted to group them in a way that provides ease of access to papers on a single subject while, at the same time, reflecting the scope of necessary labor law reform. Although many might quibble with the appropriate placement of an individual essay, it should be apparent that we have provided a representative sampling of papers that deal with all the important questions and debates.

The first section of the volume, "Historical Perspectives," provides the background necessary to understand the nearly sixty-year history of our current system of labor law. The second and third sections focus on specific aspects of the National Labor Relations Act. The second section, "Organizing and the Law," contains four papers that address the experiences of workers, unions, and managers during organizing campaigns. The third section, "Reforming the NLRA," addresses issues related to the reform of the conduct of collective bargaining. The fourth section, "The Outcomes of Bargaining Relationships," offers a look at several key economic and social benefits of collective bargaining and unionism. The fifth section, "Comparative Perspectives," draws upon experiences of other industrialized nations, particularly Canada. The sixth and final section, "Frameworks for Change," provides alternative views of the overall goals of labor law reform and the means by which to achieve them. The rest of this introduction provides a more detailed description of each of the sections and the papers contained therein.

The stage is set, in the first section of the volume, by Joel Rogers, David Brody, and James A. Gross, respectively. Rogers argues that changes in the United States and the global economy have made the U.S. legal and institutional framework for workplace representation increasingly outmoded and ill suited to contemporary economic realities. He advocates the development of a new framework that would provide minimum standards of workplace representation for all workers and a wider array of forms of representation.

Rogers advocates placing these reforms in a broader context of improvements in the "social wage" and a new international trading regime based on observance of labor standards and respect for workers' rights, enforced by a calibrated system of social tariffs. He sees the labor movement as the principal agent for achieving this ambitious and far-reaching program, but for that to happen, labor would have to once again become a mass social movement.

Brody describes and analyzes the history of the U.S. system of workplace representation, which culminated in the passage of the Wagner Act in 1935. Most important, the essay draws lessons from this historical experience that are relevant to today's labor law reform debates. Brody examines how the Wagner Act's strict prohibition against employer domination of labor organizations demonstrated a clear choice between alternative frameworks for workplace representation and a clear rejection of the national experiment with corporatism under the National Recovery Administration, prior to the adoption of the Wagner Act.

Gross calls attention to the conflicting statements of purpose in the Taft-Hartley Act and argues convincingly that, as a result, much of the original intent of the Wagner Act has been frustrated. The situation has been worsened by the extreme politicization of the NLRB and substantial intervention into labor policy by the judiciary. The core issues underlying national labor policy, according to Gross, are fundamentally moral and ethical, not legal, economic, or competitive. He advances a powerful case in support of the proposition that there should be an underlying moral basis for U.S. labor policy.

The second group of essays address the current state of workers' rights to organize under current law. Richard W. Hurd and Joseph B. Uehlein report on a survey on union organizing undertaken by the AFL-CIO's Industrial Union Department. Their essay summarizes 19 case studies that are broadly representative of the 213 that were submitted by twenty-one unions. These cases document widespread and often abusive employer opposition to union organizing efforts. Although much of this behavior is illegal, the enforcement and penalties are so weak that they do not deter the widespread violations the authors document.

Management consultants have become so bold and so contemptuous of the weakness of the labor law that repeat violations are common, even after their clients are found guilty of unfair labor practices and are required to post "cease and desist" orders. In one particularly egregious but telling case, a union-busting consultant was ordered to post a cease and desist order seven years after a representation election that was found to be tainted by his extensive unfair labor practices; he posted the notice on the seat of his employees' toilet.

Bronfenbrenner reports on a major survey of union organizers. She also found that employer opposition was widespread and often effective in thwarting organizing. Fully 70 percent of employers used a management consultant for their campaigns, and an additional 15 percent used an outside law firm. Overall, more than 75 percent of employers conducted active antiunion campaigns. Tactics used included discharges, captive audience meetings, supervisor one-on-ones, wage increases, promises of improvements, promotion of union leaders, antiunion committees, small-group meetings, letters, and leaflets. Lower union win rates were associated with most of these tactics. Stipulated or board-ordered units that were different from units requested in the petition also had a negative impact on election outcomes.

Comstock and Fox draw on the more than 150,000 telephone interviews the Wilson Center for Public Research has conducted over the last fourteen years of nonunion workers. Based on these interviews, they acknowledge a decline in interest in unionization during the late 1970s and early 1980s but report that worker interest has increased appreciably since then. Women, minority, and younger workers, in particular, make up a large and fast-growing segment of the labor force that is substantially more interested in unionization today than ten years ago. Comstock and Fox suggest that the continuing decline in union density may thus be the result not of a lack of interest in unionization by workers but of the escalating use by employers of aggressive union-avoidance tactics.

The use of these tactics has been especially pronounced, and is especially effective, in frustrating organizing in workplaces where workers want and need unions the most: in firms where job satisfaction is low, where the desire for unionization is high, and where there are high concentrations of women, minority, or less skilled workers. Comstock and Fox conclude that one important explanation for the wide gap in union density between the United States and nearly every other industrial country is the extent to which U.S. employers are allowed to campaign actively and aggressively to prevent their employees from achieving independent collective representation.

Gordon R. Pavy's essay reports on the results of a major survey by the AFL-CIO and its Industrial Union Department on the degree of difficulty unions experience in obtaining first and subsequent collective bargaining agreements after victories in NLRB representation elections. Of all the election victories by unions in 1987, for example, first contracts were not achieved a third of the time and only about half the units involved in these victories were still under contract in 1993. Pavy's essay underscores the urgent need for reforms to protect the right of workers to collective bargaining even after union certification has been achieved.

The third set of papers—by Robert J. Pleasure and Patricia A. Greenfield, Morris M. Kleiner, Robert B. Moberly, James R. Rundle, and Gladys W. Gruenberg—address specific proposals for reforming the NLRA. Pleasure and Greenfield's essay makes the case that comprehensive proposals for labor law reform should be developed through a nonpartisan process similar to the one that led to the development of the Uniform Commercial Code (UCC). Such a process would involve reviewing not only labor law as it is narrowly defined but all aspects of employment and corporate law that impinge on workers as they strive to gain a measure of democratic control over their working lives. A narrower approach that focuses on specific deficiencies of labor law, it is argued, trivializes and understates the depth of worker and union dissatisfaction with the current framework. Viewed from this perspective, the work of the Dunlop Commission is a beginning, not an end. Pleasure and Greenfield emphasize, however, that the approach they are recommending is not an excuse for inaction or delay; urgently needed reforms should be adopted promptly and do not require waiting for the results of the longer-term, comprehensive review they are advocating.

Kleiner documents the skyrocketing increase in managerial violations of the NLRA, which he argues is attributable primarily to the weakness of the penalties for these violations under current law. He surveys the empirical literature on the relationship between the penalties and deterrence of violations by management and concludes that even increasing the penalty to no more than the average union wage in the potential bargaining unit would deter up to 29 percent of serious violations. The essay presents a range of policy options to effectuate improved management compliance with the law.

Complementary essays by Moberly and Rundle, respectively, address the important debate about the relationship between the NLRA's prohibition against employer-dominated labor organizations and the goal of promoting the new methods of work organization that are required by so-called high-performance workplaces. A number of government officials, academics, and management practitioners have raised concerns, in the wake of the recent *Electromation* and *Du Pont* decisions, that the NLRA's ban is or will become an impediment to the development of high-performance workplaces and thereby undermine the nation's economic competitiveness. Moberly examines the facts of the *Electromation* and *Du Pont* cases and concludes, after extensive analysis, that they do not support repeal or weakening of the ban on employer domination of labor organizations; quite the contrary, these cases underscore the continued need for the ban.

Rundle reaches a similar conclusion by a different route. His essay reports on empirical research centering on a comprehensive search for and review of every case since 1972 in which the NLRB ordered the disestablishment of an employee committee on grounds of employer domination. Relatively few disestablishment orders were found, and the number of such orders has been declining in recent years, despite the proliferation of workplace committees. More important, Rundle did not find a single instance in which a disestablishment was ordered in the absence of one or more of the following facts: (1)

the employer in question committed one or more *other* unfair labor practices concurrently with the 8(a)(2) violation, including interrogations, threats, surveillance, discharge for union activity, and refusal to bargain; (2) the employer started the committee in response to a union organizing drive; or (3) the committee, by the employer's own admission, had nothing to do with quality, productivity, or worker empowerment. Rundle therefore concludes that there is not a single case of this type that demonstrates the need to relax or modify the prohibition against employer domination.

Legislative proposals to improve employer compliance with the duty to bargain, broadly, is the focus of Gruenberg's essay. She argues that the promise of the employer's duty to bargain is not insubstantial even under current law but that weak enforcement and inadequate penalties seriously undercut delivery on that promise. She proposes a series of specific legislative remedies to foster and promote true collective bargaining, in deed as well as in name. Among these is a proposal to eliminate the judicially imposed distinction between mandatory and permissive subjects of bargaining, an unlegislated legalism that has prevented workers from achieving redress through collective bargaining to a large and growing number of pressing workplace problems.

The fourth group of essays focuses on three important social and economic dimensions of trade unionism: (1) the special importance of trade unionism to women and minority workers and the related role of unions in narrowing the male-female earnings gap; (2) the role of trade unionism in promoting the development of a skilled workforce by encouraging investments in worker training and skill upgrading; and (3) the potential importance of unions in facilitating the application of technology and other workplace innovations in ways that are socially responsible and economically desirable.

The essay by Roberta Spalter-Roth, Heidi Hartmann, and Nancy Collins asks and answers the question "What do unions do for women?" Based on extensive, original data analysis, the authors conclude that unions are of special importance in raising the earnings of women and minority workers and of all workers with low job tenure and in reducing the gap in their earnings relative to those of older white male workers. Unions reduce wage disparities overall by raising the wages of those at the bottom of the earnings spectrum the most. Unions also raise wages the most for those workers who are the least educated and who have worked the fewest years on the job. Thus, a good way to raise wages for women, minority, and less educated workers, and to create a more equal distribution of income in the United States, would be to increase union density and collective bargaining coverage.

Unions also play an important role in skill formation and training, as the essay by Hamid Azari-Rad, Anne Yeagle, and Peter Philips makes clear. This essay presents a case study of the impact of the repeal of Utah's prevailing wage law. The authors found that the repeal accelerated the decline in the union share of Utah's construction labor market, drove down construction wages in the state, and reduced the resources available for union apprentice-ship training in construction. This decline in training has not been offset by any other public or private source and has been exacerbated by the exit of experienced construction workers from the industry. The repeal of Utah's prevailing wage law, the authors therefore conclude, has led to a market failure in training and to a looming crisis in training for construction workers in Utah.

Charley Richardson argues that technology is radically transforming the workplace. The resulting changes cannot be counted on to be socially or economically beneficial in the absence of a strong independent voice for workers, through their unions. Far from encouraging such voice, current labor law is a serious impediment to it. The distinction between so-called manda-tory and permissive subjects of bargaining, in particular, often prevents unions from addressing critical issues of workplace technology in a serious way. Technology is also altering the balance of power in the workplace, weakening the power of workers and their unions in ways that the framers of the Wagner Act could not have imagined, while underscoring the urgent need for labor law reform.

The fifth group of essays addresses labor law reform from a comparative perspective. Three—those by Gary N. Chaison and Joseph B. Rose, Richard N. Block, and Peter G. Bruce—look north to Canada; the fourth essay, by Roy J. Adams, examines Western Europe. Each seeks to draw conclusions from experiences elsewhere and considers their implications for labor law reform in the United States.

Chaison and Rose explain that there is no single Canadian model, since the regulation of labor relations takes place primarily at the provincial level in Canada. But, despite the resulting diversity, there is a common theme: Workers are provided with a more unfettered right to choose unionism than in the United States, even if this right requires substantial government intervention in labor-management relations. It has been suggested that the protection in most Canadian provinces of workers' right to organize compels protection of their right to secure a first collective agreement and their right to strike without fear of losing their jobs to newly hired replacements. As Chaison and Rose note, the issue in Canada is not whether the playing field is "level" between labor and management but rather that workers' rights must be protected. This, they suggest, is reason enough to take a hard look at our neighbor to the north as a model for U.S. labor law reform.

Bruce's essay complements Chaison and Rose's by comparing the adminis-tration of labor law by the NLRB and by the Ontario Labor Relations Board with respect to unfair labor practices. He argues that the differences in labor law and its administration account for a substantial part of the large gap in union density between Canada and the United States. Bruce finds a much higher incidence of employer unfair labor practices in the United States than in the most populous and industrialized Canadian province. He attributes this difference to the relative weakness of the remedies available under U.S. law and to the more vigorous and effective regulation of employer misconduct in Ontario. He recommends specific reforms to strengthen the regulation of employer misconduct in the United States.

Identifying the key institutional differences between the U.S. and Canadian frameworks for workplace representation is the focus of Block's paper. These differences have the effect of disadvantaging workers and their unions, systematically and substantially, in the United States, according to Block. The resulting power relationships between employers, on the one hand, and workers and their unions, on the other, are very different in Canada than in the United States. Based on his comparison, Block concludes with a series of specific recommendations for labor law reform in the United States.

Adams's essay shifts the focus to Western Europe, where, it is noted, the presumption in most countries is that workers should have workplace representation as a basic right. In Adams's view, this presumption is entirely proper and, indeed, essential to the achievement of political and economic democracy. In the United States, by contrast, there is no such presumption. Rather, a small and decreasing proportion of the workforce enjoys the right to workplace representation. Workers who do not now have this right and who seek to assert it can do so only at great personal risk and heavy cost, and they must overcome intense and widespread employer opposition. In contrast to the Western European presumption in favor of workplace democracy, the presumption in the United States is in favor of workplace autocracy. Adams argues that instead of tinkering at the margins with reforms that at best would make it easier for a small proportion of the workforce to struggle successfully for workplace democracy, there should be systemic reform to guarantee workplace democracy for all.

The volume concludes with three essays that set forth alternative frameworks and principles for fundamental change in the system of workplace representation. Included are essays by Dorothy Sue Cobble, Howard Wial, and Françoise J. Carré, Virginia duRivage, and Chris Tilly.

Cobble and Wial specify the ways in which workforce and workplace changes require a new framework for workplace representation. Cobble calls attention to the large and growing proportion of workers in the postindustrial workplace who are women or minority members. Many of these workers, as well as many white male workers, would be better served by a model of unionism more reminiscent of the occupational unionism that dominated before the rise of industrial unionism in the 1930s. A variety of legal and institutional obstacles, however, make it difficult for this form of trade unionism to take hold and spread. Cobble enumerates the obstacles and offers specific policy recommendations to remove them and to encourage the development of a new occupational unionism.

Wial examines the tidal wave of corporate restructurings, the rise in subcontracting and interfirm alliances, the decrease in job security, and the implications of all of these trends for union organizing, collective bargaining, and the employment relationship. He suggests that trade unions should rely increasingly on multiemployer organizing and multiemployer collective bargaining as partial responses to these trends. He also describes the significant legal and institutional disincentives to multiemployer bargaining and organizing and suggests that the elimination of these disincentives, and their replacement with several specific positive incentives for multiemployer bargaining and organizing, should be included among the goals of labor law reform.

The final essay in the volume, by Carré, DuRivage, and Tilly, reviews the rise of contingent employment and addresses the implications of this trend for union organizing. Limitations of current labor law effectively disenfranchise this large and growing component of the workforce from access to independent collective representation. The essay details the specific deficiencies of current employment and labor law in this regard and provides specific recommendations for reform.

As this volume goes to press, there is reason to be hopeful that its essential message will be helpful in informing a critical and long-overdue public policy debate. Recent stirrings create new possibilities for positive change in the U.S. system of workplace representation. President Clinton's election in November 1992 and the subsequent appointment by the secretaries of labor and commerce, in March 1993, of the Commission on the Future of Worker-Management Relations, chaired by John Dunlop, is a significant and noteworthy step.

Although the focus of the commission is primarily economic competitiveness and productivity, it is clearly within its realm and charge to consider the issues raised in this book. For those who value a strong and independent trade union movement as a hallmark of an advanced economic democracy, the commission could offer some hope. Whether that hope will be matched by significant labor law reform remains an open question. For those who believe that collective bargaining is a system deserving of the widest possible use, the possibility of reform looms as a positive possibility. If this volume makes a contribution to public discussion that leads to the accomplishment and advancement of those goals, we will have achieved our immodest aims.

PART I
HISTORICAL PERSPECTIVES

1

Reforming U.S. Labor Relations

Joel Rogers

Labor, management, and neutrals all recognize that the New Deal system of labor relations, codified in the Wagner (1935) and Taft-Hartley (1947) acts, no longer works for the good of the U.S. economy. While it may have been well suited to the industrial society of the 1930–50s, when it helped deliver enormous growth in real income and productivity, the New Deal system has not adjusted to the "new economic realities" of the 1990s. It currently serves neither unions nor workers nor management effectively.

The New Deal system was designed to allow worker selection of exclusive union bargaining representatives through secret-ballot elections free of management interference and to buttress collective bargaining between such representatives and management as a way of dividing the economic pie between labor and capital. At the core of the Wagner Act was the conviction that union representation within firms was not only a moral imperative but an economic and political good. The basic economic idea was that workers, acting collectively, would be able to drive up wages. In a closed economy with unemployed resources, the resulting increase in demand would stimulate private investment and job growth. The basic political idea was that worker organization would help American democracy by providing a "countervailing power" to otherwise overwhelming business domination.

In thinking about the subject matter of this essay, I benefited from ongoing collaborations with Joshua Cohen, Daniel Luria, Wade Rathke, Charles Sabel, Wolfgang Streeck, and especially Richard Freeman. See Cohen and Rogers 1992, 1993, and forthcoming; Luria and Rogers 1993; Rathke and Rogers 1993; Rogers and Sabel 1993; Rogers and Streeck 1993, 1994a, and 1994b; and Freeman and Rogers 1993a, 1993b, 1993c, and forthcoming. The following draws freely from this joint work, but I hold all coauthors blameless for errors that have survived their care.

The core ideas of this system—that workers should enjoy associational rights inside and outside the firm and that collective worker organizations can contribute to the vitality of the American economy—remain perfectly sound today. The problem is that the particular ways in which the values of free association, equality, and democratic productivism were institutionalized in the New Deal system are increasingly inapposite to present circumstance.

The New Deal system effectively premised a sharp distinction between production workers, who were assumed to be solely concerned with wages and working conditions, and management, which was assumed to have full competence in running the enterprise; an essentially closed economy, with little international wage competition; the organization of production along "Fordist" and "Taylorist" lines, in which the dominant model of efficient production was a large firm featuring assembly-line mass production of standardized goods by unskilled and semiskilled labor; and the feasibility of providing a family wage and benefit package through lifetime jobs held by single male breadwinners. Put simply, the world described by these premises no longer exists—workers have other interests, management needs more worker involvement, the economy is more open, production is more flexible and quality-driven, jobs are less stable, the workforce is more diverse—and the system based on these premises works poorly in the world that exists today.

The costs of this institutional mismatch are visited on everyone. Unions—the only form of independent collective worker organization contemplated in the system—are effectively denied their right to organize, and escalating employer opposition is rapidly "disappearing" them as a presence in national public life. Individual managements, while generally welcoming the decline of unions, are limited in their ability to support advanced forms of worker participation in the nonunion sector. Workers are denied voice, choice of its form, and protection from economic insecurity. The nation as a whole suffers from lost productivity growth, rising inequality, a failure to block the "low-road" response to rising international competition, ineffective enforcement of labor standards, and, less tangible but no less real, the erosion of democratic norms.

For all the good reasons so many people have to be unhappy with the present system, however, there is currently no consensus on the elements of its reform, or even a sense of how consensus might be organized. Organized business and organized labor remain bitterly divided over their vision of the role of worker organization in the new economy. However unfairly, both are also generally regarded as self-serving in their proposals for reform. At the same time, each retains the power to block the other's favored agenda, and neither favors wholesale transformation of the present system of the sort that now seems needed. Not surprising given this background, the Clinton administration is deeply ambivalent on this topic. And among the general public, labor law reform is simply not an issue of great salience. In brief, labor law reform lacks a public constituency, as well as an articulate and credible agent.

Still, the ascent of a new Democratic administration and its appointment of the Commission on the Future of Worker-Management Relations has again put labor law reform on the national agenda, at least formally. And diffuse but accumulating dissatisfaction with the consequences of the present system create a potential general constituency for such an effort. The questions arise: Given the changed circumstances, what appear to be the general requirements of reform, and how might their satisfaction be organized? In what follows, I attempt to answer the first question in general terms. For the sake of concreteness in addressing the second, I focus on what is needed from one of reform's natural beneficiaries and most likely leaders—organized labor itself.

Requirements of Reform

In the old days of the New Deal and the postwar era, labor unions functioned as the redistributive agent of the working class. They operated in essentially closed national economies, where the state relied on fiscal and monetary policy to regulate the macroeconomy. They demanded and got wage and benefit increases for their members—partially extracted from firms directly, partly extracted through the state. And, through the alchemy of Keynesian economics, unions brought benefits to the broader society. By delivering solid and rising wage floors to their members, they boosted aggregate demand. This gave firms markets for sales and reasons to renew investment. And that, in turn, increased productivity and lowered the costs of mass-consumption goods, which benefited everyone. In ways instructive for the present, by doing something for its members or potential members—increasing their compensation—labor helped capital solve a problem it could not solve on its own—assuring the existence of mass markets. And by doing both these things—by showing the general economic gains to be had through a more democratic ordering of the economy—labor gained the resources and political cachet that came with being an agent of the general interest.

In retrospect, it is clear that this system stood on three pillars—a Keynesian, demand-based national policy framework; large, dominant, stable firms, through which wage agreements and other deals could be cut and effectively generalized; and ready-made blocks of workers within those firms, with comparable interests and susceptible to being organized to demand and enforce those agreements. Each of these pillars has since crumbled. A combination of market saturation and the entrance of new competitors into the saturated markets undercut the autonomy of national economies, uprooting the foundations of Keynesian policy. Firm responses to new competitive pressures (whether along the high road of diversified quality competition or the low road of sweating labor) have been dominated by strategies of decentralization, internal shrinkage, outsourcing, and a restless search for strategic partners—the net effect of which has been to make firms smaller, less stable, and less determinately bounded sites of worker organization. And through its division into numberless profit and cost centers, or through increased attention to its heterogeneous skills, or both, the workforce has become increasingly divided. Most of the unskilled or semiskilled are squeezed out of stable employment; the lucky few with stable jobs often find their interests closer to those of managers than to those of their less skilled, and less employed, colleagues.

In this context, redeeming the New Deal's core values of free association, equality, and democratic productivism will require more than a bit of work. The rough outlines of necessary reform, however, are clear enough. Forms of worker organization need to be amended in ways responsive to the greater diversity of employee interest and the potentially more autonomous role of workers in governing productive enterprises. The mechanisms of wage and benefit regulation need to be changed in ways responsive to decentralization and casualization in labor markets, to permit restructuring without diminution in the quality of life and to get some lower bound on income and welfare. And, throughout, labor relations needs to be seen through a supply-side optic as much as a demand-side one. For without the alchemy of Keynes, the contribution of democratic labor organization to general economic welfare will likely arise from labor's contribution to "effective supply"—of skilled labor, technology diffusion, comparability across establishments in ways that promote flexibility, links between firms in ways that promote general economic upgrading, private multipliers and supplements to state regulatory efforts—as much if not more than from its contribution to effective demand.

Free Association

Recognizing that free association is a good thing for diverse workers as well as others, and recognizing various imperfections in the "market" of the associational choice bearing on the representation of workers' interests, reform should aim to perfect that market. This means widening the range of employees permitted collective representation, reducing the direct cost of their choosing such, and widening the range of choice itself.

Widening the range of protected employees would mean abolishing most if not all restrictions on the free choice of farmworkers, individual contractors, and supervisors, as well as on those public employees in the half of the United States that has still not recognized even minimal rights to self-organization.

Reducing the direct costs to employees of choosing representation would mean institutionalizing respect for individual freedom in that choice and for collective worker deliberation about how that choice might best be made. At present, regarding the only available form of collective representation—

unions—this condition is clearly not satisfied. Whatever one's opinion of unions, current levels and kinds of employer resistance to them clearly impose direct costs on employees and corrupt the process of deliberation. Getting closer to free deliberation would thus appear to require more effective sanctions for such employer behavior, quickly applied.

Moreover, although informed consideration of the merits of alternatives is desirable, and takes time, some significant expediting and simplification of the current election process in ways respectful of free employee choice—in the form of a return to "card check" certification or very rapid elections— seem desirable. In labor relations, as in democracy generally, the law is simplified and strengthened by a presumption that those in whose name power is exercised have the capacity to exercise that power themselves. Choosing collective representation is a choice for workers, not managers, to make.

Finally, choices for collective representation in bargaining are meaningless if they are immediately frustrated by effective refusals to bargain. At present, in the United States, only about half the units won by unions in representation elections before the National Labor Relations Board ever make it to first contract. If employees want a union to negotiate for them, they should be assured the fruits of genuine negotiation. If the union and employer reach impasse, a neutral third-party arbitrator should be empowered to force agreement.

Application of the same principle of free employee choice, however, would mandate expansion of the range of forms of representation—a move that seems recommended in any case by the diversity of the employee population. There is no good reason to reify majority unionism as the only possible form of independent worker association. If a group of individual workers short of a majority in a relevant unit wishes to concert, to join a union, to present grievances to employers, or otherwise to act to advance their interests in the employment relation, there is no compelling reason they should not be permitted to do so—absent the prior and continuing existence of a majority union. Nor—assuming conditions of employee free choice are institutionally respected—is there a compelling reason representative committees or "employee caucuses" enjoying the support of management should not also be permitted.[1]

Equality

American labor markets, where the wages of most workers have been falling for years, are now marked by punishingly high degrees of inequality in

---

1. What such "institutional" respect for free choice might look like is suggested by Alan Hyde's (1993) proposal for an "employee free choice" defense to a Section 8(a)(2) complaint. Leaving the section intact, and assuming a return to the early breadth of that denoted by "labor organization":

wages and benefit compensation. For those at the bottom of our increasingly dispersed wage structure, the results are clearly horrible, and in comparative terms increasingly anomalous. (In real purchasing power parity terms, for example, the wages of the bottom decile of American workers are now only half those of their counterparts in northern Europe.) Within the union sector and outside, moreover, inequality is exacerbated by the fact that compensation is heavily determined by firm- or industry-specific rents. Even as they share in the division of such rents, however, particular labor organizations and particular managements disagree over benefits—even basic benefits of generally recognized social importance, such as health care—often precluding their constructive cooperation. Finally, in an age of increasingly casualized employment, the firm-based character of the American benefit system—with health care, vacation time, pensions, and more determined on a firm-specific basis, and receipt of those benefits conditioned on continuance in that firm—further threatens equality in provision.

These familiar facts suggest that the basic structure of employment compensation in the United States—long defined by highly decentralized wage and benefit determination and a very low "social wage" of generic minima—is in need of reform. Equality concerns, and increasingly efficiency ones, recommend a move toward more encompassing wage setting and higher guaranteed social minima.

Raising social minima is in principle simple enough. Whether administered through firms or not, certain basic benefits would be guaranteed on a societywide basis, much as is currently being promised for health care. The efficiency benefits of doing this are many. As against other means, minima are an efficient way to redistribute income, especially when receipt is conditioned on employment. By raising the base price of labor, minima can also be an important spur to more productive labor use, setting dynamic efficiencies in motion. And, by generalizing certain standards of behavior and performance, minima facilitate flexibility in the deployment of productive resources. As emphasized in recent discussions of health-care benefits, socializing benefits promotes greater allocative efficiency in the labor market. A firm A employee

---

An employer who would otherwise violate that section by establishing or supporting a system of employee representation or communication may defend against unfair labor practice charges by showing: (a) that the system was authorized by a majority of employees in a secret ballot; (b) that before the ballot, employees were specifically advised of their right to oppose the creation of such a plan without reprisal; (c) that such authorization expires in some uniform period of time, perhaps three years, unless reauthorized.

To these provisions we might add:

(d) that the system may be abolished by a majority of employees in a secret ballot at any time; and (e) that the system cannot at any time be unilaterally abolished by the employer.

economically (given skills, taste, whatever) best suited to firm B is more likely to find her way to firm B if B does not suffer from a crippling shortfall in the benefits provided by A. The most obvious benefit, however, is to the level of equality itself. By removing a chunk of individual welfare from wage competition, minima make it more likely that those less fortunate in that competition will still live decent lives.

For all the same reasons, greater uniformity and generalization of wage bargaining are also desirable. Although the United States seems unlikely ever to contemplate truly peak bargaining between unified union federations and a unified business community, nor even anytime soon to contemplate the full use of extension laws in the unorganized sector, more modest efforts to facilitate wage generalization on a regional or sectoral basis might be considered. The law on multiemployer bargaining might be amended, shifting the presumption away from the voluntariness (and, inevitably, instability) of such arrangements and toward their requirement. And more ambitious schemes of "sectoral bargaining," of the sort now being discussed in Canada, might be usefully considered (see Baigent, Ready, and Roper 1992 and Fudge 1993).

In a given area or industry grouping or both, sectors of employees, defined by common occupational positions across different employers, could be defined (e.g., "restaurant workers in New York City"). Unions demonstrating support among members of the sector at different sites would be permitted to bargain jointly with all the employers corresponding to those sites. In subsequent organizing during the term of the resulting contract, union certification at additional sites would automatically accrete their employers to the population covered by the contract and those employers would join in the multiemployer bargaining in the next round. To make the scheme more palatable to employers and the general public, its application might be limited to traditionally low-wage, underrepresented sectors, characterized by highly uniform conditions of work.

Such efforts would facilitate greater wage coordination among stable employees of large firms. The larger and more important effect, however, would be to extend the benefits of wage generalization to employees in smaller locations—too small, under present circumstances, to support the costs of the negotiation and enforcement of separate contracts—or operating in more casualized or "independent" employment relations. There is no good reason why shifts in the structure of employment—in recent years, toward smaller firms, independent contracting, and less stable employment—should per se be associated with diminution in the quality of employment. By effectively reducing the costs of establishing a "commonality of interest" with others, such reform would permit adjustment to changed structures without sacrifice in quality.

Democratic Productivism

If the "equality" reforms of the sort just described were implemented, many of the most enduring sources of labor-management conflict would be shifted, at least slightly, to a resolution basis above or beyond that of the individual firm. If the "free-association" reforms were implemented, the forms of collective worker organization inside the firm would become more finely attuned to the variety of employee interests and identities, unions would be more self-confident, and management would be freer in the nonunion sector to experiment with its own ideas of how best to organize employee voice. In combination, this should enlarge the role of employees in productivity enhancement, both within and outside the firm.

Within the firm, as determinations about shares of the "pie" came to be determined more externally, the concentration of all parties could turn more squarely to increasing the pie itself. As the market for representation cleared, and its results were granted legitimacy, another source of haggling would be removed, and talk could again turn more easily to cooperation.

Outside the firm, the increased reach of worker organizations, and their increased definition as organizations supporting social minima and comparability across sites of employment, would yield a potentially powerful multiplier on government and firm efforts to diffuse productivity-enhancing changes in the organization of production and to secure effective monitoring and enforcement of such efforts. Effective systems of training and technology diffusion, for example, are easier to achieve when there are links across firms. Regional labor market programs are easier to administer when worker organizations are more spatially defined. Such improvements would more likely be made as a result of the reforms I have discussed.

The enhancement of firm and state efficiency through the use of workers and worker organizations might also be aimed at explicitly. The American economy currently suffers from the fact that the "low-road" sweating response to new competition is not sufficiently foreclosed by public policy, while the "high road" of advanced, high-involvement, high-wage, quality competition is not sufficiently supported. Although the reforms already suggested would go some distance toward achieving the first goal, the second also needs attention. This is where explicit efforts might be directed, in several areas.

We know that considerable gains in efficiency can be achieved within firms, and in labor markets, if information flows more freely to workers. General reporting requirements of firms to workers—on current performance, future plans, upcoming choices about products, technology, workforce restructuring, and the like—of the sort most advanced firms do already, ought to be considered.

We know that the genuine involvement of workers in solving firm problems requires not only that they see some reward from that involvement but that they have genuine power to affect the choices made. In light of this reality, where workers are organized, the ancient mandatory versus permissive distinction in bargaining seems overdue for overhaul.

We know that in most areas of workplace regulation, the sheer number, heterogeneity, and dispersion of workplaces forbid their effective monitoring by any plausibly sized state inspectorate and that "private attorneys general" pursuing civil claims can also not be relied on to achieve desired results. Increased explicit reliance on worker, or worker-manager, committees for monitoring and enforcement might usefully be explored. Occupational health and safety is one familiar area of such experimentation, but "worker-based" models of regulation might also be extended to other areas of pressing national concern—training and technology among them.

We know that in regional labor markets and (commonly metropolitan) industry agglomerations, the provision of skills and the diffusion of technology is seldom "to standard," in part because no credible institutions exist to define standards and diffuse practice based on them. Explicit efforts to promote regional skills and technology consortia, consisting of labor organizations, area employers, and relevant public authorities, and to devolve to such consortia responsibility for executing regional policies in these areas, according to national standards on performance, might also be encouraged.

In brief, we know that modernization and industrial upgrading efforts, as well as workplace regulation, require institutional supports within and across firms—to facilitate communication, organize key players, reward cooperation, punish free riders, monitor performance, diffuse best practice, use "local knowledge" to devise efficient compliance strategies with social mandates, and more. Such institutional supports extend well beyond those supplied within the markets versus states ("live free or die") governance dichotomy on which conventional policy discussion remains transfixed. Specifically, they extend to the encouragement of varied forms of *associative* governance, across as well as within firms. Labor law reform should in part be about building this institutional infrastructure of high-wage productivism. Among other things, this means explicitly encouraging our existing "social partners" to assume the socially needed tasks of economic governance—"incentivizing" the voluntary establishment of appropriate forms of association—and conditioning the special benefits and protections they receive from public authority on their willingness to assume this burden.

How Reform Might Be Organized

However desirable the reform might be, it will inevitably face opposition. It needs a committed agent to succeed.

This is not likely to be the American business community, which is sharply divided on the desirable future path of economic development in the United States—although it might, once a movement for reform got started, gain the support of some segments of the business community. Nor is it likely to be the present administration—which is deeply ambivalent about "traditional" labor organization, accepting of budget constraints so harsh that they will limit the side payments probably needed, and in general loath to enter conflicts with the business community of the sort that will inevitably be required. Nor will it come from the disorganized public, as yet far from up-in-arms about the topic.

This leaves labor.

For reasons already suggested, however, reform is also unlikely to come, even given intense labor mobilization, if it is seen as piecemeal, let alone narrowly self-serving. To put across something like the package talked about here, even to get needed discussion of that package going, reform must come to be seen as something in the general interest of the society. Its agent must be seen as an agent of the general will.

How might labor cast itself as such a paladin? Some speculations follow.

General Strategy

In very broad terms, "unions"—in our revised system, here meant only to mean "independent collective worker organizations"—need more self-consciously to create and occupy a place analogous to their old one.[2] What that means, again, is that they need to find a way to serve their members' interests in a way that also serves the interests of capital and (precisely because it serves both) enables labor to claim to advance a general will that stands above the special pleading of any particular group.

Take first the problem of serving members' interests. In the old system, unions provided job security though a combination of Keynesian demand management and internal labor market administration. Again, difficulties in controlling macroeconomic demand and the internal structures of the firm make that much more challenging today. Accepting this, the alternative is to aim more for career security than for job security and to develop mechanisms of insurance rooted more in effective supply than in effective demand. Instead of trying to define a worker's place in a fixed structure, a new unionism would seek to ensure workers power in fluid structures. The way to do that is to provide all workers with the advanced technical (and, increasingly, "business") training and counseling needed to assert power in the design of the work teams in which they are increasingly employed and to move freely in external labor markets as their current employers go under.

Notice that while workers desperately want such training and counseling services, there is little likelihood that firms themselves will provide them. After all, firms are busy forming cost and profit centers precisely because they

2. This section draws from Rogers and Sabel 1993.

have no idea what is working well enough to justify additional investment; and, as ever, firms resist assuming the costs of training workers, especially in those general skills that will increase their mobility if they might then leave. Notice too that such services cannot be easily provided through (though they might be funded by) the state, which is certainly no more able than the firms to ascertain the services needed. Services will need to be provided by institutions that are actually rooted in the economy, extend across the population of firms, and have workers' interests chiefly in mind. They will need to be supplied by unions.

Unions cannot equip members for careers independent of particular firms, however, if compensation and work rules in the corporate way stations of a likely career are so diverse that no one with an acceptable job will dare to move. As discussed, this problem, familiar today from the way people cling to jobs to preserve firm-based pension or health benefits, can only be solved by generalizing compensation and organizational practices. Barriers to mobility arising from the cross-firm differences—in performance review or dispute resolution proceedings, stock option plans or opportunities for skill acquisition, and compensation itself—that have in part arisen from decentralization now stand as barriers to worker mobility. Just as unions can serve their members' interests by making their skills more versatile, they should serve them by pressing both firms and the state to establish greater uniformity in the conditions of compensation (itself increasingly tied to skill) and employment.

Here again, unions have unique capacities to perform this role. If they are in touch with their members, they will have a much better idea than government or managers of just what underlying standards of equity need to be respected in establishing "comparable" work settings. As institutions spread across firms, unions will have wider-ranging experience concerning the different jobs that cluster into careers than even the most decentralized, joint-venturing corporation. Firms and groups of employees trying to reconcile differences sufficiently to establish a workable workplace could thus well look to unions when conflicts arise over the definition and application of rules. Moreover, as institutions of workers in the economy itself, unions are indispensable vehicles for enforcing standards—with the local knowledge and capacity for disruption needed to play that role.

Next consider how the interests of firms are advanced by this twofold strategy of new-model unions. Concerning the first interest—training and counseling—while members want a combination of technical and managerial skills to protect themselves against the risks of the labor market, firms would like to wave a magic wand over their current workforces and have employees with precisely those skills costlessly appear. If unions could help firms figure out how to make effective use of the vast public funds available for training, they could be the magic wand.

Concerning the second interest—achieving comparability across firms in the conditions of work and compensation—employers too have an interest in this goal. As firms decentralize and cooperate more and more closely with outsiders, there is less connection between who employs a person and where and with whom that person works. If an automobile firm and an airbag manufacturer codevelop a new product, a project group from one might easily spend six months on the other's site. Or if a manufacturing firm subcontracts its information system work to a data-processing firm, technicians employed by the data processor might work full time at the manufacturing site. In such cases, cooperating firms are in trouble if they tell their respective employees to treat their new coworkers as partners and then treat the partners very differently themselves. Without some generalization in work conditions, rules, and compensation, advanced forms of cooperation are far more difficult to enter into, manage, and fold when the task is done.

Just as in the old system, then, unions can play an economic role that both advances their members' interests and solves economywide problems beyond the capacity of any firm. Organizationally, their doing so will inevitably require them to be attentive to a wider variety of worker interests than they are identified with at present and—to get deals cut across diverse firms—to be more defined by geographic region and less by economic sector (here, recent signs of revival among metropolitan central labor councils are suggestive). At the same time, since people still work in particular settings (and the places are still largely described by firm ownership), it is vital that unions extend the reach of worker power in such settings throughout the economy—including in sites where unions have relatively few members. This will require getting state supports for generic baselines of worker representation and benefit.

All three changes will give unions more of a "political" flavor than they have at present. Moreover, the reemergence of unions as innovative, moral, and rational social agents of general benefit will award them a fair degree of political capital with the general public. People will see the "point" of unions more clearly than they do now.

In combination, these changes suggest a basis for a new political role for unions, at both local and national levels, as advocates for the legislated social protections and supports needed to ensure equity as well as innovation. As already discussed, the welfare state needs to be moved from a jobs-based system to one of more generic social entitlement. Public programs—as in unemployment insurance and training—need to take full measure of increases in job mobility and risk. And the state needs to help spur industrial upgrading of the desired sort not only by rationalizing its services to firms but by using its residual powers of direction (purchasing power, direct regulation of wage and production standards) to encourage movement in the right direction.

New-model unions, as agents of the general interest, could play an important role in making sure that all this happens.

Internal Reform

The labor movement that did these things would have very broad appeal. It would also, however, be a labor movement that looked rather different from the one that now exists. While many unions, in particular locals, already engage in just such practices, a commitment to egalitarian productivism is not, in general, the way unions would characterize their role. Taking that commitment seriously would imply, among other things: (1) sustained efforts within the labor movement to develop the technical capacities for guiding human capital systems, technology-diffusion programs, and firm management itself; (2) a massive increase in organizing, coupled with a willingness, even an eagerness, to accept "nontraditional" collectivities of workers as allies; (3) a much more active, and independent, political role, at all levels of government; (4) an overhaul of internal rules on jurisdiction, to get new institutional boundaries carved along genuinely functional lines and to permit interunion cooperation on issues of cross-cutting concern; (5) generalization of an "organizing" model of unionism, with much heavier reliance on membership involvement and democratic direction; (6) consolidation of directive powers, under democratic guidance, at the core of the labor movement—a two-step perhaps best accomplished by greater direct membership election of national officers; (7) and more. In brief, the labor movement would need, in ways manifest to the general public, to "reinvent" itself as a lively, democratic, intellectually self-assured, popular force for egalitarian productivism. This would involve breaking some eggs inside the labor movement.

Putting It Together

Suppose, through means best known to it, the labor movement made such moves and signaled their making to the general public. Suppose it announced, in public fashion, what it now saw as its vision, given the changed economy, along the lines suggested. Suppose it offered something like the general reform package suggested, noticing with the reader that all its elements are perfectly consistent with, even supportive of, such a transformed social role. And suppose then that it said, to business, government, and the general public:

> What we intend to do is manifestly good for the country. To do it, however, we need labor law reform. The reform we seek is not self-interested. In part, indeed, it will pose a challenge to our past practices, even as it permits us the space for internal transformation on which we are now intent. It respects free association, equality, and the requirements of a productive capitalism. It

expands choice for all, while limiting inequality and providing the basic security needed for flexible adaptation to today's economy. All evidence suggests that it will promise a vast improvement in human happiness and welfare, not to mention competitiveness. Have you got something that does all those things better?

Suppose, that is, that labor sought to make "labor law reform" congruent with "labor's transformation" and offered "labor's transformation" as something manifestly guided by a declared interest in meeting general concerns— about economic well-being, insecurity, competitiveness, some residuum of democratic feeling—alive and well in the general population. Would there be takers? Would a number of people see their stake in labor law reform, so described and understood? Would they be more prepared to join the fight that will inevitably be needed to make it happen? I think so. And I see no realistic alternative as equally hopeful.

2

Section 8(a)(2) and the Origins of the Wagner Act

David Brody

Nearly sixty years have passed since the passage of the National Labor Relations Act in 1935. So far removed are we from that time, remarked Paul Weiler on the fiftieth anniversary of the law nine years ago, that the sides are totally reversed: Management is content with it, while organized labor thinks that maybe the best thing would be to scrap the law and return to "the law of the jungle" (1985:35). Is any purpose to be served by revisiting those distant days when the Wagner Act was hailed as labor's Magna Charta? In a recent essay (1994), I made the labor historian's case for why knowledge of labor's past is important to a union movement beset by troubles. My argument contained a few sentences about the apparent anomaly of the recent decision in *Electromation, Inc. v. Teamsters Local 1049* (309 N.L.R.B. No. 163 (1992)): that, in the current vogue for employee involvement, labor-management shop committees are sharply, if not fatally, constrained by Section 8(a)(2) of the law. I cited 8(a)(2) only "to remind us that the principles and rules [the law] asserts came out of a particular history and were premised on a specific set of industrial conditions" (7–8). That history, however, turns out to have a powerful bearing on the current debate over labor law reform.

Even today, Section 8(a)(2) remains nearly pristine, without the usual encrustation of amendment and case law of a sixty-year-old provision. The National Labor Relations Board recognized this in its finding in the *Electromation* case, which is based primarily on an examination of legislative intent. Senator Robert F. Wagner is quoted extensively, and there is close attention to the successive wording of Section 8(a)(2),[1] which in the end prohibits not only employer domination in, but interference with, the formation or administra-

---

1. In the original Wagner Act, the designation is 8(2), but for consistency's sake, and to avoid confusion, 8(a)(2) will be used throughout.

tion of labor organizations, as well as any support, financial or otherwise. The reach of 8(a)(2) is determined by how the law defines "labor organization," and here too there is no mistaking the legislative intent: In its final wording, Section 2(5) leaves no shelter from the prohibitions of 8(a)(2) for workplace forms of representation insofar as concerns the terms and conditions of employment.

To the *amici* in the case who argued that changed industrial conditions call for a more flexible approach, the board responded rather plaintively that it could not be more flexible "when congressional intent to the contrary is absolutely clear."[2] One can understand why, in a law committed to fostering contractual relations between employers and employees, Congress would be eager to prevent the suborning of a collective bargaining agent by its opposite number. But what can Senator Wagner and his colleagues have had in mind by the radical constraints written into 8(a)(2) and 2(5), constraints so sweeping that they apply to employee organizations not aspiring to collective bargaining (*NLRB v. Cabot Carbon Co.*, 360 U.S. 203 (1959)) and to employer actions not tainted by antiunion animus (*Newport News Shipbuilding and Dry Dock Co. v. Schauffler*, 303 U.S. 54 (1938))? That 8(a)(2) was not inadvertent became altogether certain when Congress undertook the Taft-Hartley overhaul of 1947. The House adopted a provision permitting employers in the absence of a certified bargaining agent to form or maintain employee committees for the purpose of discussing matters of mutual interest, including the terms and conditions of work. The provision was rejected in conference, specifically (so Senator Robert A. Taft reported) because the conferees wanted the prohibitions in 8(a)(2) left "unchanged" (*Daily Labor Report*, June 8, 1959, D-3 [in the text of *NLRB v. Cabot Carbon Co.*]), and so they have remained ever since.

What has changed is an industrial environment that now places a premium on employee involvement. This takes various forms, from quality circles to production teams and up to, at its most advanced, shop committees, such as the ones disestablished by *Electromation*. At stake, argued some *amici* in that case, was nothing less than American competitiveness in the global economy. And when the Clinton administration came into office a few weeks later, lo and behold, that was exactly the position it took. The key competitive arena, says Secretary of Labor Robert B. Reich, is the workplace, and the goal, "high-performance work practice." Workplace reform is what in the Clinton admin-

---

2. The decision is reprinted in *Daily Labor Report*, Dec. 18, 1992, E-1–E-23. The quotation is in n9. In its brief survey of relevant decisions, the board notes (E-6, E-7) the one serious departure from the strict construction of 8(a)(2) by the Sixth Circuit court (*NLRB v. Scott & Fetzer Co.*, 691 F.2d 288 (1982)) and finds it wholly unconvincing. For a fuller survey of the judicial history of 8(a)(2) written under the shadow of the Sixth Circuit initiative, see Kohler 1986:534–45. For a useful listing of the scholarly commentary on 8(a)(2), see the bibliographical note in Hogler and Grenier 1992:174–75.

istration's mind calls for labor law reform. The link is explicit in the charge it gave to the Commission on the Future of Worker-Management Relations, the so-called Dunlop Commission, after its chair, John T. Dunlop.[3] Although nothing is settled yet, clearly what members of the commission have in mind, and what the secretaries of labor and commerce had in mind when they called it into being, is a system of workplace representation much more varied and collaborative than is permissible under existing law.[4]

The drift of the administration's thinking is underwritten by the most authoritative of academic voices. In his recent book *Governing the Workplace: The Future of Labor and Employment Law* (1990), Paul Weiler in fact commits himself to a specific reform—employee participation committees (EPCs)— that would be mandated by law for every workplace with twenty-five or more workers, taking as his model the German works council system. Representatives to these EPCs would be elected from within the plants, and their duties would be "to address and respond to the broad spectrum of resource policies of the firm" (285). And yet, powerfully argued and wide ranging as it is, Weiler's book contains but a single sentence (213) suggesting that this is a choice that the country considered once before and rejected when it chose the Wagner Act.

In what follows, I propose to retrace that history, taking as my central argument that what was at issue—and what accounted for the sweeping language of 8(a)(2) and 2(5)—was a systemic choice between rival forms of workplace representation[5] and, further, that it was a choice not so different from the one Weiler offers us. My method will be, in the fashion of the historian, to follow a basically chronological course, stopping along the way at major junctures—five by my count—that seem to bear on our debates over labor law. If others find in my account implications I have missed, so much the better.

Matters of Principle

The history of the Wagner Act begins two years earlier in June 1933 with the National Industrial Recovery Act, the early New Deal's misbegotten effort to fight the Great Depression through the cartelization of American

3. The commission's mission statement is reprinted in *Daily Labor Report*, March 25, 1993, F-1.

4. See the statements by Ron Brown and Robert Reich in the *New York Times*, July 5, July 27, and Aug. 8, 1993, and by commission members Thomas Kochan and Paula Voos in *Daily Labor Report*, April 30, 1993, A-17, and May 4, 1993, C-2.

5. This is not an argument that strains the historical imagination; it is entirely obvious to any reader of the legislative record leading up to Section 8(a)(2), as demonstrated, for example, in Kohler 1986:531–36.

industry, that is, through codes of fair competition. Included in the Recovery Act was Section 7(a), which said that employees had the right to organize and bargain collectively through representatives of their own choosing and in exercising that right to be free from interference, restraint, or coercion by employers or their agents. Only the historian perhaps gets excited about the question of how 7(a) got into the Recovery Act and why, once in, it stuck. For our purposes, the main thing is to understand that, although 7(a) might itself have been more or less a historical accident, something like 7(a) was certain to have been enacted, because the principles it embodied had already prevailed in an ideological struggle going back at least several decades.

Since early in America's industrial revolution, liberty of contract had been the ruling employment principle in law, applying even to agreements for which a condition of the job was not joining a union or going on strike. More palatable in later years than the yellow-dog contract, however, was the open-shop argument, which called on employers themselves to safeguard the contractual freedom of their workers by having no dealings with trade unions. But in a twentieth-century world of great industrial corporations and armies of workers, individual rights steadily lost ground to the more urgent claims of collective action. As an answer to the epidemic of strikes and industrial violence, the U.S. Commission on Industrial Relations recommended in 1915 a collective bargaining law.

During World War I, when wartime policy did briefly protect organizing rights, a threshold was crossed, notwithstanding the ugly postwar reaction. After the collapse of a national conference Woodrow Wilson had called in 1919 to find a common ground between labor and capital, Bernard Baruch assured the president that, despite irreconcilable differences, the participants "did not, at any time, reject the principle of the right of workers to organize and bargain collectively with their employers" (quoted in Brody 1965:127). And when the Norris-La Guardia Act of 1932 asserted that right as public policy, there was no audible dissent. Indeed, part of the language of Section 7(a)(1) is lifted bodily from Norris-La Guardia, and the rest is a paraphrase. There in Norris-La Guardia, moreover, are the key doctrinal words of the Wagner Act—"full freedom of association" and "actual liberty of contract." That latter phrase disposes of an expiring legal theory—*actual* liberty of contract is what public policy demands, not the fiction of freely contracting individuals—and the declaration that the yellow-dog contract is unenforceable in the federal courts drives the conclusion neatly home.

Section 7(a) advances beyond Norris-La Guardia only insofar as inclusion in the National Recovery Administration (NRA)'s codes of fair competition makes 7(a) more than a mere statement of public policy. In fact, inclusion in the codes was not much of an advance, and ineffectuality is the standard theme of 7(a) history—of the hopes of industrial workers raised and then crushed by the resistance of powerful corporate interests and the fecklessness of the New Deal. All too true.

Yet, from the perspective of our own failed labor law, 7(a) can be seen in a quite different light, for what it also demonstrated was the power of ideas whose time had come. Today, the underlying principles are masked by all the encumbering amendments, court and NLRB doctrine, and institutional interests engulfing the labor law. Section 7(a) stood quite alone, little more than an assertion of principles, but for that very reason capable of summoning up the force that brought the Wagner Act into being. Remarkably, the validity of the principles were themselves never debated, only what they required, and from this came a series of rulings, conceived of at the time as an emerging common law of labor, that finally was codified in the Wagner Act: the representation election, majority rule and exclusive representation, and a list of enjoined unfair labor practices by employers.

Once on the books, the Wagner Act developed enormous moral force. The American Civil Liberties Union (ACLU) considered it "in effect a civil liberties statute" (quoted in Daniel 1980:14) and placed it at the top of the list of First Amendment achievements for 1937. This was the atmosphere in which the Supreme Court surprised its critics and handed down the crucial *NLRB v. Jones and Laughlin* (301 U.S. 1 (1937)) decision upholding the Wagner Act. The law manifested, in fact, a new understanding of constitutional rights beginning to emerge during the New Deal. "Perhaps it is time to think of civil liberty as protection *by* the state rather than *against* the state," wrote John Dewey in 1936 (quoted in Auerbach 1966:210). The record of the ACLU—it initially opposed the Wagner Act on traditional libertarian grounds—is a perfect indicator of this remarkable shift, which was a precondition for the civil rights revolution of the 1960s. In the 1930s, however, it was labor's rights that occupied center stage.

The debate over labor law reform could do worse than to start from the proposition that "full freedom of association" and "actual liberty of contract" are rights of workers worthy of being guaranteed by the state. If that proposition no longer holds the allegiance of the country, better to know it and proceed accordingly than to remain as we are today, when the practical effect of the law is to deny to workers the rights the law says they have. If, as I believe, such a clarifying debate would serve to revitalize the established principles of the Wagner Act, the battle for reform would be three-quarters won: We know quite well what it would take to curb employer intimidation of union workers, make the representation election truly the free choice of employees, and eliminate the barriers to the first contract. More to the point for this inquiry, and where the pathway to reform is less clear, we would also have some principled criteria for assessing changes in the law intended to foster alternative forms of workplace representation.

Employee Representation

That was what Section 7(a) provided in the trial period leading up to the Wagner Act, which leads me to my second historical juncture: how open-shop employers proposed to meet the test of 7(a). The damning term commonly used by historians, and by critics at the time, was company union, but we will do better to accept the term advanced by employers and one that is more functionally descriptive—employee representation plan (ERP) or, in some companies, works council. This was a *workplace* system of representation, normally limited to single plants, and not contemplating contractual relations.

That the works council would be the first line of employer defense was obvious from the jockeying over Section 7(a) before the Recovery Act was enacted, and although industry lobbyists had not gotten what they wanted— a proviso protecting "existing satisfactory relations"—they went away satisfied that 7(a) was loose enough to encompass employee representation.[6] As soon as the law was signed, there was a tremendous rush to put ERPs into effect, sometimes with a charade of employee consultation, mostly not. The cynical motives were all too plain.

Yet employee representation also had quite respectable, well-founded roots in the advanced management thinking of the time. The most direct line into New Deal history runs back to John D. Rockefeller, Jr., the very earnest heir to the Standard Oil fortune. One of his properties, the Colorado Fuel and Iron Company, had fought a bitter strike for recognition by the United Mine Workers that had ended in the Ludlow massacre of 1914. Chastened by the public outcry, he called in the Canadian industrial relations expert (and later prime minister) W. L. Mackenzie King, and between them they devised a representation plan for the Colorado mines. Henceforth, Rockefeller became a fervent and vocal advocate, establishing a similar plan at Standard Oil (N.J.) in 1918 and taking what he considered to be an advanced position in favor of industrial democracy in the postwar period. Subsequently, he financed the most important research and consulting operation of its kind in the 1920s— Industrial Relations Counselors, Inc. (IRC).[7]

In early 1934, at the height of the battles over 7(a), the head of that group, Arthur H. Young, became vice president in charge of industrial relations at the United States Steel Corporation. From that perch, Young did the strategic thinking for the national ERP movement. And in the Steel Corporation, with its 200,000 employees and preeminent place in American industry, he had a

6. See, for example, "Memorandum to Members of the Employment Relations Committee, National Association of Manufacturers, May 26, 1933," in U.S. Senate 1937 and address of the chairman, American Iron and Steel Institute, *Yearbook 1933.*

7. The authoritative account is Gitelman 1988.

big stage for testing his program. We can get a taste of what Young thought
he was up to from a statement of principle he was fond of quoting:

> The human element in industry is the factor of greatest importance. Capital
> cannot exist without labor and labor without capital is helpless. The
> development of each is dependent on the cooperation of the other.
> Confidence and good will are the foundations of every successful enterprise,
> and these can be created only by securing a point of contact between
> employer and employee. They must seek to understand each other's
> problems, understand each other's opinions, and maintain that unity of
> purpose and effort upon which the very existence of the community which
> they constitute and the whole future of democratic civilization depend.[8]

So how did employee representation fare in practice? The plans commonly
called for joint councils, with management and labor accorded equal votes and
a majority required for any action—a transparent management veto, of
course. The details varied, but the small print invariably left the final word to
management. At International Harvester, where Arthur Young ran things in
the early 1920s, representatives who stepped out of line got a hard lesson:
They were laid off or transferred (Gilpin 1992:66–67).[9] When labor costs had
to be cut, as in the sharp recession of 1920–21, the ERPs found themselves
bypassed and thereby deflated, and, in general, on wages and the basic terms
of employment, they got nowhere.

Yet it was also true that, after the shakeout of plans initiated only to satisfy
a wartime directive or to counter a unionizing threat in the postwar strike
period, employee representation developed a good deal of staying power. The
necessary ingredients seem to have been, first, a personnel department capable
of curbing line supervisors; second, an established and progressive benefits
program; and, third, company willingness to expend the energy needed to
keep the plans from winding down into inactivity.[10]

With 7(a), of course, there was a new influx of firms not truly committed to
the ERP concept, and this was, as Arthur Young later acknowledged, a
problem he had to overcome when he joined United States Steel.[11] At the
same time, the incentives to make the ERPs work were now vastly greater

8. The statement, drawn from a famous programmatic article by Rockefeller, appears in at
least three speeches, Sept. 24, 1935, May 25, 1939, and March 11, 1941. A. H. Young Papers,
California Institute of Technology Archives (copies in possession of author).

9. Gilpin 1992, chap. 1, also includes a careful analysis of the early history of the International Harvester works council plan.

10. I am following here the assessment in Nelson 1982:335–57.

11. Talk by A. H. Young, Town Hall, Section on Industrial Relations, May 18, 1938, Young
Papers.

than before, and, in fact, over the next two years they were much rewritten and generally made more autonomous of management.

For those in the labor movement who have been wondering whether shop committees might not be a halfway house toward unionization, the answer from the history I have been describing is a qualified yes. The evidence suggests that the ERPs did foster local leadership and, insofar as they failed to produce results, did educate workers and strengthen the case for collective bargaining by outside unions. An extreme instance is to be found in the Akron rubber industry, where, after fostering its Industrial Assembly for fifteen years, Goodyear unilaterally reimposed an eight-hour day in 1935 and opened the floodgates of unionization. At Arthur Young's showcase in U.S. Steel, the ERPs in the sheet and tinplate subsidiary moved in 1935, over his objections, toward federation, and the next year the ERPs at the basic steel subsidiary were seized by union adherents, who, at a critical moment, went in a body over to the CIO.[12]

For those wondering whether the ERP experience of sixty years ago suggests that shop committees can inculcate the company loyalty and commitment we now prize, the answer is also a qualified yes. A pretty fair test would be how the ERPs fared after 1935, when they came up against CIO challenge and NLRB disestablishment. At companies that had made a long-term investment in progressive labor relations—Du Pont, for example, or AT&T— independent unions did take root. When Leo Troy surveyed this little-noticed sector in 1961, he estimated a membership of 1.5 million in two thousand organizations, although he could not specify what percentage of these unions actually stemmed from the pre–Wagner Act ERPs (Troy 1961). And, in light of current union-avoidance strategies, Sanford Jacoby (1989) has more recently given respectful attention to firms whose welfarist policies in fact worked and that retained the loyalty of their workers.

As to the big question of whether employee representation ever offered a viable policy choice, the answer is, again, a highly qualified yes. The reality was that, because employers had moved so swiftly, the works councils already occupied the ground. At their peak in 1934, they covered probably 3 million workers, more than did the unions and, in the mass-production sector where they were most heavily concentrated, very much more. Those facts—that the ERPs existed, that they were functioning, that enormous business interests stood behind them—had to be taken into account, and, initially, they more than any other set the terms of the debate. But there was another fact that also had to be taken into account: With 7(a), employee representation was no longer a private affair; on the contrary, it was deeply entangled in a massive

12. For a legislative proposal based directly on the ERP steel experience, see Hogler 1989:1–69.

program of industrial regulation, which brings me to my third historical juncture.

Workplace Representation and the State

In deciding how to square employee representation with 7(a), the country was also deciding what kind of authority the state should assert over labor-management relations. The context in which this happened nearly defies recapturing, for the National Recovery Administration represents America's one serious romance with a corporatist economy. Each of some four hundred codes of fair competition contained, in addition to comprehensive trade regulations, not only Section 7(a) but more or less detailed provisions on wages, hours, child labor, and a variety of working conditions. A profusion of agencies sprang up to interpret and enforce all this—the National Labor Board of 1933–34, the successor National Labor Relations Board of 1934–35, regional labor boards and a few industry labor boards, other labor boards under code authority, and, finally, a whole host of NRA compliance and code committees. The question of collective bargaining rights was enmeshed in this bureaucratic jungle and intermingled with other, sometimes more pressing, NRA concerns with maintaining code labor standards and settling industrial disputes. In this state of confusion or, if you will, open possibilities, what was at issue was not only the definition of bargaining rights but the scope of state responsibility.

The Wagner Act embodied one resolution—of course, the one that prevailed. But consider another. The powerful men at the head of the NRA, General Hugh Johnson and his general counsel, Donald Richberg, took the view that Section 7(a) called for a "perfect neutrality" between forms of labor organization. The company union was just as legitimate as the trade union. It was the employer's duty to deal with both of them, insofar as each was freely chosen by employees, but, by virtue of their claim to be represented, not to grant exclusive recognition to either. The Johnson-Richberg plan contemplated multiple representation, protection of the rights of minorities and individuals, no bar against company unions, and a kind of local option over the actual forms of collective bargaining—let the parties decide what they wanted, so to speak.[13]

Where this might have led is best seen in President Franklin Roosevelt's auto settlement of March 25, 1934. The initiating crisis was entirely emblematic of the time: The AFL unions were demanding representation elections leading to exclusive recognition; the companies answered that their workers

13. There is a convenient summary of the Johnson-Richberg plan in Lyon 1935:461–66.

already had representation through the ERPs but that they were willing to deal with (but not recognize or contract with) the unions for their own members (provided membership lists were turned over). Fearful that a national auto strike might set back economic recovery, President Roosevelt himself intervened and crafted a settlement embodying the Johnson-Richberg principles I have just described but implemented on the specific basis of proportional representation.

To enforce the settlement, the president appointed a special Automobile Labor Board with final and binding authority. The board first dealt with the backlog of discrimination cases, then in early 1935 administered elections for what it called "bargaining agencies" for every auto plant in the country (except Ford), the members of which were identified by affiliation and selected by a complex process to reflect the plantwide vote. Each member acted as grievance person for his or her own district and on broader issues sat on the bargaining agency (Fine 1963, esp. 222–24). The agencies replaced the ERPs, generally adopting their district lines, and became in effect the state-mandated works councils Weiler has in mind.

We might therefore pause to ask what light that experience throws on the current enthusiasm for alternative forms of workplace representation. Insofar as the works councils in Weiler's plan are intended to be supplementary to existing collective bargaining protections, not in lieu of them, as was the case with the 1934 auto settlement, to that degree, of course, the two situations are not comparable. And, in fact, the auto works councils displayed very much the same weaknesses as the ERPs they replaced, with members of the bargaining agencies complaining that in dealing with management they had no independent base of power and no claims on the latter beyond the right to be heard.[14] Yet, in the responsibilities they imposed on the state, the auto works councils do have a certain relevance for labor law reform.

The Automobile Labor Board, employing a staff of more than a hundred, ordered and administered the plant elections across the industry and, on unresolved grievances, began to function as a kind of labor court. Who would be charged with these responsibilities if the law mandates, or even only authorizes, works councils? If full freedom of association remains basic doctrine in the law, as I assume it will, will it fall to the NLRB to police the works councils against the threat of company domination and manipulation? If so,

14. For example, "Meeting of the Automobile Labor Board [ALB] with the Bargaining Agency Elected by Employees of Cadillac Motor Company, Jan. 3, 1935; Meeting of the ALB with Bargaining Agency . . . at Buick Motor Company, April 12, 1935," NRA Papers, R.G. 9, National Archives, Box 2. In the view of the ALB, the auto settlement required the employer to meet with the bargaining agency but that everything beyond that was strictly voluntary and that the actual development of collective bargaining would be a long-term voluntary process.

by what criteria? At the time, auto unionists castigated the works councils for being powerless, but the historical record also reveals them calling the councils "government unions." Most certainly, labor law reformers will want to think carefully about what functions the state will be undertaking if it becomes the author of alternative forms of workplace representation.

The auto settlement was a real alternative at the time. President Roosevelt put it forth as the basis on which "a more comprehensive, a more adequate and a more equitable system of industrial relations may be built than ever before. It is my hope that this system may develop into a kind of works council in industry in which all groups of employees, whatever may be their choice of organization or form of representation, may participate in joint conferences with their employers" (quoted in Fine 1963:224–25).[15] Think about what our labor relations might have looked like had FDR's "hope" come to pass.

The Path to Section 8(a)(2)

We come now to my fourth historical juncture—the moment of truth, so to speak—when Congress chose the path leading to the Wagner Act. From the day Senator Wagner set in motion the drafting process, in early 1934, the basic strategy proceeded on two tracks, one leading to a viable framework for free collective bargaining, the other to the expurgation of the rival workplace representation system. For the latter purpose, a serviceable weapon was at hand in a principle already well established in railway labor law: that employer domination of labor organizations was an excluded activity corollary to the right of self-organization.[16] Specifying such excluded activity was the very first problem to which Senator Wagner's team gave detailed attention when it produced the sketchy initial draft dated January 31, 1934.[17] How far to extend the curbs on employer domination, however, was not initially clear.

The finished draft of the labor disputes bill (S. 2926), which Wagner submitted to the Senate on March 1, defined as labor organizations those existing for the purpose "of dealing with employers concerning grievances, labor disputes, wages or hours of employment." A more comprehensive phrase covering "other terms of employment" ought to be added, a key academic adviser, William E. Leiserson, wrote Wagner. Otherwise, "the contention may be made that company unions may be kept in existence to deal with those

15. On FDR's commitment to the auto settlement as the basic definition of 7(a) rights, see the quotation in Bernstein 1970:191.

16. On the legal history, see Bernstein 1950:18–22. On the potency of the company-domination principle, see especially the grudging testimony of James A. Emery, general counsel of the National Association of Manufacturers, in NLRB 1985, 1:379–81.

17. The early drafts, beginning with the first, of Jan. 31, 1934, are reprinted, with commentary, in Casebeer 1989:73–131.

terms of employment that are not covered in this sub-section defining 'labor organization.'" Similar reasoning prompted Leiserson's colleague Edwin H. Witte to urge the addition of "employee representation committee" to the definition of labor organization.[18]

Logic went in one direction, but politics in another. In early May, Senator Wagner lost the initiative in the Senate Education and Labor Committee, and the powerful chair, David I. Walsh, pushed for a more accommodating bill.

Walsh's substitute permitted employers to initiate and influence, but not interfere with or dominate, employee representation committees (and other forms of labor organization) and to pay employee representatives for their time (but not to contribute financially to labor organizations) and entirely dropped the handling of grievances as a defining function of protected labor organizations. Had the preservation of employee representation been their primary concern, employers should have welcomed the Walsh substitute, but of course their real interest was not protecting the ERPs but fending off genuine collective bargaining, and here, although the Walsh substitute made the key concession of dropping the explicit duty to recognize and bargain with representatives of employees, employers could not be sure that they would not be faced with exclusive bargaining agents selected by secret ballot through majority rule, all of which was permissible at the discretion of the industrial adjustment board created by Walsh's bill.[19]

After it was too late, Arthur Young remarked that he thought that employee representation and collective bargaining were not incompatible and could fruitfully function side by side.[20] If that was Young's belief, he had blown his chance. Employers, Young included, fought Walsh's bill and helped get it killed in June 1934. In a revealing letter, Young figured that time was on his side: The efforts to enforce 7(a) could be stonewalled until it expired, and there would never "be given as good a chance for the passage of the Wagner Act as now."[21]

But time proved to be on Wagner's side, not Young's. The steam went out of the pro-business NRA experiment; the 1934 congressional elections swept

18. William L. Leiserson to Wagner, March 8, 1934, Folder 14, Box 1, Leon Keyserling Papers, Georgetown University; Edwin E. Witte, Hearings on S. 2926, in NLRB 1985, 1:271–73; Gross 1974:68. The successive drafts of the labor disputes bill incorporate Leiserson's and Witte's suggestions but are denoted "Confidential Committee Print" and seem not to have been formally added to the March 1 version. They are not reported in NLRB 1985 but can be found in Folder 20, Box 1, Keyserling Papers.

19. Walsh's bill is reprinted in NLRB 1985, 1:1084–98, and Walsh's explanation is on 1099–27. One change, not especially noted at the time but of peculiar relevance today, was the deletion from the definition of "employee" (Sec. 3(3) of the labor disputes bill) of a proviso stating that strike replacements were not employees; the deletion survived in the drafting of the final Wagner Act.

20. Town Hall Speech, May 28, 1938, Young Papers.

21. A. H. Young to L. H. Corndorf, June 16, 1934, in NLRB 1985, 2:2225.

out the Republican right wing and created the most liberal Congress in memory; and the futile struggle to enforce 7(a) exposed ever more sharply the cynicism behind all the fine talk about the rights of workers (not least by the publication of Young's damaging letter). There is no way of understanding what drove the campaign for a labor law without taking account of the nature of management's opposition—above all, to the prospect of genuine collective bargaining with independent unions—and, of course, the miscalculations that come so easily to people bent on preserving their power.

When Senator Wagner resumed the battle in the 1935 Congress, the gloves were off. The definition of employer domination of a labor organization becomes airtight, and likewise the meaning of labor organization, in 2(5). On reading the draft, Secretary of Labor Frances Perkins noted that labor organizations were defined as organizations created for the purpose of *"dealing with* employers." Would not *bargain collectively* be the preferred term? No, came the vehement rejoinder from Senator Wagner's key aide, Leon Keyserling. If Perkins's amendment were accepted,

> then most of the activity of employers in connection with the company unions we are seeking to outlaw would fall outside the scope of the Act. If, as employers insist, such "plans," etc., are lawful representatives of employees, then employers' activity relative to them should be clearly included, whether they merely "adjust" or exist as a "method of contact," or engage in genuine collective bargaining. It is for this reason that the bill uses the broad term "dealing with."[22]

The architects of the bill are entirely clear about the fact that they are forcing a systemic choice, hence, to take another example, the insistence on retaining grievance handling as a defining function of labor organizations. Because employee representation plans are mostly "nothing but agencies for presenting and discussing grievances and other minor matters . . . to exclude the term 'grievances' particularly would exclude from the provisions of this act the vast field of employer interference with self-organization by way of such plans or committees."[23] This statement, in its remarkable negativity, defines the drafting strategy: Workplace organization is encompassed by 2(5) so that it can be excluded in 8(a)(2).

So did the Congress not contemplate a need for workplace representation or recognize grievances as a legitimate expression of employee discontent? Of course it did, only not through company-dominated labor organization or— just as important—not by legislative enactment. The shaping of 8(a)(2) has to be placed in its true historical context, which was the massive NRA

22. Leon Keyserling, undated memo (1935), Folder 9, Box 1, Keyserling Papers.
23. "Comparison of S. 2926 and S. 1958," NLRB 1985, 1:1320, 1347.

experiment that was in place during this entire period. (The Supreme Court killed it only on May 27, 1935.) By introducing separate labor legislation, Wagner was intent on an act of *disengagement* from that corporatist morass, and the evolution of the law was driven by this intention. Thus, the NLRB ends up a public board, not tripartite; free-standing, not associated with the Labor Department; concerned strictly with collective bargaining rights, not with mediating and arbitrating labor disputes; and endowed with independent, adequate powers of enforcement, which, under the NRA, had been utterly lacking.

To define the NLRB as quasi-judicial was empowering but also, in the freewheeling NRA context, delimiting. It was this quite precise combination—of state authority powerfully mobilized yet narrowly applied—that gave the Wagner Act its distinctive cast and, indeed, its particular programmatic thrust: The law protected the right to organize and bargain collectively; collective bargaining itself remained free. Section 8(a)(2) is part of that great settlement, disengaging workplace relations from the meddling NRA structure and leaving it in the realm of free collective bargaining.

Workplace Contractualism

This brings me to my final historical juncture. When collective bargaining began in 1936 and 1937, there was little argument about what would go into the first contracts: a provision for shop stewards or committeemen, a formal grievance procedure, and the principles of seniority in layoff and rehire, pay equity across jobs, and just cause in discharge and disciplinary actions.[24] The hallmarks of the unionized workplace were present at its birth. Where had they sprung from? From a history of shopfloor struggle accompanying, and in my view driving, the legislative history I have been describing. The starting point went back long before the New Deal to the emergence of mass-production technology and the parallel development of internal labor markets and hierarchical command structures. In the 1920s and even earlier, one can already spot the key elements in various firms—pay equity as job classification systems appeared, rules for regulating job opportunity among permanent employees, due process in disciplinary matters, and a felt need for some formal mechanism for eliciting the views of workers and for processing their grievances, which was of course the best argument for the employee representation plans. The problem was that corporate employers were only imperfectly committed to what they themselves had created. And when the Great Depression struck, these failures became magnified in the minds of workers, who,

24. In the following discussion I am drawing on my article in Lichtenstein and Harris 1993:176–205.

facing unemployment and speedup, had an enormous stake in predictable, rule-bound treatment. This was the source of the explosive response to 7(a)—not from workers on the streets, but from those at work embittered by capricious and arbitrary treatment that violated the very precepts of bureaucratic order of the corporate enterprise itself.

The workplace events of the pre–Wagner Act era all moved in a common direction. Even at their most pliant, the employee representation plans mark a kind of beginning for the grievance procedure. The AFL unions themselves strenuously resisted the ERP system, but, given their impotence on the bargaining front, they had little choice but to channel their energies into workplace organization. At General Motors, shop committeemen had won the right to process the grievances of union members well before there was any contract.

The sense of formal process inherent in these emerging workplace structures was fostered as well by the NRA's halting efforts at adjudicating violations of Section 7(a). Among the entitlements springing from these proceedings, most interesting perhaps was seniority. One of the charges to the Automobile Labor Board had been to handle discrimination cases by testing discharge and rehire against fixed criteria, which included marital status, efficiency, *and* seniority. Invoked for this specific purpose, seniority almost at once became a general entitlement, accepted as such by the Auto Board and by the industry.

When it signed with the United Automobile Workers (UAW) a month after settling the great Flint sitdown strike, General Motors took the position that it was embodying in the contract practices that were already in place. What remained implicit, but was perfectly evident in its future actions, was that General Motors was satisfied that it was accepting a workplace system that met the requirements of a great manufacturer of mass-produced automobiles.

Now that we have arrived at the moment when that no longer seems to be the case, it might be worthwhile to bear in mind that, historically, the workplace contractualism now so much in disfavor actually represents a triumph of accommodation to the industrial world as it then was. And so, perhaps more to the point, does the labor law. It left workplace representation to collective bargaining because it was confident of the result and swept out alternative forms of workplace representation because no compelling case was made for conserving them. The ban against company domination, after all, is linked to the right to self-organization. No one argued at the time that anything else was at issue or, rather, no one on management's side, because there were indeed union people such as Walter Reuther and Clinton Golden who believed that workers had a contribution to make to production practice. A case, indeed, has recently been made that, by empowering workers, Senator

Wagner and his advisers thought they were laying the basis for high-trust cooperative workplace relations (Barenberg 1993). Management harbored no such vision; running the plant was their job.

The management rights clause in union contracts, as Barry and Irving Bluestone (1992) have been at pains to point out, stands as a monument to management's determination. In its heyday before the Wagner Act, the works council was never conceived to be of any serious relevance to better plant operations. Now that it is, we ought not to read the past as a cautionary tale but rather for what it tells us about the ways we earlier fashioned the right responses to our economic environment and, in particular, about just what it was that our labor law contributed once before—and might once again—to high-performance workplace relations.

Let me conclude by mentioning the fate of Arthur H. Young. In February 1937, the Supreme Court had not yet validated the Wagner Act, and Young was still trying to keep the ERPs at U.S. Steel going. Young was vice president in charge of labor relations, but he did not know that his boss, Myron C. Taylor, had been secretly negotiating with John L. Lewis since early January. On March 1, 1937, the astounding news broke that the steel corporation was recognizing the CIO union. After a decent interval, Young resigned. He had thought himself ahead of the curve as a progressive labor manager, but in fact he had fallen far behind. He was not even in on the decision that launched collective bargaining in the steel industry.

3

The Demise of the National Labor Policy: A Question of Social Justice

James A. Gross

The conclusions and policy recommendations in this chapter are based on evidence set forth in my three-volume study of the National Labor Relations Board and the development of U.S. labor policy from 1933 to the present. The first volume, *The Making of the NLRB: A Study in Economics, Politics, and the Law* (1974), begins with the creation of the National Labor Board in 1933 and culminates in the Supreme Court's historic decisions in 1937 sustaining the constitutionality of Senator Robert Wagner's National Labor Relations Act. The second volume, *The Reshaping of the NLRB: National Labor Policy in Transition, 1937–1947* (1982), continues the analysis from constitutionality to the passage of the Taft-Hartley Act in 1947. The third volume, which will be published by Temple University Press in its Labor and Social Change Series, analyzes and documents how labor policy has been made and changed from the enactment of Taft-Hartley to the present time.

The research for the entire study was based on NLRB records at the NLRB and the National Archives; records at the Roosevelt, Truman, Eisenhower, Kennedy, and Johnson libraries; the personal papers of former NLRB chairmen and members, as well as those of other influential people inside and outside the board; records in the National Association of Manufacturers Archives at the Hagley Museum and Library; papers from the George Meany Library; and oral history interviews with more than a hundred people prominent in the making of post–Taft-Hartley Act labor policy.

I have chosen not to repeat that evidence here but rather to write a "keynote essay" that in a sense summarizes almost twenty years of study and sets forth some conclusions, interpretations, and policy recommendations most relevant to the issue of labor law reform.

Conflicting Statutory Purposes

Ever since Congress incorporated two conflicting statements of purpose in the Taft-Hartley Act in 1947, our national labor policy has been at cross-purposes with itself. The concept added to Taft-Hartley of the federal government as a *neutral guarantor* of employee free choice between individual and collective bargaining, and indifferent to the choice made, is clearly inconsistent with the Wagner Act's concept, retained in Taft-Hartley, of the federal government as a promoter of collective bargaining. The Taft-Hartley Act contains both conceptions of government's role.

NLRBs applying quite different policies can choose between these contradictory purposes and still claim they are conforming to congressional intent. For that reason, there have been not merely revisions in NLRB case law (that would be expected and even necessary over the years) but radical changes that swing labor policy from one purpose to its direct opposite. These swings directly affect the ability of unions to organize and managements to resist organization as well as the relative bargaining power of the parties. In sum, they determine the extent to which there will be mutuality of decision-making at the workplace. As a consequence, after more than forty-seven years of Taft-Hartley (and fifty-nine years since the Wagner Act) we have no coherent or consistent national labor policy.

Under the Wagner Act, the right of workers to participate in decisions affecting their workplace lives was considered an essential component of social justice, and collective bargaining was considered essential for a free and democratic society. The Wagner Act statement of purpose was carried over into Taft-Hartley, and Robert Taft claimed his and Fred Hartley's amendments did not change the essential collective bargaining theme of the Wagner Act labor policy. Yet employers used Taft-Hartley to resist unionization and avoid collective bargaining. Taft-Hartley's emphasis on the right to reject collective bargaining, the protection of employee and employer rights in their relations with unions, the inclusion of union unfair labor practices, and the federal government's new statutory image as neutral between individual or collective bargaining encouraged employers to resist unionization and collective bargaining. The same law, therefore, can be read as encouraging collective bargaining and encouraging resistance to it.

The current state of U.S. labor policy cannot be fully understood without knowledge of the existence and influence of these conflicting statutory purposes on the development of that policy. Any reconstruction of national labor policy must begin with a resolution of this fundamental disagreement about what the purpose of the law should be.

NLRB's Role in Making Labor Policy

In the meantime, however, the existence of these conflicting statements of purpose in the act has given the NLRB, and the political officials who appoint its members, a de facto power far beyond that ordinarily necessary for the interpretation and application of any statute. Lawmaking by the NLRB or by any other administrative agency is inevitable under any circumstances. The NLRB, in applying the act, must give specific meaning to broad statutory language, interpret where neither congressional intent nor statutory language is clear and unambiguous, and even fill in gaps in the legislation. The board, therefore, is never neutral. In carrying out its statutory mandate, the board must choose among competing alternatives. Those alternatives represent the vital interests of opposed constituencies and conflicting views of what the national labor policy is or should be. Because of the conflicting statutory purposes in Taft-Hartley, however, successive NLRBs, over time and political administrations, are in the uniquely powerful position of choosing between fundamentally different national labor policies.

NLRB chairmen with strong personalities and convictions have exercised this power most dramatically. Frank McCulloch, chairman during the Kennedy-Johnson era, for example, was influential in fashioning a labor policy that encouraged collective bargaining. McCulloch and a majority of his colleagues relied on the collective bargaining policy in the Wagner Act that had been incorporated into Taft-Hartley to justify their encouragement of collective bargaining and the facilitation of unionization.

To McCulloch and his colleagues, particularly Gerald Brown, collective bargaining required employers to bargain not only about many traditional management prerogatives but also to accept unions as joint participants in the resolution of labor-related problems affecting wages, hours, and working conditions. To them, the statutory collective bargaining policy was more than an effective way of settling labor-management disputes. It was a form of employer-union joint decision-making. McCulloch, as did Wagner, saw collective bargaining as a means to the realization of social justice through the development of democratic institutions to correct industrial injustices. Unionization and collective bargaining would replace industrial autocracy with industrial democracy.

The decisions of the Republican-appointed Guy Farmer, Edward Miller, and Donald Dotson boards, by contrast, freed employers from many of the most important constraints of unionism and collective bargaining. Rather than encouraging collective bargaining, these boards preserved and increased employers' *unilateral* decision-making power in matters affecting their employees. Their focus was not on the collective bargaining policy in the Wagner Act that was incorporated into Taft-Hartley but on the newer provisions concerning individual free choice and the right to reject collective bargaining. As Chairman Miller put it, individual employee freedom of choice, not the encouragement of collective bargaining, is the "keystone of the act." He pointedly renounced, as did Farmer, any sense of "social mission" or "crusade" to help unions organize and gain collective bargaining rights (oral history interview, Edward Miller, Oct. 23, 1984, 13 and 38, on file in the Labor-Management Documentation Center, New York State School of Labor Relations, Cornell University).

The Farmer, Miller, and Dotson boards, however, were not neutral protectors of employee choice between individual and collective bargaining who were indifferent to the outcome of that choice. Their decisions deregulating employer conduct while tightening regulation of the use of economic weapons by unions increased employers' ability to use their economic power to resist unionization and avoid collective bargaining. The Miller board effectively blocked or reversed the major thrusts of the decisions of the McCulloch board. This time, however, those decisions were not short-term reversals of U.S. labor policy.

With the exception of Jimmy Carter's one term in 1976–80, Republican administrations controlled appointments to the NLRB for more than twenty years after the McCulloch board. During that time, these Republican-appointed boards, particularly the Dotson board, elevated management's authority to manage above employers' statutory obligation to bargain. During the Reagan presidency in particular, the Dotson board seriously diminished the statutory obligation to bargain, once considered central to the act, by excluding management decisions considered too important to an employer's business to have to be negotiated with a union. Many of these decisions have the most direct and severe impact on jobs.

The national labor policy became one of maximizing employers' ability to compete in domestic and foreign markets by deregulating the management end of labor-management relations. Dotson's NLRB subordinated collective bargaining to the economic interests of employers. Pursuit of that policy was particularly devastating to union organization and collective bargaining because it came at a time when the nation's major industries were in serious economic trouble and organized labor was already in serious decline.

A historical perspective discloses how the NLRB, which in its early years contributed greatly to the growth of the strongest labor movement in the world, has contributed to its decline, particularly in the last twenty-five years. It also reveals how a presidential administration can make or change labor policy without legislative changes through appointments to the NLRB.

The national labor policy is in a shambles in part because its meaning seems to depend primarily on which political party won the last election. This is an unacceptable way to make labor policy. These shifts cause not only instability in labor policy but also loss of respect for the NLRB, confusion and cynicism among practitioners, and fear among workers that they will not be consistently protected in the exercise of their statutory rights. Labor law reform, therefore, must not only consist of changes in NLRB case doctrines, because it will be only a matter of time before the appointees of another political party will reverse those doctrines once again.

Congress, the Supreme Court, and the White House

Congress over all these years has defaulted on its responsibility to make and change labor policy. Congress has not been able to get past short-term maneuverings for political advantage and support, political horse-trading, ideologically inspired emotion, unfounded and unsubstantiated beliefs about unions and labor relations, and the manipulation of labor policy in any way necessary to achieve other more important political objectives. The beauty of the Wagner Act was that almost every one of its provisions was rooted in the experience of two pre–Wagner Act labor boards whose personnel played major roles in writing the law. Since then, empirical evidence has had little or no place in the formulation of labor policy. Legislation is neither formulated on the basis of what actually happens at workplaces nor evaluated on the basis of its effects on the workings of labor-management relations. The same is true of NLRB decisions. Politics and speculation, not evidence, control.

Senate and House labor committees have also failed to conduct the thoughtful, dispassionate, and expert investigations needed to inform lawmakers of how the country's labor relations are actually working and what needs to be done as a consequence. Congressional committees are often used, for example, to prepare an agenda of doctrinal changes for a new board of the same political party rather than to inform Congress about needed legislative changes.

As a consequence, the roles of Congress, the NLRB, and the Supreme Court in making national labor policy have been blurred and confused. When Congress abdicates its legislative function, the NLRB assumes a far greater than normal role in making labor policy. As a result of the legislative vacuum and ambiguity, moreover, the making of national labor policy has also passed by default from Congress to the Supreme Court.

Early in the Reagan administration, for example, the Supreme Court, also without empirical evidence, made fundamental labor policy choices solely on the basis of the ideological value judgments of a majority of the justices. In many ways, the Supreme Court took the lead in freeing management from the constraints of the law on the basis of pure speculation and value-laden dicta about the inviolability of management rights. (A good example is the Court's majority opinion in *First National Maintenance Corp. v. NLRB*, 452 U.S. 666

(1981)). This is of major significance for U.S. labor policy and for those who propose to change it. Congressional pressure and White House appointments can reorient an NLRB, but normally legislation is needed to reverse the Supreme Court.

Nor has there been courageous leadership from the White House, no matter who the occupant. No president has been willing to take the political risk involved in pursuing a clear and definite statement of the rights of workers or in delineating statutory solutions to serious labor relations problems. Instead, administrations have done only the minimum necessary to respond, or at least appear to be responding, to political pressure, to gain political backing, or to reward business or organized labor for its support in election campaigns. They then go through the motions of seeking reform while manipulating the situation for maximum political gain or minimum political loss. As a result, any effort to reform the labor law must calculate carefully the seriousness and depth of the incumbent administration's commitment.

Employer Resistance

Labor law reformers, moreover, must be aware of the extent to which the most powerful employers in the country will resist any threat to their management prerogatives. For many years, it was presumed that employer hostility and resistance to unionization and collective bargaining came from ideologues at the margins of business and industry. On the contrary, the determined opposition of American employers taken as a whole has been the biggest obstacle to the acceptance of the congressionally declared national labor policy of collective bargaining. This pervasive opposition is a major reason this country stands almost alone among democratic nations in leaving the great majority of its workers without any organization and representation at the workplace. Widespread employer defiance of the law has continued to the present time, almost sixty years after the Wagner Act and forty-eight years after Taft-Hartley.

For example, a secret and coordinated effort was undertaken by the country's major employers, including those already organized and considered models of the collective bargaining process, to combat the McCulloch board on a series of fronts. Their secret campaign included the manipulation of both the media and public opinion. As the leaders of this resistance put it, they would never accept an industrial society in which a worker's voice was equal to management's or in which all management decisions were bargainable. For them, industrial democracy and free enterprise were fundamentally incompatible. (This coordinated employer resistance is thoroughly documented in my forthcoming book.)

Employers who accepted collective bargaining used it advantageously as a way to provide stability, predictability, and control within their plants. Bargaining, moreover, was limited to negotiating with unions about the effects of management's business decisions on wages, hours, and working conditions. Employers definitely were not bargaining with unions as part of the management decision-making process itself. The combination of the Kennedy-Johnson board's codetermination concept of collective bargaining and its commitment to spreading the practice of collective bargaining caused even these employers to push for the elimination from Taft-Hartley of the language making it the policy of the federal government to encourage collective bargaining.

The defeat of organized labor's reform bill in 1978 marked the beginning of a far more open employer resistance to unionization and collective bargaining. The bitter labor-management confrontation over the bill manifested a growing conviction among employers that successful competition in domestic and international markets required either evading or resisting unions. It has become a virtual article of faith that survival (and jobs) in this new era of economic competition depends upon unencumbered and creative management responses to change; the end of high-cost contracts with unions; the retention or regaining of management prerogatives, power, and flexibility; and the freedom to overcome other labor cost advantages enjoyed by competitors. Business leaders argued then, and are arguing even more effectively now in poor economic times, that these responses enable the country to run economically, the wheels of the free enterprise system to turn, and workers' pay envelopes to be filled.

Employers went on the attack with what one national news magazine called a "green light" from the Dotson board to bash unions ("Dotson's Exit" 1987). There has been an all-out push since then by employers to free themselves or to keep themselves free of union-imposed limitations on their managerial authority. Euphemistically named "union-avoidance" programs have flourished. Unorganized employees understand the consequences of employer hostility to unions and the likelihood of retaliation against union supporters. At the same time, employers control jobs, and economic recovery and development depend on their ability to compete successfully. Consequently, organized employers have powerful political influence that could block any serious labor law reform.

Unions and the National Labor Policy

Because Wagner-Taft-Hartley is a collective bargaining law, the fate of organized labor in this country and the fate of the national labor policy and the NLRB are intimately interrelated. Organized labor is in serious decline. Unions lose more representation elections than they win. In 1992, union membership sank to a record low 15.9 percent of all employed wage and salaried workers in the country. Between the early 1960s and 1979, that percentage decline masked an increase in union membership that simply was growing at a slower rate than overall employment. Since 1979, however, union membership has fallen while employment continues to rise.

Much of this decline can be attributed to widespread employer opposition to unionization and to NLRB decisions permitting and even facilitating that opposition. It is clearly shortsighted, however, to put all the blame on the Reagan administration, because union membership has been on a downward trend since the mid-1950s. Organized labor, for example, has not yet been able to shake the unsavory image created by the McClellan hearings in the late 1950s. Those dramatic televised hearings fixed in the public mind the still-powerful image of exploited union members controlled by corrupt and dictatorial leaders whose only true devotion was to their personal enrichment. In an extraordinary reversal of public perception, unions, seen by many as liberating forces for social and economic justice in the 1930s, have come to be commonly regarded as instruments of oppression and exploitation.

Organized labor's political influence also declined after the late 1950s, not only because of decreases in membership but because both political parties began moving toward an ideological consensus that espoused a politics of moderation. Many liberals in the Democratic party, moreover, no longer considered organized labor a force for social reform and saw little difference between "big labor" and "big business." Organized labor's legislative agenda was consistently given low priority. The AFL-CIO became a captive of the Democratic party because it had no reasonable political alternative. What the Democratic party did do for organized labor, however, was to appoint and reappoint to the NLRB people such as Frank McCulloch and Gerry Brown, who greatly advanced the collective bargaining national labor policy.

Organized labor has also been guilty over the years of following a strategy that produced several costly legislative blunders. Among the most damaging was its uncompromising demand for total repeal of Taft-Hartley after Harry S. Truman's upset election victory in 1948. Labor at that time rejected proposed changes in Taft-Hartley that the AFL-CIO would still be jointly pleading for thirty years later in its reform bill.

Unions must also bear some of the blame for limiting the scope of bargaining far short of its potential as envisioned by Senator Wagner. Unions, in general, defined for themselves far too narrow a role in the operation of the enterprise. The views of most unions on management prerogatives, for example, have been indistinguishable from those of most corporation chief executive officers. The McCulloch board, in effect, pushed more for power sharing through collective bargaining than did organized labor. One commentator has called labor's renunciation of power sharing the "longest running mistake in the history of labor" (Geoghegan 1991:246). The "social compact" between organized labor and management, in which labor was junior partner—bargaining only in limited areas while allowing management unrestricted authority to manage—was the product of limited vision.

Among the volumes of advice given to organized labor about how to revive itself, the best echoed Senator Wagner:

> The brightest hope may lie in a return to appealing to that fundamental interest that unions have advanced so effectively in the past: the dignity of the individual working person and his [or her] full, genuine participation in the life of the workplace and of the broader community. That, at any rate, would be a reflection without distortion of the principles of social justice informing our national labor policy (St. Antoine 1980:556).

Thoughts on a National Labor Policy

This country needs a definite, coherent, and consistent national labor policy. That requires more than changing NLRB case doctrines or amending Taft-Hartley to tighten or loosen government regulation of the labor-management relationship. The recrafting of a national labor policy must begin with a precise and certain statement of its purpose and objectives. Fundamental questions must be confronted and answered.

It is most important to understand that at their core these questions are moral and ethical more than legal, economic, or political. In our economic system employers, particularly corporations, are the dominant agents in producing and distributing most of the means by which people live and earn their living. The control these employers have over jobs, the use of scarce resources, and the distribution of products and services gives them the power to affect peoples' lives, to harm them, to benefit them, to violate or protect their rights, to favor some over others for various reasons, to make or break their communities, and to make many of the rules that govern who gets what in the economy and what they have to do to get it.

Consequently, the overwhelming number of working people, even when prospering, are subject to the arbitrary will of others, or to the allegedly impersonal forces of economic markets. Although the impact of employer decisions on human life is much more direct than the impact of most political decisions, the nation has been preoccupied with issues of political democracy while most people are subjugated to economic forces over which they are allowed to have little or no control. That is contrary to the promise this nation made to itself that it would be a democracy. In a democracy private power is a public trust. The very purpose of this nation, although too rarely realized, was to enable the powerless to restrain the powerful. Neither private nor government power would be permitted to control human lives because both would be subject to the public will. All of this nation's public policies, therefore, must stand up to moral scrutiny in the context of the nation's purpose and promise. Democracy is working in this country only when it meets this test.

It is not possible to be morally neutral about these issues. It is also not possible to separate moral and ethical questions from questions of economics and law in fashioning a labor policy. At its most basic, for example, a national labor policy would determine the extent to which employers would be allowed to make decisions in isolation from the people, particularly employees, affected by those decisions, or whether that decision-making power would have to be shared in some way under some circumstances. The current national labor policy is muddled and ambiguous because the Taft-Hartley Act provides contradictory answers to this basic question.

Many possible policy alternatives have been proposed. Some advocate managerial decision-making autonomy in an unregulated market, while others propose a strengthening of the collective bargaining industrial democracy approach by making it easier for employees to become organized, increasing restrictions on employers' ability to resist unionization, providing more effective remedies for violations of employees' statutory rights, and expanding employee participation in the decisions of the enterprise. Still others favor a mandatory system of elected employee participation committees modeled after the German works councils; new forms of cooperative workplace arrangements, such as quality circles, joint labor-management committees, and various employer-created worker participation schemes; or some blend of all these proposals. There has also been support for increasing the legal protection for individual employees, for example, by replacing the current common-law rule of employment at will with a law to protect some or all employees against unjust discharge.

It does not follow, however, that one national labor policy is just as morally good as another. One needs to ask by what standards and for whose benefit government shall act in developing a national labor policy. For example, in March 1993, when Secretary of Labor Robert Reich announced the formation of a commission to reexamine the assumptions underlying the national labor policy, he emphasized evidence showing that when workers have a voice the "yield is higher productivity" (*Daily Labor Report*, May 25, 1993; *Trade Union Advisor*, April 27, 1993). He did not define "voice." Ventriloquism can provide a voice. Earlier, the secretary had discussed with the AFL-CIO Executive Council the role organized labor could have "in advancing the administration's agenda of giving all workers greater participation in their companies to improve productivity." The commission was asked to recommend changes in the law and practice of collective bargaining that would increase workplace productivity through labor-management cooperation.

Increased efficiency and labor peace are appealing objectives, particularly in hard economic times. But the sole or even primary purpose of a national labor policy should not be to increase worker productivity and employer competitiveness, although these may be byproducts. The primary purpose of a national labor policy should be to find a moral basis for achieving human dignity, solidarity, and justice for all parties at the workplace and in the larger communities affected by what goes on at the workplace.

There are costs, even inefficiencies, in having an ethical society. The compelling argument for a national labor policy, however, is not that it increases employer competitiveness but that it embodies fundamentally just moral values. Senator Wagner's primary concern, to which he always subordinated the Wagner Act's other important legislative goals of economic recovery and industrial peace, remained the achievement of social justice through collective bargaining at the workplace.

Collective bargaining has given many employees an opportunity to participate in the determination of their wages, hours, and working conditions and other aspects of their lives on the job. Possibly the greatest single contribution of unions and collective bargaining has been the grievance and arbitration process. These systems of industrial justice substituted more humane rules for arbitrary treatment and unilateral dictation and developed formal procedures to resolve claims of unfair treatment during the term of a collective bargaining agreement either by voluntary settlement or by recourse to an impartial, outside third party. Unions also provide many working people with otherwise unavailable access to political forums. As the national labor policy is used to discourage unionization and collective bargaining, the protection and opportunities for legitimate participation that unions brought to even a minority of workplaces are lost.

For the past twenty-five years, in the main, Taft-Hartley has been interpreted and applied in ways that put federal government power in private employers' hands by strengthening the managerial authority of employers who already have great power over their employees. That, together with the decline of unionism, leaves unprotected the great majority of employees whose economic and political power are not sufficient to protect themselves. Almost sixty years after the Wagner Act, the overwhelming majority of employees are unorganized and unrepresented and work unprotected by grievance and arbitration systems in situations in which they may be fired at will for almost any reason.

Basic justice and the dignity of the human person demand a national labor policy that protects individual workers from arbitrary treatment and provides ways for them to participate in the decisions of the workplace that so deeply affect their lives, the lives of their families, and their communities. A national labor policy rooted in respect for human life and democratic principles would be committed to the promotion at every eligible workplace of a system of labor organizations through which employees could engage in collective bargaining with their employers concerning issues and decisions affecting their jobs. The federal government, therefore, would be an active promoter and facilitator of such a democratic system, not an indifferent neutral. A truly democratic government would not be indifferent to the lack of democracy at the workplace.

Although a law embodying this national labor policy would itself influence community attitudes, a cultural climate also must be created that emphasizes democratic values and the importance of carrying those values over into employer establishments. The organization of employees certainly would be facilitated, as it was during the early days of the Wagner Act, by a truthful claim by the national administration that unionism and collective bargaining are in the public interest. The federal government could demonstrate its commitment to organization and collective bargaining and its desire to have employees choose to participate by guaranteeing those who vote for representation a grievance procedure and arbitration. At the least, such a guarantee could be made whenever a chosen representative failed to negotiate a first contract with an employer. This would discourage employers from deliberately rendering fruitless the employees' choice of collective bargaining. It would also provide the protection against arbitrary action to which every employee is entitled.

It would be foolish or deceitful to commit to a national labor policy of encouraging collective bargaining and then allow employers to block the implementation of that policy by increasing their ability to resist unionization. A national labor policy favoring collective bargaining should minimize employer involvement in the process of employee choice. Recommendations by experts such as Paul Weiler (1990) to shorten the period of preelection campaigning by going to an election within a matter of days on the basis of signed authorization cards would help reduce the opportunity for employer interference. It would also enable the board to avoid the bottomless pit of litigation over the meaning and intent of speech and its effect on employee choice.

Employers could also be discouraged from committing unfair labor practices that interfere with employee choice by automatically certifying labor organizations that are the victims of such unfair labor practices even when there is no evidence that the labor organizations ever had the support of a majority of the employees. This severe remedy would be justified not only because it would prevent employers from benefiting from their violations of the law but also because the unlawful behavior violates human dignity and the democratic process. In other words, the legislation expressing a labor policy favoring worker organization and participation through collective bargaining and prohibiting discrimination for union activities should be and would be treated as a civil rights law and violations should be treated as violations of civil rights.

Consequently, the national labor policy should commit the NLRB to vigorous enforcement of the act. It should also encourage the board to develop and use the full extent of its broad remedy power to encourage voluntary compliance with the law. At the least, violators must no longer be able to profit from their violations. The vigor with which the law is enforced is an excellent test of the federal government's commitment to a national labor policy.

The national labor policy should also continue to permit employees to form and select labor organizations as their representatives for collective bargaining, as long as those organizations are free of employer control. The federal government's support of and deference to labor organizations and collective bargaining, however, would not automatically result in democratic participation. These labor organizations must themselves be democratic and operate on the basis of workers' genuine consent and participation.

Finally, the national labor policy should encourage employers and labor organizations to bargain about all issues and decisions directly or indirectly affecting employees' working lives and, consequently, their families and communities. The current approach leaves it to the preordained and unsubstantiated value judgments of Supreme Court justices and board members to assert what should or should not be an inviolate management prerogative. Opponents of codetermination have portrayed it as a foreign and un-American concept. Codetermination through worker participation, however, is more consistent with this country's conception of democracy than having workers treated as outsiders whose livelihoods depend on the decisions of others over whom they are denied any control or influence.

There should be no doubt that a fundamental moral objective of the national labor policy is to help the powerless restrain the powerful by eliminating the vulnerability that leaves them at the mercy of other people or supposedly impersonal economic forces—either of which can transform them from self-reliant participants into helpless victims. The national labor policy, therefore, must not only protect the powerless from the arbitrary will of others but also give them the opportunity to be actively engaged in securing their own rights and interests through participation in workplace decision-making.

This was the underlying philosophy and purpose of the Wagner Act. Many reject it today because it allegedly espoused a now supposedly archaic and unproductive confrontational approach. That is simply incorrect. Although the pursuit of justice and fairness often requires confrontations, the ultimate objective of the Wagner Act was the establishment, through collective bargaining, of a system of labor-management cooperation based on mutual interest in the success of the enterprise. It was Taft-Hartley that was confrontational, because it enabled and encouraged employers to contest and resist organization and collective bargaining.

The collective bargaining policy carried over from the Wagner Act to Taft-Hartley has been diminished over the years by some NLRBs, Congress, the Supreme Court, presidential administrations, employer resistance, and even organized labor. As a result, the current national labor policy favors and protects the powerful at the expense of the powerless. In the essential moral sense, therefore, the current national labor policy is a failure.

PART II
ORGANIZING AND THE LAW

4

Patterned Responses to Organizing: Case Studies of the Union-Busting Convention

Richard W. Hurd and Joseph B. Uehlein

In June 1993, the Industrial Union Department (IUD) of the AFL-CIO initiated a project to gather cases from affiliated unions that would highlight aspects of the National Labor Relations Board process deserving attention from those shaping labor law reform proposals. Based on the cases submitted, we conclude that in its current form the National Labor Relations Act serves to impede union organizing. Particularly problematic are NLRB policies that allow employers to wage no-holds-barred antiunion campaigns. Even where there are legal restrictions on specific actions, the penalties for violations are so meager that they serve no deterrent effect. The cases described below cover many industries, all parts of the country, large units and small, and collectively suggest that union busting has become the convention among U.S. employers.

Overview of the IUD Case Studies Project

The request for case studies that the IUD circulated was relatively broad but focused primarily on union organizing. By October 1, 1993, we had received 213 case studies from twenty-one national unions. Of these, 167 reported on organizing campaigns; included were campaigns in thirty-six states, the District of Columbia, and Puerto Rico. Most were submitted as brief summaries of one to four pages. This chapter highlights aspects of nineteen representative cases for which additional information was gathered through database searches and requests from the organizing and legal departments of the unions involved.

The picture that emerges from a review of the cases is clear. Under the current legal structure, companies faced with an organizing drive are free to conduct intense antiunion campaigns. Even those companies that have good relations with unions at other facilities often bitterly oppose union organizing. Union avoidance routinely involves the use of a management lawyer or consultant who is expert at defeating worker efforts to organize. Although many antiunion campaigns are run within the limits of the law, many others openly violate NLRB policies. The most common violation is discrimination against union activists in job assignments, discipline, and discharge. If the union manages to win the election, the employer often appeals certification to delay bargaining, in some cases for years. Even if the union is ultimately certified as bargaining agent, management may engage in hard bargaining as part of a long-term strategy to decertify the union.

The remainder of this chapter is devoted almost exclusively to summaries of the cases themselves. We believe that they offer compelling testimony to the need for labor law reform. In each topical section below, we offer several brief examples plus one case summary to give the reader a taste of the intensity of employer hostility toward workers who attempt to organize.[1]

Union-Avoidance Routine

A typical scenario has evolved for the employer's response to an organizing campaign. Consider, for example, the case of Aero Metal Forms in Wichita, Kansas. When twelve of the fifteen employees approached the International Association of Machinists (IAM)[2] about organizing a union, the company hired an attorney to design an antiunion campaign. Supervisors were trained to identify and combat union supporters, and captive audience meetings were held. Workers were warned that the union would take them out on strike and that they could be replaced; they also were threatened with plant closure. The two most vocal union supporters were fired. The April 22, 1991, election resulted in a 6–6 tie with three challenged ballots. By the time the NLRB reached a final decision and declared the union a 7–6 winner on April 5, 1993, only one union supporter still worked for Aero Metal.

Even in the face of overwhelming evidence that their employees want union representation, some companies will go to great lengths to avoid recognition and bargaining. On May 27, 1992, Local 26 of the United Food and Commercial Workers (UFCW) requested recognition from Home Style Foods in Hamtramck, Michigan, based on thirty-four signed cards from the thirty-five employees. The company denied the request, hired a consultant, and implemented a textbook union-resistance campaign: captive audience meet-

---

1. The examples and case summaries are based on material submitted by the unions involved. A list of contact persons and supporting citations will be provided by the authors on request.
2. Standard union abbreviations are used throughout, as indexed in Gifford 1992.

ings, a suggestion box, letters to employees at home, warnings about union strikes and permanent replacements, advance payment of bonuses, a new arbitration system to resolve worker complaints, discipline and dismissal for vocal union advocates, and even a promise from the owner to "fight this to the very end and that could take years." In spite of the campaign, the UFCW won the July 21, 1992, election and has prevailed on every subsequent NLRB decision. Nonetheless, there was still no contract in October 1993, seventeen months after 97 percent of the employees expressed their desire for union representation.

Although most management campaigns attack unionization on many fronts, some are more narrowly focused. In February 1993, the Amalgamated Clothing and Textile Workers Union (ACTWU) collected authorization cards from a majority of workers in a two-plant unit in Louisiana—Crowley Manufacturing and Jennings Manufacturing. The employer adopted a single theme: Vote union and you will lose your job. This message was repeated via captive audience meetings, one-on-one discussions, written communications, bulletin boards, lawn signs, and radio ads. Walls of the factories were covered with newspaper articles, blown up to five feet by three feet, about plant closings. A twelve-foot-by-three-foot banner proclaimed, "Wear the union label—UNEMPLOYED." Sets of two identical pairs of pants were hung around the factories, and supervisors explained that the only difference was that one pair was made in Crowley or Jennings for five dollars per hour and the other was made in Mexico for three dollars per day. The NLRB refused to issue a complaint on unfair labor practice charges, in essence condoning the threats. The union lost the election 275–222.

CWA v. HarperCollins, San Francisco

HarperCollins in San Francisco, owned by Rupert Murdoch, publishes psychology, feminist, and religious books. Half of the 150 highly educated employees are eligible for union membership, 80 percent of them women. Months of effort on employee-management task forces produced very little change, prompting a group of workers to contact the Communications Workers of America (CWA). On December 18, 1992, CWA filed an NLRB petition for a unit of eighty-three employees (sixty-two signed the petition).

HarperCollins sought to exclude twenty employees from the unit (CWA agreed to four). The NLRB held eight days of hearings in January and February 1993. The hearings were prolonged by management lawyers, who, for example, questioned a receptionist for three hours about her duties. The NLRB ultimately ruled with the union and included all sixteen contested employees in the unit. The decision was not issued until May 28, however, and the election was scheduled for June 18.

During the intervening months the company implemented a standard union-resistance campaign. Letters were sent to all employees at home, one from Vice President Clayton Carlson opposing "the insertion of an outside factor like CWA"; another was signed by all the managers, who argued that unionization "would not serve to promote cooperation and solidarity." CEO George Craig flew in from New York and held captive audience meetings. He declared, "This is war," and labeled as "disloyal" all employees involved with the CWA. He then promised to negotiate with an in-house association if employees dropped the union.

The company also made a series of personnel changes. Two workers were promoted out of the unit, and four were laid off. Five of these six were on the organizing committee, and the other was a vocal union supporter. Subsequently, eleven new employees were hired who voted in the election.

The aggressive resistance campaign succeeded. The CWA lost the June 18 election 31–36 with four ballots challenged. On August 31, the NLRB issued a complaint against HarperCollins on twelve violations charged by the union, including the four terminations. A hearing on the charges was scheduled for December 1993.

Legal Delays

Legal delays are a major barrier to organizing. As described above, management lawyers frequently challenge unit determinations to buy time for a union-resistance campaign. In many situations, though, legal delay is more than a temporary stalling device. In 1964, the Service Employees' International Union (SEIU) won the right to represent maintenance employees at Long Island College Hospital in New York City. The hospital pursued a ten-year legal challenge to the appropriateness of the unit that went all the way to the Supreme Court. The parties then began bargaining, but the passage of the 1974 health-care amendments to the NLRA prompted a second round of legal challenges by the hospital, which lasted five years. The SEIU won a second election in January 1979 and was certified in August 1980. The employer refused to bargain, prompting a series of ULPs filed by the union and nine more years of hearings and appeals. When the NLRB issued rules establishing appropriate units for the health-care industry in 1989, the hospital again challenged the unit. In April 1993, the NLRB upheld an administrative law judge's (ALJ) decision and issued a bargaining order. As of October 1993, there was still no contract, twenty-nine years after the workers first voted for representation.

A number of unions report that employers now are using the *threat* of legal delays to defeat unions. In an ACTWU organizing campaign at BMP American in Medina, New York, the company successfully undermined support for the union with the aid of a June 8, 1993, memo to employees:

> This outside union has filed two sets of charges against the com-
> pany. . . . Unfortunately, we have started on the road of a very, very long
> process. Our attorneys have advised us that generally the steps involve:
> an investigation, a possible trial, . . . a possible appeal to an NLRB
> panel, . . . and even a possible appeal to a Federal Appellate Court. . . . Many
> cases have lasted 5, 6, or 7 years until they become final.

A similar approach was used by Crown Cork and Seal while opposing organizing by the United Steel Workers of America (USWA) at its Puerto Rico facility in 1990–91. The aggressive resistance is particularly noteworthy because the USWA has a good bargaining relationship with this employer in thirty-six plants in the United States and Canada. But this did not stop the company from making threats explicitly tied to legal delays in a lengthy December 11, 1991, memo sent to each worker at home (translated from Spanish):

> 5. The company has prepared ULP charges for the NLRB. . . . The judge
> can issue a decision between two and twelve months. Either party can
> appeal. . . . The board can reasonably issue a decision between two months
> and two years. Either party can appeal. . . . It can reasonably take between six
> months and eighteen months for the court of appeals to issue a decision.
> Either party can appeal. . . .
>   6. If there is an election and the Steelworkers win, the company would
> challenge the results. . . . This means that the company would nullify the
> need to negotiate with the USWA.
>   7. If the USWA does not like the company's refusal to negotiate, it would
> have to file ULP charges—the company would appeal to the NLRB and the
> court of appeals. This process could take two years or more.

AFSCME v. Fountain Valley Regional Hospital, Fountain Valley, California

In May 1986, an affiliate of the American Federation of State, County, and Municipal Employees (AFSCME) was contacted by registered nurses and other professional employees at Fountain Valley Regional Hospital. After collecting 520 authorization cards from a unit of 650 (80 percent), AFSCME filed for an election in November and the delays began. The hospital challenged the unit and presented lengthy testimony on a wide variety of technical and confidential employees. The hearings stretched over eight days in December 1986 and January 1987. The NLRB issued its decision on the unit on April 1, 1987, and scheduled the election for April 30 and May 1.

Management used the five-and-one-half-month delay to implement an antiunion campaign replete with the standard threats, promises, and captive audience meetings. The campaign was coordinated by the West Coast Industrial Relations Association (WCIRA), a consulting firm known for its "Maintaining Your Union Free Status" seminars. Based on papers filed by WCIRA with the U.S. Department of Labor, Fountain Valley paid more than $365,000 for union-avoidance assistance during the first year.

The election results were 278 for AFSCME and 274 for no union and 28 challenged ballots (24 by the employer, 4 by the union). The regional office of the NLRB considered the challenges and issued a decision on November 16, 1987. Both sides requested a review by the NLRB, which concurred with the regional office but not until October 1988. The challenged ballots were finally opened, and the union won 285–279. Fountain Valley refused to accept the results, appealed the decision, and refused to bargain, claiming that the union did not represent a majority of employees.

Throughout the process of determining the election outcome, the hospital continued its antiunion campaign, prompting numerous ULP charges. A series of decisions from the NLRB were ignored, until June 12, 1991, when the U.S. Ninth Circuit Court of Appeals ordered the hospital to bargain. Over the next twenty months bargaining sessions were held once per month and progress was painfully slow. Finally, on April 12, 1993, agreement was reached when the union resigned itself to accepting the status quo on most issues. Unbeknownst to AFSCME, a decertification petition had been filed two days earlier. Union members ratified the contract on April 16, but management refused to sign it. In the meantime, ULPs continued to pile up, and management openly violated an NLRB-ordered posting while it adorned hospital bulletin boards. There was still no signed agreement as of October 1993, six and one-half years after workers voted to be represented by AFSCME.

Blatant Labor Law Violations

Some employers are not content to work within the friendly confines of NLRB regulations. Instead, they openly violate the law, most often by discriminating against the leaders of union organizing drives. Nearly half the cases submitted to the IUD for this project included specific details of workers being disciplined, laid off, or fired for union activity. In most of them, the NLRB eventually ruled against the employer—but long after the organizing campaign had been halted by worker fear.

Consider ACTWU's organizing campaign at Surgical Appliance, Inc., in Cincinnati. Nearly half the 120 employees were visited in their homes over two days in early February 1993. Approximately 70 percent of those visited signed union authorization cards. Eight workers passed out organizing leaflets at the plant gate the next morning. An hour later all eight either were laid off or had their hours reduced. This scenario was repeated over the next few days until twenty-six union supporters were laid off. The organizing campaign had been stopped cold.

Six months later, Surgical Appliances and ACTWU reached a settlement with the NLRB—$70,000 in back pay and a management agreement to cease and desist from interfering with union activity through threats, surveillance, unlawful restriction of the distribution of literature, interrogation, and discrimination. ACTWU won the NLRB case, but Surgical Appliance avoided unionization by breaking the law quickly and severely, scaring the workers into retreat.

Sheridan Manor Nursing Home in Buffalo, New York, responded similarly when faced with an organizing campaign by the CWA in late 1992. The push for unionization had originated among licensed practical nurses (LPNs), so Sheridan fired sixteen of its twenty-one LPNs on January 19, 1993, with no explanation. An election was held on August 5, but the ballots were impounded because of a company appeal of the unit determination. Subsequently, the LPNs were reinstated (without back pay) pending an NLRB hearing on the dismissals scheduled for October.

A case involving the United Mine Workers of America (UMWA) demonstrates that blatant violations of the law can be combined with lengthy legal appeals. In December 1988, the UMWA was contacted by employees of Power, Inc., an Osceola Mills, Pennsylvania, surface mining operation owned by Ryan International of Great Britain. An election petition was filed on January 6, 1989 (forty-eight of seventy-four workers in the unit had signed cards). On March 10, thirteen days before the election, the company laid off thirteen workers, all of them union activists, including the leaders of the organizing campaign. The vote at the March 23 election was twenty-seven yes, thirty no, and ballots cast by the thirteen laid-off workers were challenged by the employer.

As the case worked its way through the NLRB process over the next four years, the company committed numerous ULPs, including laying off twelve additional union supporters. As new ULPs were filed, they were appended to the previous case. All of this delayed decisions on the challenged ballots and the prior charges. The ALJ's initial decision was not issued until May 6, 1992. The company, found guilty of most of the ULP charges, appealed. The NLRB issued its decision on May 28, 1993, upholding the ALJ decision on all substantive points. The thirteen challenged ballots finally were opened on June 22, and, as expected, all were for the union; the final vote stood at forty yes, thirty no. Power, Inc., appealed the decision to the District Court.

ILGWU v. Domsey Trading Corporation, Brooklyn, New York

Domsey buys and exports used clothing, and its employees are mostly Haitian and Latin American immigrants. On December 1, 1989, a representative of the International Ladies' Garment Workers' Union (ILGWU) arrived at Domsey to request recognition. Seventy-six percent of the employees had signed cards in a unit of 243. A key union supporter with twenty-seven years' seniority informed the owner's son that the union was there to see him. Fifteen minutes later, the union supporter was fired. That afternoon, the employer's attorney told the union's attorney that he was not worried, because even if the employer had to reinstate the discharged worker, the back-pay liability would not amount to much. By late January, Domsey fired two more pro-union workers. On January 30, 90 percent of the employees walked out because of the illegal firings.

During the strike, management representatives subjected the striking workers, most of whom were Haitian, and union organizers to outrageous harassment. The owner's son placed a "voodoo table" covered with a black tablecloth in front of picketing workers, placed candles and bananas on the table, and called to the workers, "This is for you monkeys to eat." He and his cohorts called women picketers "whores" and shouted explicit obscenities at them. They called the picketers "lazy" and "stupid niggers," and they told them that they were being sprayed with water to wash off their smells.

On August 10, 1990, the 132 remaining strikers unconditionally requested to return to work. Domsey refused to rehire some of them, and those who were reinstated suffered severe abuse, including physical attacks and verbal harassment. A particularly repugnant management employee, later compared by an ALJ to Attila the Hun, physically attacked one union supporter and injured her seriously enough that she had to be hospitalized; he also screamed obscenities in the faces of others. Some union supporters quit in fear and disgust. Others were fired.

Over the next three years the NLRB took a consistent stance in opposition to Domsey's blatant disregard for the law. ALJ and NLRB decisions found the employer guilty of multiple ULPs. A court injunction ordered a halt to Domsey's discriminatory treatment of union supporters, and when the company ignored the injunction, the NLRB secured a contempt of court citation.

An election was eventually held on March 27, 1992, more than two years after the petition was filed. By this time only a third of the original union supporters still worked at Domsey, and the union lost 170–120. Although the NLRB overturned the election results, the company continued to avoid compliance with the law by appealing every decision. As of October 1993, the case was still before the U.S. Court of Appeals.

Weaknesses of NLRB Protections and Penalties

Even when the NLRB concludes that management has violated the law, its options for achieving compliance are limited. As noted above, it is standard practice for management lawyers to raise objections in order to delay an election, and in the event that the union wins, to challenge the results and delay certification. Such was the case in 1989 when the SEIU sought to represent Lakeside Community Hospital employees in Clear Lake, California. The hospital filed multiple objections, including a "concern" it had regarding the local union's method of selecting vice presidents. In response, the NLRB issued a scolding: "Objections 1, 2, 3, 6, 13, 14, 16, 18, 19, 23, 24, and 28, appear to be frivolous and border on an abuse of the Board's processes. . . . The Board *frowns* upon the filing by any party of multiple, obviously non-meritorious objections" (emphasis added). The hospital not only continued its appeals but subsequently committed numerous ULPs, prompting two additional board orders and a case before the U.S. Court of Appeals, which was heard on September 13, 1993. As Lakeside has demonstrated, frowns are unlikely to convince determined employers to alter their union-avoidance practices.

The most commonly used remedy in cases of employer ULPs is a cease and desist order, which is to be posted in central locations on the company's property. Unfortunately, many employers simply ignore the order even if they post the decision as required. For example, Dayton Hudson Corporation has openly violated the law as a response to UAW organizing at its Detroit area stores. On August 9, 1991, an election at a store in Fairlane (a narrow loss for the UAW) was set aside by the NLRB because of numerous employer ULPs. The violations included threats, coercive interrogation, discipline of union activists, following employees into restrooms, videotaping workers while they spoke to union organizers, and monitoring phone calls. Hudson's was ordered to cease such behavior and to post notices to that effect. A new election was scheduled for October 30, 1992. While the notices were still posted, Hudson's repeated the same behavior—intimidation, harassment, threats, interrogation, and spying. The NLRB canceled the election and issued a complaint detailing more than one hundred separate violations. Hearings were held, and an ALJ decision was expected in late 1993.

In situations in which discharge is clearly tied to union activity, the NLRB will order reinstatement with back pay less interim earnings from other sources. The penalty is so modest, however, that it appears to be ineffective, as every case in the preceding section demonstrates. In fact, employers that discharge union supporters during organizing campaigns typically commit multiple other violations as well; consider, for example, the behavior of Rock-Tenn.

The United Paperworkers International Union (UPIU) began organizing Rock-Tenn's Columbus, Indiana, facility in July 1989. The employer immediately started an aggressive antiunion campaign. Eight pro-union employees were discharged, union supporters were placed under surveillance, a no-solicitation, no-distribution rule was enforced, numerous employees were interrogated, and management threatened to close the plant and reduce benefits. The union lost a February 1, 1990, election 50–70. The NLRB issued complaints in October and December 1989 and in March 1990. The employer continued to harass and discriminate against union supporters, leading to more charges. Nonetheless, the union eventually achieved majority support in a second election on February 5, 1991. Over the next year the company engaged in hard bargaining while providing direct support to two employees who conducted a decertification campaign, and additional ULPs piled up. Finally, on May 25, 1993, an ALJ decision found Rock-Tenn guilty of virtually all ULPs plus violation of Weingarten rights and interfering with NLRB processes. The company appealed.

UFCW v. Gress Poultry, Scranton, Pennsylvania

The UFCW conducted an organizing campaign among 250 workers at Gress Poultry in 1986. In spite of the challenge of communicating in seven different languages to the largely immigrant workforce, the union was able to secure authorization cards from nearly 70 percent of the employees. An election was scheduled for December 23, 1986. The owners hired consultant Ray Blankenship to "run an anti-organizing campaign."

Blankenship held a series of three captive audience meetings for each of the three shifts, the first meetings in early December, the second ten days before the election, and the final meetings the day before the election. The theme at these meetings was straightforward: If the union won, the plant would be closed. Blankenship told the employees about one of his clients who had lost an election and padlocked the plant. To make sure that the message was understood by the multilingual audience, he held up a huge padlock for everyone to see. To drive the message home on election day, Blankenship held a picture of a lock and key and told employees that the employer had given him a padlock to lock the door when he closed the plant down. In addition to the threats, Blankenship took photographs of employees talking to union organizers and engaged in other acts designed to intimidate union supporters

After losing the election 114–71 with 38 challenged ballots, the union filed objections and charges of ULPs. Because Blankenship had actually delivered threats himself (most consultants stay in the background), he was charged jointly along with the employer. The case inched its way through the

NLRB process with decisions for the union at every step. During the lengthy appeals process, support for the union eroded, and the UFCW gave up on its organizing objective. Along with the NLRB, however, the union continued to pursue the case against Blankenship.

On July 18, 1990, an ALJ found that Blankenship had committed five ULPs during the election. The ALJ issued a cease and desist order and a requirement that Blankenship post the order conspicuously in his Greenwood, Indiana, offices. Blankenship appealed to the NLRB. On March 31, 1992, noting that Blankenship had a ten-year record of labor law violations in a series of cases for different employer clients, the NLRB upheld the ALJ decision. Blankenship appealed.

On July 15, 1993, the U.S. Court of Appeals enforced the NLRB order. In perhaps the ultimate statement attesting to the enforcement power of the NLRB, Blankenship submitted a certificate of posting indicating that the notice had been posted "on the seat of our employees' toilet." On September 8, 1993, the NLRB initiated civil contempt proceedings.

First-Contract Problems

As several cases we have already discussed make clear, winning a representation election does not necessarily secure union protection for workers. Utilizing the services of lawyers and consultants expert at frustrating the bargaining process, employers have been able to avoid such basic union protections as the grievance and arbitration system.

Although "surface bargaining" is considered a ULP by the NLRB, "hard bargaining" is tolerated. For example, the UMWA won an election at Shanefelter Industries in Uniontown, Pennsylvania, on April 26, 1991, by a vote of 22–6. The firm hired labor consultant Kelvin Berens from Omaha, Nebraska, to negotiate. As of October 1993, two and one-half years of monthly negotiations had resulted in no agreement on even basic issues. During bargaining the consultant displays a lackadaisical attitude by reading the newspaper while the union presents its proposals or engaging in idle banter about cattle ranching, skiing, or amusement parks to kill time and prolong the process. The union has repeatedly filed ULPs only to be told that "hard bargaining" is not a violation.

In January 1990, the International Brotherhood of Electrical Workers (IBEW) won an election in a fourteen-member unit against Coastal Electric Cooperative in Walterboro, South Carolina. The firm hired attorney Julian Gignilliat to negotiate. As of October 1993, agreement had not been reached on most key issues, including seniority, just cause, management rights, wages, and benefits. The company firmly opposes an arbitration clause, demanding that management be the last step in the grievance procedure. Gignilliat has stated that under the management proposal, if the union disagreed with the management's decision in the last step of the grievance process, it could strike "and I will replace every goddamn one of you." He also demands employment-at-will language. On September 18, 1992, an ALJ ruled for the union in a failure to bargain in good faith ULP case. The company appealed and the NLRB overturned the decision on June 30, 1993, reinstating a prior settlement agreement requiring the parties to meet and negotiate.

BCTW v. Dawn Frozen Foods, Crown Point, Indiana

In many cases the company will stall negotiations for a year then support decertification efforts by employees. The Bakery, Confectionery and Tobacco Workers' International Union (BCTW) won an election at Dawn Frozen Foods in Crown Point, Indiana, on March 28, 1991, by a 56–41 vote. Dawn hired attorney Robert Bellamy to negotiate. Negotiations were held monthly beginning in June.

There was no movement even on such simple issues as a union bulletin board. In February 1992 negotiations, Bellamy informed the union negotiating team that it would not be getting an "old '60s Baker's contract" but a contract that reflected the "realities of the '90s." The "old" clauses that the company refused to consider included union security, dues checkoff, and plant visitation rights for union representatives. A decertification petition began to circulate in the spring with supervisor support. On June 10, 1992, an employee group filed for decertification, and a vote was set for July 8.

The company made what it labeled its final offer on June 21. At this stage the union was not worried about the decertification vote because it had an internal organizing campaign in place, and seventy-plus workers were wearing union hats on the job every day. A federal mediator suggested that the union have the workers vote on the final offer, noting that management had told him that it could count hats and expected to lose the decertification election. The offer was voted down on June 28, and the union requested a new bargaining session.

Coincidentally, on June 30, Robert Bellamy conducted an all-day seminar in Indianapolis, sponsored by the Indiana Chamber of Commerce, entitled "Remaining Union Free." In the final week before the decertification vote, the company ran an intense antiunion campaign with all of the standard ingredients: captive audience meetings, supervisors holding one-on-ones, the owner promising to give the workers everything the union had negotiated without union dues, and slides of the plant with a closed sign on the door.

On July 7, Bellamy sent a letter to the union negotiator via certified mail responding to the request for a bargaining session to discuss the company's "final offer," which had been voted down:

> That final offer remains final. . . .
> —What final means is that Dawn is prepared to take a strike if its final offer is not acceptable. . . .
> —Final means you have gotten all there is to get— there is not one penny more—period.
> —If a strike does occur, Crown Point will of course exercise its right to continue operations and hire replacements. . . .
> —If you do not believe me when I say that something is FINAL, go ask the UAW in Cambellsville, Kentucky. After I gave a final offer, they went on strike over an open shop clause . . . permanent replacements were hired, the union is now gone. . . .
> FINAL means FINAL.

Copies of the letter were hand delivered on the shop floor by supervisors to every employee. The next day, the BCTW lost the decertification election 51–48.

Conclusions and Policy Recommendations

We believe that the cases collected by the Industrial Union Department lay bare the assumption of many academics and policy makers that blatant union busting is practiced only by a relatively small group of extremists in the management community. The underlying position of most employers is hostile to employee rights to organize and engage in concerted action. Given the widespread animus displayed toward unions and the current state of labor law, employer abuse of the right to organize is bounded only by the ingenuity of the lawyers and consultants who have made this field of practice their specialty.

We also believe that dramatic change in the law is needed to counteract the management union-busting convention. Based on the cases we have collected, a number of problem areas must be addressed if the right of workers to organize is to be protected.

1. Employer interference with workers' decision regarding unionization should be curtailed. Steps should be taken to limit management's ability to intimidate workers with threats, surveillance, and continuous supervisory pressure.

2. For employers who openly violate labor laws in order to defeat organizing campaigns, the costs of noncompliance must be increased. Particular

attention should be given to proposals that would protect union supporters from discrimination, especially unjust dismissal.

3. Steps should be taken to speed up the NLRB process. Election delays allow management to exploit workers' fears and intimidate union supporters. Certification and bargaining delays deny workers the right to union representation and contract protection.

4. Restrictions should be placed on the role of consultants in union-avoidance campaigns. Penalties also should be considered for consultants and law firms associated with illegal union busting activities.

5. Steps should be taken to ensure that a decision by workers to unionize cannot be circumvented by employers that refuse to engage in good-faith bargaining.

Specific labor law reform proposals that address these concerns are spelled out in detail in the IUD report *Democracy on the Job: America's Path to a Just, High Skill, High Wage Economy*. As summarized there, "The three prerequisites to rebuilding the union organizing process in this country are card majority recognition . . .; removal of employer interference from the certification process and greater union access to employees; and binding arbitration of the first contract" (AFL-CIO 1994).

The proposals offered by the IUD would place strict limits on employers' ability to thwart the right of workers to organize and join unions. They would also grant unions a reasonable opportunity to recruit new members in an atmosphere free of fear and intimidation. Finally, they would ensure that workers through their unions would have the opportunity to achieve contractual protection via meaningful collective bargaining.

5

Employer Behavior in Certification Elections and First-Contract Campaigns: Implications for Labor Law Reform

Kate L. Bronfenbrenner

Organizing is an extremely risky and arduous venture for American workers. As the experience of the last twenty years has shown, a combination of unfettered employer antiunion behavior and weak and poorly enforced labor law make for an "unlevel playing field" stacked against unorganized workers and unions. Using survey data from private-sector certification election and first-contract campaigns, this chapter will first examine the impact of NLRB practices and legal and illegal employer behavior on union election and first-contract outcomes. It will then evaluate how labor law reform would reduce the ability of employers to undermine workers' efforts to organize and win first agreements.

Although there has been a great deal of research on the relationship between employers' unfair labor practices and election outcomes, there has been very little research on the broad range of legal and illegal tactics used by employers during the NLRB election process, regardless of whether unfair labor practices were actually filed. Even fewer studies have controlled for the influence of bargaining unit demographics, organizer background, and union tactics during organizing campaigns. In addition, only a handful of studies have examined employer and union behavior during first-contract campaigns, even though a union election victory is at best Pyrrhic without a first-contract victory. This study can therefore provide new and important insights into the impact of NLRB practices and employer behavior on election and first-contract outcomes as well as the need for and ramifications of significant labor law reform.[1]

---

1. My dissertation (1993) provides an in-depth review of the industrial relations research literature relating to organizing and first-contract campaigns.

Hypotheses

This study will test the hypotheses that NLRB practices and legal and illegal employer behavior play a significant role in determining union success in elections and first agreements and that specific labor law reform will substantially diminish the negative impact of these factors. Variables relevant to labor law reform during the organizing drive include the number of days between petition and election, the percentage of cards signed, unit challenges, discharges for union activity, employer promises of improvements in wages or benefits, wage increases, captive audience meetings, company mailings, and unfair labor practice charges and complaints.

Variables to be examined during the first-contract campaign include election objections; postelection discharges, threats, and promises; unilateral changes in wages and benefits; staffing changes; captive audience meetings; full or partial plant shutdowns; the use of surface bargaining and other hard bargaining strategies; decertification drives; and attempts to undermine the committee and divide union membership.

The proposed labor law reforms include recognition after a majority card check; a consistent community of interest standard for unit determination; more vigorous and speedier enforcement of NLRB penalties for unfair labor practices, including discharges, threats, promises, unilateral changes, and refusal to bargain; financial and injunctive relief for more egregious violations, especially 8(a)(3) and 8(a)(5) charges; greater access for union organizers to the company premises; and stronger restrictions and penalties for employers that shut down operations or contract out work to avoid unionization.

Data and Methodology

This chapter relies on data collected for my dissertation, entitled "Seeds of Resurgence: Successful Union Strategies for Winning Certification Elections and First Contracts in the 1980's and Beyond" (1993). Although the primary focus of that research was to determine which union strategies had the most positive impact on union certification election and first-contract outcomes, the study also included a wealth of data on employer behavior and other unit and election background variables.

This study is based on a random sample of 261 NLRB certification elections that took place between July 1986 and June 1987. Only single-union elections involving AFL-CIO affiliates in units of fifty or more eligible voters were included. The data were collected in cooperation with the AFL-CIO, building on and refining its earlier survey of 189 organizing campaigns (AFL-CIO 1989). The 261 elections in the final sample represent approximately a third of the total elections in units with more than fifty during that period and are representative across unions, industries, regions, and types of bargaining units.[2]

Lead organizers for each of the campaigns completed a lengthy survey regarding their backgrounds, bargaining unit demographics, company characteristics and tactics, and union tactics. In addition, for 100 out of the 119 bargaining units in which the union won the election or won a second election between the election and the time the survey was completed, follow-up interviews were conducted with the union representative in charge of contract negotiations. The second survey included questions regarding the bargaining climate, the negotiation process, the negotiator's background, employer and union characteristics and tactics, as well as the outcome of bargaining.

Descriptive statistics were calculated for each of the NLRB practices and employer behavior variables to provide an in-depth portrait of the extent and nature of employer behavior and NLRB practices during organizing and first-contract campaigns. In addition, multivariate regression and logit analyses were used to determine whether specific variables had a statistically significant impact on certification and/or first-contract outcome when controlling for the influence of other election background, election environment, company characteristics, bargaining unit demographics, management tactic, union tactic, and union control variables.[3]

Results of the Certification Election Study

The results of the certification election study document both the pervasive nature of aggressive employer antiunion behavior during organizing campaigns and the negative impact that current NLRB practices and legal and illegal employer behavior have on certification election outcome.

2. There were a total of 961 single-union elections involving AFL-CIO affiliates in units with more than fifty voters during the period examined. The restriction on bargaining unit size focuses the study on significant union campaigns rather than on those involving just a handful of workers. In 1986, union win rates averaged 51 percent in the 2,635 units with fewer than fifty eligible voters, compared with 37 percent in the 1,236 units with fifty or more eligible voters. Because the failure of unions to win larger units is such a critical element of the labor law reform debate, and because it is more difficult to measure the impact of bargaining unit demographic and union and employer tactic variables in smaller bargaining units, limiting the sample to larger units helps focus the study on those units in which union and employer behavior have the most meaningful impact on election outcome.

3. For the organizing study, three different equations were used. The first two equations, with a dependent variable of percent union vote, used ordinary least squares (OLS) and weighted least squares (WLS) as the method of analysis; the third equation, with the dependent variable of election win or loss, used logit as the statistical method of analysis. For the purpose of this paper, the results for the OLS and logit equations are included. The first-contract study utilized just one equation, with the dependent variable of contract win or loss and logit as the method of analysis. A more in-depth explanation of the methodology utilized in both studies can be found in my dissertation (1993).

Impact of NLRB Practices on Election Outcome

One of the primary concerns of the labor movement is the lengthy delays between the time a petition is filed and the election is held. In this study, delays ranged from less than a month to more than two years. As we can see from table 5.1, the win rate was much higher in units in which the election was held less than two months after the petition was filed (53 percent) than when the election was held two to six months after the petition was filed (41 percent). For the 6 percent of the campaigns in which delays were longer than six months, the win rate increased to 60 percent.

This by no means tells us that delays benefit unions. Clearly, delays give employers a longer time period in which to campaign aggressively against the union. Many of the unions that were unable to maintain bargaining unit support after lengthy delays may have withdrawn from the campaign rather than going ahead with an election they were certain to lose. Because only campaigns that actually went to an election were included in the sample, the negative impact of delays is therefore underestimated.

The high percentage of campaigns in which there was a majority or near majority of signed cards makes it clear that if the election were held on the same day the petition was filed, or if certification could be achieved by card checks rather than elections, union win rates would nearly double. Although unions are required to collect signatures from only 30 percent of the unit to have an election, in more than 73 percent of the campaigns studied, unions signed up a majority of the unit on cards before the election. In addition, in more than 84 percent of the campaigns, the unions got within 5 percent of a majority and might have been able to get a majority signed up if they had known card signing would result in instant certification.[4]

Unions did especially poorly in elections in which the original unit the union petitioned for was changed by stipulation or by order of the board or courts. Unions won only 23 percent of the elections in those cases in which the unit was changed, compared with a 47 percent win rate in units that remained unchanged throughout the unit determination process. When the influence of other election campaign variables are controlled for, the results further suggest that the percentage union vote declines by 4 percent and the probability

---

4. The results for the card check variable are further substantiated by a recent study I conducted with Tom Juravich (1994), which established the first-ever national database of public-sector union certification campaigns. Several states, including New York, Washington, and South Dakota, permit certification through card check for public-sector workers as long as employers do not contest the unit and/or demand an election. Juravich and I found that in those states permitting card checks, the average percentage of the eligible voters who signed cards was 85 percent, well beyond the majority plus one required for certification. This also counteracts claims that if card signing led to certification rather than to an election, the percentage of cards signed would drop dramatically.

Table 5.1. Results of Study on Certification Elections

Independent variable	Mean or percent of sample	Percent of union-win rate (rate when not present)	Predicted impact on percent union vote	Predicted impact on probability of union win
Number of days from petition election	79 days average	N.A.	—	—
60 days or less	53	50	—	—
60–180 days	41	31	—	—
180 days or more	6	60	—	—
Percent signed cards	60% average	N.A.	3% for 10% increase in cards	5% for 10% increase in cards
More than 50%	73	51 (20)	—	—
Precampaign participation plan	7	22 (44)	-6% with plan	-22% with plan
Unit changed after petition	22	22 (47)	-4% if unit different	-15% if unit different
Management consultant used	71	40 (50)	-11% if consultant used	-3% if consultant used
Discharges not reinstated	18	37 (44)	-1% if not reinstated	-8% if not reinstated
All units with discharges	30	51 (40)	—	—
Company gave wage increase	30	32 (47)	-7% if wage increase	-9% if wage increase
Company made promises	56	34 (54)	-3% if promises made	-13% if promises made
Antiunion committee used	42	37 (46)	-6% if anti-union committee	-1% if anti-union committee
Number of captive audience meetings	5.5 meetings average	N.A.	-.2% for each additional meeting	-1% for each additional meeting
No captive audience meetings	18	42	—	—
20 or more meetings	2	18	—	—
Number of company letters	4.5 letters average	N.A.	-.5% for each additional letter	-1% for each additional letter
No company letters	21	45	—	—
More than 5 letters	30	37	—	—
Supervisor campaigned one-on-one	79	41 (43)	—	—
ULP charges filed	36	41 (43)	—	—
Complaints won on charges filed	53	53 (40)	—	—
Total for all 261 cases in sample	100	43	—	—

Note: Including predicted impact on percent unit vote and probability of a union win for all variables included in the regression and logit equations when controlling for the influence of election environment, company and unit characteristic, and union tactic and characteristic variables. Statistically significant results are in bold for all variables that were included in those equations.

of the union winning an election declines by as much as 15 percent when the unit is changed after the petition is filed.

Unit changes appear to have had an especially negative impact in those campaigns in which the final unit included other unorganized worksites or divisions of the corporation. Several unions in the sample lost elections, despite winning more than 70 percent of the votes in the unit they originally petitioned for, because the board added another branch of the company, doubling the number of eligible voters just weeks before the election.

The use of participation schemes, team concept, and other employee involvement programs appears to have been an especially effective union-avoidance tactic for the 7 percent of the employers in the sample that had these programs in place before the election campaign began. Although the number of cases is too small to come to any definitive conclusions, win rates were 22 percent lower in these units, and the predicted negative impact on the percentage union vote and the probability of the union winning the election were 6 and 22 percent respectively.

Management Tactics during Campaigns

More than 75 percent of the employers in the sample engaged in active antiunion tactics, including some combination of discharges for union activity; captive audience meetings; supervisor one-on-ones; wage increases; promises of improvements in wages, benefits, or working conditions; antiunion committees; and letters. With the exception of the consultant and discharge variables, all of the management tactics variables exhibited a statistically significant negative impact on either percentage union vote or election outcome when the influence of other election campaign variables were controlled for.

Seventy-one percent of the employers in the sample utilized a management consultant during their election campaigns. The win rate associated with campaigns in which the employer used an outside consultant was 40 percent, versus 50 percent in campaigns in which no outside consultant was used.

The failure of the consultant variable to have a strong negative effect may be due to a growing trend among larger corporations to use lawyers on retainer or to hire their own in-house labor relations specialists. These lawyers and in-house consultants play the same role as management consultants but do not have to register under the Labor-Management Reporting and Disclosure Act (LMRDA). Fifteen percent of the campaigns used outside lawyers on retainer, many of whom acted as management consultants in practice though not in name, bringing to 86 percent the number of units that used some kind of outsiders during the management campaign. Several employers in the sample, especially national chains, such as Beverly Enterprises, Inc., had in-house labor relations specialists who ran by-the-book aggressive antiunion campaigns, complete with numerous unfair labor practices. These in-house human resource specialists may have received the same training and may have served the same purpose as the outside management consultants, but they were not counted in calculating the impact of the management consultant variable.

The lead organizers surveyed claimed that employers discharged workers for union activity in 30 percent of the campaigns. Although unions filed 8(a)(3) charges in 87 percent of the campaigns in which workers were fired for union activity, complaints were issued in only 43 percent of the campaigns with discharges. Discharged workers were reinstated before the election in only 40 percent of these campaigns. In five campaigns, the NLRB ordered reinstatement after the election had taken place, too late for those workers to vote and too late to affect the election outcome positively. This meant that workers were reinstated before the election in only 34 percent of the campaigns in which there were discharges for union activity. Although win rates averaged 10 percent higher in units in which there were discharges than in units without any discharges for union activity, win rates were only 37 percent in units in which the union was unable to win reinstatement for any discharged workers before the election took place.

These mixed results for the discharge variables should not be interpreted as evidence that discharges for union activity do not have a devastating impact on workers' willingness and ability to organize. It is very likely that employers resort to discharges for union activity only during those campaigns in which the union has a good chance of winning the election. Discharges backfired for employers only in the small number of cases in which the union was able to win reinstatement for discharged employees before the election, demonstrating union power and undermining the employers' ability to intimidate workers from engaging in union activity. This contrasts sharply with the majority of elections, in which unions were unable to win reinstatement for discharged workers before the election.

The negative impact of these firings is underestimated in studies of NLRB election campaigns insofar as they do not include the large number of campaigns that never make it to an election because the employer discharged workers early in the union campaign. These include campaigns in which workers are fired after the initial union contact or the first union meeting, effectively quashing the campaign before it even gets off the ground. These also include campaigns in which, despite initial majority support, the union is forced to withdraw from the election after the employer fires some or all of the rank-and-file organizing committee, undercutting the union's ability to organize inside the workplace and intimidating workers from continuing their support for the union.

Employers granted wage increases in 30 percent of the campaigns and made promises of improvements in wages, hours, and working conditions in 56 percent, even though both of these actions can be considered violations of Section 8(a)(1) of the NLRA. In addition, employers established antiunion committees in 42 percent of the campaigns. The win rates associated with these employer behavior variables were 9 to 20 percent lower than in units in which these tactics were not used. The results further suggest that the percentage union vote would decline by 15 percent in units in which the company granted wage increases, by 3 percent in units in which the company made promises, and by 20 percent in units in which management utilized an antiunion committee. Similarly, we can predict that the probability of the union winning the election would decline by 9 percent in units in which the company gave wage increases and by 13 percent in units in which the company made promises during the election campaign.

Under the "free speech" provisions of the NLRA, employers have virtually unlimited opportunities to communicate aggressively with their employees during union campaigns, at the same time as union access is tightly circumscribed if not totally restricted. Under current labor law these employer communications can and often do include distortion, misinformation, threats, and intimidation, with very little chance of censure or penalty by the board or courts. The pervasiveness and intensity of employer communications with the bargaining unit are measured in this study by both the number of captive audience meetings held and the number of company letters sent. Union win rates declined dramatically as the number of meetings and letters increased, from more than 40 percent for campaigns in which no captive audience meetings were held or letters sent, down to 18 percent when the employer held twenty or more captive audience meetings and 37 percent when the company sent more than five letters during the campaign. The results further suggest that for every additional letter that the company mails out, the percentage of votes cast for the union declines by 2.5 percent and the probability of the union winning the election declines by 1 percent. Similarly, for every additional captive audience meeting, the proportion of union votes declines by .2 percent and the probability of the union winning the election declines by 1 percent.

The primary issues focused on by employers in these forums were strikes, dues and fines, and plant closings. According to the organizers surveyed, these messages often included blatant or veiled threats and repeated distortions or misinformation about the union. Thus, in the atmosphere created by captive audience meetings, in which the union has no access and little influence, the coercive nature of the antiunion message can be extremely damaging to the union campaign.

ULPs during the Campaign

Unions filed unfair labor practice (ULP) complaints, other than 8(a)(3) charges, in 23 percent of the campaigns, but complaints were issued in only 39 percent of the campaigns in which those ULPs were filed. Overall, including 8(a)(3)s, unions filed ULPs in 36 percent of the campaigns and complaints were issued in 53 percent of the campaigns in which ULPs were filed. Union win rates were slightly lower, but not at a statistically significant level, in campaigns in which charges were filed (41 percent), compared with campaigns in which no charges were filed (43 percent). Win rates were higher in units in which complaints were issued (53 percent), however, possibly because NLRB complaints effectively demonstrate that unions can win against the employer.

These results *do not* lend credence to those who would argue that existent NLRB law and practice effectively enforce union and worker rights in the organizing process. The NLRB failed to issue complaints in 47 percent of the campaigns in which charges were filed, despite repeated egregious and illegal employer behavior, including bribes, promises, threats, surveillance, and misinformation, in numerous cases. In addition, because of their extremely negative experience with the board in terms of both process and outcome, many of the organizers in the survey made a conscious decision not to bother filing unfair labor practice complaints even in cases of blatant violations.

Results from the First-Contract Study

Under our current labor law and in our current economic and political environment, employers have a number of legal and illegal means to thwart union attempts to bargain a first agreement. Not surprisingly, a majority of the employers in the sample used a broad range of legal and illegal tactics to resist the unions' efforts to reach a first agreement. Although the sample size and statistical method limited how many management tactic variables could be included in the estimated equation, the following management tactic variables were incorporated into the model: use of captive audience meetings; employer use of media, advertisements and public events; unilateral changes in wages, hours, and/or working conditions; use of an outside consultant or lawyer; concessionary initial bargaining proposals; discharges after the election; and surface bargaining. In addition, descriptive statistics were obtained for a broad range of other employer tactics relating to the first-contract campaign process.

As shown in table 5.2, employers continued captive audience meetings after the election in 21 percent of the campaigns, ran a media or public relations campaign in 6 percent, made unilateral changes in 37 percent, and discharged workers for union activity in 30 percent. Employers used an outside consultant or lawyer in 61 percent of the campaigns, made initial concessionary proposals in 18 percent, and engaged in surface bargaining in 37 percent. All of these actions were associated with first-contract rates 10 to 30 percent lower than in the units in which they were not used. When the influence of other contract campaign variables was controlled for, the probability of winning a first contract declined by 34 percent in units in which the employer ran a media or public relations campaign, by 13 percent in units in which unilateral changes were implemented as mandatory subjects of bargaining, by 13 percent in units in which an outside consultant was used, by 20 percent in units in which the initial proposals were concessionary, and by 24 percent in units in which, according to the union's chief negotiator, the employer engaged in surface bargaining.[5]

The weak effect of the captive audience meeting variable on first-contract outcome may be explained by the fact that the union has greater access to counteract the employer's message once the union has won the election. The results for the discharge variable may be explained by the fact that discharges after the election may serve more to spur the union to bargain an agreement that included reinstatement than to give the employer more leverage at the bargaining table.

Employers engaged in several additional legal and illegal tactics during the bargaining process that were not included in the multivariate analysis. As shown in table 5.2, employers engaged in a broad range of hard or bad-faith bargaining behaviors. These included refusal to respond to information requests (17 percent of the campaigns) and delay and stalling tactics, such as showing up late at negotiations, taking long caucuses, and failing to agree on dates for negotiation sessions (35 percent). Half the employers also bargained hard on union security language, resisting any agreement on union shop and dues checkoff clauses until the very end of bargaining, if they agreed at all.

Twenty-five percent of the employers attempted to undermine the union negotiating committee by offering bribes and promotions and by spreading rumors about individual committee members. Similarly, a third of the employers

5. The extremely strong negative effect of the employer media campaign variable is partially explained by the fact that employers are most likely to utilize the media after impasse has been reached, thus at a point when the resolution of the first contract is already in jeopardy. Newspaper advertisements, radio spots, and public forums are especially effective tools employers can use to circumvent a union and bargain directly with the employees, in order to convince them and the larger community that they will suffer permanent replacement, layoff, or plant shutdown if they fail to accept management's final offer. The effectiveness of this tactic is increased all the more by the very weak restrictions and penalties that exist under the NLRA for employer misstatements, threats, and promises included in advertisements and other public presentations.

Table 5.2. Results of Study on First Contracts

Independent variable	Percent of sample	Percent first-contract rate (rate when not present)	Predicted impact on probability of winning first contract
Included in equation			
Two months or more before bargaining begins	50	76 (84)	-5% if two months or more
Chief negotiator outside consultant or lawyer	61	75 (87)	-13% if outside consult/lawyer
Initial employer proposals concessionary	18	67 (83)	-21% if concessionary
Employer made unilateral changes	37	70 (86)	-13% if unilateral changes
Changes in wages or benefits	26	69 (84)	–
Captive audience meetings after election	21	67 (84)	-8% if captive audience meeting
Use of media, ads, and public events	6	50 (82)	-34% if media/public campaign
Surface bargaining	37	59 (92)	-24% if surface bargaining
Discharged workers for union activity	30	73 (83)	-9% if discharges
Without reinstatement or back pay	12	67	–
Not in equation[a]			
Election objections filed	23	70 (83)	–
Refusal to respond to information requests	17	82 (82)	–
Supervisor one-on-ones after election	31	77 (81)	–
Increased use of part-time and temporary workers	20	75 (81)	–
Increased use of subcontracting	8	75 (80)	–
Refusal to start bargaining	18	67 (83)	–
Stall the bargaining process	35	65 (96)	–
Undermine committee through bribes and rumors	25	60 (87)	–
Play one sector off another	31	68 (86)	–
Hard bargaining over union security	50	68 (92)	–
Offering better package to nonunion workers	10	80 (80)	–
Declared impasse and implemented final offer	7	57 (82)	–
Forced strike through unacceptable demands	7	14 (85)	–
Organized decertification campaign	14	29 (88)	–
Threatened full or partial plant closing	25	68 (84)	–
Total for 100 cases in sample	100	80	–

Note: Including predicted impact on percent union vote and probability of union win for all variables included in the logit equation when controlling for the influence of the bargaining climate, company and unit characteristic, organizing campaign, negotiating process and union tactic, and characteristic variables. Statistically significant results in predicted impact column are in bold for all variables that were included in equation.

[a] Results in bold in percent first-contract rate column were statistically significant in a chi-squared test.

attempted to divide the bargaining unit by playing one sector or interest group against another, either by job classification, seniority, gender, department, or race. In 10 percent of the units, the employer offered better wages to nonbargaining unit employees than they proposed at the table for the union employees.

A substantial number of the employers also engaged in more directly coercive behavior, such as threatening plant closings, forcing strikes, or organizing decertification campaigns. Employers threatened a full or partial plant closing in 25 percent of the campaigns, although they followed through on their promise to close the plant only 4 percent of the time. In 14 percent of the campaigns, the employer organized a decertification campaign, and unions failed to win a first contract in all but four of those fourteen campaigns. In 7 percent of the units, the employer declared an impasse and implemented the final offer, and unions won first contracts in only four of those seven units. In another 7 percent of the units, the employer forced a strike by holding to blatantly unacceptable demands. Unions were able to win a contract in only one of those strikes.

With the exception of refusing to respond to information requests and granting better wages to nonunion employees (which may just work as an incentive for unionized employees to fight even harder), the above-mentioned employer tactics were all associated with union win rates 25 to 50 percent lower than in units in which these tactics were not used. The negative differences in first-contract rates for all of these employer tactics were statistically significant in a chi-square test.

Twenty-three percent of the employers refused to recognize the union as the certified representative of the bargaining unit and instead filed objections with the NLRB and the courts to get the election results overturned. Although the challenges were dismissed without merit in every case, challenging the election still served effectively to delay the start of negotiations and appeared to have a negative impact on first-contract success, so that unions won only 70 percent of the campaigns in which the employer filed election objections, compared with an 83 percent first-contract rate when objections were not filed.

Implications for Labor Law Reform

The results from this study confirm that labor law reform could substantially improve union success rates in both certification elections and first-contract campaigns. Based on the number of campaigns in which the union lost the election even though a majority or close to a majority of the unit signed cards before the petition was filed, it is clear that the union win rate in this sample would have been nearly double if employers had been required to grant recognition after a majority card check, as is the case in some Canadian provinces.

The number of cases in the sample in which the union lost majority support because of an adverse unit determination demonstrates the importance of restricting the ability of the board and the courts to make changes in unit determination that go well beyond the community of interest standard. This is especially true in those cases in which another entire division or workplace is added to the unit at the last minute. Workers should be able to organize with workers with whom they have a true community of interest, all at the same worksite and all in the same general work classification.

The number of campaigns in this data set in which employers engaged in clearly illegal behavior during the organizing and first-contract campaigns speaks strongly to the need for more vigorous and rapid enforcement of the law and more serious penalties for employers who violate the law. NLRB staffing levels need to be dramatically expanded at the investigation, hearing, and case-processing levels. The penalties for 8(a)(3) violations need to go beyond back pay to financial penalties significant enough to act as real deterrents. Most important, workers and unions need the same injunctive penalties for egregious employer violations that are so readily applied for union violations.

The need for stiffer employer penalties is especially apparent in the area of bad-faith bargaining. As this study showed, numerous employers violate 8(a)(5) of the NLRA through unilateral changes, surface bargaining, and stalling tactics or simply by refusing to come to the table. Yet, under current law, the worst penalty an employer can get for these violations is an order to bargain in good faith. This points to a clear need for financial penalties or, in more egregious cases, actual settlement orders or interest arbitration.

The ever-expanding "free speech" rights of the employer, in contrast with the ever-shrinking access rights of unions, allowed many employers in this sample to mislead, misinform, and outright lie to employees about the union in captive audience meetings, leaflets, mailings, media campaigns, and public forums. Labor legislation that would better balance these rights would improve the ability of workers to make decisions regarding unionization without in any way constraining employers from expressing their opinions about unioni-zation in a noncoercive manner. The law should be changed to include financial penalties for threats, intimidation, lies, and distortion, whether expressed in written communications or in captive audience meetings and supervisor one-on-ones. Equally important, the law needs to be amended to offer frequent and full opportunities for union representatives to have equal time and equal access to counteract the "captive" nature of employer communication.

The campaigns in the sample in which the employer was able to defeat the union through the use of permanent replacement workers underscore the importance of labor law reform to eliminate the employers' right to hire permanent replacements in economic strikes and temporary replacements during lockouts. The cases in which employers actively organized antiunion committees, bribed or undermined organizing and bargaining committee members, used participation programs to thwart organizing drives, or initiated decertification campaigns give strong support to those in the labor movement who argue for strengthening rather than diluting the penalties and enforcement of 8(a)(2) violations.

The last and perhaps most critical area of labor law reform is suggested by the more than 25 percent of the campaigns in which the employer threatened a full or partial shutdown of the plant and the 8 percent of the campaigns in which unions lost representation because of plant closings. These campaigns demonstrate the critical need for some restrictions and/or penalties for employers that shut down operations or contract out work to avoid unionization. For, under current labor law, employers can take these actions without fear of penalty and only in the most exceptional circumstances can union internal and external pressure campaigns force a settlement.

Conclusions

These results make it clear that under current labor law organizing is an extremely difficult and risky venture for private-sector workers. The results also demonstrate that labor law reforms that would expand union and worker rights while restricting and punishing illegal employer behavior could significantly reverse the downward trend in organizing. Given that the impact of many of the individual employer tactics on percentage union vote, election outcome, and first-contract outcome ranged from 10 to 20 percent, these reforms in combination could bring union election win rates above 80 percent and first-contract win rates close to 100 percent. These labor law reforms could also dramatically increase the number of union election campaigns by greatly reducing employers' ability to crush union organizing efforts before they get to an election or even a petition.

A word of caution is in order, however. Both the larger certification and first-contract studies made it clear that union behavior also plays an extremely critical role in determining certification election outcomes. As many Canadian organizers have found, labor law alone does not organize workers. There were cases in this sample, albeit few in number, in which, despite a complete lack of employer opposition, the union still was unable to win an election. At the same time, although overall union win rates hover below 50 percent and first-contract rates run below 75 percent, some unions and some organizers are winning elections and first contracts despite labor law, despite an adverse political and economic climate, and despite aggressive employer antiunion campaigns. These unions are able to win because they are using creative, aggressive rank-and-file intensive organizing and first-contract strategies. In fact, as the findings from my broader certification election study make clear, union tactics as a group play a greater role in determining election outcome than any other group of variables, including employer behavior and NLRB practices (Bronfenbrenner 1993:301).

As union density in the private sector plunges toward 10 percent, it would be suicidal for the labor movement to depend on labor law reform for its resurrection. In fact, the only way unions will achieve significant labor law reform is to go out and organize millions of American workers, who in turn can lobby Congress and the president for reform.

Unfortunately, time is running out. If the labor movement is going to reverse the downward spiral before it is too late, it needs immediately to reevaluate the way it has organized in the past and develop a comprehensive plan to revamp its organizing structure and strategy. Only then can labor law reform be achieved and only then can we rebuild an active and vital labor movement, which is so critical to the very existence of a democratic and humanist society.

6

Employer Tactics and Labor Law Reform

Phil Comstock and Maier B. Fox

Unique among industrialized democracies, U.S. labor law allows employers actively to oppose their employees' decision to unionize. The employer's right to oppose unionization is supposed to stop short of coercion, but the law often fails to act as a deterrent or as a remedy.

The incentives to bend or break the law are considerable. Unionized workers earn much more than their nonunion counterparts in the same occupation or industry (U.S. Department of Labor 1993b). The penalties, though, are limited. Even in the case of mass firings of union supporters, the maximum penalty is net lost pay plus interest.

Since few workers can afford to be jobless, interim earnings offset the employer's liability considerably. Economic pressure can compel workers to settle for less than 100 percent of the amount due—an acceptable practice under current law that works against the interests of those who cannot afford to wait for the NLRB process to run its full course.

Changes in the political environment and in the business community's reaction to unions exacerbated the practical effect of the law's weaknesses. Union-avoidance tactics were not invented during the Reagan administration, but they were legitimized. In the highly visible mass firing of striking air traffic controllers, the Reagan administration sent a powerful message about the new balance of power in the workplace.

The first president to engage in mass firings nominated the first NLRB chairman to oppose collective bargaining publicly. In Donald Dotson's view, "Collective bargaining frequently means labor monopoly, the destruction of the marketplace" (speech to the Maryland chapter of the Industrial Relations Research Association, Sept. 28, 1983).

Under Dotson's leadership, the NLRB refused to issue bargaining orders even where employer tactics deprived unions of their majority status (W. Gould 1993:21). The increased resort to unfair labor practices by management underscores the ineffectiveness of the NLRA as a deterrent (W. Gould 1993:151, citing Weiler 1990).

By the end of the Reagan presidency, the nature of labor relations in the United States had fundamentally changed. The new emphasis was on preventing or getting rid of collective bargaining. The permanent replacement of striking employees became an acceptable practice. And advising businesses on how to block or break unions became a growth industry. Management consultants who failed to offer union-avoidance services were at a competitive disadvantage.

How do such changes affect workers' views of the benefits and risks of collective action? What bearing should this have on current deliberations regarding the reform of the nation's labor laws? Data collected by the Wilson Center for Public Research may contribute to the answers.

Wilson Center Studies

Over the last fourteen years, the staff of the Wilson Center, with which we are affiliated, has conducted 360 polls of large nonunion bargaining units in conjunction with organizing campaigns for more than fifty unions. More than 150,000 in-depth telephone interviews were completed in these polls. One limitation of the Wilson Center data is that the information comes from mid-size or larger units—comprising three hundred or more workers—since polling smaller units is not cost-efficient.

Our results are not drawn from every industry and occupation. Notable omissions include truck and taxi drivers, workers in the entertainment industry, most occupations in the building trades, and agricultural workers. But our results include all of the other traditional areas of union organizing activity, as well as nonunion bargaining units in the banking industry, in engineering, in data processing, and among university graduate students who work as teaching or research assistants.

Our studies were commissioned by labor organizations to assess the current and potential levels of support for union representation in specific bargaining units. This may lead some to assume that our results reflect cases that have been prescreened by union organizers and found to hold clear potential for majority union support. The opposite is true. In our fourteen years of operation, in not one case has a union commissioned an organizing poll because it was confident of victory. To the contrary, our 360 studies have been conducted either before the onset of organizing or after an organizing campaign lost momentum. Because of this selection process, our data may understate the demand for union representation, not overstate it.

Because these studies were conducted for union clients, some may assume a pro-union bias either in the questionnaire design or the analysis. Although each questionnaire is custom-designed, we have consistently employed benchmark questions. A questionnaire from a typical preorganizing poll is appended. (References that would identify either the bargaining unit or the client are deleted.)

With respect to the analysis, a pro-union bias on our part would serve only to mislead unions seeking to make informed decisions about large-scale organizing campaigns. We have never been asked by a union to provide less than a completely objective assessment of organizing potential. Organizing is simply too costly and resources too dear to do otherwise.

The principal strengths of the Wilson Center information are the number of workers whose views it reflects, the duration of time involved, and the fact that it reflects workers' views of union representation in a real, rather than an abstract, context.

In addition to multiple-choice questions, our interviews include many open-ended questions, designed to elicit underlying motivations. In our experience, insight into what motivates views of union representation is crucial in assessing how workers will respond. Key is the gap between expectations and outcomes, along with workers' views of a union's ability to close that gap.

Several academic students of the labor movement, notably Henry S. Farber and Alan B. Krueger (1992), have concluded that the decline in union membership since 1977 was a result of declining demand by workers for union representation. On the one hand, there can be no debate over the decline in union membership. Unions held approximately 22 to 23 percent of the total labor force throughout the 1960s and early 1970s, but the proportion dropped to below 20 percent in the late 1970s and to approximately 16 percent in early 1993. There are, on the other hand, grounds to dispute the reason for the continuing decline. Farber and Krueger hold that the explanation lies in the continuation of the lack of demand (1992:4). Their conclusion runs contrary to the trend found in the much larger number of interviews our staff has conducted.

Results of Wilson Center Polls

Our data support Farber and Krueger's position that there was a decline in demand for union representation in the early 1980s, but we find that this trend reversed in the latter half of 1985. Since then, our results show an overall increase in demand for union representation.

Farber and Krueger also note a change in the post-1984 period, but rather than finding an increase in demand, they report a leveling off of the earlier decline (1992:17). Their disparity with our results may reflect sampling differences for the period 1985–91. Farber and Krueger rely on only two studies, totaling 642 interviews, with nonunion workers (12). By comparison, during the period 1985–91 our staff conducted interviews with about 104,000 nonunion workers.

Farber and Krueger do not measure the effects of legal or illegal employer use of influence, though they concede that failure creates "ambiguity" in their findings (1992:8). Nonetheless, they maintain that "there is no evidence that any significant part of the decline in unionization is due to increased employer resistance" (18).

The assertion that increased employer resistance is not a significant part of the decline in unionization defies common sense and demands substantiation. Such proof, however, is notably absent. Moreover, Farber and Krueger take the tenuous position that "[employer] resistance in the form of harassment during an organizing campaign is not very likely to influence the responses to the anonymous survey questions we rely on" (1992:18n).

This is simply not so. Fear that responses to questions about union preference will become known to management and result in reprisals is a problem that exists even when a labor union has announced in advance that it has commissioned a survey. In our experience, without measures that reassure workers that they will not suffer reprisals for expressing union sentiments, their propensity to dissemble will be directly related to their concerns over job security.

Wilson Center data strongly indicate that workers feel employer coercion is increasing and that this tactic frustrates demand for union representation. Moreover, our data show that as desire for representation has increased, so has the frequency and extent of employer coercion.

Fourteen years ago, a common union-avoidance tactic was to portray collective representation as unnecessary. It made sense at that time. When we first began organizing polls, most nonunion workers we spoke with were not interested in union representation. Complacency and a strong sense that workers could "look out for themselves" were dominant themes then.

During 1979 and 1980, we conducted interviews with nearly fourteen thousand nonunion workers. Of these, 26 percent were clearly opposed to union representation and an additional 28 percent were firmly in favor of the nonunion status quo, although not hostile to unions per se. Pro-union workers comprised 25 percent of our interviewees, and the remainder appeared genuinely undecided.

To make matters worse, in the late 1970s, many nonunion workers blamed organized labor for high prices. Union wages were seen as the cause of, rather than the solution to, declining purchasing power.

During our first two years of operation, 16 percent of our interviewed workers volunteered "inflation" or "high prices" in response to the open-ended question "What do you feel is the single most important disadvantage, if any, of being represented by a union where you work?" Nearly one-fifth of all the workers we interviewed in this period also held the view that unions were "too powerful."

During the early 1980s, workers' desire for union representation weakened even further. The negative stereotypes initially found remained intact, and the perception that unions were too powerful gave way to concern that they were often powerless to protect job security, much less achieve real improvements.

During the period 1981–83, we conducted about twenty-four thousand interviews with nonunion workers. The clearly antiunion segment grew by 3 percent, to 29 percent of the total, and there was a 5 percent increase in the number favoring the nonunion status quo.

In this period, organizers faced a difficult, often impossible, uphill fight to gain majority status. In the typical bargaining unit polled between 1981 and 1983, only 23 percent of the workers held ingrained pro-union views and 15 percent were genuinely willing to weigh both the union's and management's arguments before making a decision.

We anticipated that the erosion in demand for union representation would continue. Surprisingly, it did not. Instead, the sentiments of nonunion workers toward representation remained almost constant throughout 1984. And then, something quite unexpected happened.

Beginning in the second half of 1985, we began to see evidence of a reversal of the earlier trend. With the exception of workers in the manufacturing sector, there has been a reduction in the proportion that could be described as antiunion. There has also been a decrease in the percentage of workers who, although not antiunion as such, favor retaining the nonunion status quo. At the same time, the segment of workers who hold pro-union views or who appear genuinely undecided has grown.

This process began slowly but has been building momentum and continues. Even when the results from manufacturing units are included, the results from the early 1980s versus the early 1990s show a significant increase in demand for union representation (see table 6.1).

At the end of 1986, in addition to analyzing the aggregate, we began looking at the demographics of the workers whose demand for union representation had increased most. Again, there were surprises. The growth of pro-union sentiments was, and has continued to be, especially pronounced among three key groups of workers.

The first group is women who have entered the workforce because of the need to increase household income, especially women who are forty-three years of age or younger and who have been in the workforce for seven or more years (table 6.2). The second group is Hispanics, including recent immigrants, who have established "roots" in the United States (table 6.3). (To date, the Wilson Center has conducted about thirteen thousand interviews with nonunion Hispanic workers, of which slightly more than half were conducted in Spanish.) The greatest surprise for us was the third group—young workers, aged sixteen to twenty-nine years, especially males from middle-class or lower-middle-class backgrounds who were not college-bound (table 6.4).

Our polls consistently show that the most important factor in the desire of nonunion workers for representation is a wide and persistent gap between what they genuinely feel they deserve and what they actually receive for their labor. Among the three groups whose demand for collective representation was increasing the most, 68 percent told us that their employer could afford to give them better wages and benefits. Only 44 percent said they felt that top management cared about their well-being. Overall, 88 percent were able to give an unprompted response to an open-ended question that asked for their most desired improvement or change at work. But only 28 percent were able to identify a way to achieve that goal. The low percentage able to identify ways to achieve job-related goals principally reflects the timing of the polls we conduct. Most often our studies occur before the onset of widespread union

Table 6.1. Attitudes toward Unions among Nonunion Workers (in percent)

	1981–83	1990–92	Net change
"Hard" antiunion	17	9	-8
"Soft" antiunion	12	16	+4
Status quo	33	24	-9
Undecided	15	22	+7
"Soft" pro-union	14	19	+5
"Hard" pro-union	9	10	+1

Table 6.2. Attitudes toward Unions among Nonunion Women Workers (in percent)

	1981–83	1990–92	Net change
"Hard" antiunion	9	7	-2
"Soft" antiunion	14	11	-3
Status quo	41	25	-16
Undecided	18	27	+9
"Soft" pro-union	12	20	+8
"Hard" pro-union	6	10	+4

Table 6.3. Attitudes toward Unions among Nonunion Hispanic Workers (in percent)

	1981–83	1990–92	Net change
"Hard" antiunion	6	6	0
"Soft" antiunion	17	11	-6
Status quo	24	15	-9
Undecided	13	18	+5
"Soft" pro-union	22	27	+5
"Hard" pro-union	18	23	+5

Table 6.4. Attitudes toward Unions among Nonunion Young Workers (in percent)

	1981–83	1990–92	Net change
"Hard" antiunion	9	7	-2
"Soft" antiunion	30	23	-7
Status quo	40	26	-14
Undecided	10	23	+13
"Soft" pro-union	7	13	+6
"Hard" pro-union	4	8	+4

activity, before the union has begun its information campaign. When we interview workers after organizing efforts are well under way, there is ready identification among those who desire representation that unionization is an effective means of obtaining their goals.

Shrinking Middle Class

Other factors also point to a broader-based increase in the desire for union representation. As work has evolved, there is ample evidence that the middle class is shrinking and that the shrinking process has been under way for years (Mishel and Bernstein 1993:13).

Those who lose middle-class status and their children are part of a large and growing new American working class. They represent a distinct reversal of a key demographic trend that shaped America for three decades following World War II. Then, many workers became middle class. Now, many in the middle class are becoming workers, in the prewar meaning of the term—that is, they lack economic security and the ability to improve their status through individual initiative. The increase in pro-union sentiment since 1985 is not surprising; it is firmly rooted in developments in the economy and labor markets.

Ronald Reagan's report on the nation's economy in 1984 showed more than a 14 percent decline in the real wages of nonsupervisory workers between 1972 and 1983. More recent figures from the Economic Policy Institute show a continuation of this trend, with real earnings of most working people continuing to drop by nearly 1 percent a year (*Economic Report of the President* 1984:264; Mishel and Frankel 1991:75).

For a while, the rise in the number of two-earner households gave Americans the impression of prosperity. A recent publication by the Joint Economic Committee of Congress, however, shows that it was illusory: "When both hours of work and work expenses are accounted for, the standard of living of the bottom 80% of families declined or showed no improvement [during the period 1979 through 1989]" (U.S. Congress, Joint Economic Committee 1992:18).

The number of people with health insurance has declined since 1980, as has the number with pension coverage. Making matters worse, part-time and casual employment among those who want to work full time appears to be increasing rapidly (U.S. Bureau of the Census 1991:101, 393, compared with other volumes).

New Working Class

The new working class is growing and will likely continue to grow. One particularly stark example is what has happened to young workers. In 1992, the Census Bureau released data showing that more than two out of every five young *full-time* workers earned wages at or below the poverty level (*Washington Post*, May 12, 1992:A7).

The new working class, especially the young, have expectations that belie their stark reality. The gap between what they feel they deserve and what they receive for their labor is especially strong among these segments of the working population. A particularly vivid indicator of this disparity is the decline in the rate of home ownership among every age group except those fifty-five and older (Mishel and Frankel 1991:225–26).

The recency of middle-class status provides ready-made expectations. The loss of middle-class status, or, among the young, the inability to maintain the living standards of their youth, is a constant reminder of unfulfilled expectations. For the new working class, the motivation is not to achieve a better way of life but to regain what they feel has been unjustly taken away.

In more affluent times, organizers often had to convince workers that they needed collective representation. The new working class is a large and growing segment of the workforce that does not need to be convinced that they deserve more than they are getting. Their own experience is sufficient.

Not all who feel this way conclude that unions are the solution. But, in the past, when they enjoyed middle-class status, few of these workers felt there was even much of a problem. Widespread downward mobility presents a major change in the organizing environment.

Why, then, have we not seen a resurgence in union membership? The key reason is the shift in the balance of power in the workplace that previous administrations actively encouraged and the current law continues to condone.

During the late 1970s and early 1980s, it was common for working people, including union members, to think unions were "too powerful." Today, a negligible 2 percent use this term. There has been a commensurate increase, especially among nonunion workers, to think of unions as weak.

Employer Pressure

The perceived weakness of unions is the flip side of the increase in employer willingness and ability to resist workers' right to bargain collectively. When outright intimidation is employed, the law offers weak protection. It provides no protection when the tactics fall just short of the statutory definition of coercion. The law implicitly assumes that there is no coercive effect short of the threshold that constitutes a violation. This ignores reality.

In practical terms, employers have many lawful ways to pressure employees who want union representation. One particularly chilling, but nonetheless lawful, deterrent is to threaten to fire all supervisors should nonsupervisory workers unionize. Another tactic is for management to predict that higher labor costs under a union contract will lead to contracting out, layoffs, or closings. In the past few years, concerns over job security have been heightened by increasing management willingness to replace permanent people with contingent workers (*Washington Post*, Oct. 20, 1993:C11, C15).

When employers threaten job security, workers do not become antiunion. In fact, such threats can actually increase the demand for union representation by widening the gap between expectations and outcomes. In such cases, however, we often find that the demand for union representation is outstripped by the perceived costs. The prospect of better earnings and treatment loses its luster when workers believe they will lose their jobs if they attempt to improve them.

Our purpose is not to list the many tactics employers may legally use but rather to underscore their effect on workers who want the benefits of collective bargaining. One clear indication comes from polls conducted after an NLRB election was held. (To date, we have conducted twenty-four of these studies. They are in addition to the 360 organizing polls.)

In the five most recent post–NLRB election polls, we asked, "What do you feel was the most important reason people voted against union representation?" Without prompting, a total of 31 percent of respondents made direct references to pressure from management, including, specifically, fear of job loss. An additional 5 percent referred to the effect of management's antiunion campaign without directly mentioning fear of what management would do.

Using this question somewhat understates the extent of management pressure in that it does not allow for the efforts of management to be listed as a secondary cause of voting behavior. Although unfair labor practice charges were filed in each of our five cases, none was sustained under the current law.

What effect does perception of employer coercion that does not meet the statutory definition of an unfair labor practice have on workers' views of representation? We have clear evidence that workers know how their employers feel about unions from the outset, or even before organizing begins. When we have asked the question "How do you feel [NAME OF COMPANY] is most likely to respond to the issue of union representation?" an average of 42 percent of the workers (N = 13,806) chose the response "make an all-out effort" to defeat the union and an additional 21 percent said "try to persuade workers to oppose union representation but stop short of an all-out effort." Only 24 percent responded that the employer would "let the employees decide on their own." (Six percent were unsure, and 7 percent refused to answer this question.)

This knowledge is pronounced among workers who in the absence of coercion would have weighed the information before making their final decision regarding union representation. At one extreme of the five postelection polls, cited earlier, 68 percent of the workers identified employer coercion as the key to the union's loss. Only 7 percent of these same workers told us they had changed their views of union representation during the organizing effort (5 percent more antiunion, 2 percent more favorable). At the other extreme, only 12 percent of the workers cited fear of employer coercion. In this case, 35 percent of the workers changed their views during the campaign (26 percent pro-union and 9 percent opposed).

The use of pressure tactics by employers is neither universal nor random. Where workers have high job satisfaction, we find less demand for union representation and a lower incidence of aggressive antiunionism by management. The workers with the lowest job satisfaction, however, usually have the strongest level of demand for representation. But it is these workers who are also most likely to be legally threatened or illegally intimidated by their employer.

To demonstrate this point, we selected twenty studies from among the 360 organizing polls conducted to date. In ten of the selected studies, the levels of job satisfaction were the lowest we have ever recorded. In the other ten, the levels of job satisfaction were the highest.

This relationship is shown in table 6.5, which includes figures for job satisfaction and worker perception of the level of antiunion pressure from the employer. The first set of data are from the ten studies that produced the lowest levels of job satisfaction. The second set is from the ten studies that produced the highest levels.

Table 6.5. Relationship between Job Satisfaction, Workers' Perceptions of Employers' Antiunion Pressure, and Views on Unionizing

Number of interviews	Net job satisfaction[a]	Pressure	Net view of unionizing
175	(30.9)	10.8	79.4
197	(28.9)	39.1	45.2
225	8.3	6.2	49.4
71	18.5	9.9	26.7
25	21.6	18.0	32.0
327	22.9	15.6	28.7
94	23.4	56.0	47.0
225	24.9	12.0	6.2
172	29.7	70.0	51.0
185	30.3	78.0	22.0
450	74.0	12.7	70.2
78	76.9	17.6	14.1
140	77.5	30.5	8.5
325	79.7	11.6	30.7
35	79.9	28.5	14.2
82	82.9	16.0	(29.0)
90	83.3	24.0	(47.0)
277	87.7	9.0	52.0
57	96.4	14.1	7.0
64	97.5	15.0	22.5

[a] Net ratings are derived by subtracting the number of negative comments from the number of positive ones.

The figures were derived from responses to the following questions: (1) "Overall, how satisfied are you with your job?" (2) "What do you feel was the most important reason people voted against union representation?" (3) "All things considered, how would you compare the advantages and disadvantages of representation by [NAME OF UNION] in terms of your experience working at [NAME OF PLACE OF EMPLOYMENT]?" The results confirm our observation that there is an inverse relationship between job satisfaction and desire for union representation.

We also found a similar relationship between the level of perceived intimidation and satisfaction levels. Those with the least job satisfaction tend to work for employers that treat their workers with disdain. Those employers, quite naturally, extend this behavior when employees wish to act collectively. The weakness of the National Labor Relations Act effectively rewards those employers that do the least for their workers—and punishes those workers whose nonunion jobs provide the least job satisfaction.

When we look at our entire set of results, we find important demographic patterns that bear out the point that the least advantaged workers—those who are most at risk—feel they cannot freely express their right to act collectively. We consistently find that highly skilled or highly educated workers report low levels of employer pressure during organizing campaigns, irrespective of other factors. For example, organizing polls of entire hospital workforces find that registered nurses (RNs) have little fear of the administration but that licensed practical nurses and, especially, service and maintenance workers are usually at the opposite end of the spectrum. Among RNs, typically fewer than 15 percent are afraid of the administration. Among service and maintenance workers, the comparable figure is 40 percent or more.

Because higher-skilled workers report less employer intimidation, deskilling has and will continue to exacerbate the weaknesses of the current law. Since deskilling is occurring while real living standards for most workers are declining, however, there is an added effect.

As skilled jobs become scarcer, an increasing proportion of those with skills (although possibly obsolescent ones) will be compelled to accept unskilled or low-skilled work. As a consequence, deskilling is also likely to contribute to the gap between expectations and outcomes. Our results indicate that this gap is the principal factor motivating demand for unionization. Thus, continued deskilling should increase the desire for collective representation while simultaneously making it more difficult for workers to achieve. This pattern is already apparent within the new working class.

Women are more likely to feel coerced by employer tactics during union organizing campaigns than are men. Overall, 26 percent of male nonunion workers say employer tactics are the main factor limiting union support in their workplace. Among women the figure is 38 percent.

In bargaining units composed almost entirely of women but supervised almost entirely by men, women report a higher than average deterrent effect stemming from employer campaign tactics. A good example comes from six organizing polls conducted among clerical workers employed by universities. In these cases, an average of 48 percent of the women interviewed made unprompted references to disapproval by, or retaliation from, the administration. In two of these cases, polls were conducted simultaneously in the predominately male maintenance units. Comparable concerns regarding employer tactics were voiced by only 28 percent of the men.

The starkest difference, however, is between whites and minorities, especially African-Americans. Only 22 percent of all white workers but nearly one-half (48 percent) of the nonunion African-Americans cited management pressure as the deterrent to unionization.

Similar variations exist in the nature and intensity of the tactics used. Among higher-skilled workers, employer pressure most often takes the form of appeals to professionalism, equating unionization with loss of individual freedoms, or references to barriers to promotions that could result under a union contract. Among the less skilled, fear of job loss is the dominant theme.

Threatening to fire an individual worker for supporting unionization is unlawful but carries a small penalty. Predicting that an entire factory will close if the workers demand union representation is legal and carries no penalty at all.

The law rewards employers who bend or even break the rules. It places those lawyers and consultants who do not practice union-avoidance tactics at a competitive disadvantage. And it fails to protect those workers who most want and need collective representation.

There is a cogent reason every other industrialized democracy excludes employers from workers' deliberations about union representation. Employers can, and absent restrictions will, exert undue pressure. That pressure is used most often and most intensely against the least skilled and least advantaged members of the workforce. Their rights are suppressed. Their opportunities for improvement are repressed. As long as U.S. employers retain their unique right to fight employees' desire for collective representation aggressively, the law will remain flawed.

Appendix to Chapter 6: Preorganizing/Early Organizing Questionnaire

Hello. My name is _____ *I'm calling from the Wilson Center for Public Research. We've been asked by* {NAME OF UNION} *to conduct a poll among people employed at the* {NAME OF COMPANY} *where you work.*

The purpose of the poll is to determine how you feel about your job and how you feel about union representation on the job.

Whether you favor union representation, oppose it, or do not currently have an opinion, what you have to say is very important. Your comments and those of your coworkers who are being asked their views will play a major role in determining whether {NAME OF UNION} *will begin an effort to represent people employed at your plant.*

May I begin?

[IF RESPONDENT REFUSES, OFFER TO CALL BACK. IF RESPONDENT STILL REFUSES, OBTAIN A REASON AND NOTE IT AND ALL AVAILABLE DEMOGRAPHIC INFORMATION ON THE REFUSAL FORM.]

1. About how long have you been employed at [NAME OF COMPANY]?
   a. unsure/refused (volunteered)
   b. less than 1 year
   c. between 1 and 3 years
   d. between 3 and 6 years
   e. between 6 and 10 years
   f. more than 10 years

2. On which shift do you work?
   a. unsure/refused (volunteered)
   b. first shift (days)
   c. second shift (afternoon)
   d. third shift (nights)
   e. varies (volunteered)
   f. swing shift (volunteered)

3. Considering all aspects of your job, including pay, benefits, working conditions and job security, how would you rate your overall satisfaction with your job; are you?
   a. unsure (volunteered)
   b. very satisfied
   c. somewhat satisfied
   d. not very satisfied
   e. not satisfied at all
   f. refused (volunteered)

4. What do you like the most about your job?

5. What do you like the least about your job?

6. If you could make just one improvement or change in your job, what would that be, if any?

7. What would be your next most important improvement or change, if any?

8. How much would you say the owners and top managers at [NAME OF COMPANY] care about your own personal well-being?
   a. unsure (volunteered)
   b. very much
   c. somewhat
   d. not very much
   e. not at all
   f. refused (volunteered)

9. What's the main reason you feel that way?

10. How effective do you feel the [NAME OF UNION] could be in helping you get needed improvements or changes at work?
    a. unsure (volunteered)
    b. very effective
    c. somewhat effective
    d. not very effective
    e. not effective at all
    f. refused (volunteered)

11. What's the main reason you feel that way?

Now I'd like to read you a list of job-related items. In each case, I'd like you to tell me how satisfied you are RIGHT NOW or if you feel the issue I mention is NOT IMPORTANT.

12. The first item is your current hourly wage rate. Thinking just about your hourly wage rate, would you say you are?
    a. unsure/refused (volunteered)
    b. very satisfied
    c. somewhat satisfied
    d. not very satisfied
    e. not satisfied at all
    f. or, is this not an important issue

13. The next item is your medical benefits. Are you?
   a. unsure/refused (volunteered)
   b. very satisfied
   c. somewhat satisfied
   d. not very satisfied
   e. not satisfied at all
   f. or, is this not an important issue

14. The pace at which you are expected to work?
   a. unsure/refused (volunteered)
   b. very satisfied
   c. somewhat satisfied
   d. not very satisfied
   e. not satisfied at all
   f. or, is this not an important issue

15. The way your immediate supervisor treats you?
   a. unsure/refused (volunteered)
   b. very satisfied
   c. somewhat satisfied
   d. not very satisfied
   e. not satisfied at all
   f. or, is this not an important issue

16. The way management disciplines employees, in general?
   a. unsure/refused (volunteered)
   b. very satisfied
   c. somewhat satisfied
   d. not very satisfied
   e. not satisfied at all
   f. or, is this not an important issue

17. The way management treats employees who become injured or ill on the job?
   a. unsure/refused (volunteered)
   b. very satisfied
   c. somewhat satisfied
   d. not very satisfied
   e. not satisfied at all
   f. or, is this not an important issue

18. The amount of job security you have?
   a. unsure/refused (volunteered)
   b. very satisfied
   c. somewhat satisfied
   d. not very satisfied
   e. not satisfied at all
   f. or, is this not an important issue

19. How satisfied are you with the fact that there is no union in your plant?
   a. unsure/refused (volunteered)
   b. very satisfied
   c. somewhat satisfied
   d. not very satisfied
   e. not satisfied at all
   f. or, is this not an important issue

20. Is there any item I failed to mention that is a special source of satisfaction for you at work?

21. Is there any item I failed to mention that is a special source of dissatisfaction to you at work?

22. Would you say that the wages and benefits you and your coworkers receive are?
   a. unsure/refused (volunteered)
   b. much more than your employer can afford to provide
   c. somewhat more than your employer can afford
   d. just about what your employer can afford
   e. somewhat less than your employer can afford
   f. or, much less than your employer can afford

23. Has anyone in [NAME OF COMPANY] management ever discriminated against you or harassed you because of your age, sex, religion, race, national origin or because of any physical disability you have?
   [IF YES, ASK FOR SINGLE MOST SERIOUS TYPE OF DISCRIMINATION OR HARASSMENT]
   a. unsure (volunteered)
   b. no/none
   c. age
   d. sex
   e. religion
   f. race
   g. national origin
   h. physical disability
   i. refused (volunteered)

24. What do you feel is the most important advantage, if any, of being represented by a union where you work?

25. What do you feel is the most important disadvantage, if any, of being represented by a union where you work?

26. All things considered, what effect do you feel having union representation would have on your own situation at work; would your own situation become?
    a. unsure (volunteered)
    b. much better
    c. somewhat better
    d. somewhat worse
    e. much worse
    f. refused (volunteered)

27. What's the main reason you feel that way?

28. All things considered, how would you compare the advantages and disadvantages of representation by [NAME OF UNION] in terms óf your experience working at your plant; Would you say?
    a. unsure/refused (volunteered)
    b. the advantages are much greater than the disadvantages
    c. the advantages are somewhat greater than the disadvantages
    d. the advantages are somewhat less than the disadvantages
    e. the advantages are much less than the disadvantages
    f. or, are the advantages and disadvantages about equal

29. What's the main reason you feel that way?

30. Leaving aside your own views for a moment, how likely do you feel it is that a majority of your coworkers will support union representation?
    a. unsure (volunteered)
    b. very likely
    c. somewhat likely
    d. not very likely
    e. not likely at all
    f. refused (volunteered)

31. OTHER THAN YOURSELF, which of the following sources would you say you would most trust for information about the question of union representation?
[ROTATE]
a. unsure (volunteered)
b. your immediate supervisor
c. coworkers who support representation by [NAME OF UNION?]
d. your plant manager
e. coworkers who OPPOSE any union
f. the company personnel department
g. letters and notices provided by management
h. members of your family
i. literature from [NAME OF UNION]
j. [NAME OF UNION] members who live or work in your area
k. articles about the union in local newspapers
m. only trusts SELF (volunteered)
n. other (volunteered—NOTE ANSWER ON COMMENT SHEET)
m. refused (volunteered)

32. How do you feel [NAME OF COMPANY] management is most likely to respond to the issue of union representation; do you feel management will?
a. unsure (volunteered)
b. make an all-out effort to oppose union representation
c. try to persuade workers to oppose union representation but stop short of an all-out effort
d. take a neutral position and leave the decision to you and your coworkers
e. other (volunteered)
f. refused (volunteered)

33. What effect, if any, would that response by your employer have on your own desire to have union representation; would it?
a. unsure (volunteered)
b. increase your desire for union representation
c. decrease it
d. or have little or no effect on your views
e. refused (volunteered)

34. If [NAME OF UNION] wins the right to represent you and your coworkers, what do you feel the union's TOP priority should be in negotiations with your employer over the terms of the union contract?

35. If you had the opportunity to speak directly and frankly with the leaders of [NAME OF UNION] about their effort to organize your workplace, what, if anything, would you tell them to do?

36. What specific type of information about the question of union representation, if any, would you most like to receive?

37. Approximately how old are you; Would you say?
   a. unsure/refused (volunteered)
   b. under 25
   c. 26 to 35
   d. 36 to 45
   e. 46 to 55
   f. 56 or older

38. How would you describe your own racial or ethnic background?
   a. unsure/refused (volunteered)
   b. White
   c. Black or African-American
   d. Hispanic or Latino
   e. Asian or Pacific Islander
   f. Native American Indian

*On behalf of {*NAME OF UNION*} thank you for your time and interest. It has been a pleasure speaking with you. Have a pleasant day/evening.*

INTERVIEWERS CODE THE REMAINING QUESTION

39. Gender?
   a. do not use this key
   b. male
   c. female

7

Winning NLRB Elections and Establishing Collective Bargaining Relationships

Gordon R. Pavy

The negative influence of corporate tactics on the right of workers to organize unions through NLRB election campaigns has been well documented. But the ability of unions to negotiate collective bargaining agreements successfully after winning elections is less explored territory. Only a few studies have attempted to measure this ability. The Industrial Union Department of the AFL-CIO did not publish the results of its comprehensive study in 1975, but partial results appeared in an article, "The Longest Season: Union Organizing in the Last Decade, a/k/a How Come One Team Has to Play with Its Shoelaces Tied Together?" (Prosten 1978). Other recent studies include *Union Organizing and Public Policy Failure to Secure First Contracts* (Cooke 1985) and "Seeds of Resurgence: Successful Union Strategies for Winning Certification Elections and First Contracts in the 1980's and Beyond" (Bronfenbrenner 1993).

The Cooke and Bronfenbrenner surveys produced results consistent with the conclusions of the IUD's 1975 study, as well as its subsequent studies on the same question, the latest of which is unveiled in this chapter. Cooke documented the significance of employer resistance to the ability of unions to win first contracts, as well as the overall rate of successful negotiation of first agreements. He used a national random sample survey of five hundred NLRB elections held during 1979–80. Cooke found that 28 percent of the units that won elections during the 1979–80 period were unable to obtain first contracts.

Kate L. Bronfenbrenner's study is based on one hundred successful organizing campaigns in 1986–87 elections. She built her sample from AFL-CIO Organizing Department files and included bargaining units with more than fifty workers. She found that in the campaigns surveyed, 80 percent of the union election victories resulted in successful first-contract negotiations.

Since 1975, the IUD has conducted two additional studies that assessed the ability of unions to negotiate collective bargaining agreements after winning NLRB elections. The second study was conducted in 1988, and the third, now in progress, began in July 1993. To get as comprehensive a reading as possible, the IUD studies included all election victories recorded by AFL-CIO affiliates for a given year.

The goal of all three studies was to measure the extent to which unions that won NLRB elections subsequently succeeded in establishing *normal, stable labor relations* with employers. The definition of normal, stable labor relations used by the IUD was "maintaining a continual bargaining relationship for at least five years following the NLRB election." In almost all cases for the periods studied, this involved the negotiation of at least two successive collective bargaining agreements following the election victory.

Even in the best of situations, it often takes a union a few weeks to negotiate a first agreement, and experience tells us that it frequently takes much longer. Assuming that most agreements during the 1970s and 1980s were no more than three years in duration, the IUD examined elections that closed five years prior to the date of the study. One would hope that the five-year lag time allowed for even the most protracted bargaining situations to be resolved.

The 1975 study analyzed NLRB election victories certified in 1970.[1] The compiled results were presented to the Executive Council of the IUD in June 1976.

At its winter meeting in January 1988, the IUD Executive Council directed its Coordinated Bargaining and Research Section to repeat the study. For the second study, the IUD selected elections administratively closed in 1982. Summary findings were reported to the IUD officers in November 1988.

The most recent study is being conducted as a joint project between the AFL-CIO's Committee on the Evolution of Work and the IUD. Question-naires for elections won in 1987 were mailed to international unions in early July 1993.

Analyzing the questionnaire responses for all three years reveals three basic points. First, over the three periods studied, unions have had a difficult time getting contracts from employers after winning elections. Unions faced stiffer employer opposition to negotiating first contracts following 1987 elections than they did in 1970–75. Almost the entire increase in the difficulty over this period was due to the use of union-avoidance tactics promoted by outside attorneys and labor-management consultants who specialize in testing the limits of the NLRA's ability to protect worker rights.

---

1. The NLRB includes only closed cases in its database. If we used the year of election to determine inclusion in the database, the database would exclude elections held during the year that had not been closed in the period between the election and the survey.

Nearly all trade unionists agree that the NLRB election process, as it is currently constituted, does not provide a fair forum for determining the desire of workers to have union representation. But even if one assumes that an NLRB election is a fair contest, the process fails to fulfill the promise of union representation for a large number of workers who vote as a majority for the union.

Second, the NLRB election process and the collective bargaining process work in opposition to each other. Workplaces where the employees are most likely to vote in a majority for the union have the most difficult time negotiating agreements. Conversely, workers in workplaces where a union will have the best chance of negotiating a contract after winning an NLRB election are least likely to cast a majority vote for the union. Unions win NLRB elections in smaller units more often than in larger units but are more likely to be able to negotiate contracts in larger units than in smaller units.

Third, unions are doing a better job choosing organizing campaigns with a high probability of victory and of getting a contract. But the number of new workers covered by labor agreements is falling.

During the 1980s, antiunion NLRB rulings and increased opposition from companies made organizing and negotiating first contracts more difficult. This hostile environment, combined with the systematic export of manufacturing jobs by companies, produced a decline in existing union membership. Lower existing membership meant fewer organizers and fewer financial resources for unions to dedicate to organizing and bargaining.

First-Contract Survey

In 1970, the NLRB closed the files on 7,773 union representation elections, excluding decertifications.[2] Unions won 4,276, or 55 percent, of those elections, covering 276,353 workers (see table 7.1). In 1982, 3,685 total elections were closed by the NLRB (fewer than were *won* by unions in 1970). Unions won 1,681, or 45.6 percent, of those elections, covering 78,153 workers. This was about one-third of the number of workers who won union elections in 1970. In 1987, the NLRB closed 3,314 elections, and unions polled a majority in 1,610, or 48.6 percent, of them. These union victories covered 81,453 workers, or 39.9 percent, of all eligible voters.

In each of the three years studied by the IUD, the survey population consisted of a subset of total union election victories. Two groups were excluded—independent local unions, because no mailing addresses were

2. All election figures exclude decertifications.

Table 7.1. *NLRB Election Victories for 1970, 1982, and 1987*

	1970	1982	1987
Union victories	4,276	1,681	1,610
	(55%)	(45.6%)	(48.6%)
Workers covered	276,353	78,153	81,453
	(48.5%)	(36.2%)	(39.9%)

available, and other unions not affiliated with the AFL-CIO or the IUD at the time.[3]

Of the 4,276 elections that unions won in 1970, the IUD solicited results on 2,656 of them (62.1 percent of all elections). Unions returned a total of 1,681 questionnaires, or 63.3 percent, of those mailed.

In 1982, unions won 1,681 NLRB elections. In 1988, the IUD mailed questionnaires to unions accounting for 1,464 (87.1 percent) of the 1982 union victories. We received 687 filled-out questionnaires, 46.9 percent of all those mailed to the unions.

In July 1993, the AFL-CIO mailed questionnaires covering 1,392 (86.5 percent) of the 1,610 total union victories in 1987 elections. As of this date, unions have returned 567 questionnaires, or 40.7 percent, of the total mailed.

Negotiating First and Second Agreements

According to the IUD's study of NLRB elections closed in 1970, unions established normal, stable labor relations in 64.5 percent of all the elections that were won, covering 209,775 workers (see table 7.2 and fig. 7.1). Of the three years studied, 1970 resulted in the largest number of new workers covered under labor agreements. But of the 1970 NLRB election victories, 35.5 percent of all units had no union contract five years after the elections. In units voting for union representation, 66,578 workers, or 24.1 percent of all the workers in those units, had no contract.

In elections closed in 1982, survey returns show that after five years only 34.6 percent of the workplaces where employees voted to join the union (49 percent of the employees) worked under a collective bargaining agreement. Units covered by a contract included 38,286 workers, less than 20 percent of

3. When the 1975 survey was conducted, the International Brotherhood of Teamsters was unaffiliated with the AFL-CIO or the IUD and was not polled. The study included responses from the then unaffiliated United Automobile Workers and the International Longshoremen's and Warehousemen's Union. All three have reaffiliated with the AFL-CIO since the 1975 study. In 1988, questionnaires were mailed to some unaffiliated unions with which the IUD had a working relationship, including the United Electrical Workers. In 1993, unions not affiliated with the AFL-CIO were excluded from the mailing.

Table 7.2. Unions That Have Stable Labor Relations after NLRB Elections

	Election year		
	1970	1982	1987
Under contract after	2,757	582	758
two negotiations	(64.5%)	(34.6%)	(47.1%)
No contract or first	1,519	1,099	852
contract not renewed	(35.5%)	(65.4%)	(52.9%)

the workers who maintained coverage by a union contract five years after winning 1970 NLRB elections.

On the opposite side of the coin, 65.4 percent of the workplaces that voted for unions in 1982 did not have a union contract after five years, compared with 35.9 percent in 1970. Projecting the results of the survey to all 1982 election victories, of all shops where workers wanted a union contract, 38,286 had one and 39,867 did not.

In the current study covering 1987 elections, returns to date indicate that the situation has improved slightly, reflecting in part the improved targeting strategies used by unions attempting to cope with the more hostile environment of the times. After winning elections in 1987, unions today maintain contracts in 47.1 percent of those bargaining units, covering 59.4 percent of the workers. Projecting this rate to all 1987 NLRB elections, 48,414 employees working in shops where the union won have a contract today, and 33,039 have no union representation. New contracts covered more workers five years after 1987 elections than five years after 1982 elections, but five years after winning elections in 1970, union contracts covered four times the number for 1987.

The results for all three years, spanning two decades, show that despite a clear expression by employees for union representation, unions have a difficult time getting employers to sign collective bargaining agreements. In fact, unions that won elections in 1982 and 1987 had a considerably more difficult time establishing normal labor relations with employers than did unions that won elections in 1970.

Workers who sign union cards and vote for the union in most cases do so in the face of harsh employer opposition. Employer campaigns against the union during the election process often continue through the contract negotiation process. During the 1980s the rate at which employers hired outside attorneys and management consultants for the express purpose of defeating the efforts of employees to unionize accelerated greatly.

Union-busting lawyers and consultants offer their services on the premise that no place of work is unionized until a contract is signed and that, regardless of the explicit expression by the employees for union representa-

Figure 7.1. Workplaces with Stable Labor Relations Following NLRB Elections

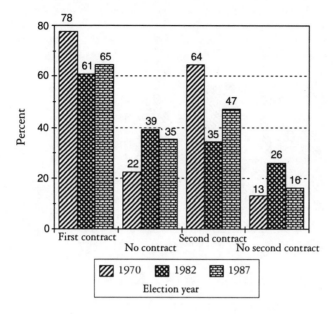

tion, employers can and should avoid signing a union contract. The services they sell are a complete package of antiunion tactics, designed for each stage of the unionization process. Their tactics test the legal and technical limits of the NLRA's provisions for protection of workers' rights and the NLRB's ability to enforce the law in a timely manner.

The current IUD first-contract study included a question not asked of respondents in previous studies: "Did the company hire an outside management consultant/lawyer to impede the first-contract process?" Responses indicated that companies hired outside consultants or lawyers during the negotiation process in 34.6 percent of the workplaces where there were NLRB union election victories in 1987. When an outside consultant or lawyer was used, companies avoided signing a contract 48 percent of the time.

Absent an outside consultant or lawyer, companies succeeded in avoiding contracts only 28.8 percent of the time following 1987 NLRB election victories. The overall rate of failure to negotiate a first agreement following 1970 NLRB election victories, a period when the use of outside management consultants during contract negotiations was almost nil, was 22.4 percent. This is very close to the failure rate following 1987 NLRB election victories absent the use of outside consultants and lawyers. Therefore, union-avoidance tactics as practiced by outside management consultants and lawyers in the 1980s have succeeded in significantly eroding the ability of unions to negotiate first contracts with employers. Consultants and lawyers often use these tactics without technically breaking the law, but their tactics circumvent the

Figure 7.2. Relationship between Unit Size and Ability to Negotiate a Contract

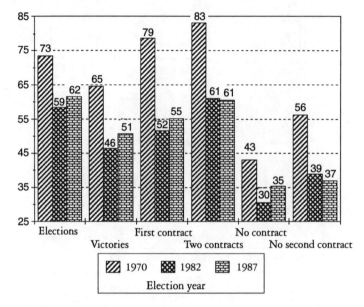

intent of the law, which is to promote collective bargaining when employees have chosen union representation.

Unit Size, NLRB Election Win Rates, and Bargaining Success

Information on unit size suggests that the number of employees at a facility has a direct impact on the ability of unions to win elections. The average size of all the units involved in NLRB elections in 1970 was seventy-three workers, and the average size of all the units with union victories was sixty-five workers (see fig. 7.2). In 1982, the average fell to fifty-nine employees for all elections, compared with forty-seven for units with union victories. In 1987, the average size of all units with NLRB elections rose slightly, to sixty-two, and the average of those with union victories rose also, to fifty-one.

In NLRB elections for each of the three years studied, as the size of the unit rose, the probability of a union victory declined (see table 7.3). In 1970, unions won in bargaining units with ten or fewer employees 64.5 percent of the time; but in units with eleven to twenty-five employees, the rate of victory fell to 56 percent. The win rate dropped to 51 percent for units with fifty-one to one hundred employees and to 42.1 percent for units with 101 or more employees. Unions held 1,207 elections with 101 employees or more, winning 508 of them, and the median size of all units with NLRB election victories in 1970 was nineteen workers.

Table 7.3. Percentage of Units That Have Normal Labor Relations after NLRB
Election Victories

Unit size	1970 Election victories	1982[a] Election victories	1982[a] Two contracts	1987 Election victories	1987 Two contracts
1–10	64.5	53.5	32.7	58.2	48.7
11–25	56.0	49.0	33.0	51.0	42.1
26–50	53.3	43.5	33.7	45.1	42.9
51–100	51.0	39.4	40.0	46.1	43.3
101+	42.1	32.5	44.6	37.5	59.2
Median	19	18	17	22	23

[a] The rate was not calculated in the 1975 survey.

The same pattern is repeated in 1982 NLRB elections. In addition, 1982
win rates were lower in each range compared with 1970. In 1982, the win rate
was 53.5 percent in units with one to ten employees, 49 percent in units with
eleven to twenty-five employees, and so on down to 32.5 percent for elections
with 101 workers or more. In 1982, unions took 493 units to election having
more than one hundred employees and won 160 of them. Bargaining units
that had union victories had a median unit size of eighteen workers in 1982.

Win rates by unit size increased slightly in 1987 compared with 1982.
Unions won elections in units with one to ten employees 58.2 percent of the
time. The win rate fell to 51.0 percent in units with eleven to twenty-five
employees, and unions won units with twenty-six to fifty employees 46.1
percent of the time. The win rate declined to 37.5 percent for units with 101
or more employees. In 1987, the NLRB held elections in 510 units with more
than one hundred employees, and unions won 191 of them. The median size of
the units with union victories was twenty-two, up by four workers over 1982.

In contrast to NLRB elections, in collective bargaining, it is the larger
units that, after beating the odds and winning elections, have the best chance
of getting a labor contract. In 1970, the average size of the bargaining units
that obtained a first contract was seventy-nine, compared with fifty-two in
1982 and fifty-five in 1987. Bargaining units that were unable to secure a
first agreement had an average unit size of forty-three in 1970, thirty-one in
1982, and thirty-five in 1987.

Relative size also played a role in a union's ability to get a second contract.
Units that were able to build a stable relationship with their employers and
secure a second agreement were larger in size on average than those that were
able to get a first contract. The size of the units that secured a second
agreement averaged eighty-three employees in 1970 and sixty-one in 1982
and 1987. The respective averages for units that were unable to secure a

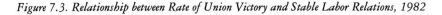

Figure 7.3. Relationship between Rate of Union Victory and Stable Labor Relations, 1982

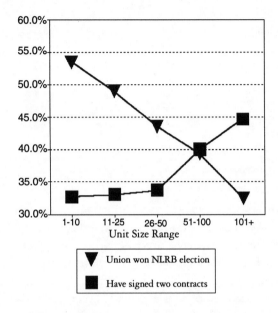

second agreement were fifty-six, thirty-nine, and thirty-seven, lower than the average sizes of units that got second contracts but higher than the averages for units that did not get first contracts.

Beyond simple averages, table 7.3 shows that in 1982, the likelihood of being able to get an agreement increased as the size of the unit winning the election increased. Figure 7.3 illustrates the relationship between the rate of union victories and unit size.

The goal of NLRB elections is to determine whether or not employees wish to be represented by a union. Contract negotiations give life to the positive expression of that desire. Data from the three IUD studies indicate that unit size is a powerful factor in determining the probable outcome of an NLRB election. In small workplaces, a union has the highest probability of winning an election. But following an NLRB election victory, a union in a small workplace is least likely to be successful in negotiating an agreement.

Conversely, a large workplace, where unions are most likely to get an employer to sign a collective bargaining agreement, is the least likely to go through the NLRB election process and vote for union representation.

Organizing Smarter Will Not Overcome Employer Opposition

The data in the 1987 survey provide support for the argument that unions are organizing more intelligently. Union membership and union resources available for organizing have been falling. In the 1980s, antiunion decisions by the NLRB, the firing of the PATCO union air traffic controllers, and shrinking union membership encouraged companies to be more aggressive in their fights with unions in both the organizing and collective bargaining arenas.

Faced with increased opposition and dwindling resources, unions learned to target their organizing efforts toward workplaces more likely to result in victory and the successful negotiation of collective bargaining agreements. Total NLRB elections and elections won by unions declined in 1987, but the rate of success in negotiating first and second agreements rose, both on a percentage basis and absolutely (see table 7.2).

In figure 7.4, the line representing the win rates by unit size for 1987 elections has shifted upward compared with the same line for 1982 in figure 7.3. Unions actually won slightly more units, on a percentage basis, in the fifty-one to one hundred range than in the twenty-six to fifty range. The median unit size for election victories in 1987 (twenty-two) is higher than the median in 1982 (eighteen) and the median in 1970 (nineteen).

In figure 7.4, the line representing the rate at which unions successfully negotiated two contracts after winning an election parallels the line for the rate of election victories in smaller bargaining units. In figure 7.3, the lines start from a divergent point and come together as unit size gets larger.

After winning elections in 1987, the rate at which smaller bargaining units negotiated contracts improved compared with 1982. Unions actually had a higher success rate negotiating contracts in units in the one to ten size range than in the next higher range of eleven to twenty-five workers. The success rate in units of twenty-six to fifty and fifty-one to one hundred stayed basically level.

In both years the two lines cross at the fifty-one to one hundred range. But in 1987 they cross at a higher percentage than in 1982. The rate of success for negotiating contracts in units with more than one hundred workers in 1987 is much higher than in 1982. Therefore, unions in 1987 NLRB election campaigns were more successful picking very small and medium-sized units based on the likelihood of securing a contract with the employer. The targeting strategy also produced improved success in contract negotiations when applied to larger units where unions traditionally achieved higher rates of success.

The NLRB election data for 1970, 1982, and 1987 show an overall decline in the number of victories in union election campaigns. Estimating from reports for the first nine months of 1992, the NLRB closed fewer than twenty-seven hundred elections involving AFL-CIO affiliated unions, and the unions won about thirteen hundred of them, or 50 percent. NLRB elections that unions won in 1992 had approximately thirty-five thousand fewer eligible voters than the union victories in 1987. The total number of elections

Figure 7.4. Relationship between Rate of Union Victory and Stable Labor Relations, 1987

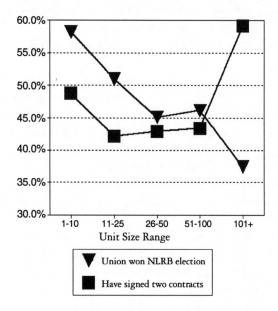

involving more than one hundred workers declined to 400, compared with 510 in 1987. The win rate in these larger units declined to 34.3 percent, compared with 37.5 percent in 1987. Out of thirty elections held in the first nine months of 1992 with one thousand workers or more, unions won five.

The win rate in the smallest units, with one to ten workers, rose to 64 percent in the first nine months of 1992. The rate of union victories in the eleven to twenty-five, twenty-six to fifty, and fifty-one to one hundred size ranges was virtually unchanged from 1987. The median size of the units in which there were union victories fell in relation to 1987, down from twenty-two to eighteen.

In the next five years, unions will have a difficult time getting contracts after 1992 election victories at the same rate and that cover as many employees compared with 1987. If unions get contracts in *every* election won in 1992, the number of workers covered by contracts will increase by 50,000, only a marginal improvement over the 48,414 workers under contract five years after winning elections in 1987.

Conclusion

From 1970 through 1992, only a fraction of union supporters, clearly expressing their desire for union representation in a system that inhibits that expression, have been able to secure the protection of a union contract.

Though protected by a contract, right-to-work laws and company opposition to union security clauses have reduced the number of union members to a small portion of the workers covered. The high hurdles erected by recent NLRB decisions and corporate opponents to unionism have prevented many unions from organizing as vigorously as they might. As a result, many workers were denied the opportunity to participate in an election and to choose whether or not they wished to join a union.

The balance of power in the workplace has shifted too far in favor of employers. The rights of employees to form, join, and assist unions need to be protected to a greater degree than the law currently allows. The recommendations for labor law reform that will come out of the Commission on the Future of Worker-Management Relations may not be all that organized labor wants and probably will have some elements that will provide new challenges for unions. But reform is needed to give new life to the promise of collective representation for those who want it.

PART III
REFORMING THE NLRA

8

Toward Fundamental Change in U.S. Labor Law: A Law Reform Framework

Robert J. Pleasure and Patricia Greenfield

The need for top-to-bottom reform of the labor and employment laws in the United States has broad support. Even those who favor less government intrusion seek reform, such as Charles Fried, who argues that "the time has come for a review of the premises, and not just the details of our employment law system" (1985:75). The current debate concerning the shape and content of labor law reform, however, has been cast in the context of proposals perceived as "pro-labor" or "pro-management." Absent a rational framework for evaluating these proposals, it is inevitable that any proposal or set of proposals for reform, even those originating from a broad-based commission, will be evaluated and judged, opposed and supported, based on the parties' assessments of whether they are being advantaged or disadvantaged. We propose an entirely different framework for putting forth and evaluating proposals for labor law reform. We find that a comprehensive framework for analyzing and evaluating labor law reform proposals can be derived from American experience with nonpartisan law reform generally.[1]

This approach makes strategic sense from a labor movement perspective. First, the tendency to focus on specific and narrow deficiencies in the labor law alone, rather than on comprehensive law reform, trivializes the depth of dissatisfaction of workers and unions with the system. Second, the force of argument for reform based on rationalization, speed, and other generally agreed-upon criteria can be broadly accepted and linked to the strong political support in the United States for more generalized law reform. Third, and finally, beginning and framing a debate built on the foundational princi-

1. Given the space constraints, this article cannot discuss or analyze all models for law reform. We have taken particular models and examined how the discussion, debate, and process relating to labor law reform might be constructed using significant law reform principles.

ples of law reform puts the labor movement in the mainstream of progressive legal and political thought in the United States.[2]

Principles

To develop a framework based on such generally accepted criteria, our starting point is jurisprudence, the empirical study of law in action. The jurisprudence of law reform—its objectives, process, and discipline—provides insights that should resonate across a wide spectrum of interests in the current debate over labor law reform. An examination of discussion and debate in this area helps us construct a framework that is based on the way the law functions for the parties, not just an ideal model based on theoretical rights and duties.

The notion of law reform was an important concept in American progressive thought at the turn of the century, and "attention to judicial administration throughout this Century has been influenced heavily by this early Progressive legacy" (Wheeler and Whitcomb 1977:28). Law reform surged as a theme in social movements in common law countries; it was a central part of the ideology of the revolution in England in the seventeenth century (Trevor-Roper 1967:244–45). Law reform, like reform generally, both in England and the United States, has its origin among ordinary people (B. Shapiro 1980:331–32). As the adage has it, if you have been dealt four aces you are not likely to ask for a new deal. And although "lawyers' law" may be the subject of reform debate in bar associations, fundamental law reform has not been a subject that has had wide appeal among practicing lawyers.[3]

Despite these obstacles, law reform received impetus from the growth of federal regulation in the twentieth century, which spurred review litigation, and "as a result case backlogs developed and judicial reformers became increasingly alarmed at what they called 'delayed justice.' Reformers . . . stepped up their demands for the principles of efficiency, integration, unification, and coordination in the federal system" (Carp and Stidham 1985:64).

These reformers began, as we do in examining labor law, with Karl Llewellyn's starting point: dissatisfaction with the existing state of the law

2. To be sure, claims of nonpartisanship in law reform, like similar claims of neutrality by nonpartisan good-government advocates, may obscure the interplay of interests in the debate concerning modernizing efforts. Although political and economic interests will determine what kind of law reform we will have, surely a consensus against obscurantism, delay, partiality, and inconsistency can be built around models from the U.S. tradition of law reform. In general, such a consensus will benefit labor. Further, labor's commitment to law reform and its extensive experience should enable it to give content to general notions of consistency, fairness, reasonableness, and speed. Adoption of these principles for labor's purposes will enable labor to engage in the debate for the common good, the broadest social purpose.

3. "Lawyers do not take law reform seriously—there is no reason why they should. They think the law exists as the atmosphere exists, and the notion that it could be improved is too startling to entertain" (Jones and Stebbings 1987:38).

(Twining 1985:313). Llewellyn, the architect of the major law reform project of this century—the development of the Uniform Commercial Code (UCC)[4]—succinctly set out similar principles for framing the law reform effort in his draft of the policy and purposes section of the code: "1. To bring law abreast of modern need, 2. To clean out needless and expensive complexity and confusion, 3. To introduce throughout standards of commercial reasonableness and safety, 4. To provide a solid and clear basis for counselling and for informal adjustments of disputes" (Twining 1985:464, n.2). This summary of the general goals of law reform is congruent with the needs and desires of the labor movement: to have a system of labor laws characterized by speed, coherence (internal to the statute and external so that the law will not be confusing to the affected parties), and the encouragement and facilitation of private dispute resolution.

Framework for a Broad-Based Law Reform Approach

In proposing that labor law reform be based on such generally accepted principles, we have no illusions that complete and universal consensus among all affected parties will be achieved. Morton J. Horwitz's discussion (1992) of a century of American law notes that although speedy justice had a strong appeal in twentieth-century American legal thinking, there has also been a growing awareness concerning the relationship between substantive deliberation and procedural efficiency. Horwitz, quoting James M. Landis in 1961, comments that the ultimate defeat of a plan to reorganize the NLRB was "'due to considerations having no relationship to the improvement of the administrative process but having a relationship to two factors, first political opposition pure and simple, and second to thwart the basic principle' of the Labor Act that collective bargaining 'should be the foundation of labor-management relations in our economy.' Landis concluded: 'As one witness for the National Association of Manufacturers bluntly put his reasons for opposing the plan: "one man's delay is another man's due process"'" (Horwitz 1992:244). Recent management reaction to current efforts at labor law reform illustrates how little certain approaches have changed (Irving 1993:12, 14).

Where, then, does the use of these principles get us if they will not be, in fact, universally accepted? The answer is that taking a clear principled position always creates opposition, and we would, in any case, expect continuing and complete opposition to true and effective labor law reform from certain management constituencies. These principles, however, put the labor movement on the "high ground" and on the side of well-established reform

4. The UCC governs the operation of commercial transactions. It has been adopted in full by forty-nine state legislatures and the District of Columbia and in part by the fiftieth state.

principles conceived in the public interest. This, in combination with the second part of our proposal, enables us to gain allies from numerous other constituencies.

The second part of our proposal relates to the substantive broadening of the labor law debate. As noted earlier, there is substantial support for law reform in the employment area generally. Before embarking on a constrained drive for narrow and limited changes in the labor law, we need to step back and look at the entire range of obstacles confronted by workers today in their attempts to gain control of their working lives and achieve some form of industrial democracy. What aspects of law, not just "labor" law, but employment and corporate law, limit workers' ability to achieve these goals? And what are the sources for support for change in these areas?

Why would we try to broaden the debate beyond the admittedly massive problems posed by the current structure, substance, and process of the National Labor Relations Act? In examining other areas of law, will we perhaps open Pandora's box? We believe that there is a far greater danger of using all our "chips" (almost inevitably necessary in any substantial battle over labor law reform) in an effort that will achieve minimal results and not really affect workers in the workplace or the future strength of the labor movement. We have a unique opportunity to frame the debate and accompanying political activity and coalition-building in a manner that builds the most broad-based support possible without diluting our central purposes, that increases our chances of success, and that ensures us that the final product will actually make a difference.

There is significant impetus for law reform on a wide front originating not only with the labor movement but with traditional law reform institutions. In 1987, the AFL-CIO Executive Council issued a statement calling on state legislatures to enact wrongful-discharge statutes and proposing minimal protections for wrongfully discharged workers. In 1991, the Uniform Law Commission's Model Employment Termination Act was adopted by the National Conference of Commissioners on Uniform State Law, and as of May 1993, it was introduced and pending in three states (Kamiat 1992:2). Whether the model act complies with the AFL-CIO minimum standards is beyond the scope of this paper. What is of first importance for purposes of this discussion is that a traditional law reform institution has approached employment law in a manner that, if followed, would profoundly affect the common law of employment contracts and, in particular, displace the already seriously eroded American rule of contract at will. Of additional significance to our discussion of labor law reform is the approach taken to the development of the model act in an area that is similarly fraught with the potential for and actuality of conflicting employer and worker interests. The official prefatory note by Theodore St. Antoine offers employers and workers justification for support of the model act in the arbitrary results of the unequal application of existing law.[5] Such an approach is instructive in dealing with the inherent conflicts in areas of labor and employment law generally.

Law reform efforts in other substantive areas developed almost simultaneously with the model act, such as the American Law Institute, which began its Corporate Law Project to reform state corporation law (American Law Institute 1984). State corporation statutes, perhaps in as much disorder as labor and employment law in the United States, are, in the words of Bayless Manning, "'towering skyscrapers of rusted girders, internally welded together and containing nothing but wind'" (quoted in Schwartz 1988:7). The drive for federal chartering of corporations comes from those reformers who are dismayed as state courts and legislatures, on the initiative of managers, cut down shareholders' remedies in the areas of duty of due care, business judgment, and fair dealing.

It is in this context of substantial ferment within traditional law reform institutions that the call for labor law reform occurs. The idea of restructuring corporate governance systems to take account of workers' interests as a significant constituency alongside stockholders should mesh well with calls in traditional law reform quarters for the federal chartering of corporations and for the revision of basic employment law. Amid calls for a new model of corporate governance, the validity of basic assumptions about corporate ownership is raised.[6] If, in the context of efforts toward labor and employment law reform, works councils are proposed, the impetus for broadening corporate constituencies among corporate law reformers should add to the strength of those efforts. If "contracts of adhesion"[7] are rejected in a model state employment termination act, as they are (see National Conference of Commissioners 1991, "Comment to Section 4," 7A:76), then the debate for generalized labor

5. St. Antoine's note demonstrates massive direct litigation costs to employers. On the workers' side, the current situation produces about 2 million discharges in the nonunion, nongovernment sector, of which 150,000 to 200,000 would have claims under a "good-cause" statute. Yet, generally, only highly paid personnel can avail themselves of the existing remedies. Further inducements to employers exist in the indirect costs in elaborate personnel policies, internal grievance systems, and other means to provide defenses in wrongful-discharge suits (National Conference of Commissioners on Uniform State Laws 1991).

6. "Are corporations merely commodities that can be bought and sold, or are they political and social institutions that must be handled in a different way? In decision making, should directors take into account only the interests of shareholders when other constituencies such as employees, creditors, and communities also have a stake in the enterprise?" (Dallas 1988:19).

7. Contracts of adhesion are usually the product of unequal bargaining power; they include elaborate and verbose provisions, often written in the most obscure terms, in a manner that advantages one side to the bargain. Examples include contractual waivers of liability on the backs of transportation tickets, bailments, and hotel registrations; grossly unfair employment contracts; and franchise agreements. Parties disadvantaged by such terms often seek equitable relief by way of rescission, or contend that the terms to which they object are unenforceable on account of unfairness or obscurity.

and employment law reform can take place on a higher plane where the existence of unequal bargaining power is both acknowledged and remedies are sought—not only by academics but by a traditional law reform institution supported by the bar and the delegates of state governors.

Substantive Labor Law Illustration

What are the implications of the law reform approach we have described above for a particular area of labor and employment law? Much has been written and litigated on the mandatory-permissive distinction and the limits this distinction and the accompanying case law have placed on workers' rights to negotiate over issues critical to their working lives, including management's decisions to invest and remain in existing facilities or to relocate work or close plants (Sockell 1986; *First National Maintenance Corp. v. NLRB*, 452 U.S. 666 (1981); *Dubuque Packing Co.*, 303 N.L.R.B. No. 66 (1991)). An effort to amend the NLRA would focus solely on 8(a)(5) and 8(d). The public debate would be along predictable lines, with the issue most likely framed around the question of management's right to retain, as *First National Maintenance* puts it, its "core of entrepreneurial control" and on what basis, if any, labor has a right to "interfere" with that control. We all probably know who will win that debate.

Let us assume, however, that we would prevail in the debate and that the current mandatory-permissive distinction were struck from the act's interpretation. The act itself still requires only "good-faith bargaining," not agreement. We all know that a clever and determined management can circumvent such a requirement if this is the only legal limitation on management's unilateral decision-making power. We also note that a number of academics and a greater number of practitioners argue that the distinction can be rendered meaningless by a smart, determined, and powerful union, which has the ability to bring economic pressure to bear on related mandatory issues.

Thus, a narrow labor law approach to this issue is likely to result in one of the scenarios we have described above. Either we will lose politically because of a constrained framing of the issue, or we will use valuable political capital to achieve results that are probably, at best, symbolic. Let us now examine how we might approach this issue using general law reform principles and an accompanying broad-based approach to interrelated areas of law.

There is today broad recognition that workers have a great deal of expertise to offer the corporation and that workers should be involved on multiple levels in corporate decision-making, including at strategic levels. In both union and nonunion enterprises, workers are involved in labor-management committees dealing with a range of issues. Workers are company stockholders, they are employee owners, and they are on boards of directors. The old Tayloristic notion of the limited role of the worker in the enterprise is no longer relevant as a notion on which to base bargaining models. The law must change to "bring it abreast of modern need." Leaving all items open for negotiation, as opposed to trying to determine on a case-by-case basis whether a certain situation meets the multiple and intricate NLRB-established tests, will "clean out needless complexity and confusion" and help provide for the informal and private adjustment of disputes. Instead of enduring the inefficiency involved in litigating whether the *First National Maintenance* or *Dubuque Packing* standards are met (and leaving aside the clear possibility that these standards may have been changed by the NLRB by the time any particular case reaches adjudication), the parties will be encouraged, if not forced, to settle their disputes privately and informally, through negotiation.

In addition to this approach to the 8(d) question, a true commitment to law reform requires us to go beyond the NLRA. Law reform requires integration, unification, and coordination. In the interests of these principles, we must ask what other issues and areas of law affect the situation just described. Three relevant areas, involving employment, contract, and corporation law,[8] surface in an initial broad-based examination of the issues: plant-closing legislation, worker and community rights relating to a company's decision to close down a plant and move out of a community, and works councils.

The interests of integration, unification, and coordination require us to evaluate existing legislation that may relate to and affect any proposals we make in the area of law reform. Thus, we must examine the Worker Adjustment and Retraining Notification (WARN) Act closely to make sure that other legislation we ultimately introduce takes into account the nature and level of protection already provided. This examination also gives us an opportunity to study evaluations of and research concerning the operation of the WARN Act over the last five years to see if there are aspects of the act that need improvement consistent with law reform principles.[9] If so, our law reform package should include proposals related to the WARN Act.

Another issue currently being debated and discussed in communities across the country is community rights in the case of plant closings and relocations. One of the most recent examples of this controversy involved a General Motors closing in Ypsilanti, Michigan, where the discussion of community

8. As our discussion in the previous section noted, these are areas that have already been the focus of general law reform efforts.

9. The Department of Labor is currently conducting a review of WARN ("DOL Favors Changes to Strengthen WARN Act" 1993). For a discussion of current research and case law under WARN, see McHugh 1993.

rights made its way into the courts. Although the debate has many complex aspects (Craypo and Nissen 1993), the central argument is that the old model of corporate mobility—which allows corporations to set up shop in a community for as short or long a time as they want, benefit from community and worker resources, and then leave at will—no longer makes sense. Corporations settling in a community frequently obtain massive tax benefits and other community services, such as special roads built by the municipality, or waivers from state and local regulation, which represent lost revenues and a substantial investment on the part of the municipality and/or the state. Much of the time these benefits have been bestowed on the basis of implicit or explicit corporate commitments to remain in the community, commitments also made to workers. The workers, in turn, have made commitments to the corporation, which, it is argued, may rise to the level of enforceable property rights.

Community rights advocates, municipalities, and unions have gone to court in an attempt to enforce these commitments, arguing that certain rights, including contractual rights, have been violated. These groups have received a sympathetic ear from the courts in several instances, but even sympathetic courts have acknowledged the limitations of the current state of U.S. law and its inadequacies in attempting to deal with these situations (*Local 1330, USWA v. U.S. Steel Corp.*, 631 F.2d 1264 (1980)).

Using a broad-based law reform approach, we argue that modern need and commercial reasonableness demand new law in this area, recognizing the impact corporations have on local and state economies and the requisite level of corporate responsibility in relation to workers and the larger community. Such an approach is consistent with general principles of law reform and also broadens the constituency for reform. Significantly, this approach and accompanying legislative proposals also strengthen any rights to notice and bargain over plant closings or relocations.

Finally, there is the issue of works councils. There is, of course, much debate about the advisability of using this model or some variation in the U.S. context in order to extend the scope of worker voice in areas that heretofore have been solely within management's discretion. If the labor movement chooses to argue for the establishment of such councils, the argument should be based on a number of the law reform principles just discussed, including bringing the law abreast of modern need and setting up systems to encourage private dispute adjustment. Because of the relationship between works councils, bargaining issues, and community rights (assuming that public representatives would be involved in works councils), any proposal in this area must be structured carefully to ensure a unified and coordinated system of workplace law and to build support among a variety of constituency groups.

Models for Creating Comprehensive and Meaningful Proposals

What process should be established to develop a comprehensive set of proposals that would achieve true reform of the law of the workplace? In the twentieth century, several different models have been used to effectuate such proposals. Two preeminent nongovernment law reform institutions, noted earlier, currently exist in the United States: the National Conference of Commissioners on Uniform State Laws, set up with the support of the American Bar Association in 1892, and the American Law Institute, established by the Association of American Law Scholars in 1922. The products of the conference on Uniform State Laws are primarily uniform acts proposed to the states and, in fewer numbers, model acts, which have a lesser order of endorsement from the commission. The primary work of the American Law Institute was conceived to be restatements of the law, specifically the common law of contract and separately of tort.

The work of the National Conference of Commissioners on Uniform State Laws has been impressive, although its successes have been limited almost entirely to the commercial law field (Twining 1985:273). In 1991, however, the conference adopted the National Conference's Model Employment Termination Act, discussed earlier. For the Model Termination Act, the conference followed its usual practice of appointing a committee of practicing lawyers to act for the commissioners by voting on draft texts for submission to the full conference for approval. Advisers with special qualifications in labor law, and representing diverse client interests, participated through comment but did not vote, and a reporter, Theodore St. Antoine, was appointed. The venture into as controversial an area as employment termination represents a new direction for the commission. Its greatest success to date has been the development, with the American Law Institute, of the Uniform Commercial Code, beginning in 1942 and finishing in 1951.

Unlike the conference, which is made up of practicing attorneys and state governors' delegates, the American Law Institute (ALI) is governed by academicians. ALI, like the conference, seeks to eliminate complexity, uncertainty, and lack of uniformity in the law, but its chosen instrument is not the uniform or model act. Rather, it is the work of academic examination, setting out the mainstreams in the law and unabashedly selecting a better view when there are multiple and conflicting doctrines with which to contend. Though it may be oversimplification, the general difference between the two organizations is that, whereas the commission is a body of practitioners with no pretense at scholarship, ALI was always an elite institution. And, quite logically, the chosen instrument of the conference is recommended legislation, while ALI develops expository restatements of "meticulous scholarship" with the express intent that the issues they undertake to examine are too complex and perhaps important to commit to the many legislatures (Twining 1985:274).

The hallmark of both the National Conference and ALI processes is the reliance on committee meetings among persons who by broad legal and political experience (in the case of the conference) or academic distinction (in the case of ALI) are presumed to be capable of crafting a uniform or model law, or, in the case of ALI, a magisterial restatement. In either case, even though witnesses may occasionally be called to testify to the law in action, the activity is humanistic law as craft, and in the process the law is drawn from the experience or scholarship of the committee participants.

Neither the National Conference nor the ALI process is an exercise in pure empiricism. But, in both venues, the process of law reform takes into account the complexity involved in understanding the law in action and the difficulty of giving it new coherence, simplicity, and speed and putting it to the service of the litigants and the community. To that end, different information-gathering models may be used. William Twining distinguishes the scientific model of law reform and a committee-room model, noting that Anglo-American tradition has been closer to the latter. The committee-room model, employed on a national scale by Karl Llewellyn, Soia Mentschikoff, and the American Law Institute in developing the Uniform Commercial Code, relies on evidence of "expert" witnesses of both an opinion and experiential nature. In the scientific model, a commission seeks scientific validation "on all matters which are relevant to the subject of reform and which are susceptible to empirical investigation" (Twining 1985:314–15). Twining reports a tendency in the United States toward a scientific model of law reform but, in a footnote, is less than sanguine about the effectiveness of the scientific approach.[10]

In drafting the Uniform Commercial Code, Llewellyn adopted a committee-room model that drew extensively on years of his own research on commercial practice:

> His questioning tended to be specific, guided principally by a concern with function and process. "If I were a cheque and I arrived in the mail, where

10. *"The Report of the Commission on Obscenity and Pornography* (1970) is an example of a recent trend of government-sponsored reports which have moved closer to a 'scientific model' in the United States. The Commission is estimated to have cost in the region of two and a half million dollars, yet the main empirical studies were admitted to be inconclusive and, at the end of 1970, it appeared unlikely that the Commission's recommendations would be implemented. The financing of the Code project was on a much more modest scale" (Twining 1985:466, n.41).

would I go? . . . What would be done to me first? Why? . . . " If Llewellyn's methods were unrigorous, his knowledge of business practice was reputedly rich in insight, "feel," and in detailed information (Twining 1985: 316).

For the comprehensive examination of labor and employment law reform, it may well be that some combination of and balance between both the scientific and committee-room model would be beneficial.

The reform of commercial law in the United States through the work of Llewellyn, ALI, and the National Conference of Commissioners on Uniform State Laws has been described here because of the complexity and range of the task undertaken and the near-universal adoption in a few years of its completion. Llewellyn, in preparing his drafts, identified values in law reform that have obvious appeal in any law reform project. Indeed, his statement of purpose describes principles not just of commercial law but of law reform generally. The UCC experience is a reminder that with sufficient political will and willingness to confront the full complexity of law in action, American legal institutions have the capacity to reform.

Conclusion

Our examination of alternative procedural models and substantive issues leads us to several conclusions. First, the usual approach to constructing legislative proposals is inadequate. Experience has shown us that general legislative language (or even language most fair-minded readers believe is clear and specific) leaves us at the mercy of judicial interpretation. As scholars have established (Atleson 1983) and trade unionists have experienced, the courts regularly revert to the use of common law, which clearly and fairly consistently works against workers and their organizations. Thus, in developing any procedural model, it is essential that its drafters be people with the expertise to confront the complexities of the law of the workplace and the patience and commitment to spell out the details that will ensure that the legislation's intended results will actually be achieved.

Second, as we noted earlier, we have no illusions that, even using general law reform principles, we can get a body of lawyers, practitioners, or academics to reach consensus on all or even most issues. To achieve law reform that is meaningful, we will need some form of commission that makes an underlying philosophical commitment to collective bargaining and the formation of workers' organizations (Gross, chap. 3) and then, in the context of that commitment, agrees and operates on the principles of true law reform. Committee membership and the sweep of substantive proposals will need to be as broad-based as possible to involve the affected and supportive constituencies, who will be our allies in the political battle ahead.[11] Third, we need to develop and be able to depend on the aggressive support of politicians who have the political will to advocate for major, fundamental change.

Fourth, and finally, we need to recognize that this will not be a short-term process. Following the principles of law reform and doing the work needed to avoid an approach that inevitably will lead to trivialization of our efforts will take time.[12]

Mere tinkering with separate sections of the current law is not sufficient, and truly fundamental change cannot occur unless we build broad-based support and consensus for such change. The framework we have discussed, based on generally accepted law reform principles and well-established models in various areas of legal practice, will help to advance a comprehensive set of proposals that can gain the support necessary to become law. And because these proposals will have been based on fundamental law reform and experience, the new law will truly help reform a system that has often worked against labor for much of this half-century.

11. To this end, active organizing of multiple constituencies around a range of issues and through a range of approaches not limited to general law reform, many of which are discussed in this volume, will benefit the drive toward labor law reform.

12. Our approach recognizes that current short-term law reform proposals and efforts such as those involving striker replacement may need to proceed on a "fast track." Such efforts, however, should not lose sight of the need for an integrated approach involving a longer-term process for fundamental reform.

9

What Will it Take? Establishing the Economic Costs to Management of Noncompliance with the NLRA

Morris M. Kleiner

Prior to the appointment in 1993 of the Commission on the Future of Worker-Management Relations by President Bill Clinton, the most recent visible effort to bring federal industrial relations legal issues to the forefront of public attention occurred in 1984 in the U.S. House of Representatives. Much of the testimony and analysis during that effort focused on problems of the American labor movement in attempting to organize and obtain first contracts (U.S. Congress 1984). A large part of that discussion centered on the growing level of unfair labor practices committed by management in the private sector and the perception that there existed huge economic incentives for management to commit those violations. If financial costs to management, like back pay to a fired employee, were so small that they failed to deter violations of the National Labor Relations Act, then a method to increase compliance would be to increase those costs to a level that would at least make management indifferent from a cost-benefit perspective.

The views of unionists on the penalty structure of the NLRA were summarized in 1984 by Richard Trumka, the president of the United Mine Workers of America, in testimony before the House of Representatives Subcommittee on Labor-Management Relations:

Fifty years of experience under this legislation have taught the American labor movement that the original promises of the Act are often little more

The author would like to thank Tzu-Shian Han for his excellent research assistance and Michael Belzer, John Budd, and Mitchell Gordon for their comments on earlier versions of this paper.

than a cruel hoax. The basic right to engage in concerted activity has little meaning to a fired union activist who must wait three or more years to get his or her job back. Nor does the token sanction of posting a notice on a bulletin board make an employer think twice before flaunting its legal responsibilities.

Robert J. Pleasure, director of the George Meany Center, views the legal environment for unions as follows: "We are living in the law of the jungle right now, except that unions are living in a cage and the employers are well armed" (quoted in *Wall Street Journal,* Nov. 6, 1984).

The primary purpose of this chapter, however, is to assist both academics and public policy makers in establishing the economic costs of noncompliance with the major provisions of the NLRA by providing a range of estimates from the academic literature on the types and levels of penalties that might cause employers to reduce their level of noncompliance. First, the study will present a rationale of the incentives for businesses and their economic agents—managers—to violate the act. The limitations of using solely an economic approach for providing estimates for this analysis will be presented. Second, this analysis will briefly document the rise in unfair labor practices by management and the economic rationale for this increase. Third, the paper will review the current literature on this issue and present an analysis that shows a range of estimates, suggesting how penalties might be developed on this issue.[1] Fourth, and finally, a presentation will be made of a continuum of alternative proposals for developing additional worker voice through the legitimacy and power of unionization. These proposals mirror the enforcement mechanism of other labor legislation from the U.S. experience (Greenfield and Pleasure 1993).

Incentive Structure for Firms under the NLRA

In most modern firms the owners, typically shareholders, put significant pressure on managers to maximize profits or shareholder wealth (Kleiner, McLean, and Dreher 1987). This policy promotes attempts to keep labor costs low. The way these incentives are developed regarding federal labor relations policies is to obtain the cooperation of lower-level managers in activities to defeat the union. In fact, a recent study found that in the 1980s the use of first-line supervisors during an organizing campaign was the most effective

---

1. The approach taken in this chapter is similar to a "meta-analysis," which analyzes correlations or develops summary statistics for key variables of interest across studies. Typically, estimated parameters or summary statistics are developed based on the number of observations per study, the estimated regression or correlation statistics, and the standard error term of the coefficient.

management weapon in causing the defeat of a union in an NLRB election. Moreover, the plant managers who were in charge during organizing drives leading to elections suffered dire consequences, such as a greatly increased likelihood of being fired or demoted (Freeman and Kleiner 1990). Given this incentive structure, it is not surprising that mid- and upper-level managers see the use of unfair labor practices as a tool that can stop organizing with little economic costs but with potentially huge opportunities for career advancement.

In addition to profit incentives, managers often view the imposition of a union as an unwanted intervention within the organization that reduces corporate control. To the extent that the domination of the rules of the workplace has an implicit economic value, it can be a major motivating factor for managers or owners of the enterprise. Therefore, any estimate based only on profits lost as a result of an organizing drive would probably understate the implicit value to employers of keeping a union out of an organization through the use of unfair labor practices.

Trends in Managerial Violations of the NLRA

One of the most documented areas of labor relations law research has been the upward trend in managerial violations of the NLRA. This section provides a brief overview and analysis of the results. The range of estimates of serious violations varies from Weiler's estimate (1984), that one in twenty workers involved in an organizing drive is terminated, to the more conservative estimates of Robert LaLonde and Bernard D. Meltzer, Jr. (1991), that approximately one in sixty organizers is terminated. Further, NLRB data reports show that, despite a downward trend in the number of elections per year, the number of violations increased fivefold from the 1950s to the late 1980s (NLRB annual reports, 1950s–80s). Moreover, the number of successful union elections leading to first contracts remained relatively constant, at about two-thirds, during the 1970s and 1980s. Finally, the percentage of unfair labor practices that were found to be meritorious remained relatively constant, at around 35 percent, during the same period (Weiler 1984; Freeman and Kleiner 1990). Even these results may understate the intimidation employers can use by testing the limits of the law, for example, by suggesting that individual workers be displaced during an NLRB-administered election campaign or making more general threats to move a plant to a new location (Suskind 1992:1).

The two sections of the NLRA that are most likely to be violated are those related to discrimination for union activity, 8(a)(3), and those covering failure to bargain in good faith, 8(a)(5). Violations of these provisions of the act do not carry punitive damages for the guilty party. If a firm discharged an employee for union activity, the likely penalty would be reinstatement plus back pay and interest. Further, there are no explicit monetary penalties for employers that violate the failure to bargain in good faith provision of the act. It is, therefore, not surprising that there has been a significant growth in violations of these provisions, in spite of the precipitous decline in the number of contracts and in union membership. As was presented in a U.S. General Accounting Office study (1982) on the impact of the NLRA on workers, 58 percent of reinstated employees were no longer working for that employer within one year and 29 percent of the total were fired following reinstatement. From these studies and the evidence on the growth of violations and repeat violations, the implication for workers is that exercising one's rights of collective bargaining can result in being fired more than once. Employees in the United States, unlike those in most other industrialized nations, are intimidated by the threatened loss of current and potential future employment through their participation in union-organizing efforts.

Empirical Analysis of NLRA Penalties on Employers

Since the 1984 publication of *Has Labor Law Failed?* by the U.S. House Committee on Government Operations, there has been an increase in the number and quality of analytical scholarly papers estimating the impact of NLRA penalties on firm behavior. Unfortunately, no one has summarized or evaluated the consensus findings of these published studies in the major labor relations scholarly outlets. This section discusses some of the major published papers on this topic, including the data sources, the analytical techniques used, and the relevant findings. It also provides a range of estimates and levels of statistical significance based on these studies, which may frame the debate on the potential economic costs and their effect in reducing NLRA violations.

The basic approach that was used in examining these studies is that the firm is indifferent in its choice between providing an increase in wages, and paying additional penalties, legal fees, or other costs related to a potential unfair labor practice charge or violation. Therefore, if there is a consistent behavioral response by employers to potential wage increases in terms of their likelihood to commit an unfair labor practice, the estimates presented in table 9.1 could provide a range of appropriate penalties to reduce violations. If the results are relatively consistent, then this method could be said to "price" unfair labor practices to employers.

The table provides results on the impact of alternative measures of wages and/or benefits and bargaining contract indexes on the likelihood of managerial violations of the National Labor Relations Act for studies that use both cross-sectional and time-series data sets. The first part of the table presents studies that examined the impact of wage levels, changes in wages, or union-nonunion wage gaps on the general category of violations that fall within the section of the act designated as 8(a) violations. These violations include both issues of individual employee discrimination and of duty to bargain. The first column of the table shows the authors and the publication date of each study. The second column shows the type of data and the statistical methodology they used. The third column presents major empirical findings relevant to the issue of employer compliance with the NLRA. The estimates are presented as behavioral relationships indicating the impact of wage levels or union versus nonunion wage gaps on the likelihood of committing a violation of the NLRA.

The following sections of the table show the impact of wage variables on the likelihood of violating specific sections of the NLRA. Initially, the results relate to the sections concerning discrimination against employees for union activities, or Section 8(a)(3). The last portion of the table shows the impact of the section dealing with failure to bargain in good faith, or Section 8(a)(5).

Since these studies used different data sets, as well as time-series and cross-sectional approaches, and alternative model specifications, any one study will probably not be sufficient to develop a convincing argument of the impact of economic variables on the commission of unfair labor practices. Other statistical issues, such as omitted variable bias or misspecification errors, may also limit the results of any one study. Taken together, however, the consensus findings provide more consistent results. These findings suggest that economic factors, such as wage differences between union and nonunion workers within a firm, are likely to provide important incentives for managers to violate the law, especially if these wage gains come out of profits. Within the general confines of current labor relations law, public policy makers attempting to obtain greater compliance could use these results as guidelines in the development of appropriate penalties that would implicitly price unfair labor practices to management.

The general picture that emerges from the results in the table is that potentially paying higher wages and the commission of unfair labor practices are positively related and statistically significant. First, the mean t-ratios for statistical significance are positive in all cases. Second, for the twenty-three regressions used to estimate the results presented in the table the "grand mean" t-ratio was a statistically significant 2.93. No one study yielded convincing evidence of a relationship between higher union wages and the commission of unfair labor practices, but taken together they provide a fairly strong pattern of consistent results.

Some of the studies provide especially relevant guidelines concerning the behavioral responses of management to potential economic incentives, such as the narrowing of the union-nonunion wage gap through labor law penalties. Using the estimates from two of the studies listed, an examination of the impact of the imposition of a 20 percent increase in wages, which might be

Table 9.1. *Studies on the Cost of Compliance with the Major Management-Focused Provisions of the National Labor Relations Act*

Author(s)	Data and methods	Results
General 8(a) Violations		
Roomkin (1981)	Time series (1952–75); least-square regression	One percent change in the average hourly earnings increases the volume of unfair labor practice cases per worker under the NLRB's jurisdiction filed by unions against employers by .012 to .068 percent.
Dickens (1983)	Cross-sectional data of 966 workers employed in thirty-one midwestern establishments in which union representation elections had been held in 1972 or 1973; probit regression	The worker's potential wage change positively affects the probability of workers' voting for a union. One dollar increase in the worker's potential wage gain increases a worker's probability of voting for a union by about 13 percent.
Elliott and Huffman (1984)	Annual report of the National Labor Relations Board 1970, 1975, and 1980; least-square regression	The gross hourly earnings of production workers on manufacturing payrolls adjusted by regional consumer price index are positively associated with the number of unfair labor practices per thousand workers under NLRB jurisdiction. One dollar increase in gross hourly earnings of production workers is associated with an increase in the number of unfair labor practices per thousand workers by .02 to .14 percent.
Roomkin and Harris (1984)	Two-digit industry-level data; the number of unfair labor practice cases per production employee in every other fiscal year from 1958 to 1978; least-square regression	One dollar increase in the average hourly earnings is associated with a .039 to .278 percent increase in unfair labor practice cases against employers per production worker.
Flanagan (1989)	Time-series data of unfair labor practice charges against employers for 1950–80; least-square regression	Natural logarithm of union–nonunion wage differential is significantly associated with the number of unfair labor practice charges by unions or individual workers against employers. One percent increase in union–nonunion wage differential is associated with increases in the number of unfair labor practices filed by unions with the NLRB by 154 to 285 per year.
Koeller (1992)	Forty-eight contiguous states for the years 1968–82; pooled data and simultaneous equation; 2SLS regression	Hourly earnings (adjusted for geographic differences in the consumer price index) are positively associated with the number of unfair labor practice cases filed against employers. One dollar increases in hourly earnings is associated with increases in the number of unfair labor practices filed by unions with the NLRB by 94 to 614.

Table 9.1. Studies on the Cost of Compliance with the Major Management-Focused Provisions of the National Labor Relations Act (continued)

Author(s)	Data and methods	Results
8(a)(3) Violations		
Kleiner (1984)	Three hundred three firms (1972–79); logit model	Firms that committed unfair labor practices in previous years are more likely to commit them in the current period. Using estimates of the value at the mean, firms that committed past violations are more than twice as likely to commit current violations. Firms that committed unfair labor practices in previous years have 37 percent higher probability of violating 8(a)(3) than firms that did not.
Freeman (1986)	Time-series data (1950–80); least-square regression	The union wage differential increases managerial opposition. One percent change in union-nonunion wage differential leads to a 2.54 percent increase in unfair labor practices per worker.
Freeman and Kleiner (1990)	Two hundred two firms (100 in Boston region and 102 in Kansas City region) in 1979–86; 15 AFL-CIO affiliates, 1982–83; logit and Tobit estimations	The potential union wage differential is positively associated with the probability that a firm will be charged with or be found guilty of an unfair labor practice. A 1 percent increase in the union-nonunion wage differential increases probability of an unfair labor practice by .37 to .41 percent.
8(a)(5) Violations		
Roomkin and Harris (1984)	Two-digit industry-level data; the number of unfair labor practice cases (per production employee) in every other fiscal year from 1958 to 1978; least-square regression	One dollar increase in the average hourly earnings is positively associated with an increase in the number of unfair labor practice cases filed against employers (duties of collective bargaining) per production employee by .516.
Kleiner and Schliebs (1991)	Cases in which a federal district judge ordered the employer to bargain in good faith in the 1970s and early 1980s; thirty-six firms (eighteen firms negotiating contracts after a bargaining order and eighteen firms without a bargaining order); simulation from regression	Firms not bargaining in good faith gain about 5.9 percent in wages and contract benefit reductions relative to comparison group, even following a court order.

imposed by a Davis-Bacon-like penalty on a firm for a serious violation of the National Labor Relations Act, is presented.[2] The estimates from Robert Flanagan's study (1989) suggest that unfair labor practice charges would be reduced by between 3,000 and 5,700 per year with penalties of the kind suggested by the imposition of the prevailing wage. This would represent a 13 to 25 percent drop in the total NLRB case load. Estimates from firm-level analysis for the 1980s by Richard B. Freeman and Kleiner (1990) show that the introduction of "prevailing wages" in a firm would likely reduce the probability of committing an unfair labor practice by management by between 7 to 8 percent. This would represent about a 29 percent drop in the number of unfair labor practice charges. Furthermore, such a significant penalty would signal to the business sector that workers' organizing rights are an important area of federal labor law, which may further increase compliance.

Such a penalty might also induce higher numbers of workers to vote for unions during NLRB-conducted elections. For example, William Dickens (1983) estimates, using a cross-sectional model for individual worker behavior, that projected increases in wages of approximately a dollar an hour would increase the probability of voting for a union in an NLRB election by approximately 13 percent, controlling for managerial threats and unfair labor practices during the organizing drive.

Studies examining the impact of potential economic costs to management for violations committed against individuals are presented in the second part of the table. First, Kleiner (1984) found that firms committing 8(a)(3) violations in a particular year were more likely to commit them in a subsequent year. This result suggests that there may be a learning-by-doing approach by organizations not familiar with the penalties. This study further shows the relatively low cost of violations relative to their economic benefits. Second, in a time-series model, the widening of the union-nonunion wage differential by 1 percent is associated with an increase of 2.54 percent in the number of unfair labor practices per worker (Freeman 1986). Moreover, Freeman and Kleiner (1990) used a cross-sectional approach to analyze 8(a)(3) violations and found that a 1 percent increase in the union-nonunion wage gap during an NLRB-sponsored election increased the likelihood of an unfair labor practice by between .37 and .41 percent. Overall, these results are consistent in showing the importance of wage differences in increasing illegal employer resistance to organizing and unionization.

2. The 20 percent figure is currently the standard estimate of the union-nonunion wage gap in the United States (Blanchflower and Freeman 1992). The Davis-Bacon Act requires that the local prevailing wage be paid for government construction contracts, which is typically the negotiated wage in an area. Suggestions that this be the appropriate penalty for failure to bargain in good faith was discussed as part of the labor law reform proposals during the late 1970s.

The last section of the table focuses on studies on the duty to bargain in good faith and the impact of wage changes, negotiated contract differences, and federal court orders on firms that violate Section 8(a)(5). The time-series analysis by Myron Roomkin and Dawn Harris (1984) shows relatively large wage effects on the commission of this type of unfair labor practice. The impact is at least twice as large as those effects cited in the previous section describing discrimination against individuals for union activity. In another study, Kleiner and Melanie Schliebs (1991) found that firms that failed to bargain in good faith gained about 5.9 percent in wages and benefits, even following a federal court order to bargain, relative to a closely matched comparison group. Given the usual three-year delay, and the potential lost earnings by employees during this process, this section of the NLRA is particularly ineffective. Overall, the results of studies of the economic incentives for employers to violate Section 8(a)(5) are even larger than the results of studies involving individual discrimination issues.

This summary is consistent in its findings. Namely, the economic benefits for noncompliance are high. This is the case because employers perceive that higher wages will result as a consequence of a successful organizing drive and contract and cause a lower level of future profits. The studies listed in the table provide the factual basis for the reasoning that greater compliance with the intent of the act could be achieved if penalties such as imposing the prevailing wage were enforced. Certainly, class-action suits, like those permitted under civil rights legislation, or imposing punitive damages for individuals whose rights are violated might provide economic incentives that would have real behavioral effects on management. This enhanced level of penalties might go a long way toward reducing noncompliance.

Increased penalties would have to be tempered by other new economic realities. First, newly unionized workers received wage changes only slightly higher than their nonunion counterparts following a union win and contract during the 1980s (Freeman and Kleiner 1990). Second, the variation in the industry wages and the distribution of wages generally favor larger union wage effects for workers with lower abilities than for those whose abilities are higher (Blau and Kahn 1993). Third, penalties would need to be constructed carefully in order not to put firms out of business and to avoid job losses that would result. The introduction of penalties such as a prevailing wage should also result in low-wage employers being less likely to violate the NLRA, because the relative penalty would be higher for such employers.

Conclusions

The purpose of this chapter has been to provide an evaluation from empirical industrial relations and economic studies of whether firms respond to the potential of wage increases by committing larger numbers of unfair labor practices. The results support the belief that a statistically significant relationship exists between the amount firms can reasonably expect to increase their wages as a result of a successful organizing drive and the likelihood of their committing unfair labor practices. These results imply that increased penalties along the lines of a prevailing wage policy would reduce the number of unfair labor charges by between 13 to 29 percent and would probably enhance workers' rights during and after an organizing drive.

The structure of appropriate public policies on penalties might vary. For example, AFL-CIO President Lane Kirkland alluded to doing away with the NLRA, including the secondary boycott provisions, and letting economic or labor market forces determine employee and union rights (Apcar 1984). This process may be the ultimate extension of "voluntarism" in labor relations. Such an outcome may not guarantee individual or union rights, however, or those of small employers, which may not have economic clout. An alternative, which might invite more legalism into the process, would be to provide workers with the same kinds of protection and legal clout enjoyed by workers covered by other forms of discrimination law, ranging from race and gender to age and disability. A related alternative would be to allow punitive damages for individuals who could prove employer discrimination under the NLRA. This legalistic approach might also provide workers in a firm who experienced discrimination with benefits such as prevailing wages, along the lines of the Davis-Bacon Act. Also, firms with serious labor law violations might be forbidden from bidding on government contracts. The results, using the estimates shown in the table, suggest that such solutions would likely reduce discrimination by employers that appear to be responsive to labor costs regarding their willingness to follow the NLRA. At a minimum, these facts should at least inform the Commission on the Future of Worker-Management Relations, which has been charged by President Clinton to rethink this nation's labor law policies, that there are clear economic incentives at work regarding managerial and worker behavior and that these incentives should be taken into account in developing greater employee representation for this nation's workforce.

10

Worker Participation after
Electromation and *Du Pont*

Robert B. Moberly

For more than a decade, employers, unions, governments, and others have paid considerable attention to the development of worker participation programs. These programs have taken the form of worker representation on company boards of directors, worker ownership, quality of work life programs (QWL), quality circles, productivity gainsharing, and profit-sharing (Moberly 1985, 1988; State and Local Labor-Management Committee 1993).

Observers have reacted both positively and negatively to worker participation programs. Some proponents of such programs argue that Congress should amend or repeal Section 8(a)(2) of the National Labor Relations Act, which prohibits employer assistance or domination of labor organizations, in order to promote the development of employee participation programs (Perl 1993; Bowers 1992; Clarke 1987; "Collective Bargaining" 1983). Conversely, those who oppose amending Section 8(a)(2) frequently are critical or skeptical of employer-employee cooperation and participation efforts (Herrnstadt 1992; McLeod 1990; Kohler 1986). This paper takes a somewhat different position, arguing that employer-employee cooperation and worker participation are beneficial and ought to be encouraged, yet that Section 8(a)(2) remains a vital part of our efforts to protect against employer interference with union organization.

Proponents of modification of Section 8(a)(2) point to two recent NLRB cases, known as *Electromation* and *Du Pont*.[1] In this chapter I argue that these

The author is grateful for the research assistance of Scott Atwood.

1. *Electromation, Inc. v. Teamsters Local 1049*, 309 N.L.R.B. No. 163, 142 L.R.R.M. 1003 (1992); *E.I. Du Pont de Nemours & Co. v. Chemical Workers Ass'n*, 311 N.L.R.B. No. 88, 143 L.R.R.M. 1121 (1993).

cases do not unduly restrict efforts at employee participation. Rather, the cases restrict employers' ability to carry out actions that threaten employees' legitimate right to organize. I also argue that eliminating or modifying Section 8(a)(2) as suggested by its critics would probably allow employers to use employee participation programs as union-busting mechanisms. At the very least, the suggested changes would permit management to control such programs, a result Section 8(a)(2) was expressly designed to prevent.

Section 8(a)(2)

A major purpose of the 1935 Wagner Act was to curtail company unions. The initial draft of the act contained only a ban on company unions, and the issue was "the most important in the political fight over the drafting and passage of the Act" (Barenberg 1993:1386). Most company unions were sham unions. Employers created and dominated such unions to give their employees the outward appearance of good-faith collective bargaining. For the most part, the establishment of company unions was designed to keep independent unions out of American industry.

Senator Wagner's goal was to promote true collective bargaining by prohibiting sham or company unions. His efforts were memorialized in Section 8(a)(2) of the act, which makes it an unfair labor practice for employers to "dominate or interfere with the formation or administration of any labor organization or contribute financial or other support to it."

Early NLRB decisions on employer domination or interference under Section 8(a)(2) focused on rather blatant examples of employer misconduct and also established the basic parameters of acceptable employee groups under the act. Three years after the Wagner Act's adoption, the Supreme Court handed down *NLRB v. Pennsylvania Greyhound Lines*, 303 U.S. 261 (1938). Greyhound management established a classic employee representation plan stacked with pro-management employees. Management established the union's bylaws, which gave the company direct control over union meetings and the selection of union representatives. Management also strongly urged employees to join the union and threatened to fire workers who contemplated joining an independent outside union.

Greyhound did not dispute the facts of the case but maintained that the NLRB improperly ordered the disestablishment of the representative plan. Management maintained that a cessation of the unfair labor practice was the only possible remedy if the company were found to have violated the NLRA.

The Court initially determined that the company employee association was plainly a sham union. It found that management had committed unfair labor practices when it improperly dominated and interfered with the association. Such actions stymied employee attempts to "bargain collectively through representatives of their own choosing." The Court thus considered whether the board could properly disestablish a company union. Examining the legislative history, the Court concluded that Congress clearly intended to promote the disestablishment of labor organizations that management had improperly influenced. The Court conceded that disestablishment may not be appropriate in every instance of employer domination. Yet the Court then determined that the control that Greyhound wielded over the employee association made it "incapable of functioning as a bargaining representative of employees" and ordered the union's disestablishment.

The next year, the Supreme Court solidified its rather blanket prohibition of company unions in *NLRB v. Newport News Shipbuilding & Dry Dock Co.*, 308 U.S. 241 (1939). The organization had existed for more than twelve years, and Newport News argued that the organization had the support of its employees. The Court held, however, that neither employer motive nor employee satisfaction is a pertinent factor in determining whether a company union is prohibited. Rather, the only question is whether there is employer domination or interference. The Court found that regardless of how innocuous the company's actions or unions appeared, company-dominated organizations could not be allowed if the Wagner Act's goal of promoting collective bargaining was to have a chance for success.

Section 8(a)(2) remained intact despite efforts to legalize company unions or their progeny in the Taft-Hartley Act of 1947 ("Participatory Management" 1985:1766–67; Cox 1947–48). But significant questions arose concerning the precise definition of a labor organization. Section 8(a)(2) prohibits dominating or interfering with a labor organization. Under Section (2)5, a labor organization is broadly defined as "any organization of any kind, or any agency or employee representation committee or plan, in which employees participate and which exists for the purpose, in whole or in part, of dealing with employers concerning grievances, labor disputes, wages, rates of pay, hours of employment, or conditions of work."

In the only Supreme Court case on this issue, *NLRB v. Cabot Carbon Co.*, 360 U.S. 203 (1959), the Court held that if an employee group "deals with the employer" on any of the enumerated topics, the employee group has no ultimate control over disposition of the issue and therefore will per se be a labor organization. A majority of the circuits have followed the *Cabot Carbon* view that any employee committee that "deals with" management on any issue enumerated in Section (2)5 is deemed a labor organization, except when such organization is an independent entity. A minority of circuits, however, have narrowly interpreted the *Cabot Carbon* analysis and have used employer motive and employee satisfaction as determining factors on the question of whether Section 8(a)(2) was violated.[2] Some courts have also concluded that actual rather than potential domination needed to be shown.[3]

The NLRB has not accepted the analyses of the minority circuits that consider factors such as free choice, employee satisfaction, or lack of employer antiunion motive. It has applied a fairly strict test to employee representation plans and has been unwilling to read *Cabot Carbon's* holding narrowly. This outcome has sometimes been criticized as nostalgia and as an impediment to change in the modern workplace.[4] Yet the board has upheld a number of worker participation programs and has indicated it is not adverse to the recent proliferation of quality of work life and other employee participation programs. For example, in *Sparks Nugget, Inc.*, 230 N.L.R.B. No. 43 (1977), the board determined that an employee committee established by management to resolve grievances was not a labor organization because it was actually adjudicatory in nature. It resolved grievances, rather than simply proposing solutions for management's review. All decisions of the committee were final. Thus, the committee was a management tool performing a function for management, rather than interacting with it. The committee did not act as the employees' advocate, and the board therefore concluded that *Cabot Carbon's* definition of "dealing with" did not include this committee.

Current Status of Section 8(a)(2)

The National Labor Relations Board recently decided two cases that directly addressed Section 8(a)(2) and worker participation issues. *Electromation, Inc. v. Teamsters Local 1049*, 309 N.L.R.B. No. 163 (1992), arose in a nonunion setting, while *E.I. du Pont de Nemours & Co. v. Chemical Workers Ass'n*, 311 N.L.R.B. No. 88 (1993), arose in a unionized workplace. The cases were highly publicized in advance as landmarks.

Electromation Case

Electromation, an electronics manufacturer, employs approximately two hundred people, and the company was not unionized at the time in question. In 1988, Electromation decided to cut expenses by altering the employee attendance bonus policy and, in lieu of a wage increase for 1989, distributing

2. *NLRB v. Streamway Div. of the Scott & Fetzer Co.*, 691 F.2d 288 (6th Cir. 1982); *Hertzka & Knowles v. NLRB*, 503 F.2d 625 (9th Cir. 1974); *Chicago Rawhide Mfg. Co. v. NLRB*, 221 F.2d 165 (7th Cir. 1955).

3. See *Streamway*, 691 F.2d at 295.

4. See "Quality Circle Busters" 1993 (referring to the NLRB as "an antique New Deal agency that can't seem to get its mind around to the modern economy").

a lump-sum payment based on length of service. Employees were displeased with this reduction in benefits, and in January 1989, sixty-eight employees signed a petition expressing dissatisfaction with the new attendance policy. The company president then met with a selected group of eight employees and discussed a number of issues, including wages, bonuses, incentive pay, attendance pay programs, and leave policy (all of which are conditions of employment). Management then proposed establishing "action committees" as a method of involving employees. After meeting again with the same eight employees, the company announced the formation of five action committees and posted sign-up sheets for each. Each action committee was composed of six employees and one or two members of management, as well as the benefits manager, who coordinated all of these committees. No employees were involved in the drafting of the policy goals expressed in the sign-up sheets; the company determined the number of employees permitted to sign up. After the committees were organized, the company posted a notice to all employees announcing the members of each committee and designating action committees in the areas of (1) absenteeism-infractions, (2) no smoking policy, (3) communication network, (4) pay progression for premium positions, and (5) attendance bonus program. The management coordinator testified that the posting was to ensure that anyone who wanted to know what was happening could contact the people on the committees. The action committees began meeting in late January and early February of 1989. Management representatives participated in the meetings, which were held on a weekly basis in conference rooms on the company premises. The company paid employees for their time spent participating and supplied necessary materials. A manager facilitated the discussions.

On February 13, 1989, a union sought recognition. There was no evidence that the company was aware of organizing efforts by the union until that time. The company informed employees that it would be unable to participate in the committee meetings and could not continue to work with the committees until after the union election. The union then charged the company with violating Section 8(a)(2) when it created the employee action committees.

An administrative trial judge found that the action committees constituted a labor organization within the meaning of Section 2(5), since employees, supervisors, and managers served as committee members; the committee acted in a representational capacity for employees; and their discussions concerned conditions of employment. The judge also found that the company dominated and assisted the committees, since it organized the committees and determined their nature, structure, and functions. The judge noted that meetings took place on company property, supplies and materials were provided by management, and members were paid for time spent on committee work.

On appeal, the board scheduled oral argument, usually reserved for significant cases, and framed the pertinent issues as follows: (1) At what point does an employee committee lose its protection as a communication device and become a labor organization and (2) what conduct by an employer constitutes domination or interference with the employer-employee committee?

In its majority opinion, however, the board restricted its findings to the specific facts of the case. The board first determined that the statutory language alone was insufficient to determine whether the statute should apply to particular facts. Consequently, it sought guidance from the legislative history. In the board's view, this history revealed that the prohibition against company-dominated labor organizations was a critical part of Senator Wagner's goal of eliminating industrial strife through encouraging collective bargaining. The board concluded that Wagner, in fact, thought that employer-dominated unions constituted the greatest obstacle to true collective bargaining. Quoting Wagner, the board observed that such a union "makes a sham of equal bargaining power. . . . Only representatives who are not subservient to the employer with whom they deal can act freely in the interest of employees." Thus, the first and most important step toward genuine collective bargaining was to abolish company-dominated unions as an agency for dealing with grievances and other conditions of employment. Because he intended to eliminate employer-dominated unions, Senator Wagner defined the term "labor organization" broadly. Edwin Witte of the University of Wisconsin was also influential in securing a broad definition of "labor organization." He wanted to include the most prevalent form of company-dominated union, the employee representation committee, including those that merely "deal" or "adjust."[5]

In adopting a broad definition of labor organization, the board determined that Congress and Wagner wanted to include not only highly organized groups such as labor unions but also loosely organized representation committees. The latter group was a prevalent form of company union at the time the Wagner Act was passed. To avoid creating a loophole that could conceivably emasculate the entire act, Wagner advocated a strict interpretation of labor organization in determining the nature of an employee group.

The NLRB further explored the legislative history with respect to the type of employer conduct Congress intended Section 8(a)(2) to prohibit. The board concluded that by prohibiting domination, interference, or assistance, Congress intended to provide a broad assurance that employee groups would be

---

5. Mark Barenberg's research (1993) even more firmly establishes the intention of the framers to create a broad definition of labor organization.

protected in their freedom to act independently of employers when representing employee interests.[6]

Proceeding to the merits, the NLRB first considered whether the action committees were labor organizations under Section 2(5). An organization is a labor organization, said the board, if (1) employees participate; (2) the organization exists, at least in part, for the purpose of "dealing" with employers; and (3) those dealings concern "conditions of work" or other statutory subjects. Further, if the organization has as a purpose the representation of employees, it meets the statutory definition of "employee representation committee plan" under Section 2(5).[7]

The board noted that the Supreme Court broadly defined "dealing with" in *Cabot Carbon.* The board observed that some unilateral mechanisms, such as suggestion boxes or brainstorming groups or other information exchanges, do not constitute "dealing with." Rather, "dealing with" involves a bilateral mechanism involving proposals from the employee committee concerning statutory subjects, coupled with real or apparent consideration of those proposals by management. The organization could escape the "dealing with" label if it limited itself to performing essentially a managerial or adjudicative function, such as independently resolving employees' complaints without dealing or interacting with the employer.

Applying the above principles to the facts of this case, the board first found that Electromation's action committees were labor organizations. There was no dispute that employees participated in the group. Second, the committees were actively "dealing with" management by sending proposals to management for consideration. Third, the subject matter of that dealing, which included the treatment of employee absenteeism, bonuses, and other monetary incentives, clearly concerned conditions of employment. Fourth, the employees acted in a representational capacity, because they were to discuss committee issues with other employees and were to elicit ideas from other employees regarding solutions that would satisfy the employees as a whole.

The board then examined whether the committees were autonomous entities or whether they were dealing with the employer about conditions of employment. The board concluded that a purpose of the action committees,

6. This conclusion was recently affirmed by an even more extensive analysis of legislative history in Barenberg 1993.

7. The majority opinion, because it found that the employee members of the action committees acted in a representational capacity, expressly declined to determine whether an employee group could ever be found to constitute a labor organization without a finding that it acted as a representative of other employees. The majority noted that member Dennis Devaney, who separately concurred, would have reached that issue. Devaney concluded that such a finding is necessary to find that a group is a labor organization within the meaning of Section 2(5). Thus, it appears that this remains an open issue.

in fact their *only* purpose, was to address employee dissatisfaction by creating a bilateral process to reach bilateral solutions on the basis of employee proposals. Nothing in the record indicated that the company either limited the purpose of the action committees to achieving "quality" or "efficiency" or designed the committees to be solely a "communication device" to promote efficiency or quality. Thus, the board did not answer the question of whether an employer-initiated committee existing for quality, efficiency, or communication purposes may constitute a labor organization under Section 2(5). The concurring opinions of members Dennis Devaney and Clifford R. Oviatt, Jr., however, clearly indicated that they did not view such committees as labor organizations.

On the question of whether the employer's conduct constituted domination in the formation and organization of the labor organization in violation of Section 8(a)(2), the board easily concluded that it did. It was the company's idea to create the action committees. The company drafted the purposes and goals of the committees, which defined and limited the subject matter each committee would cover. It determined how many members would compose a committee and the number of committees on which a single employee could serve. It appointed management representatives to the committees to facilitate discussions, and it contributed financial and other support, such as paid leave time to serve on them. On this record, the board concluded that the company dominated the action committees in their formation and administration and unlawfully supported them. The purpose of the action committees was not to enable management and employees to cooperate to improve quality or efficiency but rather to create an impression that disagreements were being resolved bilaterally, when in fact the company imposed its own unilateral form of bargaining or dealing on the employees.

In concurrence, members Devaney and Oviatt made it clear that they felt that quality of work life programs would be permissible, so long as they did not impair the right of the employee to free choice as a bargaining representative. For example, the board has upheld self-regulating employee teams that are given unilateral power over their job duties. Oviatt noted that *Electromation* involved "garden variety 8(a)(2) conduct," but nonetheless expressed approval for a broad spectrum of worker participation programs, including quality circles and quality of work programs, that draw on the creativity of employees.

A third concurring opinion, by member John Raudabaugh, completely disregarded the Supreme Court's opinion in *Cabot Carbon* and seemed to have very little credibility with any of the other board members.

The NLRB's decision in *Electromation* should not be surprising. Contrary to critical editorial opinion from the *Wall Street Journal* ("Quality Circle Busters" 1993), the ruling does not outlaw most existing employee participation programs that are aimed at productivity and efficiency. The case does not prohibit productivity teams, quality circles, or quality of work life programs, so long as those programs are not used for employee representation concerning conditions of employment. These plans must not usurp the right of employees to pick their own representatives by giving employees the illusion of a bargaining representative without the reality of one. Worker participation programs are likely to continue unharmed to the extent that they deal with improving quality, productivity, or such matters as customer relations, rather than working conditions. The *Electromation* case reaffirms the protections of labor organizations and employees, without impairing legitimate worker participation efforts.

Du Pont *Case*

The NLRB issued its decision in *Du Pont* in May 1993, just six months after the *Electromation* decision. Du Pont, unlike Electromation, was union-ized. Du Pont is a diverse corporation that specializes in chemicals. Its Deep Water, New Jersey, plant employs more than thirty-five hundred persons. The Chemical Workers Association ("union") has been active at Deep Water for about fifty years and represents the plant's clerical, production, and maintenance employees.

In 1984, Du Pont began experimenting with cooperative programs. The company established a number of committees that included management as well as bargaining unit employees. The committees discussed "conditions of work," such as safety and incentive awards, and benefits, such as employee picnic areas and jogging tracks. A major question was whether the commit-tees existed, at least in part, for the purpose of "dealing with" the employer. The board made it clear that there is room for lawful cooperation under the act, specifically listing "brainstorming" groups, information-sharing groups, and suggestion boxes as legitimate activities not involving the bilateral mechanism of "dealing with" the employer. The Du Pont committees, how-ever, went much further. Each committee had management representatives who were full participating members. The management representatives interacted with employee committee members under rules of consensus decision-making. Thus, management representatives could reject employee proposals, and so the board found that there was "dealing" within the meaning of Section 2(5). The board also concluded that there would be no "dealing with" management if the committees were governed by majority decision-making, management representatives were in the minority, and each committee had the power to decide matters for itself, rather than simply make proposals to management. There would also be no "dealing" if management representa-tives participated on the committees as observers or facilitators without the right to vote on committee proposals.

The board noted that committees could exist for the purpose of planning educational programs without there being dealing. These committees did much more, however, including deciding on incentive awards, which clearly are benefits and mandatory subjects of bargaining. Since management and employees determined the incentive awards under a rule of consensus decision-making, the board found that the committees existed for the purpose, in part, of dealing with the employer on a statutory subject.

Moreover, the board found that management dominated the administration of these committees. First, management retained veto power over any committee action, because decisions were by consensus. Second, a management member served as either the leader or the resource person of each committee and therefore had a key role in establishing the agenda for each meeting and in conducting the meeting. Management also controlled how many employees could serve on the committee and which employee volunteers would be selected if there were an excess number of volunteers. The employees had no voice in determining any aspect of the composition, structure, or operation of the committees. Moreover, management could change or abolish any of the committees at will. The board therefore determined that the evidence clearly established that the company dominated the administration of the committees.

Unlike *Electromation*, *Du Pont* involved the additional question of whether management violated its duty to bargain under Section 8(a)(5) of the NLRA by holding safety conferences and establishing safety and fitness committees. The board held that the safety conferences amounted to brainstorming and information sharing and noted that nothing in the act prevented an employer from encouraging its employees to express their ideas or to become more aware of safety problems in their work. Management did not establish the conferences as bilateral mechanisms for making specific proposals and responding to them. Thus, the board set forth the safety conferences as a labor-management cooperation technique that would be permissible under the act.

By contrast, the safety and fitness committees did not separate their activities from those properly within the union's authority. Some committees dealt with issues identical to those with which the union dealt and in fact brought about resolutions that the union had attempted and failed to achieve, such as establishing a new welding shop, a recreation area with picnic tables and other amenities, and, as previously noted, incentive awards. Thus, the company bypassed the recognized labor union, in violation of Section 8(a)(5). Further, the company dominated other labor organizations in the form of safety committees, in violation of Section 8(a)(2).

Following the *Du Pont* case, the *Wall Street Journal* ("Quality Circle Busters" 1993) proclaimed the NLRB the "quality circle busters," while the *New York Times* reported that "employers, lawyers, and business trade associations expressed dismay" about the decision (Noble 1993:A22). Such commentators would have one believe that Du Pont was merely attempting to improve worker productivity and company efficiency. If this were true, the committees probably would have withstood scrutiny. Nothing in the board's opinion indicates that quality of work life programs that concern themselves solely with production and efficiency are unacceptable. The issues addressed by the committees at Du Pont were far more wide ranging than production and efficiency. They involved monetary safety incentives, employee fitness programs, and related matters that clearly were subjects of bargaining. The committees were used, as is common in company union situations, to place mandatory subjects of bargaining before company-dominated groups, rather than to deal with the lawfully recognized independent union on the subjects. These were precisely the evils Senator Wagner was addressing in Section 8(a)(2) (Barenberg 1993:1386), and there is no evidence that the protection against such action should be relaxed. Relaxation would only result in further diminution of the bargaining power and effectiveness of lawfully recognized unions.

As this case demonstrated, the wrongs Section 8(a)(2) was meant to correct still exist. Supposed employee committees supplanted the union and were actually controlled to some degree by management, while the authorized representative of the employees, the recognized union, was weakened. Without Section 8(a)(2), some employers would undoubtedly attempt to retain as much control as possible over so-called cooperative programs.

Labor-management cooperation programs (or jointness programs)[8] often serve an important function even in unionized workplaces, but they should be negotiated with the union when they involve conditions of employment. Certainly there is no lack of examples of successful cooperative programs that major employers and unions in the United States have negotiated. Such agreements normally contain certain negotiated principles, including joint determination of the goals of the program; sharing of information; a clear indication that the program serves as a supplement rather than a substitute for collective bargaining; certain expressed indicia of mutual respect and trust; and further statements of support and leadership from both top management and union representatives (Moberly 1985, 1988).

The board recognizes the importance of cooperative efforts such as quality of work life programs. Productivity and efficiency issues clearly are legitimate subjects for employee committees. In *Du Pont*, however, management used the committees to undermine the union's representational capacity, rather than truly to cooperate. The *Wall Street Journal* ("Quality Circle Busters"

---

8. The term "jointness" is preferred by some, to indicate a coming together of equals for mutual benefit. See Getman and Marshall 1993.

1993) scoffed at this idea, sarcastically remarking that the committees obtained a picnic area and "the union had promised picnic tables too, but never delivered." The implication was that the union was lackadaisical. The board noted that, in reality, the union had repeatedly been turned down on the picnic tables, ostensibly because they were too expensive. By granting the committees benefits that the company denied through collective bargaining, management used the committees to undermine collective bargaining. The effect of such conduct, if allowed to continue, would be to diminish union power even further and to establish management clearly as the dominant party in labor relations.

Proposals to Amend or Repeal Section 8(a)(2)

There have been numerous proposals to amend or repeal Section 8(a)(2). These include recent congressional proposals reacting to *Electromation* and *Du Pont* and consideration of the issue by the recently established Commission on the Future of Worker-Management Relations.

With respect to congressional proposals, in March 1993, Representative Steven Gunderson (H.R. 1629, 103rd Cong., 1st Sess.) and Senator Nancy Kassenbaum (S. 669, 103rd Cong., 1st Sess.) proposed an amendment to Section 8(a)(2) that would allow an employer to establish, assist, maintain, or participate in an organization or entity in which employees participate and discuss matters of mutual interest and that does not have or seek authority for a collective bargaining agreement. This proposed legislation apparently would allow the employer-dominated committees at both Electromation and Du Pont. Some have justified this proposal by arguing that the Wagner Act was established for, and only contemplates, an adversarial model of labor-management relations; accordingly, the section must be altered to reflect the changing times (Perl 1993; Bowers 1992; Clarke 1987). This is clearly inaccurate, however. Recent work shows rather conclusively that Senator Wagner in fact was a cooperationist and had as his primary goal a system in which employers and independent unions would be able to cooperate through collective bargaining to create a more stable and productive work environment (Barenberg 1993). This opinion has also been noted by Archibald Cox and his coauthors, who state (1991:86–87): "The Wagner Act . . . embodied a conscious, carefully articulated program for minimizing labor disputes. Its sponsors urged that enforcement of the guarantees of the rights to organize and bargain collectively would be the best method of achieving industrial peace."

Of course, collective bargaining will not always be a cooperative enterprise; as in any form of negotiation or bargaining, there will be adversarial or positional examples as well as examples of cooperation. Moreover, there is likely to be a continuum of behavior from a cooperative to a competitive or adversarial stance, depending on the bargaining relationship and many other factors. Further, deep-seated employer resistance has prevented the model from becoming as cooperationist as intended (Sockell 1989:1014).[9] Nothing in the legislative history or experience of Section 8(a)(2), however, requires an interpretation that prohibits cooperative efforts.

Nor do *Electromation* and *Du Pont* prohibit worker participation programs. To the contrary, the majority and concurring opinions support such programs when limited to issues of productivity, quality, and efficiency or when negotiated through collective bargaining. Thus, no NLRB or court decision has struck down an employee participation program properly so limited. Eliminating Section 8(a)(2), or drastically amending it as suggested above, however, would seriously threaten employees' right to organize and engage in collective bargaining, as recognized by Congress in 1935 and again in 1947. Such removal or amendment would undoubtedly lead to the creation of participation schemes designed, at least in part, to avoid, break, or evade unionization. This would seriously damage the credibility of all employee participation programs, including those properly limited to productivity, efficiency, and quality, as well as broader programs created through collective bargaining. Consequently, repeal or amendment could have the opposite effect of that intended; that is, participation groups could become discredited and employees could avoid them wherever possible. Based on the past history of labor relations, some employers would undoubtedly use such programs to counteract union activity and to diminish the visibility and effectiveness of existing unions.

Amendment of Section 8(a)(2) could only be justified if such action were part of a comprehensive overhaul of our labor laws to encourage genuine employee participation that is not employer controlled. For example, one proposal is that every American workplace above a certain size have an employee participation committee that voices the interests of employees in dealing with management about a wide range of employment issues (Weiler and Mundlak 1993; O'Connor 1993). Even with this arrangement, many serious technical questions would have to be resolved. At the very least, this would require employers to comply with minimum standards of representation, such as holding secret-ballot elections, providing information and financial resources, and protecting representatives from reprisal.

Another possibility would be to provide for worker councils, workers on boards of directors, or minority representation, as is done in many European countries (Summers 1979, 1980, 1982, 1987). Employee committees might

9. Donna Sockell (1989) notes that an AFL-CIO survey of union organizers estimated that employers actively resisted 90 percent of organizing drives in 1982–83.

also be established by statute, with appropriate representation procedures and protection from reprisal, to consider certain statutory rights, such as job safety.[10] If any such plans to create truly independent employee participation are adopted by Congress, it would be a simple matter to exclude such plans from Section 8(a)(2). It would not be necessary to repeal or otherwise amend the statute.

Conclusion

Worker participation programs are a vital part of American industry today, in both the unionized and nonunionized sectors. Section 8(a)(2) does not hamper the development of such programs when they are legitimately directed toward improvements in productivity, efficiency, and quality. But Section 8(a)(2) does prohibit employer efforts to create employee groups that deal with employers on conditions of employment, because the employer inevitably controls such groups and thereby undermines the rights of workers and unions.

Electromation and *Du Pont* do not inhibit the proper use of employee committees to improve productivity, quality, and efficiency. No court or board decision has struck down an employee participation plan aimed at those goals, provided they did not also establish employer-controlled groups that dealt with conditions of work. Therefore, these decisions do not call for repealing or amending Section 8(a)(2).

Amendments to Section 8(a)(2) should be considered only as necessary to accommodate comprehensive labor law reform that would broadly increase employees' representation rights. Although there is much to be considered in the creation of such additional forms of representation, other industrial countries have established some models through the use of worker councils, workers on boards of directors, minority representation, and related schemes. Moreover, the notion of employee participation committees is certainly worthy of further consideration. These changes must be approached with great caution, however, and only as part of broad labor law reform that would not decrease the right and ability of employees to obtain adequate representation through labor organizations that are truly independent.

10. For example, proposed legislation would require employers with more than ten employees to establish safety and health committees involving both management and labor representatives. H.R. 3160, 102d Cong., 1st Sess. Sect. 201 (1991); S. 1662, 102d Cong., 2d Sess. Sect. 201 (1992).

11

The Debate over the Ban on Employer-Dominated Labor Organizations: What Is the Evidence?

James R. Rundle

Background

The debate over the National Labor Relations Act's ban on company unionism has taken center stage in the deliberations of the Commission on the Future of Worker-Management Relations, yet the debate has been informed by little factual evidence.

Section 8(a)(2) of the National Labor Relations Act makes it an unfair labor practice for an employer to "dominate or interfere with the formation or administration of any labor organization." The definition of a "labor organization" (Section 2(5)) is very broad: "any organization of any kind . . . which exists for the purpose, in whole or in part, of dealing with employers concerning grievances, labor disputes," and so on. This means that if an employee committee deals with issues that a union would have a right to bargain over and if the committee is dominated by the employer, then the committee is illegal, and the National Labor Relations Board can order the committee to be disestablished.

The focus of most employee involvement programs, including teams, quality circles, total quality programs, and the like, is ostensibly on quality, efficiency, and customer satisfaction. Although these issues might not appear to be bargainable, many argue that bargainable issues are inevitably implicated in such programs (see *Electromation, Inc. v. Teamsters Local 1049*, 309 N.L.R.B. No. 163 (1992)). This would make the programs vulnerable to legal

The author thanks Patricia Greenfield for valuable advice and encouragement and Elizabeth O'Leary for diligent and expert research assistance.

challenge, and several proposals have been advanced to modify Section 8(a)(2), or Section 2(5), in order to protect them from such challenges.

Who Favors Modifying the Ban?

These proposals arise from astonishingly diverse sources. Business leaders and Republican politicians say that Section 8(a)(2) must be changed if American business is to use employee involvement to compete in the world market.[1] In a variant of this argument, some members of the Commission on the Future of Worker-Management Relations have asserted that employee involvement is necessary for the creation of high-skill/high-wage jobs. But they also point to a "representation gap" in the American workplace owing to the decline of organized labor, arguing that Section 8(a)(2) needs modification if workers are to explore new channels for exercising "voice." Most of those advocating modification of Section 8(a)(2), however, also accept the employer's argument: that Section 8(a)(2) stands in the way of employee involvement (see Freeman and Rogers 1993a; Gould 1993; Weiler 1990:218). Commission chair John Dunlop views the legal constraints on employee involvement as the first issue the commission should address.

Altering Section 8(a)(2) is the only issue employers have advanced in the labor law reform debate, apart from their resistance to labor's proposals. It therefore stands as labor's only bargaining chip. The sole commission member drawn from the labor movement, former UAW president Douglas Fraser, has suggested trading some part of 8(a)(2) for better organizing rights.

Purpose of Section 8(a)(2)

There are reasons to worry about this developing bandwagon. The independence of workers' organizations is central to the purpose of the National Labor Relations Act. Section 7 gives workers a right to "*self*-organization" and "to bargain collectively through representatives of their *own* choosing" (emphasis added). Section 8(a)(2) was intended to safeguard this independence, and therefore it concerns the heart of the act.

The need for Section 8(a)(2) became clear in attempts to enforce Section 7(a) of the earlier National Industrial Recovery Act (1933). The NIRA established a right to organize and bargain collectively, but it did not distinguish company unions from independent unions. The result was that employers

---

1. See for example, Perl 1993; remarks of Rep. Steven Gunderson (R-Wisc.), in the *Daily Labor Report*, March 31, 1993, A-14; remarks of Jeffery C. McGuiness, Labor Policy Association, in the *New York Times*, Dec. 18, 1992; *amicus curiae* briefs to the NLRB in *Electromation* for the Manufacturers' Alliance for Productivity and Innovation, for the Chamber of Commerce of the United States of America, and for the Coalition of Management for Positive Employment, Training and Education, the National Association of Manufacturers, and the American Iron and Steel Institute.

organized employee representation plans much faster than workers organized unions, prompting Senator Wagner to state, "The very first step toward genuine collective bargaining is the abolition of the employer dominated union" (NLRB 1985, 1:15). In fact, the new National Labor Relations Board did root out many ERPs in its early years (Hutson 1992).

Furthermore, precedents under Section 8(a)(2) give unions important bargaining rights when employers propose these plans and empower unions to reject plans they do not believe to be legitimate.

Does Evidence Support Altering Section 8(a)(2)?

Altering a section of the National Labor Relations Act that was conceived as central to its purpose should not be contemplated on the basis of unexamined assumptions that "good-faith" employee committees are threatened by legal action. Nor should it be based on an unproven belief that most existing committees are fundamentally different from ERPs or that something like ERPs would never again stand in the way of organizing if Section 8(a)(2) were weakened. This is particularly true when the proposed alteration is the only one employer organizations favor and for which they have campaigned in a vigorous and, as we shall see, highly misleading manner.

One missing key is the record of Section 8(a)(2) in practice. Has the application of this section of law actually thwarted employee committees that empower workers and improve competitiveness through group processes? Since the belief that 8(a)(2) thwarts these efforts is so pervasive and influential, it is remarkable that no one has made a systematic effort to find out if this is actually true. Instead of information, we have heard mostly a fog of confusion created around a recent case, *Electromation*.

"Industrial Age Rules Bog Down Modern Economy"

In the Electromation case, employer organizations such as the National Association of Manufacturers, the Labor Policy Association, the Chamber of Commerce, and others waged what Charles Morris (1992) suggested was a deliberate "campaign of disinformation."

The Labor Policy Association's brief claimed that the decision of the administrative law judge (later upheld by the NLRB) allows for "only two options: traditional collective bargaining, based on the threat of economic warfare, or no involvement in work improvement efforts whatsoever," and asked whether the act would recognize "emerging workplace realities and maturing labor-management relationships, or will its gaze be frozen forever upon the adversarial labor relations landscape of 1935?" The Chamber of Commerce's brief warned, "The Board must find a way to accommodate the new organizational concepts in American industry, under which an employer and groups of employees work cooperatively to improve quality, productivity, and overall performance in order to be competitive at home and abroad."

Eleven Congress members filed a brief declaring that Section 8(a)(2) "sounds a potential death knell for what could be the key to economic rebirth" (Zurofsky 1992). Newspaper and magazine accounts echoed these apocalyptic warnings: "Firms Fear NLRB as Hurdle in Global Race," "Putting a Damper on That Old Team Spirit," "Setback for Labor-Management Teamwork Efforts," "A Wedge in the Workplace," "Remove the Cloud over Teamwork," "Quality Circle Busters," and "Industrial Age Rules Bog Down Modern Economy."[2]

Real Meaning of Electromation

This clamor was created without the slightest basis in the facts of the case. Electromation's committees dealt only with mundane terms and conditions of employment. Neither the employer nor the numerous *amici* filing briefs in the case ever argued that the committees were teams or quality circles or were formed with any intention of improving efficiency or product quality. What really is remarkable about *Electromation* is that the use of labor law by the employees and the Teamsters union was a stunning success. The Teamsters filed a Section 8(a)(2) charge after losing a certification election. A judge found that the employer had established and dominated committees that were functioning as labor organizations and ordered them to be disestablished. Then, through a stipulated election agreement arising out of efforts to settle the case, a second election was held, which the union won. Thus, as a direct consequence of acting on Section 8(a)(2), the employees gained a labor organization under their own control and used it to win enforceable rights.

Advocates of altering Section 8(a)(2) would greatly strengthen their position if they cited cases of thriving employee involvement programs, established in good faith and demonstrably beneficial to both company and employees, that were struck down by the NLRB. Indeed, if they cannot do this, then they are asking for a change in a major, long-standing statute without a single test case to show why the change is needed. That such a proposal has reached the top of the commission's agenda, at a time when unions are reeling from discriminatory firings, refusals to bargain, and hiring of permanent replacements, calls for prompt scrutiny.

It is my hypothesis that in actual practice, Section 8(a)(2) has had virtually no impact on good-faith experimentation with employee involvement. This hypothesis is tested through a review of 8(a)(2) disestablishment cases over the past twenty-two years.

Methodology

How can we know whether the board had disestablished committees of the type employers say they need to be competitive or that have "empowered"

---

2. From, respectively, the *Memphis Commercial Appeal*, May 31, 1992; *Business Week*, May 4, 1992; *New York Times*, Dec. 18, 1992; *Houston Chronicle*, May 22, 1992; *Chicago Tribune*, July 12, 1993; *Wall Street Journal*, June 9, 1993; *Denver Rocky Mountain News*, June 27, 1993.

employees? There are thousands of employee involvement committees and hundreds of different plans. Are they *all* good and necessary? What criteria can we use to decide?

Employers simply say they want to make "good-faith" efforts to involve employees and point to their need to be competitive through improved quality and so forth. Some add that committees empower employees by increasing responsibility and decision-making authority. Although these criteria are vague, they proved to be easy to test in the existing cases.

To find the cases in which the board disestablished employee committees, I did a Lexis search of NLRB cases from 1972 to 1993 using "8(a)2" and "disestablish!" "disband!" or "dismantle!" as key words (the exclamation mark is a truncation symbol). This twenty-two-year period is the full range covered by Lexis. During this period employee involvement grew slowly at first and more rapidly later (Ichniowski, Delaney, and Lewin 1989) despite the existence of Section 8(a)(2). If Section 8(a)(2) had limited this development, we would expect a rise in the number of disestablishment cases over time.

There is no certainty that this search yielded every disestablishment case during the twenty-two-year period, but a check of several law review articles and briefs revealed no additional cases.

"Good-Faith" Criterion

The disestablishment cases were then checked for (1) other unfair labor practices; (2) whether the charge arose out of a union organizing campaign and, if it did, whether the committee was established during the campaign, revitalized at the time of the campaign, or engaged in new activity that might make the committee a more attractive alternative to unionism; and (3) whether a certified union was in existence and, if so, whether the employer had refused to bargain with it.

Antiunion motivation need not be shown to establish domination of a labor organization, so the board has not always determined whether a committee's formation or actions had the purpose of thwarting union activity. Also, other ULPs do not necessarily have any connection to the Section 8(a)(2) violation. For our purposes, however, if "good-faith" efforts at employee involvement are being thwarted by board decisions, we would expect to find cases in which no such indications of bad faith exist.

"Quality" and "Empowerment" Criteria

The decisions of the administrative law judges attached to board decisions are a rich source of information about the cases. The ALJ scrutinizes the employers' arguments and, in particular, the issues the committees discuss.

Using this resource, the cases were checked for evidence that the committees were created primarily to improve the quality of a product or service; to improve efficiency; to introduce new technology or new work practices, such as total quality management; or to expand the scope of employee decision-making. If board decisions hampered experimentation with such activities, there should be evidence in the ALJ's record. We would expect to find that some committees engaged mostly in those activities but were struck down because they included some bargainable issues in their deliberations. We would expect some employers to argue that their committees' accomplishments were critical to the success of the firms and that the committees occasionally had to discuss bargainable issues to be fully effective. And if the committees empowered employees, we would expect to find in some cases that employees gained decision-making authority, not just the opportunity to make suggestions. Certainly, if any of these situations occurred, the employer would present the evidence and the ALJ would discuss its merits.

Results

Have Disestablishments Increased over Time?

The Lexis search yielded 101 citations, of which 58 proved to be cases in which the board had disestablished one or more employee committees (table 11.1). In the case of 19 citations, the board declined to disestablish. The other 24 citations proved irrelevant. If we divide the search period into two eleven-year blocks, 1972–82, and 1983–93, we find that the number of disestablishments has *decreased markedly* in recent years, not increased as we would expect if Section 8(a)(2) were limiting employee involvement (table 11.2). *In the last eleven years, the board disestablished in only seventeen cases, or less than two per year.*

Have "Good-Faith" Efforts Been Struck Down?

During the entire twenty-two-year period, the board ordered disestablishment in only five cases in which it found no other ULPs (table 11.2). Typical of the ULPs were interrogations, threats to shut down and lay off, surveillance, discriminatory discharge, soliciting grievances, promises, and granting improvements. In one case, charges of discriminatory discharge were settled by reinstatement (*North American Van*, 288 N.L.R.B. 11 (1988)), and in two others the committee was formed during an organizing campaign (table 11.1). *This leaves two cases in twenty-two years in which there were no other ULPs found and the committee that was disestablished had not been established in the course of a union organizing campaign.*

Have Quality or Empowerment Efforts Been Thwarted?

The two cases remaining are *Electromation*, in which the committees had nothing to do with quality, productivity, or empowerment, and *Alta Bates*,

Table 11.1. NLRA Violations Concurrent with the Order to Disestablish Employee Committees, 1972–93

Abbreviated case name	Board number	Year	Organizing campaign [a]	Union in existence [b]	Other sections violated [c]	Violations or other circumstances
DuPont	311 N.L.R.B. 88	1993		Yes	8(a)(1) 8(a)(5)	Refusal to allow union communications, soliciting grievances, refusal to bargain, unilateral change, warnings, discharge
Ryder	311 N.L.R.B. 81	1993	Yes		8(a)(1)	Threats to withhold raises and to lay off
Salt Lake	310 N.L.R.B. 149	1993	Yes	Yes	8(a)(1) 8(a)(3) 8(a)(5)	Interrogations, threats, promises, discharges, refusal to bargain, unilateral change
Yukon	310 N.L.R.B. 42	1993	Yes	Yes	8(a)(1) 8(a)(3) 8(a)(5)	Interrogations, promises, surveillance, threats, eliminating benefits, discharge, refusal to bargain, unilateral change
Research Fed.	310 N.L.R.B. 13	1993	Yes	Yes	8(a)(1) 8(a)(5)	Threats, soliciting grievances, promises, granting benefits, refusal to bargain, unilateral change
Electromation	309 N.L.R.B. 163	1992	Yes [d]		none	Organizing drive shortly after committees established; union lost, but then won board-ordered election after committees were disestablished
F.M. Transport.	306 N.L.R.B. 156	1992	Yes		8(a)(1) 8(a)(3)	Discharge, questioning, promises, threats
Camvac	288 N.L.R.B. 92	1988	Yes	Yes	8(a)(1) 8(a)(5)	Interrogations, promises, threats, granting benefits, unilateral change
Airstream	288 N.L.R.B. 28 [f]	1988	Yes		8(a)(1)	Threats, granting improvements, discriminatory prohibition of literature distribution
North Am. Van	288 N.L.R.B. 11	1988	Yes		none	Union supporter fired but reinstated in settlement of 8(a)(3) charge; refused to allow on committee

Table 11.1. NLRA Violations Concurrent with the Order to Disestablish Employee Committees, 1972–93 *(continued)*

Abbreviated case name	Board number	Year	Organizing campaign [a]	Union in existence [b]	Other sections violated [c]	Violations or other circumstances
UARCO	286 N.L.R.B. 7	1987	Yes		8(a)(1) 8(a)(3)	Interrogations, threats, soliciting grievances, discharge
Ona Corp.	285 N.L.R.B. 77	1987		Yes	8(a)(1)	Soliciting grievances, promises; bargaining order in previous case, then refusal to bargain in another
Memphis Truck	284 N.L.R.B. 99	1987		Yes	8(a)(3) 8(a)(4) 8(a)(5)	Refusal to sign collective bargaining agreement, violating contract, refusal to bargain, unilateral change, refused to rehire
Superior Cont.	276 N.L.R.B. 55	1985	Yes		8(a)(1) 8(a)(3)	Impression of surveillance, threats, expressing the futility of organizing, discharge
Jet Spray Corp.	271 N.L.R.B. 32	1984	Yes		8(a)(1)	Overly broad rules, threats, interrogations, urging employees to abandon union drive
Predicasts	270 N.L.R.B. 170	1984	Yes [d]		8(a)(1)	Promises, interfering with distribution of union materials
Lawson Co.	267 N.L.R.B. 75 [f]	1983	Yes		8(a)(1) 8(a)(3)	Granting unprecedented benefits, threats; asking employees to withdraw authorization cards and deal directly, saying they'd never deal with a union
Comet Corp.	261 N.L.R.B. 188	1982		Yes	8(a)(1) 8(a)(3) 8(a)(5)	Discharge, refusal to bargain
Homemaker	261 N.L.R.B. 50 [f]	1982		(Yes) [g]	8(a)(1)	Impression of surveillance, interrogation
Marhoefer	258 N.L.R.B. 71	1981	Yes	Yes	8(a)(1) 8(a)(5)	Soliciting complaints, promises, telling employees company would never sign a contract, threats

Table 11.1. NLRA Violations Concurrent with the Order to Disestablish Employee Committees, 1972–93 (continued)

Abbreviated case name	Board number	Year	Organizing campaign [a]	Union in existence [b]	Other sections violated [c]	Violations or other circumstances
K & E Bus	255 N.L.R.B. 137	1981	Yes		8(a)(1) 8(a)(3) 8(a)(4)	Threats, interrogation, promises, granting improvements, discharge, layoffs, discriminatory refusal to hire or rehire
Walker Die Cast.	255 N.L.R.B. 34	1981		Yes	8(a)(1) 8(a)(3) 8(a)(5)	Threats, surveillance, removing picket signs, discharge, refusal to reinstate, advising employees to resign, unilateral changes
Classic Industries	254 N.L.R.B. 149[g]	1981	Yes		8(a)(1)	Threats to subcontract or close down if union won
Streamway	249 N.L.R.B. 54f	1980	Yes		8(a)(1)	Interrogating about union views
Wisconsin Beef	249 N.L.R.B. 34	1980	Yes		8(a)(1) 8(a)(3)	Interrogations, threats, lay off due to union activity
American Feather	248 N.L.R.B. 147	1980	Yes	Yes	8(a)(1) 8(a)(3) 8(a)(5)	Refusal to recognize union and bargain, assuring striker replacements that strikers would never be reemployed, failing to place strikers on hiring list, granting wage increase, withholding cost-of-living allowance
St. Vincent's	244 N.L.R.B. 20	1979	Yes		8(a)(1)	Threats, promises, surveillance, interrogation
G.Q. Security	242 N.L.R.B. 84	1979	Yes		8(a)(1) 8(a)(3)	Decertification election, Teamsters intervened; threats, discharge solicitation and remedying grievances through committee
Worldwide	242 N.L.R.B. 40	1979	Yes	Yes	8(a)(1) 8(a)(5)	Campaigning for competing labor organization, announcing negotiations for benefits, refusing to recognize union and bargain, interrogations, threats
Stephens Inst.	241 N.L.R.B. 71	1979	Yes		8(a)(1) 8(a)(3)	Interrogation, threats, bribing employees to abandon union activity, soliciting employees to observe a union meeting, discharge

Table 11.1. NLRA Violations Concurrent with the Order to Disestablish Employee Committees, 1972–93 (continued)

Abbreviated case name	Board number	Year	Organizing campaign[a]	Union in existence[b]	Other sections violated[c]	Violations or other circumstances
Fry Foods	241 N.L.R.B. 42	1979	Yes[d]	Yes	8(a)(1) 8(a)(3) 8(a)(4) 8(a)(5)	Assults, thirty-three discharges, interrogations, threats, surveillance, harder working conditions, refusal to bargain, unilateral change
Kurz-Kasch	239 N.L.R.B. 107	1978	Yes		8(a)(1)	Falsifying hiring dates, interrogations, threats
Mattiace	239 N.L.R.B. 4	1978	Yes		8(a)(1) 8(a)(3)	Discharges, interrogations, threats, promises, surveillance, polling
Morbark	237 N.L.R.B. 105	1978	Yes		none	Formed and bargained with committee during drive
Liberty	236 N.L.R.B. 201	1978	Yes		8(a)(1) 8(a)(3)	Impression of surveillance, threats, interrogations, transfers, layoffs, and discharge of union supporters
Ace Mfg.	235 N.L.R.B. 113	1978	Yes		8(a)(1)	Interrogations, promises, surveillance
Northeastern U.	235 N.L.R.B. 122[f]	1978			8(a)(1)	Denied "9 to 5" supporters access and refused to deal with them, but bargained with committee
Metrop. Alloys	233 N.L.R.B. 145[g]	1977	Yes		none	Created and dominated committee and claimed it would be "just like a union"; presented a "collective bargaining agreement" to employees
Kux Mfg.	233 N.L.R.B. 50	1977	Yes		8(a)(1)	Interrogations, threats, coercing employees to designate committee as their bargaining agent, polling, granting benefits

Table 11.1. NLRA Violations Concurrent with the Order to Disestablish Employee Committees, 1972–93 (continued)

Abbreviated case name	Board number	Year	Organizing campaign[a]	Union in existence[b]	Other sections violated[c]	Violations or other circumstances
Federal Alarm	230 N.L.R.B. 78	1977	Yes	Yes	8(a)(1) 8(a)(3) 8(a)(5)	Interrogations, threats, refusal to bargain with union, recognizing and bargaining with committee
Interstate Engin.	230 N.L.R.B. 3	1977	Yes		8(a)(1)	Interrogation, impression of surveillance, threats of closure and discharge, promises
Mid-Continent	228 N.L.R.B. 98	1977		Yes	8(a)(1) 8(a)(5)	Refusal to bargain, polling, telling employees union could be voted out by a poll and they could bargain through committees
Internat'l Signal	226 N.L.R.B. 97	1976	Yes[d]		8(a)(1) 8(a)(3)	Discharge, discriminatory enforcement of no solicitation rule
Alta Bates	226 N.L.R.B. 65	1976		Yes	none	Found "dealing with" mandatory subjects, but not bargaining; no evidence of anti-union intent
Freemont Mfg.	224 N.L.R.B. 79	1976	Yes		8(a)(1) 8(a)(3)	Discharge, interrogation, surveillance
Surface Industr.	224 N.L.R.B. 35	1976	Yes	Yes	8(a)(1) 8(a)(5)	Interrogations, threats, surveillance, shutdown, refusal to bargain, unilateral changes
M-W Education	223 N.L.R.B. 67	1976	Yes		8(a)(1)	Interrogations, threats, raises, free meals
STR	221 N.L.R.B. 103	1975	Yes		8(a)(1) 8(a)(3)	Threats, suspensions, interrogations
Contract Knitter	220 N.L.R.B. 30	1975	Yes		8(a)(1) 8(a)(3)	Threats, surveillance, economic reprisals
RPI	219 N.L.R.B. 85	1975	Yes[d]		8(a)(1)	Interrogations, threats, promises

Table 11.1.   NLRA Violations Concurrent with the Order to Disestablish Employee Committees, 1972–93   (continued)

Abbreviated case name	Board number	Year	Organizing campaign [a]	Union in existence [b]	Other sections violated [c]	Violations or other circumstances
Rupp Industries	217 N.L.R.B. 65	1975	Yes		8(a)(1)	Threats, interrogation, pay raise
Hertzka & Knowles	206 N.L.R.B. 32[e]	1973	Yes		8(a)(1)	Threats of closing, laying off, and blacklisting
Lowen	203 N.L.R.B. 86	1973	Yes		8(a)(1)	Threats; committee established 2 months after union lost
Versatube	203 N.L.R.B. 87	1973	Yes		8(a)(1)	Promises, threats to close, chair of committee solicited grievances in presence of foremen
Money Olds	201 N.L.R.B. 22	1973	Yes		8(a)(1)	Granting rate increases
Gibbons	199 N.L.R.B. 88	1972	Yes		8(a)(3)	Discharges, refusal to reinstate
Solmica	199 N.L.R.B. 41	1972	Yes	Yes	8(a)(1) 8(a)(5)	Interrogations, promises, granting of benefits, refusing to bargain
Goulds Pumps	196 N.L.R.B. 118	1972	Yes		8(a)(1)	Warnings, interrogations, telling employees they didn't need to comply with Board subpoena

[a] Means that the 8(a)(2) charge was the result of an organizing campaign. Except as noted (see "d"), the committee was formed or changed its activity in apparent response to the campaign.

[b] Means a union coexisted with the committee. Where a union organizing campaign is also indicated, it means a union won an election, or a bargaining order was issued, during the period under investigation.

[c] The number listed is the 8(a) violation found in addition to the 8(a)(2) violation. An 8(a)(1) violation is indicated only if cause was found other than the 8(a)(2) violation itself. So if the 8(a)(1) violation is just "interference" resulting from an 8(a)(2) domination of a committee, then a 8(a)(1) violation is not listed.

[d] The committee was in existence before the organizing campaign, and there was no evidence that it changed its activity in order to undermine the campaign.

[e] U.S. Court of Appeals denied enforcement. No court of appeals ordered disestablishment when the board did not.

[f] U.S. Court of Appeals enforced.

[g] The union itself was dominated and actually amounted to no more than a committee.

Table 11.2.   *Employee Committees Disestablished by the NLRB, 1972–93: Summary Statistics*

	1972–82	1983–93	Total
Number of disestablishment orders	41	17	58
Number of cases in which *no* ULPs were found (other than 8(a)(2) violations)	3	2	5
Cases in which the committee was formed or used in apparent response to organizing activity	32	12	44
Cases in which a union existed and the employer refused to bargain[a]	11	7	18
No other ULPs; committee was not formed or used in apparent response to organizing activity	1	1	2

[a] Some cases involve both union organizing and refusal to bargain, as explained in note b of table 11.1

266 N.L.R.B. 65, a 1976 case. In the latter case, a union was present, yet every issue taken up by the committee was an ordinary grievance of the type unions handle every day (with the possible exception of a request for a suggestion box). In every other case in which a union was present and a committee was disestablished, the board found a refusal to bargain. Not one of the fifty-eight cases contained any evidence that the committee in question had increased productivity, quality, or the decision-making authority of the employees.

All of this leaves us with a simple, stark conclusion: *There is absolutely no evidence that the NLRB has ever in the past twenty-two years disestablished a committee of the type employers say they must have to be competitive.*

Cases That Do Not Reach the NLRB

For the last three years, Lexis has included ALJ decisions that have not reached the NLRB. Among these were five cases in which the ALJ ordered disestablishment of a committee. None deviated from the pattern of NLRB cases described above.

Discussion

Employee Committees as Alternatives to Unionism

What of the arguments that employee committees could be a new form of representation that could fill the gap left by union decline? Richard B. Freeman and Joel Rogers (1993a), arguing for modifying the ban on company unionism, state that current labor law presents workers with an "'all or nothing' choice in representation—traditional labor unions or none at all." But that is not true.

First, workers have the right "to form, join, or assist labor organizations" (Section 7), and, as we have seen, a nonunion committee can be a "labor organization." Workers also have a right under Section 7 "to engage in other concerted activity for mutual aid and protection." So workers can form organizations and act concertedly to attempt to persuade or pressure an employer even without unionizing. Clyde W. Summers (1990a) advocates doing exactly that.

Second, as this study shows, there is little chance that the board will disestablish more than a handful of the thousands of existing employee committees. If opportunities to experiment with alternative forms of "voice" are wanted, then they exist already. An overlooked tool is the Labor-Management Reporting and Disclosure Act. Sections 3(i) and (j) define the term "labor organization" similarly to the way it is defined in Section 2(5) of the NLRA. This means that people who are represented by employee committees that are "labor organizations" have a right of access to meetings, to address the committee without fear of reprisal, to elect the heads directly, and to be informed of those rights, and the committee must disclose its finances.

At Polaroid Corporation, a committee was challenged as undemocratic under the LMRDA. Polaroid's CEO abolished the committee rather than allow elections for its chair and vice chair (*Daily Labor Report*, June 23, 1992, A2–A3; *Scivally v. Graney*, 143 L.R.R.M. 3043 (1993)). The potential for exercising LMRDA rights has not been tapped; unions could use them to educate workers about democracy in the workplace.

A more serious problem with the promotion of nonunion committees is that they are assumed to have value as an alternative to "traditional" unionism. The value of unionism has been painstakingly documented. Unions are known to improve wages and benefits, reduce turnover, increase equality of wages, protect the jobs and income of older workers (Freeman and Medoff 1984), and make the Occupational Safety and Health Act (OSHA), useless in nonunion firms, into an important tool for safety (Weil 1991). They make substantial gains even in first contracts (Bronfenbrenner 1993:471). In contrast, the value of employee committees is simply taken on faith.

Should Labor Trade 8(a)(2) for Something Else?

Would some degree of change in 8(a)(2) be worth trading for something that would make it easier to organize? First of all, what would employers give up to get such a change? Probably not much, because, as we have seen, they are not actually harmed by 8(a)(2). But more important, the employers used the employee involvement issue phenomenally well to derail the Commission on the Future of Worker-Management Relations and just about everyone else from the issues that matter to labor and working people. Employers have accomplished this without a single argument they could back up with facts. They are very powerful in Congress. Against that opposition, if labor engages in horse-trading, what will come of it? Consider this scenario: By the time such a trade gets through Congress, Section 8(a)(2) will be dead, and the labor movement will wind up with a pale ghost of the new rights it thought it was getting.

Furthermore, any change would present real hazards, no matter how carefully drafted. The recent *Du Pont* decision (311 N.L.R.B. No. 88 (1993)), along with earlier cases, provides valuable precedent that should not be lightly cast into doubt. No one can predict what the altering of 8(a)(2) or 2(5) would be used to justify in years to come. Who would have guessed when the Taft-Hartley Act was drafted that forty-five years later a board member would argue that, in adding new language to the first section, Congress must have intended a change in 8(a)(2), even though Congress specifically rejected such a change? Yet that is what member John Raudabaugh did in his concurrence in *Electromation*.

What Labor Stands to Lose

The *Du Pont* decision affirmed that unions can insist on bargaining over employee involvement plans that deal with bargainable issues and employers cannot implement such plans without the union's agreement. This is not just a right to bargain; it is veto power. It may even apply to plans that deal only with nonmandatory subjects.[3]

Whether unions should participate in employee involvement is the subject of rich debate within the labor movement. But it would be a mistake to inject that controversy into the debate over labor law reform. Those who reject employee involvement obviously do not want to lose their legal basis for challenging it, but it should be just as obvious that unions engaged in employee involvement must preserve their right to bargain over the plans and to reject anything that they believe is not legitimate.

Could weakening 8(a)(2) hurt organizing? The small number of disestablishment cases, as well as their decline during the 1980s, contrasts sharply with the rise in 8(a)(3) discharges (Freeman and Medoff 1984). This suggests that employee committees are not often the employers' weapon of choice in organizing drives. But two independent studies show that union win rates are exceptionally low where employee committees exist (Bronfenbrenner 1993:313;

---

3. The April 15, 1993, memorandum of NLRB general counsel Jerry M. Hunter leaves open this possibility and directs the regional offices to submit such cases for advice. *Daily Labor Report*, April 26, 1993, G-9.

AFL-CIO 1984:6). This fact will not be lost on employers if unions begin to make organizing gains.[4]

Section 8(a)(2) is a fifty-nine-year-old law forbidding a practice that has historically proven to be a potent antiunion device. It cannot prevent employers from using committees during organizing campaigns, but it places important limits on them. If it is weakened, a future generation of organizers may scorn us for it.

Finally, the principle of unionism independent of employers represents a vital human need in our society, no matter how dire labor's decline may be. There is dignity in creating one's own organization, in choosing one's own representatives, and in recognizing and acting on the common interests and vulnerabilities of workers dependent on property owners for a livelihood. There is no substitute. Weakening Section 8(a)(2) would be a portentous event, a death knell of an entirely different sort from the one predicted by the eleven members of Congress who lobbied the NLRB in *Elecromation*.

What It Will Take to Achieve Positive Reform

The call for modifying 8(a)(2) is based on a bold misrepresentation of its impact in the workplace by employers, combined with uncritical acceptance of the employers' arguments and other assumptions by many others. It has reached a crescendo that has nearly drowned out the real needs of working people.

In 1988, the Massachusetts building trades faced a referendum campaign against the prevailing wage law. The campaign was organized by the Associated Builders and Contractors, joined by a tax revolt group. The trades defeated the campaign by creating alliances with other unions, civil rights organizations, religious organizations, and other groups and by convincing voters that the law was in the public interest (Erlich 1990). If that is what it took to save an existing law, what will it take to achieve positive reform? Even granting that labor law is not made by referendum, can it really be accomplished without organizing public support well beyond the labor movement itself?

---

4. A recent article entitled "Scary New Union Activism . . . How to Fight It and Win," urges, "Despite some discouraging rulings by the (NLRB), . . . we strongly recommend that all companies find ways to set up more employee involvement opportunities" as a way of countering new organizing tactics (Cabot 1993:5–6). The activities it advocates, however, are clearly limited in important ways by 8(a)(2).

12

Status of Workers' Rights to Bargain Collectively

Gladys W. Gruenberg

If I were a health-care professional asked to comment on the current status of the patient named "Collective Bargaining," I would be inclined to give a guarded diagnosis: "Critical and unstable." Some academics have already prescribed a new health regimen (Kochan, Katz, and McKersie 1986; Weiler 1990). Some union advocates have suggested that the patient would be just fine if released from shackles (Friedman and Prosten 1993). Some management advocates do not even think the patient is sick (Batten 1986; DiGiovanni 1986). My prescription concentrates exclusively on the decisions of the National Labor Relations Board in enforcing Section 8(a)(5) of the National Labor Relations (Wagner) Act, which was designed to prevent employers from refusing to bargain with the majority representative of employees in an appropriate unit.

First, a disclaimer is in order to avoid charges of partiality. I realize that Section 8(b)(3) of the NLRA also forbids union refusal to bargain. My study of NLRB annual reports from 1947 to 1990, however, indicates that at no time have 8(b)(3) allegations exceeded 17 percent of all charges filed against unions (*NLRB Annual Report* 1949), and such charges have been primarily technical (failure to comply with notification requirements) or heavy-handed ("take the same contract other employers in the industry have signed or else") (table 12.1). This tends to limit analytical potential except in the context of mandatory versus permissive bargaining proposals, which are discussed later.

At the same time, Section 8(a)(5) allegations have risen as high as 43 percent of all charges against employers (*NLRB Annual Report* 1973) and have remained higher than 25 percent since 1962, whereas 8(b)(3) charges have consistently hovered around 8 percent in the same period. In addition, employers tend to approach their collective bargaining duty from a somewhat different perspective; their alleged violations of Section 8(a)(5) are more

Table 12.1. Charges Alleging Violation of Section 8(a)(5) Received During
Fiscal Years 1946–85

Year	Number	Percent of all charges[a]	Five-year average (in percent)
1946	1,241	32.5	
1947	1,347	31.8	
1948	705	27.6	
1949	1,070	25.8	
1950	1,309	29.3	29.4
1951	1,235	29.7	
1952	1,226	28.5	
1953	1,347	30.6	
1954	1,212	27.7	
1955	1,213	27.8	28.8
1956	838	23.8	
1957	827	22.6	
1958	1,039	17.1	
1959	1,311	15.9	
1960	1,753	22.7	20.4
1961	1,676	20.6	
1962	2,294	24.9	
1963	2,584	27.1	
1964	3,088	28.9	
1965	3,815	34.9	27.2
1966	3,811	35.0	
1967	3,819	33.9	
1968	4,097	34.5	
1969	3,967	33.0	
1970	4,489	33.0	33.8
1971	5,018	32.4	
1972	10,131	42.1	
1973	9,760	43.4	
1974	9,501	42.7	
1975	5,633	27.7	37.4
1976	6,729	28.6	
1977	7,848	30.1	
1978	8,136	30.1	
1979	8,754	30.2	
1980	9,866	31.5	30.1
1981	9,815	31.4	
1982	10,898	39.3	
1983	12,211	42.1	
1984	10,349	40.2	
1985	9,479	42.4	39.0

Source: NLRB annual reports, 1946–85. Table 2 in the appendix of the annual reports details
data for allegations of specific unfair labor practices under Section 8 of the NLRA.

Note: Fiscal year 1946 was the last year for the original Wagner Act, passed in 1935, and is
included merely for comparison purposes. Congress enacted extensive amendments to the
National Labor Relations Act in the Labor Management Relations (Taft-Hartley) Act, 1947,
including a new Section 8(d) defining collective bargaining. Employer unfair labor practices
were unchanged under Section 8(a). An employer's refusal to bargain is an unfair labor practice
under Section 8(a)(5).

[a] Includes all allegations of unfair labor practices against employers. A charge is merely a
request for an investigation by the NLRB. Only about 1 percent of all charges reach the
formal adjudication stage. Annual report data do not differentiate among charges after
investigation has begun.

subtle, and the nuances beg for extensive analysis. So much for apologia on subject matter selection and limitation.

Wagner Act

When Congress passed the NLRA in 1935, collective bargaining was in about the same critical and unstable condition it is today, albeit for other reasons. It was confined almost entirely to the skilled trades in construction and to other fixed locations, where employers found it difficult to move facilities or to replace workers on short notice; hence, strikes could be effective in interfering with economic activity. In less skilled, more replaceable occupations, collective bargaining could be effectively avoided.

The preamble of the NLRA suggests that its primary purpose is to offer alternative dispute resolution for strikes seeking recognition.[1] Until 1945, as figure 12.1 suggests, 75 percent of the cases filed with the NLRB involved "representation," that is, petitions for elections so that workers could decide whether they wanted unions to represent them in bargaining with their employers. Since 1980, that percentage has been exactly reversed; only 25 percent are representation cases.

Majority rule is the first test the NLRB applies in deciding whether an employer has a duty to bargain. Under the NLRA, an employer has always had the right to challenge a union's majority claim, provided the challenge is bona fide and not an attempt to undermine the union's status. Thus, the NLRB has consistently coupled the workers' right to bargain collectively with the employer's right to question whether the collective entity truly represents the employees' wishes.

Even before the Labor-Management Relations (Taft-Hartley) Act (LMRA) added to Section 7 of the NLRA the seemingly innocuous proviso reminding employees of their right to "refrain" from concerted activity,[2] the NLRB required proof of majority status, usually through the conduct of an election but sometimes through a check of authorization cards signed by employees to indicate their desire for union representation (*NLRB Annual Report* [hereafter *NAR*] 1954:96; *Aiello Dairy Farms*).[3]

1. National Labor Relations Act, Findings and Policies, Section 1: "It is declared to be the policy of the United States to eliminate the causes of certain substantial obstructions to the free flow of commerce . . . by encouraging the practice and procedure of collective bargaining."

2. National Labor Relations Act, Section 7: "Employees shall have the right to self-organization, to form, join, or assist labor organizations, to bargain collectively through representatives of their own choosing, and to engage in other concerted activities for the purpose of collective bargaining or other mutual aid or protection, and shall also have the right to refrain from any or all such activities."

3. Complete case citations are given at the end of the chapter.

Figure 12.1. Filings of Unfair Labor Practices Cases and Representation Cases, Fiscal Years 1945–1980

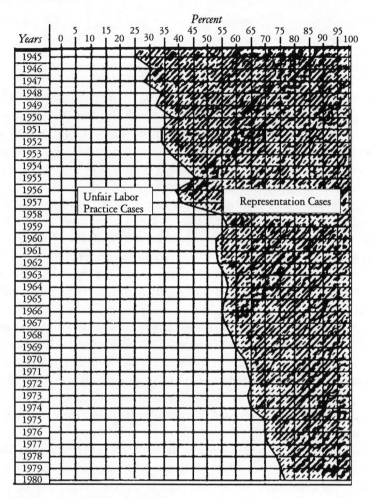

Source: NLRB, 1980 Annual Report, chart 15, 22.

Thus, on the one hand, the primary purpose of the NLRA has always been to create an environment wherein representatives of the employees and of the employer can engage in peaceful collective bargaining ultimately leading to a signed agreement designed to stabilize the relationship. Congress hoped that harmonious industrial relations would improve productivity, leading to higher profits, higher wages, greater consumer purchasing power, and finally to increased employment. On the other hand, if collective bargaining does not take place, the whole purpose of the NLRA is frustrated.

Taft-Hartley Act

When World War II began in 1941, employers were encouraged to accept collective bargaining agreements as evidence of stable industrial relations, a condition required by the War Production Board before awarding government contracts. This helped expand collective bargaining, so that by the war's end union membership had almost doubled. Reaction forces succeeded in passing the LMRA over President Truman's veto in 1947, emasculating the secondary boycott and sympathy strike weapons of the old-time craft unions through mandatory injunctions and damage suits, while spelling out in Section 8(d) that collective bargaining did not require employers to agree to anything.[4] This was again seemingly innocuous language; the NLRB had never forced employers to sign contracts they had not agreed to (*NAR* 1950:125). And, since the language applied equally to both sides of the bargaining table, no one could doubt its complete impartiality. Right? Wrong!

What could compel agreement if the federal government could not do it? Obviously, in the face of employer opposition, workers had only their last resort—the strike. But strikes are effective only when employers suffer economic hardship. Permitting employers to continue making profits by selling goods and services provided by strike substitutes reduces the employer's hardship while increasing the striking workers' insecurity. Under those conditions, striking employees are hit by a double whammy—lost wages and lost jobs. Here again there is ample evidence that the NLRB has always permitted employers to hire strike substitutes, so where's the beef? (Boudin 1941; Estreicher 1987; Gillispie 1972; P. Hirsch 1970; Janes 1975; Perry, Kramer, and Schneider 1982; Sales 1984; Schatzki 1969).

Bargaining Obligation

In the NLRB annual reports, the definition of the employer's bargaining obligation has remained virtually unchanged since the 1947 Taft-Hartley amendments. The NLRB has seldom directly and explicitly changed the rules governing bona fide collective bargaining; however, even NLRB members have bemoaned the differences in fact finding (Dennis 1985; Zimmerman

---

4. National Labor Relations Act, Section 8(d): "For the purposes of this section, to bargain collectively is the performance of the mutual obligation of the employer and the representative of the employees to meet at reasonable times and confer in good faith with respect to wages, hours, and other terms and conditions of employment . . . but such obligation does not compel either party to agree to a proposal or require the making of a concession."

1985). The apparently innocuous language of Section 8(d) has become the overriding consideration in deciding whether an employer is bargaining in good faith. Here are the principles that the NLRB has generally applied since 1947 in deciding Section 8(a)(5) obligations (Morris 1983; Ross 1965; St. Antoine 1992; *NAR* 1948:59: "The basic elements of a finding of unlawful refusal to bargain appear to have remained unchanged by this [Section 8(d)]."):

1. An employer must recognize the union representing a majority of employees in an appropriate unit (Westfall 1991; *NAR* 1949:70: "Majority status is presumed to continue until shown to have ceased or until such time as circumstances arise which indicate that the presumption no longer holds true." *Dorsey Trailers, Inc.*).

2. An employer must meet at reasonable times and confer in good faith (Axelrod 1986; *NAR* 1948:61: "The question of good or bad faith is primarily one of fact and turns on the circumstances surrounding bargaining negotiations in each case." *Andrew Jergens Co.*).

3. An employer must give the union the information needed to bargain intelligently (Carron and Noecker 1982; Hexter 1992; *NAR* 1948:62: "Refusal to give the union information as to rates of pay and wage adjustments necessary to a proper disposition of grievances [is a violation of the act]." *National Grinding Wheel Co.*).

4. An employer must make proposals and counterproposals with respect to wages, hours, and other terms and conditions of employment (Costello and Weinberg 1993).

5. An employer must sign the agreement reached in the course of negotiations (*NAR* 1949:75: "Although the Act does not compel agreement, it does require the parties to enter into negotiations with a sincere desire to reach and sign an agreement." *Tower Hosiery Mills*).

6. An employer must maintain the status quo on all agreed employment conditions during the contract term unless changed by mutual agreement (Boltuch 1991; Chicoine 1992; *NAR* 1948:68: "The employer failed in its statutory duty to bargain by unilaterally granting merit wage increases to individual employees and by refusing to furnish their accredited representative with information regarding such increases." *J. H. Allison & Co.*).

7. An employer must bargain about any changes in employment conditions not covered by the contract before attempting to impose them unilaterally (Cohen 1985; Connor 1992; Green 1986; Kolick and DeLancey 1993; Wheeler and Murray 1991; Zurofsky 1987; *NAR* 1949:73: "An impasse does not constitute a license to avoid [subsequent bargaining] where the circumstances which led to impasse no longer remain in status quo." *Boeing Airplane Co.*: fourteen months of bargaining culminating in a deadlock permits the employer to terminate the contract at will without violating the NLRA.).

8. An employer must bargain about grievances and arbitrate if the contract so provides (*NAR* 1984:106: sets forth six principles for deferral to arbitration).

Employers who fail to carry out these duties may be charged with refusal to bargain under Section 8(a)(5) of the NLRA. If a strike occurs as a result of this or any other alleged unfair labor practice, the strike may be transformed from an economic strike, which jeopardizes strikers' jobs by threat of permanent replacements, into an unfair labor practice strike, wherein the employer may be required to reinstate the strikers, regardless of replacements. The uncertainty lies in the NLRB's fact-finding responsibility in connection with the eight specific items listed above.

1. *Recognition of the majority union.* A finding that the employer is unreasonably challenging the union's majority status supports a refusal to bargain charge (*NAR* 1956:88: "[Employer's doubt about the union's majority status was merely] to gain time to dissipate the union's strength." *Joy Silk Mills*). But it has become more and more difficult for the NLRB to find such a challenge unreasonable (*NAR* 1952:162: "Employer had reasonable grounds for believing that the union lost its majority . . . when more than half of the strikers were lawfully replaced." *Old Line Life Insurance Company of America*). After winning an election in which a union's majority status is dissipated by an employer's antiunion campaign, the union has exactly one year in which to convince the employer to sign an agreement or its majority status may be challenged (*NAR* 1959:75: "Majority status is a rebuttable presumption after the first year, subject to confirmation by election." *Celanese Corp. of America*). Thus, if the employer holds out for a year and the employees strike, they are on their own—a refusal to bargain charge is unlikely to turn their action into an unfair labor practice strike warranting reinstatement, absent any other violations (*NAR* 1968:133; *Fleetwood Trailer Co.*).[5]

2. *Meet and confer.* A finding that an employer is unreasonably recalcitrant where negotiations drag on for months supports a refusal to bargain charge. An employer may continue to talk every proposal to death, however, and then declare an impasse and implement the last offer (*NAR* 1967:105: "The determination of whether an impasse exists is a matter of judgment." *Taft Broadcasting WDAF*). The NLRB has always permitted this, but the definition of what constitutes an impasse may be based on a technical finding as to whether a particular proposal is a mandatory or a permissive subject of bargaining (*NAR* 1958:104: "The Act does not permit a party to insist on inclusion of a nonmandatory clause to the point of impasse as a condition to

---

5. The *Fleetwood* decision to reinstate strikers, based on *Mackay Radio & Tele. Co.*, was reversed by the Ninth Circuit: ("[We] cannot penalize those who decide not to strike in order to benefit those who do . . . [the strikers' gamble has proved] unsuccessful"), but was enforced by the Supreme Court ("An employer's refusal to reinstate strikers necessarily discourages employees from exercising their right to organize and to strike guaranteed by the Act.").

agreement on mandatory matters." *Borg-Warner Corp., Wooster Div.*). This finding of fact is crucial. If a bargaining subject is mandatory,[6] the employer may declare an impasse and take unilateral action without risking a refusal to bargain violation, and a strike protesting such action is an economic rather than an unfair labor practice strike (*NAR* 1951:198: "[There is] futility in further negotiations . . . leaving the employer free to take [unilateral action] without the mutual consent of the union." *Reed and Prince Mfg. Co.*). But if the bargaining subject is merely permissive, strikers who protest employer unilateral action are not necessarily guaranteed reinstatement under the NLRA. The main problem is that the parties cannot be sure whether the NLRB will decide a subject is mandatory or permissive. This uncertainty is debilitating to efficient collective bargaining.

3. *Request for information.* Upon request of the union before or during negotiations for a contract or for settlement of a grievance, an employer is required to supply relevant information if it is reasonably needed for intelligent consideration of the bargaining subject (*NAR* 1955:94: "[Information requested must be] relevant and necessary to collective bargaining." *Whitin Machine Works*). The NLRB's decision rests on a number of findings: (1) whether the request involves a mandatory (yes) or permissive (no) bargaining subject, (2) whether the information is really necessary for the union to make an intelligent evaluation of the employer's proposal or counterproposal, again depending on whether the bargaining subject is mandatory (yes) (*NAR* 1956:123: Financial records must be produced when the employer claims inability to pay a wage increase. *Truitt Mfg. Co.*) or permissive (no), (3) whether supplying the information imposes an unreasonable burden on the employer (no), and (4) whether the request involves confidential data (no) (e.g., health records). These findings are not the usual objective fact finding but tend to be based on subjective judgment, depending on the NLRB members' attitudes toward management rights and union responsibilities. Turnover among board membership has created so much uncertainty in this area that union requests for information are routinely questioned by employers, causing delays and unwarranted animosity in negotiations (Hexter 1992).

4. *Proposals and counterproposals.* Here again the word "reasonable" is crucial. When is an employer's proposal or counterproposal so preposterous as to

---

6. The NLRB labels bargaining subjects "mandatory" in the context of the Section 8(d) definition of collective bargaining, that is, limited to "wages, hours, and other terms and conditions of employment." All other subjects, except illegal proposals (e.g., closed shop), are merely permissive; that is, they may be bargained for and included in the contract if the parties mutually agree to them, but the employer may not declare impasse over them; nor can strikers gain unfair labor practice protection if the employer refuses to bargain about them.

warrant a refusal to bargain charge? May an employer propose restrictions on what matters are grievable, on appeals to arbitration? May an employer insist on a management rights clause that for all practical purposes emasculates the rest of the agreement? These are not merely academic questions (*NAR* 1982:145: "The employer engaged in surface bargaining . . . proposed a broad management rights clause, a no strike clause, and limits on arbitration so predictably unacceptable that no self-respecting union would accept it." *Chevron Chemical Co.*). The NLRB may find an apparently innocuous management rights clause to be a waiver of the union's right to bargain about the subjects listed as management prerogatives, permitting the employer to make unilateral changes during the contract's term (*NAR* 1965:76: "Broad management rights clause effectively authorizes employer unilateral action to discontinue a department and transfer employees to other jobs . . . essentially a change in method permitted by the management rights clause." *Fafnir Bearing Co.*). And a so-called zipper clause[7] may foreclose bargaining on any subject that the NLRB finds is not specifically covered in the agreement (*NAR* 1982:143: "[A zipper clause constituted] a waiver of the union's right to bargain on matters covered by the contract." *GTE Automatic Electric Co.*).

5. *Signing a contract.* When the NLRB finds that an employer has violated Section 8(a)(5) by refusing to sign an agreement that has been negotiated, can the NLRB so order? Section 10 seems to give the NLRB that power,[8] but that remedy has been used rarely and does not have judicial approval (*NAR* 1968:132: *H.K. Porter*).[9] The usual remedy for a refusal to bargain violation is an order to bargain, putting the parties right back to square one (*NAR* 1948:63: "If [the employer] has refused to bargain with the statutory representative of his employees, he is ordered to do so upon the union's request. In all cases the employer has to post a notice in his plant, stating that he will comply with the Board's order."). For some of the more egregious violations, the NLRB has sought injunctions under Section 10(j) (*NAR* 1967:171: "A simple order to bargain in good faith would not be sufficient . . . [because] employer would have everything to gain and nothing to lose." *N.L.R.B. v. George E. Light Boat Storage*). But in 1986, a year noted for refusal to bargain

7. A zipper clause may provide that the agreement represents everything the parties have bargained about, and no other matters may be raised during the contract term.

8. National Labor Relations Act, Section 10: "The Board is empowered . . . to prevent . . . any unfair labor practice. . . .. This power shall not be affected by any other means of adjustment or prevention."

9. In *H.K. Porter*, the NLRB's order that the employer grant a checkoff clause was remanded by the circuit court: "[The NLRB] may not force an employer to agree to any provision as a remedy for an unfair labor practice [but may only] force negotiations." The Supreme Court agreed but enforced other parts of the NLRB's order.

charges (see table 12.1), only a dozen court orders were sought to restrain 8(a)(5) violations, and there were seven favorable judicial rulings (*NAR* 1986:269).

6. *Maintaining the status quo.* Stability in industrial relations is a stated objective of many NLRB orders involving 8(a)(5) violations. Once a contract is signed, an employer has an obligation to abide by its terms. If unforeseen circumstances arise, making it unprofitable or seemingly impossible to carry out the express provisions of the agreement, the employer is required to bargain with the union to seek relief (*NAR* 1967:111: "Economic factors must be so compelling as to limit meaningful bargaining . . . as it must be carried on within a framework of a decision which cannot be reversed." *Ozark Trailers*). In the absence of mutual agreement, the original bargain should stand. Any employer attempt to implement change unilaterally may result in an appeal to arbitration and/or an 8(a)(5) charge. If the NLRB finds that the matter is covered by the agreement, deferral to arbitration is the usual remedy. The NLRB has never considered enforcement of a collective bargaining agreement a proper matter for NLRB action (*NAR* 1966:145: "The Board has no jurisdiction to enforce a collective bargaining agreement." *C&C Plywood Corp.*). In fact, before arbitration clauses became de rigueur, the NLRB usually told a union charging violation of an agreement to invoke court action under Section 301 of the LMRA[10] (*NAR* 1954:100; *Textron Puerto Rico-Tricot Div.*).

7. *Bargaining about changes.* When the contract is apparently silent or when a zipper clause forecloses bargaining during the contract term, no refusal to bargain charge can be sustained, if the NLRB finds that the union has waived its right to bargain about such matters (*NAR* 1951:196: "[There must be] a clear and unmistakable showing of a waiver." *Tidewater Associated Oil Co.* was revised by *United Technologies*: *NAR* 1988:82: "Employer has a right to change rules regarding absenteeism under a management rights clause which constitutes a contractual waiver of the union's right to bargain over disciplinary rules."). In these cases the NLRB's interpretation of the NLRA is as uncertain as an arbitrator's interpretation of a collective bargaining agreement. This approach is not what should be expected from a quasi-judicial body acting under a section of a statute that has remained unchanged since 1947 (Dennis 1985; Zimmerman 1985).

8. *Deferral to arbitration.* In appropriate cases the NLRB has deferred to arbitration since 1955 (*Spielberg*). At that time the NLRB subjected arbitration awards to rigid guidelines aimed at implementing the purposes of the NLRA. As arbitration gained wider acceptance by the parties, the NLRB has

---

10. Labor-Management Relations Act, Title III, Section 301: "Suits for violation of contracts between an employer and a labor organization . . . may be brought in any district court of the United States."

gradually loosened its restrictions on deferral, leading to greater uncertainty. This is especially true in connection with refusal to bargain charges. The NLRB is likely to defer to arbitration any matter that alleges a violation of both the NLRA and the collective bargaining agreement (*NAR* 1982:35). Whether the arbitrator's award conforms with NLRB decisions is no longer relevant so long as it disposes of the issue (*NAR* 1984:21: "We do not require total consistency but only that the arbitration award must not be palpably wrong." *Olin Corp.*). This is a far cry from the policy enunciated in *Collyer Insulated Wire* and *General American Transportation Corp.*, which emphasized the need to effectuate the policies of the NLRA. The NLRB seems to have limited its jurisdiction in a manner comparable to the way the Supreme Court has limited lower courts on appeals from arbitration decisions. It should be noted, however, that the NLRB has a statute to enforce, which is quite different from enforcement of a private agreement. And, again, the resulting uncertainty does not bode well for stable industrial relations.

Proposals for Legislation

Based on this analysis, the conclusion is inescapable that NLRB decisions have become so uncertain as to make intelligent prediction almost impossible, especially as NLRB membership changes. When we couple this uncertainty with no change in the statute, what can we hope to gain from labor law reform? Amending the law can accomplish little if enforcement remains in the unstable hands of political appointees. The old saw about "government giving and government taking away" is certainly operative in this environment. But that is the cynical excuse for doing nothing. Here are some specific proposals for legislation:

1. Make Section 10(j) discretionary injunctions mandatory. After all, mandatory injunctions for Section 8(b)(4) violations, coupled with the threat of million dollar damage suits under Section 303 of the LMRA, have effectively forced unions to refrain from those activities or pay a heavy price. Authorizing the NLRB to seek a priority mandatory injunction where there is reasonable cause to believe that an employer has violated Section 8(a)(5), and permitting punitive damages for a proven violation, may provide greater incentive for employers to abide by the law.[11] Administratively prioritizing these cases,

---

11. The NLRB has admitted that its remedies in 8(a)(5) cases have been inadequate on many occasions (*NAR* 1971:91: "[We] agree that the current remedies of the Board designed to cure violations of 8(a)(5) are inadequate, but we cannot agree with the [ALJ's] remedy that the employer pay wage increases retroactively [which employees would have received but for the employer's unfair labor practices]." *Excello Corp.*; *NAR* 1982:222: "[We seek the injunction] to maintain the status quo to prevent the Board order from being rendered meaningless and ineffective in protecting employees." *Bohn Heat and Transfer Group*; *NAR* 1989:127: "[We

similar to the requirement for 8(b)(4) violations, would also help effectuate the purposes of the NLRA.[12]

2. Remove the distinction between mandatory and permissive subjects of bargaining. This amendment to Section 8(d) has the potential for making negotiations less technical, hence less adversarial. Technicalities tend to encourage more legalism, leading to further disagreement and disruption. Section 8(d) does not specifically refer to mandatory or permissive subjects of bargaining. Why then does the NLRB use this technical distinction to decide whether an employer may declare an impasse and implement the last offer during negotiations? In addition, if an employer decides to declare an impasse, the matter should be subject to arbitration rather than to unilateral action, especially for a first contract.

3. The notification provisions of Section 8(d) were designed to encourage unions to seek mediation services, not to deprive employees of their right to bargain collectively. Tying this requirement to violations of the NLRA that may jeopardize the employees' jobs and the union's majority status does not encourage harmonious collective bargaining (*NAR* 1949:77: Workers who engage in a strike in the absence of Federal Mediation and Conciliation Service notification lose their status as employees).Time limits are important to prevent egregious mishandling of negotiations by union representatives, but they should not become a technical excuse for depriving workers of collective bargaining rights. In the alternative, if notification requirements are demanded of a union, they should also apply to an employer. No unilateral change should be permitted without at least sixty days' notice to the union and to the mediation services (*NAR* 1984:82: A three-day notice to employees of a plant was found to be sufficient to avoid tipping off competitors. *Creasy Co.*).[13] Unilateral action by an employer is likely to be as unstabilizing to industrial relations as a union request for changes in the existing agreement.

4. Remove from the NLRA semantic language that waters down workers' rights to bargain collectively. In a law that purports to favor collective bargaining, rights of employees gain protection through the collective entity. Other laws have been and should be enacted to protect individuals who do not

---

require] proof that a return to the status quo ante would be unduly burdensome [for the employer]. . . . Our previous test was continued viability of the enterprise, which was too stringent." *Lear Siegler, Inc.*, revising *Woodline Motor Freight*).

12. National Labor Relations Act, Section 10(j): "The Board shall have power, upon issuance of a *complaint* . . . charging . . . an unfair labor practice, to petition any United States district court . . . for appropriate temporary relief or restraining order" (emphasis added). Section 10(1), however, requires the NLRB to seek an injunction if preliminary investigation (given priority over all other cases) indicates that there is reasonable cause to believe the *charge* is true. It applies only to certain alleged union violations of Section 8(b)(4), 8(b)(7), and 8(e) of the NLRA.

13. Congress has already recognized the rationale for such advance notice in connection with large-scale layoffs by enacting the WARN Act, effective February 4, 1989.

desire representation.[14] Innocuous as the language in Section 7 may seem, it suggests that employees should refrain from collective bargaining, which runs counter to the stated goals of the NLRA. This same reasoning applies to the definition of collective bargaining in Section 8(d), which states that an employer is not required to agree to anything. This two-faced approach to industrial relations in the law itself exacerbates the uncertainty characterizing the current status of collective bargaining in the United States. It's time for Congress to end this forked-tongue legislative drafting process.

14. The promulgation of the Uniform Employment Termination Act by the National Conference of Commissioners on Uniform State Laws, providing just-cause protection for all private-sector employees to be adjudicated by arbitration, is a promising step in this direction.

Appendix to Chapter 12: NLRB and Court Cases

Aiello Dairy Farms, 110 N.L.R.B. 1365 (1954).

J. H. Allison & Co., 70 N.L.R.B. 377 (1947), enforced, 165 F.2d 766 (6th Cir. 1948), *cert. denied*, 355 U.S. 814 (1949).

Andrew Jergens Co., 76 N.L.R.B. 363 (1948).

Boeing Airplane Co., 80 N.L.R.B. 447, *rev'd*, 174 F.2d 998 (D.C. Cir. 1949).

Bohn Heat and Transfer Group, 110 L.R.R.M. 3013 (D.C. Ill. 1982).

Borg-Warner Corp., Wooster Div., 113 N.L.R.B. 1288 (1956), *rev'd*, 236 F.2d 898 (6th Cir. 1957), *enforced*, 356 U.S. 342 (1958).

C&C Plywood Corp., 148 N.L.R.B. 414, *rev'd*, 351 F.2d 224 (9th Cir. 1966), *enforced*, 385 U.S. 421 (1967).

Celanese Corp. of America, 95 N.L.R.B. 664 (1951).

Chevron Chemical Co., 261 N.L.R.B. 44 (1982).

Collyer Insulated Wire, 192 N.L.R.B. 837 (1971).

Creasy Co., 268 N.L.R.B. 1425 (1984).

Dorsey Trailers, Inc., 80 N.L.R.B. No. 89 (1949).

Excello Corp., 195 N.L.R.B. No. 20 (1971).

Fafnir Bearing Co., 151 N.L.R.B. 332 (1965).

Fleetwood Trailer Co., 153 N.L.R.B. 425 (1965), *rev'd*, 366 F.2d 126 (9th Cir. 1967), *enforced*, 387 U.S. 375 (1968).

General American Transportation Corp., 228 N.L.R.B. 808 (1977).

GTE Automatic Electric Co., 261 N.L.R.B. 1491 (1982), *revising* 240 N.L.R.B. 297 (1972).

Joy Silk Mills, 85 N.L.R.B. 1263, *enforced*, 185 F.2d 732 (D.C. Cir. 1955), *cert. denied*, 341 U.S. 914 (1955).

Lear Siegler, Inc., 295 N.L.R.B. No. 83 (1989).

Mackay Radio & Tele. Co., 304 U.S. 333 (1938).

National Grinding Wheel Co., 75 N.L.R.B. 905 (1948).

N.L.R.B. v. George E. Light Boat Storage, 373 F.2d 762 (1967).

Old Line Life Insurance Company of America, 96 N.L.R.B. 499 (1952).

Olin Corp., 208 N.L.R.B. 573 (1984).

Ozark Trailers, 161 N.L.R.B. 561 (1967).

H. K. Porter, 172 N.L.R.B. No. 72, *rev'd*, 380 F.2d 295 (D.C. Cir. 1970), *affirmed in part*, 397 U.S. 99 (1970).

Reed and Prince Mfg. Co., 96 N.L.R.B. 850 (1951).

Spielberg Mfg. Co., 112 N.L.R.B. 1080 (1955).

Taft Broadcasting WDAF, 163 N.L.R.B. No. 55 (1967).

Textron Puerto Rico-Tricot Div., 107 N.L.R.B. No. 142 (1954).

Tidewater Associated Oil Co., 85 N.L.R.B. 1098 (1951).

Tower Hosiery Mills, 81 N.L.R.B. No. 120 (1949).

Truitt Mfg. Co., 110 N.L.R.B. 856, *rev'd*, 224 F.2d 869 (4th Cir. 1955), *enforced*, 351 U.S. 149 (1956).

United Technologies, 287 N.L.R.B. No. 16 (1988).

Whitin Machine Works, 108 N.L.R.B. 1537, *enforced*, 217 F.2d 593 (4th Cir. 1954), *cert. denied*, 349 U.S. 905 (1955).

Woodline Motor Freight, 278 N.L.R.B. 114 (1986).

PART IV
THE OUTCOMES OF
BARGAINING
RELATIONSHIPS

13

What Do Unions Do for Women?

Roberta Spalter-Roth, Heidi Hartmann, and Nancy Collins

Currently, the United States has the lowest rate of union membership among all industrialized countries except France. Without labor law reform, unions may represent only 5 percent of the U.S. labor force in the year 2000 (Rothstein 1993). Is this prediction good news or bad news for the economy and for the living standards of U.S. citizens? How would this prediction, if it came to pass, affect women workers?

Many economists argue that declines in union monopolies and the resulting declines in union wage premiums result in economic growth. Capital can be freer to move into new markets; to create new, more flexible jobs; and to increase efficiency and productivity (Rothstein 1993; Hirsch 1991; Freeman 1990; Kochan, Katz, and McKersie 1986).

Other researchers argue that the higher wages generated by union membership not only result in higher living standards for workers but, because unions reward seniority and reduce turnover, encourage investment in technologies and work processes that enable workers to be more efficient and productive (Freeman 1990; Belman 1989; Freeman and Medoff 1984). Researchers also suggest that the decrease in union membership has contributed to the growth of inequality in the U.S. wage structure (Freeman 1993). Lawrence Katz (as cited in Rothstein 1993:34) claims that fully one-fifth of the increase in the wage differential between lower- and higher-wage workers during the 1980s can be explained by the decline in union membership. Because of the impor-

The research on which this paper is based was funded by the Women's Bureau, U.S. Department of Labor. An earlier version of this paper was presented at a symposium sponsored by the Women's Bureau on October 14, 1993. Points of view or opinions stated here do not necessarily represent the official position or policy of the U.S. Department of Labor. We would like to thank Jill Braunstein for her assistance in the many stages of the development of this paper and Nicoletta Karam for her help in preparing the final manuscript.

tance of union membership for increasing living standards and productivity and for decreasing wage inequality, the decline in membership is seen as a cause for concern.

Much of the analysis of the role of unions in increasing wages and productivity is limited largely to studies of male blue-collar workers in manufacturing industries. During the last few decades, along with the general decline in union membership, the map of unionization by industry, occupation, and gender has changed. The unions with declining membership are largely male blue-collar unions, while the unions with increasing membership are more likely to include workers in occupations that are predominantly female and white collar (S. Eaton 1992).

In 1992, only 16 percent of U.S. workers were union members, and an additional 2 percent were represented by unions or associations in which they were not members (U.S. Department of Labor 1993:238). As figure 13.1 shows, the proportion of male workers who were unionized fell from 39 percent in 1965 to 22 percent in 1990. The proportion of women workers who were union members increased from 16 percent in 1965 to 19 percent in 1975 and then fell to 14 percent in 1990. Figure 13.2 shows changes in the absolute numbers of union members. Even as the proportion of all workers who were union members fell, the total number increased through 1980. The

Figure 13.1. Union Membership as a Percentage of the Female, Male, and Total Workforce

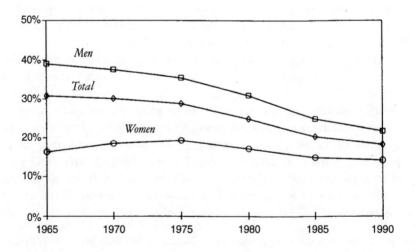

Sources: Institute for Women's Policy Research estimates based on published and unpublished data from the Current Population Survey, the Bureau of Labor Statistics, and the Women's Bureau, U.S. Department of Labor.

Figure 13.2. Union Membership, 1955–1990

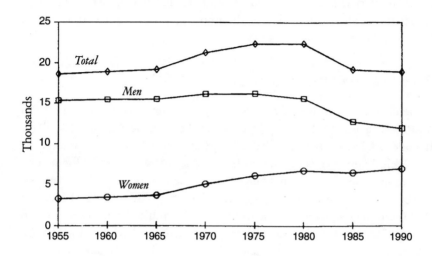

Sources: Institute for Women's Policy Research estimates based on published and unpublished data from the Current Population Survey, the Bureau of Labor Statistics, and the Women's Bureau, U.S. Department of Labor.

number of women workers has continued to increase since 1980, but that gain has been more than offset by the decline in the number of members who are men. Because of the decline in the number of men and the increase among women, women currently represent 37 percent of organized labor's membership, a higher percentage than at any time in the history of the U.S. labor movement.[1]

This chapter maps the distribution of union women and men workers across occupations, industries, firm sizes, and education level. It examines the impact of union membership on women's wages and job tenure. It explores whether being unionized contributes to increased wages, controlling for variation in other factors that affect earnings, and whether unionized low-wage workers have greater job tenure than their nonunionized counterparts. If

1. No consistent series of data on union membership or on union membership by gender exists. Up through 1980, the Bureau of Labor Statistics collected membership data from unions and, beginning in 1970, from associations. Between 1973 and 1980, the Current Population Survey (CPS) asked a sample of individual workers (in May of each year) about their union status. Each month since 1983, the CPS has asked the members of the sample's outgoing rotation group about their union status and, if they are not members, whether they are represented by a labor organization that bargains collectively over wages or working conditions. For the purposes of this overview, the authors developed a new series that attempts to

that is the case, then encouraging collective bargaining can lead to increased job tenure, productivity, and wages in currently low-productivity, low-wage service industries, where women are disproportionately employed. The chapter concludes with a discussion of the implications of the new diversity in union membership for union policy.

Data Set and Sample Size

The data used in this study are for the 1987 calendar year from the 1986 and 1987 panels of the Survey of Income and Program Participation (SIPP) for all workers (civilian, nonagricultural, wage and salary), ages sixteen to sixty-four (excluding teenagers living with their parents) who worked for at least seven months and five hundred hours during the calendar year. This data set, developed by the Institute for Women's Policy Research (IWPR) includes 17,200 sample members, representing about 79 million U.S. workers, or 66 percent of the total U.S. civilian labor force (sixteen and over) in 1987, or 80 percent of the employed, wage and salary, nonagricultural labor force. To focus our analysis on committed adult workers who are likely to be relying on employment as their main source of income, we excluded those with limited work effort (fewer than seven months or five hundred hours of work), as well as older workers and teenagers living at home.[2]

Findings

Who Are the Union Workers?

The percentage of women union members is at an all-time high, but this is because unionization rates among women have declined more slowly than among men. As figure 13.3 shows, however, unionization is not declining among all categories of women workers. A comparison of IWPR's SIPP-based data sets for 1984 and 1987, in which workers can be identified as low-wage workers (worked at least seven months at or below an average hourly wage,

achieve consistency by adjusting the different data sets. For example, because the individually reported data are lower for the years in which both union-reported membership data and individual-reported membership data exist, we adjusted post-1980 data upward. We also adjusted pre-1970 data upward to include estimates for professional association members. Our estimates are for membership, not representation status. The labor force base with which we compare union membership in order to estimate union density is the civilian wage and salary employed labor force sixteen and over, including agricultural workers.

2. In the SIPP data set, information on union status was missing for fully 50 percent of the "less committed" workers—those in our sample who had worked five hundred hours but not necessarily in seven out of twelve months. Since differences between union and nonunion workers are the focus of our investigation, we excluded this group of 2,736 less committed workers for whom the information on union status was unreliable.

Figure 13.3. Unionization Rates among High-Wage versus Low-Wage Workers, 1984 and 1987

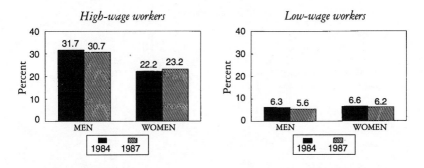

Source: Institute for Women's Policy Research calculations based on the 1984, 1986, and 1987 Survey of Income and Program Participation.
Note: Low-wage workers are those who earned an average hourly wage of less than $5.80 for at least seven months out of the year; high-wage workers are those who earned an average hourly wage of less than $5.80 only one month or never.

$5.80 in 1987, that would equal the annual poverty level if they worked full time full year) or high-wage workers (worked at least seven months, no more than one of which was at an average hourly wage that would qualify as low), shows that the unionization rate among high-wage women workers actually increased from 22 to 23 percent during this period. The unionization rate among high-wage men, which is about 10 percentage points higher than among high-wage women, declined by 1 percentage point between 1984 and 1987. Among low-wage workers, unionization rates are substantially lower (at about 6 percent) and do not vary significantly by gender; they declined slightly between 1984 and 1987 for both women and men.

How have the declines in union density in blue-collar industries and the increases in some of the more female-dominated occupations and industries affected the current distribution of unionized workers? What differences do we see between the distribution of unionized males and females? Table 13.1, which presents data on our sample of unionized workers by occupation, industry, firm size, and education level, shows the dramatic differences between the genders. The differences reflect the very different places women and men hold in the labor market. They reflect the differential rates of unionization across the economy, with "male" areas being generally more unionized than "female" areas. They also reflect the differential rates of unionization for men and women in similar economic areas, with, for example, male blue-collar workers having a higher rate of unionization than female blue-collar workers.

Occupation. Table 13.1 shows that the modal male union worker is blue collar. Men in blue-collar occupations are more unionized than men in other

Table 13.1.   Distribution of Union Members by Occupation, Industry,
Firm Size, and Education Level

Variables	Women (in percent)	Men (in percent)
Occupation		
Administrative support	27	9
Blue collar	18	60
Managerial/professional/technical	39	18
Sales	5	3
Service	11	11
Industry		
Finance/trade	8	10
Manufacturing	17	34
Mining/construction	0	12
Public administration	9	10
Public utilities	12	18
Service	54	16
Firm size		
Less than 25 employees	3	6
Between 25 and 99 employees	8	10
At least 100 employees	89	84
Education level		
Less than high school	12	17
High school diploma	33	44
Some college	22	24
College or more	32	15

Source: IWPR calculations based on the 1986 and 1987 panels of the Survey of Income
and Program Participation.

occupations (60 percent of male union members are blue-collar workers but
only 44 percent of all males in our sample were employed in this occupational
category). In contrast, fewer than 20 percent of unionized male workers were
in the next largest occupational category: managerial, professional, and technical workers. Unlike blue-collar workers, skilled white-collar workers are
underrepresented among unionized male workers.

Unlike men, unionized women are most likely to be found among managerial, professional, and technical workers. Women in this occupational category are more heavily unionized than women in other occupations relative to
their representation in the employed workforce (39 percent of all women
union members are in professional, managerial, or technical occupations,
while only 31 percent of all women workers in our sample worked in these
occupations). Within this category, professional specialty workers are especially likely to be represented by unions and provide the largest share of
women members to unions of any single occupational category.

The administrative support occupations provide the next largest category
of unionized women; more than one-quarter of unionized women workers
come from this occupational category. Although this is the largest single
occupational category among women (31 percent of all women workers in our

sample), administrative support workers are somewhat underrepresented among unionized women workers. The small proportion of women employed in blue-collar occupations is relatively well organized (representing 18 percent of women union members but only 12 percent of the female workforce). But despite their relatively intensive rate of unionization, blue-collar women constitute a small proportion of unionized women overall.

Industry. Although fewer than three out of ten male workers in our sample were employed in manufacturing, this industry still provides the largest share of unionized male workers—34 percent (see table 13.1). Workers from transportation, communications, and public utilities provide the next largest share. Service industry employees are the third largest group of unionized male workers. They are, however, slightly underrepresented when compared with their representation in this industry.

In striking contrast, more than half (54 percent) of all unionized women workers come from the service industries, and almost all of these women are from the professional and related services (including hospital workers, educators, and social service workers). Women in this industrial subcategory represent 35 percent of all women workers in our sample, but they contribute 51 percent of the women workers in unions. In contrast to men, a substantially smaller share of unionized women workers come from manufacturing, since fewer women are employed in this industry. The third largest category of unionized women workers are in transportation, communications, and public utilities. Although only 5 percent of employed women workers are in this category, they represent 12 percent of the unionized female workforce. (Spalter-Roth and Hartmann 1992 provides a detailed discussion of unionization among women in the communications industry.)

Firm size. Unions have organized successfully in larger workplaces using an industrial model; not surprisingly, therefore, table 13.1 shows that workers in firms with more than one hundred employees constitute the largest share of union members by far, more than 80 percent for both men and women. Both male and female employees in larger firms are substantially more likely to be members of unions, and women union members are even more likely to be in larger firms than their male peers.

Education. Table 13.1 shows dramatic differences in the education of union men and women. Among men, the largest group of union members (44 percent) have a high school diploma but no college education; these men are overrepresented among members of unions. Men with a college degree are underrepresented, while those with less than a high school diploma or those with some college are represented about equally.

The findings for women are reversed. High school graduates are somewhat underrepresented (38 percent of all employed women workers, compared with 33 percent of the women in unions). In contrast, college graduates are more represented in unions—about one out of three union women has a college degree, compared with about one in five employed women.

This map illustrates the changing face of unions as women become a higher proportion of their membership. It reflects the changes in union membership from blue-collar to white-collar occupations, from manufacturing to professional specialty industries, and from high school to college graduates. The findings help explain the increase in union membership among higher-wage women workers between 1984 and 1987. They suggest that union membership is increasingly characterized by a new diversity, which needs to be reflected in union policies and leadership.

Impact of Unionization on Women's Wages

Union workers have historically earned more than nonunion workers, although the relative size of the pay gap (or the union wage premium) found in any particular study depends on the data set used, the employment status of the workers included, the calendar years covered, and the multivariate statistical techniques used to control for other factors along with union status.

We use statistical regression techniques, specifically an ordinary least-squares (OLS) model, to estimate the importance of union membership, relative to other factors, in increasing hourly wages for women. The data for this analysis are limited to the 1987 panels; the 1986 SIPP panel is excluded because of the lack of certain key variables. In addition, Asian-Americans are excluded because their labor market patterns do not correspond well to those of either white women or other women of color and because there are too few of them to analyze separately.

The OLS model tests the impact of various human capital characteristics, work-related information (including union status, firm size, hours worked, occupation, and industry), and demographic and geographic information on women's hourly wages in 1987.[3] Table 13.2 provides the results of the predictive equations. Since the model for all women workers showed that being a woman of color negatively affected hourly wages (it decreased them by $.53), separate models were calculated for white women and women of color. All estimated coefficients that are statistically significant at the .05 level are marked with asterisks.

The table shows that union membership or coverage under a collective bargaining agreement increased women's hourly wages by $.90. White women received $.91 in union wage premiums, and women of color received $.87. In percentage terms, however, women of color gain more from union member-

---

3. Hourly wage is calculated by summing the income earned from the primary job across all months of 1987 and dividing by the total hours worked at the primary job in 1987. There are a few minor differences between this model and the model used in our previous study using the 1984 SIPP (see IWPR 1989).

Table 13.2.   Estimates of the Impact of Various Variables on Women's Average Hourly
Wage in 1987

Independent variables	All women	White women	Women of color
Intercept	$-0.10	$-0.35	$0.34
Union status	0.902***	0.914***	0.868**
Human capital			
Highest grade completed	0.173***	0.175***	0.164***
Work experience	0.179***	0.177***	0.168***
Work experience squared	-0.004***	-0.004***	-0.004**
Any job training	0.301**	0.266*	0.504*
Job characteristics			
Hours worked/1,000	0.674***	0.631***	0.899***
Work site more than 100 Employees	1.040***	1.121***	0.688**
Firm Size less than 25 Employees	-0.339*	-0.323*	-0.459
Occupations (professional/managerial)			
Technical, sales, and administrative	-1.541***	-1.582***	-1.293***
Service	-2.238***	-2.224***	-2.240***
Blue collar	-2.358***	-2.358***	-2.364***
Industry (manufacturing)			
Mining	3.830***	3.802***	a
Construction	0.394	0.477	-0.484
Transportation and other public utilities	3.431***	3.363***	3.632*
Wholesale trade	0.244	0.646	-2.181*
Retail trade	-1.154***	-1.199***	-0.883*
Finance, insurance, and real estate	0.539*	0.589*	0.248
Service, excluding personal	-0.712***	-0.697**	-0.799*
Personal service	-1.432***	-1.791***	-0.741
Public administration	0.078	0.350	-0.694
Demographics			
Age	0.220***	0.239***	0.145*
Age squared	-0.002***	-0.003***	-0.001
Black or Hispanic	-0.526***		
Married with spouse present	-0.054	-0.166	0.374
At least 1 child under 6	0.093	0.227	-0.368
Region (Western resident)			
Southern	-0.710***	-0.682***	0.735**
Northern	0.442**	0.409*	0.666*
Midwestern	-0.759***	-0.769***	-0.502
Adjusted R-squared	0.3739	0.3574	0.4690
F Value	100.48***	82.23***	25.42***
Sample size	4,664	3,944	719

Source: Institute for Women's Policy Research calculations based on the 1987 Survey of Income and
Program Participation.
***p<.001.
**p<.01.
*p<.05.
[a] Estimates could not be made for this variable because there were no women of color in the sample
working in the mining industry.
The reference groups for "Occupation," "Industry," and "Region" appear in parentheses: coefficients
shown are relative to the value for this reference group.
Asians and Pacific Islanders were excluded from the 1987 data used for analysis.

ship than do white women (just as we found in our earlier study, IWPR 1989). White women gained 11.8 percent from union membership or coverage, while women of color gained 12.6 percent.

Unionization has a greater impact on women's hourly wages than do individual human capital variables. Each year of education completed by women increases their wages by $.17 per hour; each year of additional work experience in the type of work of their primary job in 1987 adds $.18 per hour. Having any formal job training increases their wages by $.30. Except for training, the effects of human capital variables did not differ substantially in absolute terms between white women and women of color. Women of color received significantly greater rewards from job training ($.50 per hour, compared with $.27 an hour by white women). The effects on hourly wages of union status compared with these human capital variables is shown in figure 13.4.

Along with union membership, occupation and industry are unquestionably important in determining women's hourly wages. With professional and managerial occupations as the reference group, our results show that technical, sales, administrative occupations, service occupations, and blue-collar occupations negatively affect women's wages (decreasing wages by $1.54,

Figure 13.4. Impact of Union Coverage, Years of Education, Formal Job Training, and Years of Experience on Hourly Wages of Women, 1987

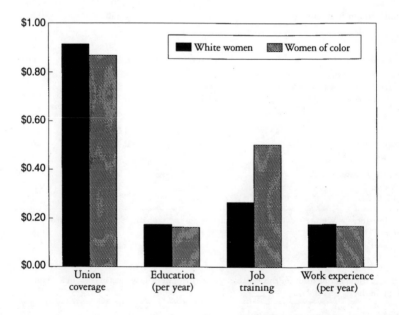

Source: Institute for Women's Policy Research regression results based on the 1987 Survey of Income and Program Participation.

$2.24, and $2.36 per hour, respectively). The results were similar for both white women and women of color. With the manufacturing industry as the reference group, our results show that working in the mining industry (there were a relatively small number of cases in the sample) and working in transportation, communications, or public utility industries brought the greatest benefits to women's wages ($3.83 and $3.43 per hour, respectively). The finance, insurance, and real estate industries increased women's wages by $.54 an hour. Though there appears to be no significant effect for white women from working in the wholesale industry, women of color are negatively affected by $2.18 per hour. Industries that have negative effects on women's wages compared with manufacturing are retail trade (-$1.15), personal services (-$1.43), and all other services (-$.71).

Other factors that had a large impact on wages include the number of hours worked, whether the worksite had more than one hundred employees, and whether the firm employed fewer than twenty-five workers. Each additional one thousand hours of employment increased hourly wages by $.67. In other words, working full time (two thousand hours) increases earnings by $.67 per hour compared with working half time (one thousand) hours. Women of color benefitted more than white women from added hours worked. Working at a large worksite (more than one hundred employees) contributed $1.04 to the hourly wages of all women; white women added $1.12 to their hourly wages, compared with $.69 for women of color. Working for a firm with fewer than twenty-five employees negatively affected the wages of white women (by $.32 per hour). For women of color, the results were inconclusive.

Age and region had the expected effects on women's wages, but, surprisingly, family status had no significant effect. Neither being married with the spouse present nor having at least one child under six years old affected women's wages (see table 13.1).

In sum, although women's wages are significantly affected by their hours of work, their human capital, and their distribution among occupations, industries, firms, and regions, the independent net effect of unionization is strong and positive.

Impact of Unionization on Job Tenure

As noted, most of the studies of union effects on job tenure and productivity are based largely on male blue-collar workers. Table 13.3 shows the uncontrolled effects of unionization on job tenure for women workers. We find that women union members have more than twice the median years of job tenure of nonunion workers (8.3 years compared with 4.0). (OLS regression analysis [Spalter-Roth, Hartmann, and Collins 1994] indicates that women gain an additional 1.2 years of tenure as a result of union membership, controlling for variation in other factors.) Among higher-wage women, unionized women workers have about three additional years of tenure com-

Table 13.3.   Percentage Distribution of Union and Nonunion Women Workers by Job Tenure, 1987 (uncontrolled results)

	All	*Nonunion*	*Union*
All workers			
Number of workers	38,630,000	30,770,000	6,160,000
Total	*100.0*	*100.0*	*100.0*
Less than 1 year	7.9	8.2	3.4
1 to less than 2 years	17.8	18.5	9.7
2 to less than 4 years	19.7	21.1	15.0
4 to less than 10 years	27.1	27.7	28.7
10 or more years	22.5	19.9	40.7
Median job tenure (years)	4.3	4.0	8.3
Observations with missing tenure	5.0	4.6	2.6
Low-wage workers			
Number of workers	12,760,000	11,220,000	750,000
Total	*100.0*	*100.0*	*100.0*
Less than 1 year	11.6	11.2	7.7
1 to less than 2 years	25.7	25.1	23.9
2 to less than 4 years	23.8	25.1	18.7
4 to less than 10 years	20.6	21.3	25.3
10 or more years	10.0	9.9	20.6
Median job tenure (years)	2.5	2.6	3.6
Observations with missing tenure	8.3	7.3	3.8
High-wage workers			
Number of workers	17,970,000	13,440,000	4,050,000
Total	*100.0*	*100.0*	*100.0*
Less than 1 year	4.6	4.7	2.5
1 to less than 2 years	12.9	13.6	7.7
2 to less than 4 years	16.3	17.4	13.7
4 to less than 10 years	31.1	32.4	29.2
10 or more years	32.3	29.2	45.4
Median job tenure (years)	6.7	6.1	9.3
Observations with missing tenure	2.7	2.6	1.6

Source: IWPR tabulations based on the 1986 and 1987 Survey of Income and Program Participation.
Note: Low-wage workers are those who earned an average hourly wage of less than $5.80 for at least 7 months out of the year; high-wage workers are those who earned an average hourly wage less than $5.80 only 1 month or never.

pared with their nonunion counterparts (9.3 versus 6.1 years). Low-wage workers have substantially less job tenure than higher-wage workers, regardless of union status. But unionized low-wage workers have an additional year of job tenure compared with their nonunion counterparts (3.6 years versus 2.6 years, respectively). The distribution of women across the categories for tenure show that among the low-wage unionized women workers, twice the proportion have ten years' job tenure or more than among the low-wage nonunion women. Although all low-wage union women do not receive a wage premium that moves them into the category of higher-wage workers, they do appear to gain job security. Their additional years of job tenure may also result in higher productivity.

Union Effects on Wages by Tenure

Figure 13.5 shows the union wage premium as a percentage of the median nonunion hourly wage for women workers by years of job tenure (the figures shown result from tabulations of the sample data; they represent "gross" rather than "net" effects of union membership on wages and do not statistically eliminate the effects of other factors on wages). The data show that the wage premium varies inversely with years of job tenure. Those workers with the fewest years of job tenure appear to benefit the most from unionization. Union women with less than one year of job tenure gain a premium of 43 percent; for union women with one to two years of job tenure, the union premium falls to 30; while those with ten or more years receive a smaller union premium of 22 percent. These findings indicate that unions decrease wage inequalities among women workers.

Conclusions

The decline in union membership is a cause for concern for women workers because membership or coverage under collective bargaining agreements is associated with higher wages for women and longer job tenure. Unions appear to benefit black and Hispanic women's wages especially. Since families headed by women are disproportionately poor, increasing these workers' earnings through collective bargaining would reduce poverty and increase living standards. Unions also appear to reduce wage inequality overall and to

Figure 13.5. Union Wage Premium for Women by Years of Tenure

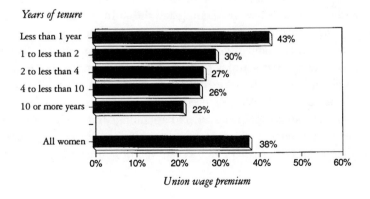

Source: Institute for Women's Policy Research regression results based on the 1986 and 1987 Survey of Income and Program Participation.

bring up the wages of less experienced workers relatively more. Unions also appear to increase job stability. Among low-wage workers, women union workers have an additional year of job tenure: among higher-wage workers, union women have three more years of job tenure than do nonunion women. Unionization gives low-wage women job security as well as higher wages. Additionally, employers may reap productivity gains from these more stable, unionized women workers.

If unions are important for women workers, some positive trends are apparent. The number of women workers in unions is still growing; unionization has shifted to areas where women work disproportionately: the public sector, nursing, teaching. And, as the analysis presented here shows, between 1984 and 1987, even the rate of unionization, not only the number of union workers, increased among higher-wage women workers.

As the increased proportion of unionized women in service occupations and industries has changed the face of labor unions, new issues and styles of organizing and bargaining have emerged. Unions with a high proportion of women members (such as AFSCME, SEIU, and CWA) have become active in negotiating for policies and programs that promote pay equity, affirmative action, family leave, child care, and women's awareness of their right to work free of sexual harassment, along with more traditional issues of wages and job security (Cobble 1993; S. Eaton 1992). Local unions composed of clerical workers or nurses have developed new methods of organizing and bargaining, including "one-to-one" organizing drives, more flexible "ruleless" contracts that move away from traditional job-control unionism, and grievance procedures that are problem-solving rather than adversarial processes (Albelda 1993; Hoerr 1993; S. Eaton 1992).

The issues and models of employee-employer relations that emerge from the increased participation of women in unions can have a vital impact on the content and style of collective bargaining and the ability of unions to increase workers' living standards and productivity. For this new diversity to be reflected in the content and style of collective bargaining, however, women need to play a greater part in union leadership. Currently, women comprise 37 percent of all union members but only 8 percent of elected and appointed officials (Albelda 1993). Women need to gain access to union leadership positions so they can decide issues, affect bargaining strategies, and organize the remaining 86 percent of women workers who do not benefit from the increased wages and job security gained through unionization.

14

The Effects of the Repeal of Utah's Prevailing Wage Law on the Labor Market in Construction

Hamid Azari-Rad, Anne Yeagle, and Peter Philips

The government has always been a major purchaser of construction services. In 1987, federal, state, and local governments jointly accounted for 20 percent of all construction purchases (U.S. Bureau of the Census 1987). As a primary customer of construction services, the government holds the potential to use its bargaining power to force down wage rates. Whether the lowering of wages lowers the overall cost of state construction by reducing the wage bill or raises overall construction costs by impairing quality and thereby raising repair and maintenance costs over the lifetime of the project remains an open question. Nonetheless, absent legal restrictions, government entities purchasing construction services may be tempted to save on initial construction costs by letting bids to contractors who are paying wages below the going rates in an area.

As early as 1881, the AFL argued for the passage of state prevailing wage laws that would prohibit the government from using its market power to lower wages. Kansas passed the first state prevailing wage law in 1891, and by 1969 forty-one states and the District of Columbia had prevailing wage laws in effect. Several cities also passed local prevailing wage laws in construction. A federal law was first proposed by New York representative Robert Bacon in 1927. Bacon justified his measure as follows:

> The Government is engaged in building in my district a Veterans' Bureau hospital. Bids were asked for. Several New York contractors bid, and in their bids, of course, they had to take into consideration the high labor standards

We wish to acknowledge the assistance and comments of Randy Brown, Van Hemeyer, Matt Hotchkiss, Garth Mangum, Gary Ray, Scott Smith, and Bob Wood.

prevailing in the State of New York. . . . The bid, however, was let to a firm from Alabama who had brought some thousand nonunion laborers from Alabama into Long Island, N.Y.; into my district. They were herded onto this job, they were housed in shacks, they were paid a very low wage, and the work proceeded. . . . It seemed to me that the Federal Government should not engage in construction work in any state and undermine the labor conditions and the labor wages paid in that State. . . . The least the Federal Government can do is comply with the local standards of wages and labor prevailing in the locality where the building construction is to take place (U.S. Congress 1927).

The federal government passed the Davis-Bacon prevailing wage law in 1931 during Herbert Hoover's administration (Gould and Bittlingmayer 1980). These local, state, and federal laws effectively took wages out of the competitive strategies of contractors preparing bids for government jobs.

State governments began experiencing fiscal crises in the late 1970s. In 1978, Proposition 13, restricting state expenditures, was passed in California, and the Labor Law Reform Bill failed in Congress. In this political and economic context, many state legislators argued that to save tax dollars, the government should use its bargaining power to lower its construction costs, even if the probable effect of this action would be the lowering of construction wage rates and a possible effect might be the lowering of quality in the construction industry. In 1979, Utah and Florida repealed their prevailing wage laws, both of which had been on the books since 1933. Utah's repeal was successfully vetoed by Utah's governor. In arguing to override the governor's veto, Representative S. Garth Jones, the sponsor of the repeal, wrote in the *Deseret News* (Feb. 23, 1979):

> The prevailing wage rate is substantially the union pay scale. In 1933 the law was designed to place money into a depressed economy, to increase wages to get the economy moving. The law does the same today. But today, the economy is not depressed; inflation is the problem and the cost of government is too high. Repealing the prevailing wage rate will allow the free enterprise system to establish the wages of tradesmen at a substantial savings to taxpayers. The prevailing wage law is inflationary. Additionally, the prevailing wage rate discourages non-union contractors from bidding public contracts. It encourages union contractors to bid public contracts. The effect is to force people looking for work to go to union contractors. The law is inconsistent with Utah's Right to Work law.

In debating the veto override in the Utah House, Representative Jones claimed: "At a time when unions are suffering major defeats in the Congress of the United States and elsewhere, the Governor of Utah has decided he can give the unions something the Legislature never would" (Utah House audiotapes, Feb. 1979). Despite these arguments, Jones failed in his appeal to override the governor's veto, although the Utah prevailing wage law still lasted only two more years. In 1981, the Utah legislature successfully overrode a second veto to repeal its forty-eight-year-old prevailing wage law. Because of the opposition of Utah's governor, Florida was the first state to repeal its prevailing wage law. In the next nine years, seven additional states repealed their laws—Alabama and Utah (1981), Arizona (1984), Colorado, Idaho and New Hampshire (1985), and Louisiana (1988). Nine states have never had prevailing wage laws—Georgia, Iowa, Mississippi, North Carolina, North Dakota, South Carolina, South Dakota, Vermont, and Virginia (Thieblot 1986).

This chapter is a case study of the effects of the repeal of prevailing wage law in Utah. We found that the Utah repeal accelerated the decline in the union share of the state's construction labor market, drove down average construction wages in the state, and decreased union apprenticeship training for construction. No public or private source has offset the latter decline. In response to the decline in union membership and training, contractors have reduced turnover in order to retain skilled workers and to minimize screening and training costs. In response not only to the decline in construction wages but also to the coincident decline in health and pension benefits, however, experienced construction workers are leaving their trades for careers in other industries. Thus, while construction firm turnover is on the decline, turnover in the industry is on the rise.

There is a looming crisis in training for construction workers in Utah. This crisis is the result of the market's failure to provide effective incentives to elicit training programs from those capable of paying for general training in construction skills and sufficient incentives for those trained in construction to remain in the industry. This looming crisis is currently in abeyance as contractors use skilled workers trained by unions before the 1981 repeal of the prevailing wage law. The crisis has been further masked until recently by a slow-growth construction economy in the state. As the generation of union-trained construction workers ages, however, the training crisis will slowly emerge. If the Utah construction market expands rapidly (as may be happening currently), the training crisis will come to the fore more rapidly.

Effect of Repeal on Construction Unions and Wages

When Utah repealed its prevailing wage law in construction, wages became a focus of competition between contractors bidding on state jobs. Many contractors went nonunion or double-breasted to match or beat the lower wages of nonunion contractors, and other union contractors lost market share. Mike Gibbons, a unionized heavy and highway contractor, recalls:

> The [Utah] little Davis-Bacon applied to cities, counties, state, all the
> government agencies. There was always a lot of open shop around, but

whenever they came up to any of these jobs, which tended to be the bigger jobs, we were always on an even playing field, labor-wise. As soon as the law was repealed, some of these nonunion people that had been doing small work around town suddenly just took off, and the union people, like ourselves, our market share decreased. We were paying twenty-five dollars, and they were paying fifteen dollars or even maybe ten. There were times when we could bid a job at cost and they would still beat us. What it did to us is our market share just plummeted and continued to plummet over a period of ten years (personal interview, president of Gibbons and Reed Contractors, May 14, 1993).

Because construction employment was falling, many union members went nonunion with their traditional employers to stay employed. Terry Wright, the vice president of the large industrial and commercial general contracting firm Jacobsen Construction, notes that after the repeal "there were a lot of union workers that carried their card in their shoe. They worked open shop until a union job came available. A lot of folks all of a sudden started to find homes over there [in the open shop] and never came back" (personal interview, May 15, 1993). Consequently, contractors that remained union did not have a significant labor productivity advantage over many of the newly nonunion contractors. This effectively forced remaining union contractors out of much of the construction market.

With the decline of union contractors, union membership fell (fig. 14.1).[1] The decline in membership was accelerated by the 1982 recession. Union membership appeared to recover from the recession, but many dues-paying members were working open shop. With the onset of the next downturn in Utah construction in 1986, union membership began to fall steadily. These data are consistent with the story that union members working in the open shop eventually found a home there and quit paying their union dues.

With the repeal of the prevailing wage law and the resulting decline in unionization in Utah, average wages in construction fell relative to the average Utah wage (fig. 14.2). Construction wages, which ranged from 120 to 125 percent of the average Utah wage before the construction boom of the 1970s, rose to above 130 percent during the boom. When construction employment growth stopped in the late 1970s, construction wages fell back toward the high end of their normal premium over average Utah wages. But with the repeal of the prevailing wage law, construction wages fell to a new lower range of 110 to 115 percent of the average wage in Utah.

1. Data are based on quarterly per capita dues contributions to the Utah AFL-CIO Building and Construction Trade Council. Payments underestimate union membership because of underreporting of membership from participating locals as well as other exemptions and withdrawals of locals.

Figure 14.1. Union Membership in Construction in Utah, 1977–1989

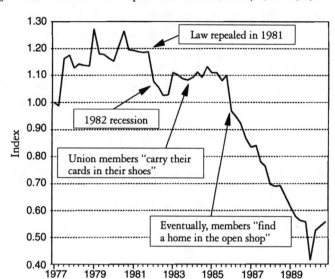

Union membership begins to decline with the prevailing wage law repeal and the onset of the 1982 recession. Membership recovers somewhat in 1983 but not as fast as overall construction employment. With the 1985 downturn in Utah construction employment, union membership begins a steady decline to less than half its late 1970s peak.
Source: Utah State Building and Constuction Trades dues records.

Because many factors changed together, it is difficult to estimate the wage effect of the repeal of Utah's prevailing wage law. But, by comparing relative wages in construction after the repeals in all eight states that annulled their prevailing wage laws with those in states that kept theirs and states that never had prevailing wage laws, it is possible to estimate the effect of these repeals. Table 14.1 reports the results of a generalized linear regression model of the determinants of the wages in construction relative to average state wages for all fifty states and the District of Columbia.[2] Construction wages in each state are broken down by contractor type corresponding to four-digit-level standard industry codes. Residential and heavy and highway contractors are excluded because residential contractors typically do not do state work and heavy and highway contractors typically are covered by the federal prevailing wage law. The model makes the relative wages for each type of contractor in each state for each year between 1975 and 1991 a function of an annual time trend. Unionization in construction fell throughout the time period studied,

2. This is a fixed effects model in which separate state and industry intercepts are calculated but not reported.

and this probably accounts for the 1 percentage point per year loss in the construction wage premium evident from the model. Additionally, the model demonstrates that as unemployment rises, construction wages fall faster than average wages within a state. A 3 percentage point rise in unemployment results in a 1 percentage point decline in the construction wage premium. States that never had a prevailing wage law have construction wage premiums that are 4 percentage points lower than states with prevailing wage laws. Finally, our focus is the impact on wages of repeals of prevailing wage laws. The model estimates that construction wage premiums fell 2 points after the repeal compared with before, controlling for the aforementioned factors.

This is an underestimate of the effect in part because the model does not include benefits. Typically, unionized construction workers receive better health and pension benefits than do nonunionized workers. The shift to nonunion work with lower benefits is not measured by the model. Also, although the model estimates an overall decline in the construction wage premium of 2 points, the decrease in the wages of unionized workers moving to open-shop employment would be much larger. Finally, the result that the negative effect of never having had a prevailing wage law is greater than the negative effect of having repealed such a law suggests that the final effect of these repeals has not yet been felt. By 1992, state prevailing wage law repeals had been in effect for an average of 8.5 years, and assuming that the final effect will be equal to the negative wage effect in those states that never had prevailing wage laws, our results suggest that the effects in 1992 were 80 percent felt.[3]

Decline in Training

With the decline in union membership and in relative wages, training for construction, both in union apprenticeships and through vocational schools, declined in Utah. Union apprenticeships are tied to the availability of union jobs. For example, unionized plumbers and pipe fitters in Utah historically have attempted to maintain apprenticeship rates at between 10 and 15 percent of the number of union journeymen plumbers in the state (fig. 14.3). As employment boomed in the 1970s, however, the union (the United Association of Journeymen and Apprentices of the Plumbing and Pipe Fitting Industry of the United States and Canada) could not meet the demand for journeymen from the unionized contractors. Consequently, the union increased

3. Because states that repealed the law were not heavily unionized, the effect of a repeal on average construction wages was less than it might have been had a heavily unionized state repealed its prevailing wage law.

Figure 14.2. Wages and Employment in Construction in Utah Relative to Wages Statewide

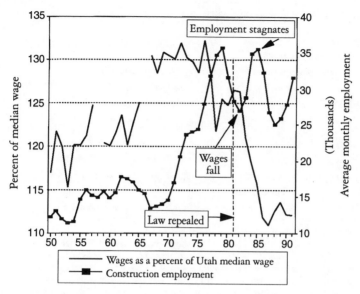

Construction employment in Utah grows rapidly in the 1970s, but growth stops in the 1980s and cyclical fluctuations become more pronounced. Wages that ranged between 120 and 125 percent of the Utah median wage prior to the construction boom of the 1970s rise above 130 percent of Utah's median wage during the boom. As the boom ends, wages trend back down to their normal range, but with the repeal of Utah's prevailing wage law, wages plummet.

Source: Utah Job Security, Division of Labor Market Information Annual Report, Table 5.

apprenticeship rates to a peak of 25 percent in 1975. The boom persisted, but the backlog had been remedied. So the union lowered its apprenticeship rate back to normal ranges by 1978. Employment during the construction boom peaked in 1979 and membership in the union peaked in 1981. With the repeal of the Utah prevailing wage law, the union dropped its apprenticeship rate to 10 percent, a historical low. Union membership fell slightly in 1982 and then began a steeper decline in 1983. Faced with these sustained declines in membership, the union cut its apprenticeship rate to historical lows in 1986 and thereafter. Unions hit harder by declines in membership have scaled back their apprenticeship programs further. The carpenters' union, Utah locals 184 and 1498 of the United Brotherhood of Carpenters and Joiners of America, which graduated seventy in a class in 1977, graduated five in 1992 (personal interview, Paul Hansen, Carpenters Union instructor, Weber Basin Job Corps, Sept. 2, 1993). The Utah International Union of Bricklayers and Allied Craftsmen suspended its apprenticeship program altogether.

Table 14.1. Effect of Repeal of Prevailing Wage Laws in the Wage Premium in Construction Nationwide, 1975–1991

Dependent variable = Construction workers' wage as a percent of the state average wage

Independent variables[a]	*Effect on wage premium*[b]
General annual trend in wages	-1 percentage points
State-by-state unemployment rate	-.4 percentage points
State never had prevailing wage law	-4 percentage points
State repealed its prevailing wage law	-2 percentage points
Constant	131% of average state wages

Adjusted R square	= .74	Percentage states and years of repeals = 9%	
Number of cases	= 27,660	Percentage states and years never	
Years	= 1975–91	had prevailing wages	= 16%
Contractor type	= four-digit SIC	1975 construction premium	= 122%
		1991 construction premium	= 105%

Source: U.S. Department of Labor, *Employment and Wages.*
Note: The construction wage premium over average wages in a state fell 1 percentage point per year in the model, covering the years 1975–1991. Each percentage point in a state's unemployment level lowered construction wages relative to average state wages by 4/10ths of a percentage point. The repeal of a states prevailing wage law lowered the construction premium by 2 points. The construction premium in states that never had a prevailing wage law were 4 points lower than in states that retained this law throughout the period.
[a] State and industry effects not reported.
[b] All variables are statistically significant at the 1 percent level.

The decline in union apprenticeship training in Utah has not been offset by a rise in other sources of training. Because the repeal of Utah's prevailing wage law was motivated by a desire to limit state expenditures, state legislators were not eager to raise funding for state-sponsored vocational training. Delmar Stevens, who has taught building trades construction at Salt Lake Community College since 1971, chronicles the decline in enrollment:

> I started at the college in 1971. We went about two or three years and then the enrollment just really started to grow. [When I started we had] probably about forty-five students with the first-year and second-year programs. Then about 1973 or '74 it really started to grow. It jumped up to two hundred students, [but] then the crunch came in the last part of the '70s and early '80s and it just dropped back to thirty or forty students. Right now we let in anybody who can walk or crawl. We'll probably graduate six or seven this year (personal interview, Sept. 14, 1993).

Although the number of graduates of vocational programs in construction grew in the 1970s, the construction labor force grew more rapidly. Thus,

Figure 14.3. Apprentice Plumbers as a Percentage of Journeymen Plumbers in Utah, 1961–1991

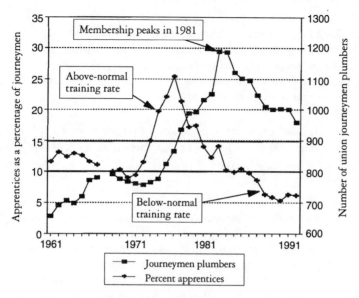

The plumbers' union in Utah has historically attempted to train apprentices at a rate of 10 to 15 percent of their journeymen members. As employment boomed in the 1970s, the union could not meet the demand for journeymen and consequently expanded apprenticeship training rapidly. As the numbers of journeymen grew to meet demand, apprenticeship training was reduced back to normal rates. But with the repeal of the prevailing wage law, union membership declined and apprenticeship training rates were cut to all-time lows.

Source: Utah plumbers and pipe fitters locals' membership records.

while the 1970s was the heyday of vocational training at Salt Lake Community College, graduates as a percentage of the construction labor force had already begun to decline.[4]

Stevens argues that the decline in enrollment is driven by a lack of demand for training: "The staff is hanging on by their fingernails because there's not enough students that want to get into the program." He adds that many of his graduates do not stay in construction: "They get out, and they find out that they don't want to work in the cold in the winter and they want to get into something more secure, something that's got benefits." Construction has always required workers to work in the cold, but the loss of benefits and security has occurred since 1980, along with the stagnating employment, declining rate of unionization, and falling relative wages.

4. Data available upon request.

Stevens also argues that the decline in construction training is a function of shifting government priorities in education:

> I can't speak for the school—I don't want to get in trouble that way—but we do have more general ed classes feeding the university [than in the past], and the vocational programs are really suffering. You look at Weber State. They used to have vocational programs, and with academic drift, they don't have any vocational programs anymore.

Tom Lewis, director of the apprenticeship program for the plumber and pipe fitters' union, agrees with Stevens that there is an institutional tendency to move away from vocational education:

> We used to have a pretty good relationship with the community colleges. The reason we bought our own building and moved out here [away from Salt Lake Community College] is that you have an administrator of a vocational school and they don't want to remain the administrator of a vocational school. They move to an applied technology center, then they're a community college, and then they're a university. I started my apprenticeship at Weber Vocational Center, which is now Weber State University. Vocational training seems to get set aside as this evolution happens and we eventually just get moved out the back door (personal interview, Sept. 3, 1993).

The steady decline in vocational training as a percentage of the construction labor force through good times and bad supports the notion that the state has simply tried to get out of the business of vocational training in construction. The fall in union membership and wages has made construction a less attractive career. At the same time, unions are less able to train construction workers. As unions are weakened and schools drift toward academic offerings, the capacity to respond smoothly to an upsurge in construction jobs is undercut. And federally sponsored Job Corps vocational training is not in a position to fill in the gap.

Federal revenues pay for Job Corps training in Utah at both the Weber Basin and Clearfield centers. Federal funding in real terms for these centers has not expanded, but the Weber Basin Job Corps Center, which draws predominately from the Utah population, significantly contracted its construction worker training throughout the 1980s. This center committed itself to changing from an all-male student population in 1980 to 50 percent female by 1990. To accommodate this switch, training for traditionally male occupations, such as construction, have been scaled back to accommodate new offerings in traditionally female occupations, such as office management and clerical work. Cement masonry and heavy-equipment training have been eliminated, and instruction in carpentry, painting, and bricklaying has been cut in half.

The Clearfield Center has graduated approximately one hundred construction trainees per year since the early 1970s. Fewer Clearfield graduates go into the Utah labor market compared with Weber Basin because most of Clearfield's students are from out of state. On the whole, perhaps 10 percent of Clearfield's graduates go into the Utah labor market, but this percentage rises during periods of local labor shortage. It is estimated, however, that at most only 25 percent of Clearfield's graduates will stay in Utah (personal interview, Merle Hill, vocational education manager, Clearfield Job Corps, Sept. 9, 1993).

Even without union pressure, a skill shortage in Utah construction may raise wages and induce a new generation of young people to enter vocational training. When that happens, however, high-quality training programs, which take time to create, may not be in place to meet that demand, which will add an additional lag to the natural time it takes to train a skilled laborer.

Market Responses: Training, Turnover, and Careers

The market has not successfully made up for the decline in union and state-sponsored training. At the national level, the nonunion Association of Building Contractors (ABC) has attempted to replicate the union system of bargaining for hourly contributions to a training fund. It is difficult, however, to induce ABC's member contractors to include general training costs in their bids. Each contractor fears his competitors will not include training costs. Thus, in an attempt to be low-cost bidder, ABC contractors often refrain from including training costs despite the ABC's initiative. Consequently, very little ABC training has occurred in Utah.

Nonunion apprenticeship programs operate, however, in the licensed trades of electricians and plumbers. In 1992, there were 846 nonunion licensed apprentice electricians in Utah and 2,068 nonunion journeymen. Thus, there are 4 apprentices for every 10 journeymen in the nonunion sector. In contrast, there were 123 apprentices and 607 journeymen in the union sector in 1992, or 2 apprentices for every 10 journeymen. In the nonunion sector, apprentices begin at about six dollars per hour with no benefits. Over a four-year period, the state mandates that their wage rise to 80 percent of a journeyman's pay. In the union sector, apprentices begin at seven dollars per hour with an additional three dollars in benefits. Their wages rise to fourteen dollars per hour plus three dollars in benefits over a five-year period (phone interview, Julie Leroy, assistant business manager, IBEW Local 354, Sept. 25, 1993).

Nonunion apprentices are sponsored by a particular contractor that oversees their on-the-job training, and these apprentices also take classwork at a participating community college. Union apprentices work under the direction of an apprenticeship coordinator, rotate among employers for on-the-job training, and take classes at community colleges and union apprenticeship centers. Roughly 90 to 95 percent of the union apprentices complete their programs and graduate to journeymen status, while only 15 to 20 percent of the nonunion apprentices graduate (personal interview, Frank Dean, electrical instructor, Home Builders Institute, Clearfield Job Corps, Sept. 9, 1993). Given these rates, in four years, out of 846 nonunion apprentices, we should expect 125 to 170 journeymen to be graduated. In five years in the union sector, out of 123 apprentices, 110 to 115 apprentices would graduate to journeymen electrician. Thus, while the nonunion sector accounts for more than 85 percent of all electrician apprentices, it accounts for about 60 percent of journeymen graduates. Economic theory is consistent with this pattern wherein nonunion apprentices are paid less and graduate at a lower rate than union apprentices.

Economic theory posits that in the absence of marketwide institutions or government subsidies, individual workers will have to pay for their own on-the-job training when the skills learned are general to an industry and not specific and unique to the activities of a particular firm. The worker-learner pays for training by accepting a wage that is lower than the value to the firm of that worker's marginal product. By working for less than what the worker is worth to the employer, the worker pays the employer for on-the-job training. That beginning nonunion electrician apprentices earn six dollars per hour while union apprentices earn ten dollars per hour (including benefits) is consistent with the theoretical proposition that nonunion apprentices pay for their own training by taking a discounted wage below their marginal value to the contractor.

Because the employer does not pay for nonunion training, the theory suggests that the employer has no stake in the worker's training. Consequently, if the worker leaves, the employer does not lose any investment in the worker's human capital. Thus, the employer will tolerate high levels of turnover. Because the worker is receiving less than what the worker can earn in other jobs with no on-the-job training, the worker may be tempted to exit jobs with training when current personal budget needs become pressing. So, on both the employer side and the worker side, turnover is tolerated in the nonunion sector. This is consistent with the higher turnover rates among nonunion apprentices, but other factors also contribute to the 15 to 95 percent differential in nonunion to union graduation rates.

Because the nonunion employer prices new hands at discounted wages that shield the employer from investing in the human capital of the new workers, the employer does not screen new workers extensively to forestall subsequent turnover. Failure to preselect new workers for aptitudes and attitudes consistent with a long-term attachment to construction work adds to the turnover among nonunion construction apprentices. In contrast, the joint apprenticeship boards of unions and union contractors do considerable preselection for both aptitude and attitude before letting a candidate into an apprenticeship program. This is because both the union contractors and unions will invest in the union apprentices' training. Not wanting to lose their up-front investment, they seek to eliminate exit once the apprenticeship is begun.

In the nonunion sector, workers may also leave apprenticeships if it becomes apparent that the employer offering training at a discounted wage is not delivering on that promise to train. Because employers are able to discount wages of apprentices below their current worth to the employer, it is tempting to engage in bait-and-switch tactics whereby training is promised but not delivered. By saving on training costs, the employer can earn an additional profit from employing green hands at discounted wages. In the union sector, because employers and union journeymen invest in the training of the apprentices, bait-and-switch tactics are less attractive. Because the apprentices' wage is not discounted as much below what they could earn elsewhere, the apprentices are not as tempted to leave. Thus, economic theory predicts the observed pattern whereby the nonunion sector must begin training five apprentices to graduate one journeyman while the ratio in the union sector is close to one to one.

While nonunion contractors tolerate high levels of turnover among apprentices, with the decline in training and union membership, nonunion Utah contractors have sought to reduce the turnover among trained journeymen. Figure 14.4 shows that there has been a long-term decline in labor turnover in construction. Table 14.2 presents a pooled, cross-sectional, time-series linear regression model explaining this long-term decline, as well as the differences in turnover rates in Utah by contractor type from 1956 to 1991. Not surprisingly, this model shows that turnover was higher in years in which variations in monthly construction employment were great. It also shows that contractors with larger crews tolerated proportionately more turnover. Contractors employing more expensive labor sought to reduce turnover. When union membership was a high percentage of the construction labor force, turnover was higher simply because contractors losing one good worker could turn to the hiring hall for a reasonable substitute at little additional cost. When vocational schools were graduating a large number of construction-trained students relative to the Utah construction labor market, contractors tolerated more turnover because the market had proportionately more trained substitutes. Union membership and vocational graduates have been on the decline, however. Thus, this regression model shows that over time, contractors have responded by reducing the turnover among journeymen.

Although turnover to the firm has been on the decline, it may be that workers are entering and leaving construction at higher rates than twenty

Figure 14.4. Turnover in Construction in Utah versus Statewide

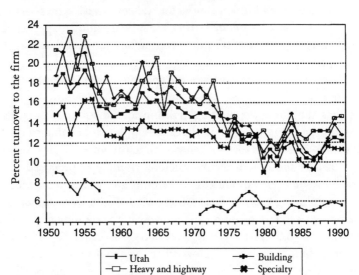

As the number of trained journeymen in the union hiring halls declines and the number of nonunion journeymen declines, firms respond by reducing turnover.

Source: Utah Job Security, Division of Labor Market Information, annual report, table 5.

years ago. In 1970, Utah construction workers on average were forty-two years old (U.S. Bureau of the Census 1970). By 1990, the age had fallen to thirty-three (U.S. Bureau of the Census 1989–91). Much of this decline may be due to the construction expansion in the 1970s, which brought in a new generation of younger workers. But the decline in age may also be due to the decline in health and retirement benefits and to the decline in relative wages associated with the decline in unions. As Delmar Stevens points out, many young construction workers he has trained leave the field when they form families, seeking other occupations that provide needed health and retirement benefits. Although nonunion contractors are increasingly providing health and retirement benefits especially to their key people, the health benefits tend to be more expensive for a given level of care, and the retirement 401K plans lack the insurance component associated with union-defined benefit plans. Further research on the effect of union decline on career turnover in Utah construction is needed.

Conclusions

Employment in the construction industry is inherently unstable because the industry fluctuates cyclically and seasonally while firms expand and

Table 14.2.   Linear Regression Model of Turnover Rate in Construction in Utah

Dependent variable = firm turnover in construction[a]

Variable[b]	Actual coefficient	Standardized coefficient
Union members[c]	1.76	.24
New vocational graduates[c]	2.45	.20
Real wage	-.076	-.62
Seasonality	2.12	.15
Workers per contractor	.052	.40
Constant	-1.88	
Adjusted R square	= .24	
Number of cases	= 351	
Time period	= 1956–91	
Contractor type	= four-digit SIC	

Source: Utah Job Security Annual Report, table 5.
Note: Contractors in Utah tolerate higher labor turnover when union membership is a high percentage of the labor force and when new vocational school graduates are plentiful. Turnover is more common in years when monthly employment fluctuates a lot. Contractors are more willing to tolerate turnover among lower-paid workers, and contractors with larger work crews must accept higher levels of turnover. Standardized coefficients indicate that worker skill and crew size have the largest impact on variations in employer turnover rates, while both the availability of union members and new vocational graduates have larger effects than seasonal fluctuations in employment.
[a] The actual variable is ln(turnover/(1-turnover)) to meet the technical requirement in linear regressions of being an unbounded dependent variable.
[b] All independent variables are statistically significant at the 1 percent level.
[c] As a percent of the construction labor force.

contract their employment as they win and lose job bids. Unions have acted like a flywheel within the industry, creating career workers when there were only casual jobs. Unions did this by facilitating the movement of journeymen from employer to employer and minimizing the employers' transaction and screening costs in the process. Unions also lowered training turnover by providing a mechanism whereby employers and journeymen could rationally invest in the human capital of apprentices. This raised the wages of apprentices so they would stay with the training program and induced the union and employers to promote the passage of apprentices to journeymen in order to preserve their investment. Unions also encouraged the career attachment of trained journeymen by providing relatively high wages and wages in the form of health and retirement insurance, which are increasingly attractive to workers as they age. By creating career jobs in a casual labor market, unions created the institutions needed to make human capital investment a rational market activity.

With the decline of unions in Utah, the formation and preservation of human capital skills have become less rational market behaviors. Self-investment on the part of apprentices becomes more precarious as the differential between the apprentices' wage and alternative wages in other industries widens. It simply becomes more reasonable for apprentices to leave construction if unforeseen current budget problems emerge. The high turnover among non-union apprentices represents in the aggregate a considerable loss of human capital to the construction industry, even though it is not a loss the employer or the state pays for directly. With the lowering of construction wages, it becomes reasonable for young construction workers to limit the amount of human capital they invest in themselves. With a lower stake in construction skills and the disappearance of wages in the form of health and old-age insurance, it becomes more reasonable for journeymen construction workers to abandon the construction field when they start families. This represents an additional loss of built-up human capital.

Contractors have attempted to minimize the effect of this increased skill volatility within the industry by encouraging firm attachment. Still, despite initiatives, such as profit-sharing, 401K plans, and health insurance, designed to attach key workers to the firm, construction turnover remains well above the average for the Utah labor market. In short, union decline has meant the decline of the career worker within Utah construction, a diminution in incentives to invest in construction skills, and an increased loss of accumulated human capital as apprentices and journeymen leave the trade.

Although the loss of human capital and career jobs in this industry do not appear as a private cost on the ledgers of any one contractor, both the industry and society at large pay a price for the loss of middle-class occupations in construction. Not only is quality in the industry put at risk when human capital stocks are allowed to dwindle, but the quality of social life is imperiled when we dismantle the institutions that generate stable jobs out of unstable working conditions.

15

The Role of Technology in Undermining Union Strength

Charley Richardson

The subject of labor law and its relevance in current form to the realities of modern economic and social conditions has been thrust onto center stage. The declining percentage of the workforce that is unionized, the decreasing standard of living of workers, and the increasing incidence of intimidation and firing of workers who try to organize are, for many, reason enough to revisit the basic tenets of labor law. The oft-repeated refrains that "unions want changes in labor law to make up for their own failures" or that "unions are failing because they are no longer relevant" ignore the fundamental changes that have occurred in the economy, in the workplace, and in the relative power of labor in its dealings with management. In particular, technological change has altered the field on which the game of labor-management interaction is played in ways that are not accounted for in labor law as it currently exists and require that labor law be revised and updated.

I will argue that the accelerating pace of technological change, and the increased scope and power of the technologies that are being introduced, are critical in explaining the weakening of unions and their decreasing ability to negotiate improved wages and working conditions. The weakening of labor law and labor law enforcement that occurred over the twelve years of the Reagan-Bush era has been matched by a rapid, technologically enabled increase in the ability of management to undermine and bypass both traditional sources of union bargaining power and the controls imposed by labor law. Thus, not only does the system of protections for the right to bargain collectively have to be rebuilt to overcome the legacy of Reaganism, but it also must be updated to reflect and counteract the tendency of technological change to place increasing power in the hands of management. In this context, I will point to particular areas of labor law that are affected by technological change and suggest changes in labor law that would begin to rebuild the system of collective bargaining in the United States.

Goal of Labor Law Reform

I begin from the assumption that the purpose of labor law is to provide a means for workers to improve their conditions of work and have an effective voice in defining their futures. The method of labor law is to impose order and rules on the process of achieving and maintaining union representation, rules that should give employees the right *and* the realistic ability to bargain collectively. The corollary to this assumption is that absent the ability to bargain collectively, the needs, hopes, and aspirations of the workforce will not be attended to appropriately. The purpose of labor law reform, therefore, must be to strengthen the right of workers to bargain collectively and their ability to bargain successfully.

The issue of purpose cannot be dismissed lightly. Unfortunately, much of the current discussion of labor law reform is not driven primarily by a concern for the rights of workers but rather is a reflection of a national focus on competitiveness (or the failure of competitiveness) and the search for new forms of "worker input" into the workplace and work processes that can revive the profitability of firms. To the extent that improving the competitiveness (profitability in the face of international competition) of American business dominates the labor law reform debate, the needs of the workforce will not be directly met, and at best will be relegated to second-class status and the hopes of trickle-down.

The federal government, in placing its mark on the debate, has defined the issues narrowly. The mandate of the Commission on the Future of Worker-Management Relations, for example, carefully avoids any mention of the rights of the workforce and focuses on productivity. Although it is probably unnecessary to repeat that mandate here, it provides an important backdrop for the discussion that follows:

> What (if any) new methods or institutions should be encouraged or required to *enhance workplace productivity* through labor-management cooperation and employee participation?
> What (if any) changes should be made in the current legal framework and practices of collective bargaining to enhance *cooperative behavior, improve productivity and reduce conflict and delay?*
> What (if anything) should be done to increase the extent to which workplace problems are *directly resolved by the parties themselves*, rather than through recourse to state and federal courts and regulatory bodies? (emphasis added)

The particular focus of the mandate, and its failure to recognize the nature of the crisis *for the workforce*, obviously limits the range of "acceptable" proposals or solutions. To discuss, for example, the reduction of conflict and the direct resolution of problems by the parties themselves without recognizing the existing and growing imbalance of power in the workplace is to ignore social reality and betray the needs and rights of the workforce. Worker input, cooperation, and participation when placed in the context of a vicious attack on unions and on the rights of workers become shallow, and even dangerous, concepts. Recognizing the role of technology (and management control over technology decision-making) in creating the imbalance of power between labor and management is crucial to determining the appropriate direction for labor law reform.

Technological Change and Workplace Restructuring

America's workplaces, be they hospitals, schools, factories, retail stores, or construction sites, are in the midst of a technological revolution. From computerized engine analyzers at the local gas station to robots moving parts in the factory (or dinner trays in the hospital), from laser bar code scanners in the supermarket to optical character readers at the post office, from computerized information systems that track and schedule production from the arrival of raw materials to the shipping of finished products (whether the raw materials are stock metals to a machine shop or patients in a hospital) to new types of ceramics and plastics, the changes in workplace technology are evident all around us.

Understanding the impact of technology on the workplace requires looking beyond its physical manifestations in equipment and tools. Technology is the end result of a social process of gathering and embedding knowledge in a machine, a tool, a piece of software, a technique, a material, *or* a way of organizing work. The social nature of that knowledge (who controls it and its application and how critical it is to the production of goods and services) has a significant impact on the relations among, and relative power of, the parties involved in the production process (Braverman 1974; D. Noble 1984).[1]

Although the concept of technology as embedded knowledge may be more intuitive when applied to computers or software, it is equally applicable to other technologies. For example, new materials and techniques emerge from a research process (developing and organizing knowledge) and can have a significant impact on the knowledge and skills required by any particular

---

1. It is unfortunate that much of the vocabulary of technological change is oriented toward the manufacturing sector. Technological change is equally active in the services and construction. The terms "production" and "production process" are used throughout this chapter to refer to the social process of creating and delivering goods *and* services.

production process. The switch from steel to plastic pipes by gas utilities, for example, is transforming the skills needed to install new pipe (critical production skills) and is thereby reducing the demand for workers with the "old" skills. Statistical process control (SPC), a technique for analyzing and controlling production, ultimately takes production decision-making out of the hands of the workforce, embedding it in formulas or algorithms. It therefore provides a mechanism for devaluing the knowledge and skill of existing workers within the production process.

Technological change is, of course, not a new phenomenon. We have, however, entered a period characterized by continuous technological change and by the introduction of technologies of such scope and power that they affect whole workplaces, occupations, and even industries. Change has become the only constant in America's workplaces.

Rapid and deep change in technology and work organization, according to the conventional wisdom, is required by the new competitive reality. According to Secretary of Commerce Ron Brown, speaking at the Conference on the Future of the American Workplace in 1993: "Competitive success now requires constant, sustained innovation. That means for governments and businesses and workers, we must constantly be reinterpreting, reevaluating, and reinventing how we work."

The perceived challenge of technological change and global competition has placed a premium on the collection and use of the ideas of the workforce and on workforce acceptance of ongoing change and have therefore pushed the issue of labor-management relations onto the front burner. The business necessity is, on the one hand, to tap the innovative potential and flexibility of the workforce (Best 1990; Jaikumar 1986), while, on the other hand, minimizing loss of control over the work process, over the direction of change, and over the distribution of gains (Parker and Slaughter 1988).

Business needs the input of the workforce—but it also needs to control the process of technological change and work restructuring. Toward this end, elaborate programs of empowerment have been developed to align employees with the goals of management and at the same time gather their ideas, insights, and knowledge. This approach envisions the elimination of the contradictions between workers and owners (the recognition of which is fundamental to our labor law) with the arrival of "a greater competitive enemy" on the horizon. Labor Secretary Reich spoke at the Conference on the Future of the American Workplace about the need for a new "compact" between labor and management: "This new compact recognizes that we're in a different world now, where the enemy is not a nasty boss or a stubborn union head, but rather all the obsolete ways of working that no longer work."

The faddish "rebellion" against Taylorism (because it rejects the ideas and capabilities of the workforce) is in one sense a recognition of the importance of the workforce. It is not, however, a commitment to implement workers' ideas that do not meet management's needs; nor is it a commitment to workers' right and ability to negotiate their future. The current hemorrhage of jobs at such companies as Xerox, IBM, and Digital Equipment Corporation is a grim reminder that the rights of employees are not secure (and in fact do not exist) without an independent source of power to back them up. Promises of lifetime employment and the rhetoric of empowerment, which were used to invoke extra effort and innovation from employees, are now being ignored with impunity.

Impact of Technological Change

New technologies have significant impact on two general arenas of importance to the workforce—working conditions and the strength, or potential strength, of worker collective voice. Working conditions affected by technology include the pace of work; control over work processes; skill; health and safety issues, such as exposure to toxics, repetitive strain injuries, and stress; job security; job opportunity or career ladders; and wages. The impact of technology in these areas is well described elsewhere (Richardson 1993a, 1993b; Garson 1988; Howard 1985; Shaiken 1984; Karasek and Theorell 1990). Here I will only make the point that although technology as such is not the final determinant of working conditions, it does provide the base of options from which the struggle to improve conditions commences.

The auto assembly line provides a good example. Autoworkers did not design the assembly line. There are certainly many reasons autoworkers would not pick the assembly line as their core production technology, among them the stress, repetitive strain injuries, and boredom (Hamper 1991). Autoworkers have, however, struggled over the years, both individually and collectively, to improve conditions on the lines. The potential for success in that struggle is limited, however, by the problems inherent in assembly-line operations, and much of the focus has therefore been diverted to increasing wages, benefits, and the right in later years to move away from the line into easier jobs.[2]

The increasing use of computers in the workplace has brought with it many concerns about working conditions. The impact of computerization on working conditions depends on who (or whose needs) controls the design and implementation processes. At this point there are few if any significant

2. In heavily unionized Sweden the auto industry was moving toward limitations on, and even the elimination of, the assembly line, in large part because workers were displaying their dissatisfaction with that form of production by simply not showing up for work. The Volvo plant in Uddevalla, for example, relied on teams of workers to build whole cars. This trend is currently being reversed because of global competition from "lean" producers.

mechanisms for unions or workers to have input into these processes. Computerized monitoring and the stress that it creates, job intensification, deskilling, exposure to electromagnetic radiation, job loss, and the undermining of wage rates are some of the negative effects that are created, or enabled, by computerization (Garson 1988).

Although improvements in working conditions can certainly be achieved within the confines of particular base technologies, so-called retrofit solutions often are ineffective and expensive, run up against structural limitations, and take years to negotiate, design, and implement. It is extremely difficult for unions to negotiate better working conditions as long as they are excluded from decisions concerning the core technology, especially given the current situation of rapid technological change.

Changes in technology also inevitably alter the strength of the workforce in relation to management in that they affect the number of workers, the location of critical skills, the ability to relocate production, and the ability of management to divide and monitor the workforce. Although there are certainly examples of technological change that have increased the power of the workforce, historical experience points primarily in the other direction. The decline of many of the early craft unions, for example, was in great part secured by technological changes that allowed management to bypass the critical production skills that were the basis of the unions' strength.

The strength of the Amalgamated Association of Iron, Steel and Tin Workers in the 1800s, for example, was based in the skills required to make iron and steel and the unity of those who possessed these skills: "The companies could not produce raw or finished iron or steel without them" (Hoerr 1988:46). But technologies were developed and implemented that allowed these critical skills to be bypassed:

> Later in the 1890's, two growing trends undermined the Amalgamated's
> position. One was steel's increasing displacement of iron as America's basic
> metal, thus making obsolete the skills of the iron foundrymen who formed
> the core of the Amalgamated. At the same time, steelmakers were
> introducing new machinery which could be operated by relatively unskilled
> laborers (Hoerr 1988:46).

Thus, two significant changes in technology, one in materials technology and the other in machinery, formed the basis for undermining the strength of the union and ultimately ensuring the union's total destruction.

Similarly, Henry Ford's assembly line allowed the bypassing of critical skills. The standardization of parts and operations, which were the heart of the assembly-line process, allowed increased control over the workforce, at the same time that large gains in productivity were achieved. The skilled fitters who had been the core of the fledgling auto industry were displaced as Ford "not only perfected the interchangeable part, [but] perfected the interchangeable worker" (Womack, Jones, and Roos 1991:30).

Although one should never underestimate the significance of the disruption and realignment of labor relations that accompanies large-scale technological restructuring such as occurred in the steel industry in the late 1800s and in the auto industry in the early 1900s, given the implications for the particular unions involved and for the labor movement as a whole, historically such change has happened relatively sporadically. Periods of disruption have generally been followed by long and technologically stable periods during which the workforce "learned" how to exert power in the newly configured workplace by gaining control over strategic skills and engaging in collective action. Using this power, they were able to negotiate improved working conditions and bring more balance to labor relations. Certainly, the steel and auto industries are clear examples of this process.

The effectiveness of worker voice—that is, the ability of the workforce to bargain with management—is determined in large part by the ability of the workforce to exert economic pressure—that is, to prevent production or otherwise to threaten the ability of the employer to make money. The ability to prevent production is affected by two groups of factors that can be characterized as organized and inherent. The organized factors include the involvement and solidarity of the workforce and the strategic vision of the leadership. The inherent factors are those closely tied to the actual production process and therefore to technology. These include the portability of work, the level of skill required by the production process, the proportion of critical skills that are controlled by the unionized workforce, the general skill level of the workforce (particularly in relation to the skill levels in the broader population), and the proportion of the sector's workforce that is unionized. Although this last factor is clearly affected by the organizing ability of the unions, it can also be greatly affected by management's ability to move work and by changes in technology that allow sectoral shifts that dilute the unionized core of an industry. Mini-mill technology in steel and microwave technology in telecommunications are examples of technologies that enabled significant shifts in the form and location of production, which in turn affected the proportion of the sectoral workforce that was unionized.

The new technologies that are being introduced into America's workplaces, and the very fact of rapid technological change, have a significant impact on all of these inherent factors. The printing sector provides us with a clear example of how computers can change power relations in an industry. For approximately one hundred years the linotype machine was a core technology used in the process of creating plates for newspaper presses. The strength of the International Typographical Union was based primarily on the critical role of the linotype machine in daily newspaper production and on the union's control over linotyping and layout skills. Since the 1960s, several generations of typographic technology have come and gone. The layout work can now be shifted geographically because it is done electronically. The overall demand for typographers has dropped precipitously as the new technologies have become increasingly productive. And many machine-specific skills are simply no longer necessary. As a result, the union has lost much of its ability to control working conditions and to protect its membership over the long run.

In the situation described below, the unions at a major newspaper in Richmond, Virginia, went on strike to prevent the production of a financial paper using an early version of computerized production, cold-type photocomposition:

> The management, which had expected the strike and laid its plans, brought new photo-setting equipment into the main newspaper area. They brought lorries in past the picket lines and loaded the hot lead linecaster machines onto them and drove them out of the plant and simply sold them, mostly for scrap. Meanwhile, management and advertising people, helped by secretaries and others who were simply recruited off the street, set about working the new photo-setting equipment. The first photo-set copies were late and they were terrible to look at for several months. But they came out.
> The union had of course walked out in the belief (well founded in the days when there was only hot lead) that the paper could not be got out without them. Its members then had to watch the management literally scrapping the machinery that had been their livelihood (Winbury 1975:24).

Management's ability to bypass the skills of the workforce allowed management to make this move. The historic power of the union to push management to the bargaining table by threatening production was rendered useless.

A sheet metal shop south of Boston provides another example of the impact of technology on labor-management relations. At this shop, the latest in CAD/CAM (computer-aided design and computer-aided manufacturing) software is used to fabricate ventilation system duct work. The vast majority of the layout work is done on a computer, which in turn sends instructions to a computer-controlled plasmarc cutting machine and simultaneously creates bar code labels that aid in work-piece alignment and tracking. According to the owner of the shop, this equipment has drastically changed the skill requirements: "Ten years ago we did 5 million dollars worth of business and we had fourteen cutters [the most skilled of sheetmetal workers]. Today we do $25 million worth and we have one" (personal interview, 1992). Even the one cutter who is left is not an integral part of the production process but rather is there to do special jobs and repairs.

The effect of computerization on worker voice in this case is quite clear. The key skills that used to reside with the cutters, and without which no work could be done, are now bypassed and made irrelevant by the use of the computer. The ability of management to move work geographically through electronic communication and to bypass historically critical skills weakens the union's ability to threaten economic action and gives management increased power within the bargaining relationship. Similar situations occur in practically every industry.

Technological change in this country has historically been guided by, and primarily responsive to, the needs and goals of management (D. Noble 1984; Shaiken 1984; Howard 1985; Braverman 1974). Thus, the needs of the workforce for improved working conditions are generally ignored by, and often in conflict with, the predominant methods of technology design and implementation. The ability of the workers to negotiate their own futures is also increasingly undermined by the particular paths of technological change.[3]

Labor Law and Technological Change

Without delving into a historical analysis of the reasons behind the passage of the NLRA, it is safe to say that the framers of the law sought "to provide a legal climate in which the union movement could grow and operate effectively" (Taylor 1975:158). Such a climate would have to be one in which pressure could be applied on employers to be responsive to issues of importance to the workforce. Thus, the law required that employers negotiate over wages, hours, and conditions of work. The law also sought to improve the *balance of power* between labor and management, so that negotiations could be productive for both parties and increase the likelihood of industrial peace and improve the functioning of the economy: "Collective bargaining, if it was to serve the cause of industrial peace, presupposed an arrangement in which the contesting parties possessed equality in bargaining power. Should one side be very weak and the other very strong, the possibilities for industrial warfare would be increased" (Taylor 1975:158).

As discussed above, technological change has allowed management to bypass many of the pillars of workers' collective power and has thereby facilitated a significant shift in the relative strengths of labor and management. Thus, any move toward equality that was created by the passage and

3. Although, as Harry Braverman (1974) argued so persuasively, changes in technology are used to deskill the workforce and thereby to weaken collective voice, it is also true that every technological change creates a demand for new skills, particularly in a highly competitive environment. Skilling versus deskilling is not the issue. Rather, it is whether critical production skills are controlled by those who ideologically and organizationally are aligned with the needs and goals of management or with those of the workforce and whether the opportunity exists for the creation of a collective voice that can exert real power within the production process.

application of labor law is being counteracted by the rapid pace and broad scope of technological change, a change that the framers of the law did not foresee and could not have predicted. This country's labor law was developed during a time when significant or fundamental technological changes were relatively rare, at least relative to current experience.

The focus of labor law is on conditions bargaining—the right of workers to bargain over the conditions of work within the confines of the technologies of the day. The law gives workers the right to exert economic pressure, with collective voice as the mechanism:

> The central idea of section 7 is to give workers the legal right to negotiate with their employer as a group instead of as individuals. Congress created this right because individuals have little bargaining power when they deal with employers, particularly large corporations. The result of this lack of power is that workers can be forced to accept low wages and poor working conditions (Gold 1989:9).

The workforce in the United States is clearly experiencing such a lack of power, with all its consequences. The right to collective economic action exists in theory but is very difficult to apply in practice, for both political and technological reasons. Many unions, especially in industries that have successfully implemented new technologies, have reported that the right to strike has become essentially meaningless, in part because of the threat of permanent replacements, but also because of technological changes that have made it easier to transfer production or simply to keep production running using "supervisors," outside contractors, and scabs. The collective power of the workforce is not being successfully utilized, at least in part because (1) it is harder to create and maintain the collective when it is constantly being technologically altered, and (2) the collective itself, as currently defined, is losing much of its inherent strength through the mechanisms of technological change.

Although the technologically enabled power shift is a general phenomenon, there are particular sections of the labor law that are problematic during times of rapid technological change.

Mandatory Subjects of Bargaining

The list of mandatory subjects of bargaining presumably covers the issues of primary importance to the workforce. Although wages, hours, and working conditions may be the most important issues for the vast majority, it is now necessary to recognize that a primary determinant of the conditions of work, and of both wages and hours, is the technology of production, both directly and through its impact on the relative strengths of labor and management.

Thus, if the goal is to give the workforce the ability to bargain over wages, hours, and working conditions, then the ability to bargain over technology is a prerequisite.

The duty to bargain over mandatory subjects must also be analyzed in light of the relative strengths of labor and management. If their relative strengths are, as I have argued, becoming increasingly skewed by the changes in technology, then the duty to bargain becomes a hollow imperative.

Definition of Bargaining Unit

Determining the appropriate unit for bargaining is highly problematic in a time of rapid technological change. Many unions have units that are defined based on either job titles, departments, or job descriptions. All of these are at risk as technology is used to change the work that is actually done. In many cases, this leads to an erosion of the bargaining unit over time, either because work is moved outside the unit or because it is outsourced. In either case, technological advances enable this process to occur.

For new bargaining units, the standards of community of interest as defined in the NLRA and in case law are increasingly difficult to apply. Social contact and interaction are being eliminated and replaced by electronic contact. Work has become increasingly portable, untethered from the limits of geography that once existed. The form of work changes regularly, as do routes of transfer and advancement.

Under current law, for example, data entry workers in the Caribbean would certainly be ruled to have no community of interest with insurance workers in Boston, even though moving the work back to Boston is entirely feasible. The geographic dislocation of this work was made possible by advanced communication technologies. Programmers in India, who are using satellite communications linked to mainframes in the United States, could certainly be seen as the third shift of the local operation. A community of interest and social interaction with their fellow workers in the United States could be created using the same technology, but the workers do not control it (Zuboff 1988). As the relationship between the workforce and the physical manifestations of their jobs (like the assembly lines, blast furnaces, post offices, and so) is weakened, so too is the social bond and interaction that the NLRB has used as a basis for determining community of interest and appropriate bargaining unit.

Definition of Supervisor

The definition of a supervisor interacts with the definition of a bargaining unit to allow and even promote the removal of critical skills from the bargaining unit, thereby weakening the union's collective voice. In general, the definition of supervision within the act accepts the Taylorist division between "thinking supervision" and "doing workforce" (F. Taylor 1972). For example, the application of independent judgment is one of the criteria used to delineate supervisory positions. As the locus of work moves increasingly into the electronic world, removed from direct physical manipulation of materials and machines, many companies are taking advantage of the cultural and legal definitions to create new "management" positions that in another time would be called craft. At AT&T, a new class of highly skilled technicians has been created called subject matter experts, who are outside the bargaining unit but not responsible for direct supervision. Particularly as expert systems are used to take over more "routine" problems, the numbers of "nonsupervisors" who are members of the union or available to organize drops precipitously. Managers are also then available to perform critical tasks during any possible work stoppages.

Deunionization

The process of deunionization envisioned by the act is an orderly and democratic one of decertification. With advanced communication and computer technologies, many more options for deunionization have become readily available to management. Although the NLRA defines the decertification process, preventing management from removing union status without a vote, there is nothing in the law that prevents management from removing union status by moving the work. New technology has made moving work easier in many different ways.

Organizing

A somewhat less direct but exceedingly important factor in analyzing the relationship between technological change and the effectiveness of labor law is the difficulty of organizing workers in a highly technological and rapidly changing world. Any worker can see the power of technological change in their lives and the tight grip management has on the direction of technology. As long as unions are excluded from exerting influence in this crucial arena, the lessons learned by the workforce about management control over technology and the impact it has on job security, job quality, and the possibilities for worker input will stand as a barrier for workers who are contemplating organizing. If technology is a large factor in creating the future, and management controls technology, then the possibility of a positive return from unionization can seem minor compared with the risks involved in an organizing drive.

Limitations on Economic Pressure

The NLRA places limits on (or bans) the use of certain tools of economic pressure, including sitdown strikes, secondary boycotts, and sympathy strikes. At a time when the primary economic weapon, the strike, has become difficult to use and the employment relationships that are key to defining secondary boycotts and sympathy strikes have become less stable and open to manipulation, these limits condemn the workforce to a weakened position in that they increase rather than mitigate the imbalance of power in the workplace.

Suggestions for Reform

There are obviously many changes in the labor law that are needed to give workers a realistic right to bargain and improve their lives. I will focus here on suggestions for reform that will help counteract the effect of technology on the imbalance of power and that would, if implemented, give workers a better opportunity to negotiate effectively over wages, hours, and conditions of work.

Expand the mandatory subjects of bargaining. Simply put, technological change must be made a mandatory subject of bargaining. This is necessary to give unions the opportunity and ability to exert influence over key technological decisions before they are made. Only in this way will the workforce be able to bargain collectively and effectively over wages, hours, and working conditions and have a real voice in determining their own futures. And only in this way can the potential negative impact of new technologies on society as a whole be mitigated successfully.

Develop a new definition of bargaining unit. The changes in production, and therefore in social relations, have made the definition of bargaining unit at best difficult to apply and at worst a major barrier to collective voice. Shifting employment relations, new types of work, and ongoing skill realignment must all be dealt with. New definitions are needed that seek to build a larger community of interest.

Building appropriate bargaining units may also require that employers be mandated to provide employees with access to the technologies of interaction to counteract the technologically enabled destruction of community. Union bulletin boards, lunch rooms, and break rooms provided some of this sense of community in the past. Electronic mail, bulletin boards, and interactive media, all under union control, may have to provide it in the future.

Provide resources. Bargaining over technology requires expertise and effort on the part of unions. This includes the ability and focus to engage in what will, of necessity because of the nature of technological change, become continuous bargaining over technology. Without appropriate resources, unions will find it difficult to keep their issues on the table and to develop options and monitor results effectively. Although the resource imbalance between companies and unions has always been a problem, continuous bargaining will increase it several fold. Companies will continue to dominate the technology agenda.

In order to provide resources to the unions, the rules of company domination must be revisited to allow *negotiated* access to company resources to support the union's continuous bargaining activities. Forms of support would include lost time for union technology activities (to prepare for bargaining) and resources to do research on new technologies and technological options, to attend trade shows, and to hire expert support. Access to company information about trends in the industry, options in technology, and strategic plans should also be required. New forms of public support for union efforts to research technological change and to educate their members to understand and negotiate about new technology should also be created.

Care must be taken to ensure that in revisiting the rules of company domination, the company does not influence union activities and goals.[4]

Support additional forms of economic pressure. Sitdown strikes, secondary boycotts, and sympathy strikes should all be reanalyzed in terms of the new imbalance of power between labor and management and the shifting employment relationship. Other forms of economic pressure that recognize the new technological reality might include electronic picket lines (if the work is electronic, then the picket line should not be in the street) and worker control over data that are gathered by the production process (workers used to control that data because it was in their heads).

Increase limitations on deunionization. The law needs to be revised to counteract the increased ability of firms to deunionize or disorganize by moving and/or changing work. Such changes could include automatic following of work, whether it is moved geographically or shifted technologically; increased penalties for shutting a plant down or moving work; and union veto power over strategic and technological moves that are detrimental to the workforce.

Remove barriers to unionization. Union efforts to change the law to improve the chances of organizing are often dismissed as efforts to "unbalance" the labor law. Instead, they should be seen as attempts to rebalance a system that has been undermined by the increasing rate of technological change, as well as by other significant factors. Card check recognition, rapid resolution of illegal firings, and first-contract arbitration are all reforms that should be on the list. These are all discussed in greater detail elsewhere in this volume.

Strengthen the ban on company-dominated unions. The ban on company-dominated unions has to be strengthened instead of weakened. Current proposals to weaken Section 8(a)(2) seek to support management's access to workers' ideas without providing the workforce with an independent source of power and ability to bargain over the use of those ideas. As unions move into

---

4. Company influence over union goals is in fact envisioned by many promoters of total quality management and employee involvement. The role of the union is presented as one of junior partner, accepting the primacy of the goals and mission of management. See, for example, Gitlow and Gitlow 1987.

new areas of negotiation, such as new technology, the difficulty of developing, implementing, and maintaining a union agenda grows. The potential for subtle dominance by management is increased. In this environment, independence of thought, organization, and action are more, not less, important. Without these mechanisms, the discussion of change becomes, de facto, employer dominated. The ability of management to dominate the workplace and the direction of workplace change is increased by the current uses of technology. It should not be increased further by legal changes that undermine the protections that workers are now provided.

Conclusions

Technology, and in particular management's control over the course of technological change, raises a significant challenge to the labor movement in meeting its goals of negotiating improved working conditions and a voice in determining the future. Management's control also is a challenge to society's commitment to collective bargaining. Within the context of rapidly changing technology, many aspects of U.S. labor law actually stand in the way of workers having the voice they need.

Unfortunately, many of the "mainstream" proposals for labor law reform respond insufficiently to this challenge. Giving employees a forum for the discussion of issues with management, without the necessary legal support and concrete mechanisms of power, will probably provide management with what it wants, access to the workers' ideas, but is unlikely to bring significant return to the workforce. The discussion of labor law reform must be refocused based on a recognition of the reality of power in the workplace, a reality that is deeply affected by technological change.

PART V
COMPARATIVE PERSPECTIVES

16

The Canadian Perspective on Workers' Rights to Form a Union and Bargain Collectively

Gary N. Chaison and Joseph B. Rose

It is a standard practice for American proponents of labor law reform to include elements of Canadian labor policy in their proposals. They often argue that if Congress were to adopt the "Canadian approach," workers would have greater freedom in their choice of union representation and the declining fortunes of American unions would be at least partially reversed (e.g., Weiler 1983, 1984; Freeman 1988). The resiliency of Canadian unions during the turbulent 1980s is cited as evidence of the importance of a supportive legal framework (e.g., Rose and Chaison 1988, 1990; Chaison and Rose 1991a). But despite numerous analyses and proposals, the variants of the Canadian approach are seldom fully appreciated in the United States. In this chapter, we examine four prominent components of Canadian labor policy—union certification, first-contract arbitration, bans on striker replacements, and the content of collective agreements. We argue that underlying these policies are values worthy of careful consideration as labor law reform is debated in the United States.

Canadian versus American Labor Policy

In contrast to the U.S. federal system of labor relations, the constitutional division of powers in Canada establishes a decentralized system in which the federal government and the ten provincial governments have independent authority over labor relations. Nevertheless, in the early decades of the twentieth century, the practice of labor relations was regulated by Parliament rather than by the provinces. Even though there was increasing provincial

The authors thank Cara MacDonald for her excellent research assistance.

experimentation by the 1930s, the federal government set the tone for labor policy reforms and there was substantial uniformity among jurisdictions. Over the past twenty-five years or so, labor policy innovations have shifted to the provincial level, with the result that it is increasingly difficult to speak of a uniform Canadian model (Woods 1973; Weiler 1986).

The development of Canadian labor policy has been a by-product of Australian and American influences. The former influence is reflected in the Canadian system of state intervention in the negotiating process, for example, the use of compulsory conciliation in interest disputes throughout most of the twentieth century. Commentators have observed that the limitation "of early Canadian legislation was that it concentrated on protecting the public from work stoppages without providing for the protection of employees to organize, negotiate and resort to economic sanctions" (Woods et al. 1969:19).

Although Canada embraced the principles of the Wagner Act by the mid-1940s, there remained important differences in labor policy between the two countries. As described by H. D. Woods (1973:49), the American system is "concerned with establishing the framework of the relationship rather than with the actual bargaining process itself," whereas the Canadian thrust has been "with disputes, the negotiating process, and the machinery of administration of agreements." In a broad sense, the American system gives the parties substantial autonomy to fashion their bargaining relationship. In contrast, the Canadian system imposes greater restraints on work stoppages and relies on compulsory procedures for the prevention and settlement of interest and rights disputes.

Recent American Interest in Canadian Labor Policy

The recent scrutiny of Canadian labor policy in the United States was undoubtedly started by two landmark articles written by Paul Weiler. Weiler (1983) examined the limitations of the American certification election procedures and concluded that the system needed to be reformed. He proposed adoption of the Canadian method of certifying unions on the basis of either membership card counts or expedited ("instant") elections. In a companion article, Weiler (1984) addressed the broader issue of the protection of employees' bargaining rights and argued that the arbitration of first collective agreements, as practiced in some Canadian jurisdictions, "offers the strongest hope of adding teeth that have long been lacking from the enforcement of the duty to bargain in good faith" (411–12). In subsequent work, Weiler continued to argue the benefits of Canadian-American comparisons (1986) and added a ban on striker replacements to the list of suggested reforms (1990).

Apparently impressed by Weiler's analyses of organizing procedures and union membership gains in Canada, an AFL-CIO committee commented in its widely read report *The Changing Situation of Workers and Their Unions*:

> The Canadian experience is especially instructive. Canada has roughly the same type of economy, very similar employers and has undergone the same changes [e.g. labor market shifts] that we previously have described with respect to the United States. But in Canada, unlike the United States, the government has not defaulted in its obligation to protect the right of self organization; rather Canada's law carefully safeguards that right (AFL-CIO 1985:15).

Interest in Canadian labor law was clearly growing in the United States by the mid-1980s. Richard Freeman became a strong and prolific advocate of the Canadian approach, claiming, "The clearest scenario for union resurgence is enactment of labor laws comparable to those in Canada, where provincial laws essentially impose neutrality on management in organizing drives" (1987:36). Favorable evaluations of the Canadian process for union certification appeared in Freeman's analyses of union growth in the United States (e.g., Freeman 1988, 1989a, 1989b) as well as in our comparisons of the state of the unions in North America (e.g., Rose and Chaison 1985, 1990; Chaison and Rose 1991a).

New proposals for repealing the National Labor Relations Act and for shifting the locus of labor policy to the state level were based on the decentralized system in Canada. This reflected the provinces' proclivity for laws that were innovative and generally supportive of unionization (Bredhoff 1987; Freeman 1989b). Descriptions of the Canadian approach were found in congressional testimony about the limitations of American legislation (e.g., "Statement of Gary N. Chaison and Joseph B. Rose" 1992b). Canadian procedures were prominent in labor law reform bills; for example, during the last session of Congress, the proposed Workplace Democracy Act (H.R. 6041) included first-contract arbitration and union certification by membership card counts, and the Workplace Fairness Act (S. 55) restricted the hiring of striker replacements. In the following sections we discuss the innovations that have been so widely heralded in the United States.

Characteristics of Canadian Labor Policy

Certification

There are a number of distinguishing features of Canadian certification procedures, including the reliance on card counts rather than votes, provisions for expedited elections, and broader remedies for labor boards. Although there appears to be a general misunderstanding of what constitutes the Canadian approach to certification, the theme underpinning the legal framework is to allow employees to choose their bargaining agent freely, to provide a reasonably expedited procedure for doing so, and to minimize conflict over union recognition. Compared with American unions, the certification success rate is higher in Canada, protracted employer campaigns are less prevalent, and the incidence of employer unfair labor practices is lower (Rose and Chaison 1990; Chaison and Rose 1991a; Bruce 1993). Recent studies by Terry Thomason (1993, 1994) show that expedited certification procedures in Canada reduce the opportunity for employers to commit unfair labor practices aimed at influencing the employees' choice of union representation.

Although each jurisdiction provides a procedure for trade union certification, there is substantial variation across jurisdictions in the level of employee support to apply for and gain certification, whether certification is based on signed membership cards or a vote, and the authority of labor boards to certify a union automatically where there is employer misconduct. Typically, but not universally, a union must obtain a 35 to 45 percent showing of interest to apply for certification, and elections are required when membership support is between 40 and 55 percent. Several jurisdictions permit prehearing votes with a minimum showing of interest, for example, 35 to 45 percent. This allows labor boards to determine the employees' wishes close to the time of application and to resolve other matters, for example, the appropriateness of the bargaining unit, at a later date. Although certification elections are normally decided on the basis of majority support among employees casting ballots, some jurisdictions require a minimum level of voter participation (for example, 55 percent in British Columbia), while others require unions to obtain majority support from all eligible voters in the bargaining unit (George Adams 1993).

In contrast to the United States, most certifications in Canada are based on signed membership cards. Although the majority of Canadian labor boards retain a discretionary power to order a vote regardless of the level of membership support, they normally grant automatic certification when the union demonstrates majority support (50 percent plus one in most jurisdictions and 55 percent in Ontario and British Columbia). Two provinces, Alberta and Nova Scotia, require representation votes, but each relies on expedited elections essentially "to avoid the 'pitched battles' associated with lengthy American-style representation campaigns" (George Adams 1993:7–49).

Automatic certification may also result from employer misconduct during an organizing campaign. In Ontario, this may occur regardless of the level of union membership support. In contrast, the labor board in British Columbia must satisfy itself that the union would have likely achieved the requisite support in the absence of employer unfair labor practices, and in Nova Scotia, the union must achieve at least 40 percent membership support. Both Ontario and British Columbia recently adopted mandatory expedited procedures to allow their labor boards to hear and decide discipline or discharge complaints arising out of organizing drives (George Adams 1993).

First-Contract Arbitration

First-contract arbitration has been enacted in six jurisdictions covering 80 percent of the Canadian workforce. Its adoption recognized first-contract negotiations as a major source of conflict, producing 10 to 15 percent of all strikes (Labour Canada 1970–85). In addition, a committee studying labor reforms in British Columbia recently observed that "some of the most pro-tracted and bitter disputes have arisen out of the first collective agreement negotiations" (Committee of Special Advisors 1992). The original intent of the legislation was to provide a trial marriage effect, that is, to lay the foundation for establishing a mature bargaining relationship, and a deterrent effect, that is, to pressure employers to bargain with newly certified unions by raising the possibility that the labor board will impose a costly first agreement if a settlement is not reached. This labor policy initiative recognized the need for additional third-party assistance in the bargaining process to deal with what often amounted to recognition disputes (for example, the employer's refusal to accept the legitimacy of a newly certified union).

As in the case of certification, first-contract arbitration procedures vary among Canadian jurisdictions. Typically, applications are made to the appro-priate minister of labor or to the labor board, which has the discretion to refer disputes to arbitration. Manitoba is the only province where applications are automatically referred to first-contract arbitration (Sexton 1991); Ontario provides automatic access in specified circumstances (described below). There is also variation with respect to the trigger mechanism for referral to arbitra-tion (some jurisdictions require evidence of employer misconduct), whether mediation is required, whether arbitration is performed by the labor board or by private arbitrators, and the duration of first contracts (most jurisdictions impose one-year agreements; others permit two-year agreements) (George Adams 1993).

The diversity of approaches can be illustrated by comparing two systems. In Ontario, there are two methods for processing first-contract arbitrations. First, the labor board may direct the settlement of a first contract when there is evidence of employer misconduct, for example, a refusal to recognize the union's bargaining status or the adoption of uncompromising bargaining positions. Second, if an application is made to the minister of labor thirty days after the parties are in a legal position to strike or lock out, the dispute is automatically referred to arbitration. In British Columbia, an application can be made to the labor board's mediation division for a mediator following the parties' failure to achieve a first contract and the employees' authorization of a strike. If mediation fails, the mediator must report to the labor board and may recommend one or more of the following options: (1) propose terms of settlement; (2) appoint a mediator-arbitrator; (3) refer to a single arbitrator or a board of arbitration; and (4) allow the parties to resort to economic sanctions. If the parties fail to reach a settlement, the labor board directs whether the first collective agreement will be resolved by arbitration or a work stoppage (George Adams 1993).

The effectiveness of first-contract arbitration as a remedy in union recognition disputes is related to the design features of the system. Initial experience in British Columbia provided little support for the trial marriage effect—imposed first contracts were infrequently followed by renewal agreements, and unions often were decertified (Weiler 1980; Walker 1987). A recent study of first-contract statutes in Canada found the procedure did have a deterrent effect. In addition, "the Quebec and Manitoba experience suggests that the more time passes and the greater the number of cases referred, the more successful this remedy will be not only in terms of putting an end to a current dispute but also in terms of getting the parties used to each other and into a more mature and enduring relationship" (Sexton 1991:239–40). Jean Sexton suggests that the system of first-contract arbitration could be improved by making greater use of mediation-arbitration, referring cases to arbitrators rather than labor boards, and imposing longer first contracts, that is, two- or three-year agreements.

Striker Replacements

It is important to note that restrictions on the use of striker replacements have an impact beyond altering the relative power of the union and management at the bargaining table. To varying degrees, Canadian procedures preclude the employer's strategy, still available in the United States, of forcing a union into a strike, permanently replacing strikers with workers hostile to unions, and then petitioning the labor board for decertification of the union. Weiler (1990:266) observed that "although continued operation of the business during the strike has an immediate effect on the terms of the particular bargain between the parties, hiring permanent replacements puts in doubt the future of the collective bargaining relationship itself."

The ban on striker replacements is not uniformly regulated throughout Canada. Prior to the adoption of striker replacement legislation in Quebec (1978) and Ontario and British Columbia (both in 1993), the rights of strikers were protected in two broad ways. First, six jurisdictions provided for either the reinstatement of strikers once a collective agreement was concluded or made it an unfair labor practice if the employer failed to do so (Labour Canada 1993). Second, three jurisdictions prohibited the use of professional strikebreakers. Currently, only Quebec and Ontario prohibit the use of striker replacements and guarantee strikers their positions at the conclusion of a work stoppage (George Adams 1993).

Restrictions on the use of striker replacements and on the performance of bargaining unit work vary among the three provinces with protective legislation. This undoubtedly reflects an attempt to achieve a balance of interests, that is, the desire to protect vulnerable groups of employees and minimize strike violence on the one hand and to provide employers with some flexibility to continue operations on the other (Ontario Ministry of Labour 1991). In British Columbia and Quebec, the restriction on striker replacements is commensurate with a work stoppage, whereas in Ontario the provision also requires the union to obtain 60 percent support in a secret-ballot strike vote (George Adams 1993).

As a general rule, all three provinces prohibit the use of "outside" workers as striker replacements. Bans apply to employees (including managerial staff) from other facilities operated by the struck employer and to individuals employed, engaged, or supplied by another person, including subcontractors. Differences exist with respect to regulating the staff of the facility experiencing a work stoppage. Although all three provinces ban employees hired after the commencement of bargaining from working as striker replacements, only Quebec and Ontario have blanket prohibitions on bargaining unit members working during a stoppage. In British Columbia, strikers and nonbargaining unit employees (including managerial staff) may individually agree to work during a stoppage. The law stipulates that there can be no reprisals against employees who refuse to perform struck work. Ontario and Quebec permit managerial staff at a struck facility voluntarily to act as replacements. Quebec also prohibits the contracting out and/or relocation of struck work to other facilities (permissible in both Ontario and British Columbia). All three provinces make exceptions for emergency situations and essential services, so that, for example, the parties or the labor board (or other agency) may designate employees to provide for the continuation of essential services (British Columbia Ministry of Labour 1992; Ontario Ministry of Labour 1992a; George Adams 1993).

There is some evidence of the effects of replacements on strikes in Canada. For example, a recent Ontario survey found that a majority of work stoppages involved the use of replacement workers, the average strike lasted longer when striker replacements were used, and only a small percentage of these disputes involved major violence (Haywood 1992). It has been more difficult to isolate the impact of striker replacement legislation on strike activity. Evidence from Quebec has been inconclusive about the effects of banning replacements on the incidence of strikes and their duration (Gunderson and Melino 1990; Ontario Ministry of Labour 1991). Anecdotal evidence suggests that picket line violence and hostility declined and that the collective bargaining climate improved. Perhaps these broad generalizations are all that can be expected given the laws were adopted only recently and the difficulties of establishing cause and effect. As noted in Ontario, restricting the use of striker replacements has been justified on the basis that replacement workers contribute to "bitter and violent confrontations" that reduce the parties' willingness to "engage in meaningful and effective collective bargaining" and discourage unionization among employees who are most vulnerable to replacement, that is, "relatively unskilled and economically insecure workers" (Ontario Ministry of Labour 1991:32). Clearly, research is required to determine empirically whether these outcomes have been achieved.

Content of Collective Agreements

There are two broad differences in the Canadian approach to the scope of bargainable issues. First, Canadian labor boards have rejected the American distinction between mandatory and permissive subjects of collective bargaining. As a result, virtually any issue may be pursued to impasse. Second, there are statutory requirements regarding the content of collective agreements. For example, collective agreements typically must contain a minimum one-year duration clause, a union recognition clause, and, with the exception of Saskatchewan, a clause providing for the final and binding resolution of grievances (rights arbitration).

There are also some differences in the collective agreement requirements across jurisdictions. Most jurisdictions do not prevent the parties from negotiating union security clauses making union membership a condition of employment. Dues checkoff is regulated, albeit in different ways. Five jurisdictions require compulsory dues checkoff, and the remainder require the employer to deduct and remit dues to the union when individual employees authorize it. In five jurisdictions, collective agreements must contain a technological change provision dealing with such issues as advance notice and disputes procedures (George Adams 1993).

This brief review indicates that labor policy in Canada is both interventionist and normative. There is a tendency not only to remove selected items from the bargaining process but to establish uniform standards for collective agreements. Note that where the parties fail to satisfy the statutory requirements for certain issues, for example, grievance arbitration and technological change, the model clauses specified in the legislation are deemed to form part of the collective agreement. In one sense, the Canadian approach tends to narrow the scope of bargaining by disallowing negotiations below the minimum standards. Overall, by establishing minimum requirements for collective agreements and not restricting the scope of negotiable subjects, Canadian labor policy seeks to minimize conflicts over the boundaries of collective bargaining.

Conclusions

Our brief discussion of Canadian labor policy should dispel any beliefs that there is a unitary Canadian model. As Weiler (1986) observed, the Canadian provinces have become laboratories for labor law innovation, experimenting within their borders and adopting and modifying procedures that proved successful elsewhere. In a decentralized system, labor laws also reflect regional interests and the relative power of labor and management organizations.

Despite these differences, we do see common values underlying the procedures for union certification, first-contract arbitration, striker replacements, and the content of collective agreements. The Canadian approach is predicated on the unfettered freedom of choice of employees to select unionism and the pursuit of this objective through state intervention in union-management relations. Furthermore, Canadian jurisdictions explicitly recognize the interrelatedness of the four features discussed earlier; that is, the meaningful expression of employee free choice extends well beyond union certification and includes the negotiation of first agreements and the ability to strike.

In all likelihood, the strongly interventionist character of Canadian labor policy would prove objectionable to American lawmakers, employer groups, and perhaps even some unions. It is important to recall that Canadians have become conditioned to state intervention in labor relations through a system of compulsory conciliation that dates back to the turn of this century. We believe, however, that the Canadian experience can help define the basic contours of labor law reform in the United States. Too often, debates over reform proposals are sidetracked by questions of how to balance the power of labor and management (creating a level playing field or "correcting the tilt against labor" ["Senate Vote Kills Bill" 1992:647]) or questions of whether public policy has led to union membership declines and if new laws can create a resurgence (e.g., Troy 1993). Proposals tend to be evaluated in terms of the countervailing rights of unions and employers or the potential changes in union membership. The Canadian approach provides an opportunity to redirect the debate because it emphasizes the employees' right to select union representation, rather than the outcome of that choice in union strength or size. There will always be disagreements about the portability of specific Canadian procedures and the appropriate degree of state intervention in the establishment of bargaining relationships, but can there be any doubt about the compatibility of the values implicit in the Canadian approach and the fundamental principles of American labor law?

17

Reforming U.S. Labor Law and Collective Bargaining: Some Proposals Based on the Canadian System

Richard N. Block

The divergence in unionization rates between the United States and Canada has been increasing over the last thirty-five years. In 1955, both countries had rates of about 32 and 33 percent. In 1991, the rate in Canada stood at approximately 33 percent, while the U.S. rate was about 16 percent (Chaison and Rose 1991b; Chaykowski and Verma 1992; "Union Membership Unchanged" 1992).[1]

Seymour Martin Lipset (1989) explains the divergence by what he believes is the antistatist and individualistic culture in the United States and the more statist and more collectivistic culture in Canada. Peter G. Bruce (1989) and Noah Meltz (1989) argue that the parliamentary system in Canada is more susceptible to the political pressure that unions can exert through a third party than the two-party, separation-of-powers system in the United States.

Most of the work on this paper was completed while the author was a research associate at the Centre for Industrial Relations at the University of Toronto. The research was supported by the Canadian Studies Centre at Michigan State University and the Centre for Industrial Relations at the University of Toronto. The author would like to thank Roy Adams, Peter Bruce, Donald Carter, Richard Chaykowski, Morley Gunderson, Pradeep Kumar, Joseph Rose, and participants in seminars at the Industrial Relations Centre, Queen's University, the Centre for Industrial Relations, University of Toronto, and the School of Labor and Industrial Relations and Canadian Studies Centre, Michigan State University, for helpful comments on an earlier draft of this paper.

1. Leo Troy (1992) has argued that private-sector unionization in the two countries is converging and that the major reason for the higher rate of unionization in Canada compared with the United States is the higher rate in the Canadian public sector. Although this observation is accurate, the rationale for distinguishing between the public and private sectors in Canada is much less compelling than the rationale for making this distinction in the United States. The provincial laws in Canada generally cover both public- and private-sector employers (George Adams 1985). In the United States, by contrast, with the exception of the U.S. postal service, public employees are not covered by the NLRA.

Weiler (1990) argues that the U.S. unionization process, with its lengthy election campaign and minimal penalties for employer unfair labor practices, places a very heavy burden on unions.

In contrast to the macro approaches of Lipset, Bruce, and Meltz and the micro approach of Weiler,[2] this chapter will stake out a middle ground. It will be argued that the differences in unionization rates are due in part to industrial relations legal institutions that have institutionalized collective bargaining in Canada to a greater extent than in the United States. I will analyze these institutions and present some policy proposals based on these institutional differences.

U.S. versus Canadian System

What are the differences between the United States and Canada that may have contributed to the differential rates of unionization?[3] An analysis of the Canadian legal system suggests at least five differences that are relevant: (1) the method of processing unfair labor cases, (2) the role of judicial review, (3) tripartitism, (4) evolution by legislation, and (5) government involvement in collective bargaining.

Processing of Unfair Labor Practice Cases

The processing of unfair labor practice cases under the NLRA is controlled by the general counsel, who has unreviewable authority to issue complaints on unfair labor practice charges (Hardin 1992). Board regional offices investigate all such charges. Approximately 70 percent of charges are found to be "without merit" (NLRB annual reports 1976–91) and are either withdrawn or dismissed. If the charge has "merit," it will be settled (about 24 percent of all cases for the period 1976–91) or a complaint will be issued and the case taken to the board (about 6 to 7 percent of all cases for the period 1976–91) (NLRB annual reports 1976–91).

In Canada, case processing is quite different. In Ontario, for example, the Ontario Labour Relations Board (OLRB) will examine a charge and attempt to obtain a settlement or voluntary withdrawal. During 1980–92, 59.4 percent of all cases were settled, and 21.1 percent of all charges were with-

2. Like Weiler, Bruce, and Lipset, I essentially make the argument that the differences in the unionization rates in the two countries are due primarily to differences in societal institutions that enhance unionization. W. Craig Riddell (1993) estimated that only about 15 percent of the differences in unionization rates between the two countries was due to labor force occupational structures and that the remainder was due to the greater likelihood that a given worker would be unionized.

3. A full discussion of the similarities and differences between U.S. and Canadian labor law is beyond the scope of this chapter. For such a discussion, see Weiler 1983 and 1990.

drawn (OLRB annual reports 1980–92). If a settlement or withdrawal is not forthcoming, the case is sent through the normal board processes. There is no procedure for a dismissal at the investigation stage.[4]

The problems associated with the general counsel system can be illustrated by a hypothetical employer who wishes to test an interpretation of the NLRA. The employer can act on its interpretation. If no complaint is issued, the employer prevails. If a complaint is issued, the employer can make its case before the board and other appropriate tribunals (Block and Wolkinson 1986).

Unions, by contrast, generally must wait for the employer to act and then file a charge. If the charge is found to be without merit, no complaint will be issued. Thus, the union has no independent means of getting a good-faith interpretation of the law litigated.[5] Although unions may have their rights explored for them if the general counsel believes that the law is ambiguous or that the courts of appeals are in error, this is a decision for the general counsel rather than for the union.[6]

The Canadian systems provide no official screen on the cases. Thus, Canadian unions have an access advantage into their legal system not possessed by their U.S. counterparts. The implications of this difference are illustrated in table 17.1, which presents average annual data on the percentage of cases closed informally and with a formal proceeding. The data from the NLRB are for all cases closed for the fiscal period 1976–90. The data from Ontario are for cases involving "contravention of the act" for fiscal 1981–92; from British Columbia, "unfair labor practices" for fiscal 1977–91; and for Canada, "unfair labor practices" from fiscal 1975–92.

Only a small fraction of the cases in the United States actually receive a full hearing before the board; more than 90 percent are closed at the regional level. This suggests that cases that could result in a change in the law that might be more favorable to unions do not receive a hearing. In the Canadian jurisdictions, only 59 to 81 percent of the cases were closed without a hearing, suggesting that unions in Canada can get their issues aired more easily. The preferred access of employers in the United States would be expected to

---

4. Bruce (1990) has also commented on these differences in case processing procedure between the NLRB and Canadian labor boards, specifically in Ontario.

5. Although, in theory, the union would have the same privileges as employers in secondary activity cases, such cases receive high-priority processing. If the general counsel believes the charge has merit, Section 10(l) requires that an injunction must be sought halting the activity. See Block and Wolkinson 1986.

6. This occurred between 1956 and 1989 as the board dealt with the issue of whether union organizers have right of access to the employer's property. See, for example, Block, Wolkinson, and Kuhn 1988 and Avery 1989.

Table 17.1. Percentage of Canadian and U.S. Cases Disposed of Informally and Formally (annual averages)

Jurisdiction	Closed without formal hearing	Closed with formal hearing
United States (1976–90)	93.4	6.6
Ontario (1981–92)	81.2	18.8
British Columbia 1977–91	62.9	37.1
Federal jurisdiction, Canada (1975–91)	59.0	41.0

Sources: Annual reports of the NLRB, Ontario Labour Relations Board, and Canada Labour Relations Board for years noted; annual reports of the Labour Relations Board of British Columbia, 1977–85, and annual reports of the British Columbia Industrial Relations Council, 1986–91.

Note: Canadian labor board data are not comparable to NLRB data. All NLRB unfair labor practices cases are listed as "C" (charge) cases. The Canadian boards provide data on unfair labor practice cases but provide separate data on such issues as refusal to bargain, which would be subsumed in C cases in the United States. This analysis uses only unfair labor practice cases in Canada and British Columbia and contravention cases in Ontario. These cases generally represent practices involving union organizing that are unfair labor practices in the United States, that are generally comparable across jurisdictions in Canada, and account for the overwhelming majority of the noncertification nonconstruction industry case load in these Canadian jurisdictions.

permit the industrial relations system to drift more toward their interests in the United States than in Canada.[7]

Judicial Review

Under the NLRA, a party aggrieved by a decision of the board may appeal to the court of appeals. Alternatively, the board must request enforcement by the court of appeals. Although judicial review is also available in Canada, courts in the United States have taken a far more active role in reviewing the actions of the NLRB than courts in Canada have in reviewing the actions of the Canadian boards.[8]

Table 17.2 illustrates the greater activism of courts in the industrial relations system in the United States compared with Canada. It provides data on cases closed by court action as a percentage of unfair labor practice cases or contravention cases (Ontario). In reality, the percentages for Canada are even smaller relative to comparable U.S. data, since the former data exclude cases in

7. Block and Benjamin W. Wolkinson (1986) tracked NLRB nondecertification representation election outcomes during the period 1936–81. Their analysis shows a correspondence between the expansion of employer rights in election campaigns and the decline in the percentage of elections won by unions.

8. This discussion of judicial review is consistent with that of Bruce 1990.

Table 17.2. Total Canadian and U.S. Labor Cases Closed with Court Decisions as a Percentage of Unfair Labor Practice Cases Disposed of/Closed with Formal Hearing (annual averages)

U.S. National Labor Relations Board, 1976–90 (compliance orders)	32.2 (C cases)
	33.6 (CA cases)
U.S. National Labor Relations Board, 1976–90 (dismissals)	8 (C cases)
	8 (CA cases)
Ontario Labour Relations Board, 1980–81 to 1991–92 ("contravention of act")	7.1
British Columbia Industrial Relations Council, 1988–91	5.2
Canada, federal jurisdiction, 1980–91	6.4

Sources: Annual reports of National Labor Relations Board, Ontario Labour Relations Board, British Columbia Industrial Relations Council, and Canada Labour Relations Board for years noted.

British Columbia and the federal jurisdiction involving violations of the duty to bargain. The U.S. data, by contrast, contain all unfair labor practices.

Litigation occurs in about one-third of all NLRB cases closed with a compliance order (a finding that the respondent, usually the employer, has violated the act), while the rate of litigation in the Canadian jurisdictions is from one-fifth to one-seventh as much, even with these very high Canadian estimates. Why is this the case? In Canada, parliamentary supremacy provides the legislatively established labor relations boards with substantial status. The role of the courts is to ensure that the boards stay within their jurisdiction and do not violate the procedural rights of the parties (Carrothers, Palmer, and Raynor 1986). All the statutes give the labor relations boards exclusive jurisdiction to make determinations essential to collective bargaining. Most of the Canadian statutes have privative clauses, which generally limit the scope of judicial review in labor board cases (Carrothers, Palmer, and Raynor 1986).

Courts in the United States, however, have generally been willing to review board decisions based not only on whether the decision is supported by substantial evidence on the record as a whole but also on whether the board has interpreted the NLRA consistent with the intent of Congress. Although the NLRB's sole role is to interpret the NLRA, the courts have the authority to interpret the NLRA in the context of other well-established legal and constitutional principles (Block and Wolkinson 1986).

For example, in cases involving union access to the employer's property (*NLRB v. Babcock and Wilcox W,* 351 U.S. 105 (1956)), although the board consistently attempted to balance the rights of unions and employers, the courts have generally analyzed the cases in a trespass and private property framework, reducing the access of unions (Block and Wolkinson 1986; Avery 1989). The general narrowing of the scope of the employer's duty to bargain over business decisions affecting employment, a 1960s line of cases culminating in the Supreme Court's rejection of a board decision in *First National Maintenance* (452 U.S. 666 (1981)), was the result of a series of court decisions in the 1960s and 1970s that overturned more expansive board interpretations of the scope of bargaining.[9] Essentially, courts have generally been unwilling to adopt board decisions that would grant rights to unions that infringe upon traditional employer property rights in the absence of clear statutory language that it was the intent of Congress to grant unions such rights (Atleson 1983; Block and Wolkinson 1986; Avery 1989; *Lechmere Inc. v. NLRB*, 139 L.R.R.M. 2225 (U.S. Sup. Ct. 1992)).

Such court behavior provides an incentive for employer aggressiveness. This provides an explanation for the much greater frequency of appeals (usually by employers) on compliance cases than on dismissals.

Further understanding of the reason for employer aggressiveness under the NLRA can be seen by examining case disposition data. As noted, the board dismisses or obtains a withdrawal of 70 percent of all unfair labor practice charges against employers. This implies that, if the employer can make a good-faith argument, the chances are only about 30 percent that a complaint will be issued. Board decisions result in a finding of a violation only 69 percent of the time (NLRB annual reports). In the courts, for the period in question, the board claims that its position prevails, in whole or in part, in about 83 percent of cases (NLRB annual reports 1976–91). Based on these numbers, the probability of ultimate employer success in a representative unfair labor practice case is about 83 percent (1-(.30*.69*.83)). This analysis indicates that employer appeals can substantially increase the probability that an employer will prevail in the case.

Tripartitism

Although both the United States and Canada use labor relations boards as the primary means for adjudicating disputes over the interpretation of labor laws, the compositions of the boards differ. The NLRB is composed of political appointees with five-year terms, while seven Canadian provinces have tripartite boards consisting of representatives of labor, management, and the public (George Adams 1993).[10] This difference results in substantially different institutional outcomes (Meltz 1990; George Adams 1993).

The NLRB is a quasi-judicial, neutral adjudicative body. The tripartite provincial boards, however, include representatives of the parties. Tripartitism

9. See, for example, *Hawaii Meat Co. v. NLRB*, 321 F.2d 397 (CA 9, 1963); *NLRB v. Adams Dairy Co.*, 350 F.2d 108 (CA 8, 1966); and *Ozark Trailers, Inc.*, 161 N.L.R.B. 561 (1966).

10. Ontario, Manitoba, British Columbia, Newfoundland, Saskatchewan, Nova Scotia, and New Brunswick have tripartite boards. Alberta, Prince Edward Island, and the federal jurisdiction have nonpartisan boards. Quebec has its own system of labour courts (George Adams 1985).

increases the chances that both parties will have their cases and point of views understood. It also enhances the chances that the result will be accepted, since the losing party knows there will be a representative of its point of view hearing the case. As George W. Adams notes, "The tripartite regulatory approach in Canada permitted the manning of the dispute resolution machinery, at least in part, by labour and management representatives and in this way created a commitment in the parties of interest to the workability of the system" (1985:219.) The NLRB, which addresses rights issues, has no obligation to make the collective bargaining *system* workable.

Legislation

The NLRA has seldom been amended, having undergone major amendments only in 1947, 1958, and 1974. Indeed, it was not designed to be frequently amended, since the NLRB, composed of presidential appointees who must receive Senate confirmation, was the means of adjusting the administration of the NLRA to the changing political consensus.

Practice, however, has not conformed to the administrative model. Because of a lack of union access to the NLRB and court decisions that have narrowed the board's influence, the United States has seen a continuing movement toward employer interests in the labor law system, with little opportunity to adjust the system the other way. There has been an atrophying of the mechanisms for striking the balance among employer, union, and employee interests.

In Canada, the provinces continually amend their collective bargaining laws (Bruce 1989; George Adams 1993) as employer and union influence increases and decreases with the changing political consensus in Canada. For example, through 1985, Alberta amended its statute in 1947, 1950, 1954, 1957, 1960, 1964, 1968, 1970, 1973, 1974, 1975, 1980, 1987, 1983, and 1988. All of the other provinces demonstrate similar patterns (Kumar, Coates, and Arrowsmith 1989; Coates 1991; "BC Moves to New Labor Bill" 1992; Ontario Ministry of Labour 1992b; George Adams 1993). Although not all of the amendments are of equal importance, the frequency of amendments demonstrates a vibrant industrial relations legal system in Canada in which both parties are able to have their interests represented and the laws do not tilt too far in either direction for too long a period of time. In essence, Canada has developed a system of "normal maintenance" of the industrial relations system through legislation that does not exist in the United States.

Government Involvement in Collective Bargaining

In the United States, there is generally minimal government involvement in contract negotiations and labor conflict. Canada, however, presents a somewhat different picture. New Brunswick, Prince Edward Island, Nova

Scotia, Newfoundland, Ontario, and the federal jurisdiction all require conciliation as a precondition to a legal strike or lockout. Most Canadian jurisdictions require strike votes before a legal strike may be authorized (George Adams 1993). Six jurisdictions have provisions for first-agreement arbitration, and Canadian statutes often impose requirements on the content of agreements (George Adams 1993; Chaison and Rose, chap. 16).

Although designed to curb strikes (Gunderson, Kervin, and Reid 1989), such government involvement also implies that the government has an obligation to protect collective bargaining and the integrity of the parties. The Canadian legal structures provide a monitor and constraints on the parties' behavior during negotiations. Although they cannot prevent outcomes from being primarily a function of bargaining power, government pressure makes it difficult for Canadian employers who have bargaining power to use the bargaining process to eliminate the collective bargaining relationship.

Policy Proposals for the United States

The foregoing discussion suggests that the greater unionization rate in Canada is at least in part associated with the legal and institutional structure, which is far more supportive of collective bargaining than the legal and institutional structure in the United States. To what extent can the lessons from Canada provide a basis for policy changes in the United States? In this section, I will develop several broad proposals for a new structure of labor law institutions in the United States based on the foregoing discussion.

Proposal: Reconstitute the NLRB as a tripartite national body with regional boards. It is proposed that the NLRB be reconstituted as a tripartite decision-making body with regional boards modeled on the World War II War Labor Board. The current board structure of administrative law judges should be replaced with a structure of regional boards based on the regional structure of the War Labor Board.[11]

This change would shift the U.S. industrial relations legal system from sole reliance on a model that adjudicates rights to a model that also has a practical dispute resolution component. It would bring management and union perspectives to unfair labor practice charges and ensure that practical problems and concerns of both parties are addressed. It would increase voluntarism and reduce the amount of legalism in the system by making sure that the views of both sides are represented in disputes.

11. See, for example, *The Termination Report* (1947), especially vol 1; Witte 1946; Taylor 1948, especially chaps. 3–4.

Actual investigation, resolution, and adjudication would be done at the regional level by the regional board. Regionalization would encourage speed in decision-making and thus resolution of the dispute or, if necessary, a decision in the dispute closer to the parties while still being made by a tripartite body.[12]

Proposal: Abolish the general counsel, permitting all parties access to board procedures; add priority processing for cases involving charges of unlawful discharge under Section 8(a)(3). The purpose of this change would be to provide all parties equal access to board procedures while still retaining priority handling for those cases involving parties not involved in the primary labor dispute. Priority processing for charges alleging discriminatory discharge should be added to the act to minimize wage losses for the employee and the back-pay liability for the employer. Since there would no longer be a merit determination, the Section 10(l) injunction would be eliminated in these cases. Presumably, priority processing of secondary activity cases and the expeditious handling of cases by the regional boards should mean that cases would be processed in a timely manner.

Proposal: Make regional board orders immediately effective and automatically enforceable by a court; narrow the scope of judicial review of national board decisions to whether the board has jurisdiction over the case and whether the board granted the appellant due process. This change would increase the status and importance of the NLRB by limiting the scope of judicial review of board decisions to a scope similar to that used in Canada. It would help ensure that industrial relations problems and issues are addressed and resolved by the NLRB, the body that is most expert in industrial relations and represents all interests in industrial relations. Making regional board orders immediately effective and enforceable by a court eliminates the possibility of delay and also the need for costly enforcement proceedings.

Proposal: Include in the legislation a statement that the new NLRB is not bound by a previous decision of the board or any court. The purpose of this proposal is to permit the reconstituted board to reexamine all labor law doctrines without being constrained by previous board, court of appeals, or Supreme Court

---

12. The advantages and disadvantages of tripartism vis-à-vis neutral adjudication have been the subjects of much debate. The basic strength of tripartism is its participatory aspects. Its major weaknesses are that it is inefficient compared with neutral adjudication. It should be pointed out, however, that the current neutral NLRB has been severely criticized for delays. For a discussion of tripartism, see *Termination Report* 1947:xvii–xix (George W. Taylor, "Voluntarism, Tripartitism and Wage Stabilization") and 571–781 ("Reports from the Regions") and Taylor 1948.

decisions. It will provide employers and unions with the opportunity to argue that old doctrines should be changed or retained. The tripartite board would ensure that persons who have experiences similar to the parties' would be hearing the case. Releasing the reconstituted NLRB from precedent would, over a period of several years, probably develop a system that is fair to all parties and takes into account the needs and interests of employers and unions.

Proposal: Create a standing tripartite national labor law commission that would make periodic recommendations to the board and to Congress regarding changes in the provisions of the NLRA, in interpretations of existing provisions, and in board procedure. The creation of a tripartite national labor law commission is designed to provide the United States with the "normal maintenance" of the labor law system that is provided by the parliamentary system in Canada. Since the courts would no longer be providing substantial oversight of decisions of the reconstituted NLRB, there would need to be a mechanism for parties dissatisfied with doctrines developed by the board to make their views known and to have those views acted on, if appropriate. The commission could take comments from interested parties on the state of the NLRA as interpreted by the NLRB but could act on its own as well. If the commission believed the comments that changes in doctrines or the law were warranted, it could so recommend to the board and to Congress.

Proposal: Give the regional board the option to direct the Federal Mediation and Conciliation Service to mediate a dispute in which there has been a charge of unlawful refusal to bargain. This change would give the reconstituted board a vehicle to ensure the institutional integrity of both parties in refusal-to-bargain cases and aid the parties in carrying out bargaining when the board believed such support was needed. It would help ensure that the bargaining process will not be used by a union to place undue burdens on an employer or by an employer to undermine the status of a union.

Conclusions

This paper has attempted to explore differences between industrial relations institutions in the United States and Canada and how those differences may affect the level of unionization. It also developed some policy proposals for the United States based on the Canadian systems and the U.S. experience with the World War II War Labor Board. The focus of these proposals has been on process and institutions; if the processes and institutions are well conceived, the interests of employers and unions will be well protected. If this work can expand the focus of U.S. debate on labor law reform from primarily rights to rights and institutions, it will have accomplished its purpose.

18

Union Certification as an Instrument of Labor Policy: A Comparative Perspective

Roy J. Adams

In comparative perspective, the North American practice of union certification is very unusual. Generally, other countries do not divide the labor force into tiny bargaining units and do not require representatives of employee interests to win the support of the majority of employees in each microunit to acquire government support for recognition. This chapter briefly reviews the genesis, justification, and experience with certification and compares the North American experience with functional equivalents in Europe (especially Britain, Germany, and Sweden) with a view toward suggesting alternatives to North American practice.

Theory of Certification

In 1918, the United States National War Labor Board (NWLB) investigated the labor unrest that was holding up war production at the Bethlehem Steel Company. The board found that the troubles were due primarily to the refusal of Bethlehem's management to deal collectively with its employees. It insisted on dealing with workers individually. After futile attempts at mediating a settlement, the board imposed it own solution. The award called for the establishment of shop committees, with policy-making responsibilities, in each department. The committees would, for example, be responsible for negotiating piece rates. The award also called for the creation of a "mediation board," composed of three representatives elected by the employees, three chosen by management, and a neutral chair appointed by the secretary of war, whose duty it would be to settle all "disputed issues not covered by the award," with final appeal to the NWLB itself (Conner 1983:123). Although the labor board had no formal powers of enforcement, during the war the

Wilson administration stood behind it with a threat to intervene up to commandeering the factories of recalcitrant employers—a threat that it carried out in a few cases. In short, the mediation board would have wide discretion to negotiate terms and conditions of employment, and the NWLB in effect assumed the power to arbitrate impasses.

In addition to establishing the new structures, the board forbade Bethlehem management from discriminating against employees for involvement in a union or for otherwise becoming active on behalf of employee interests. This award, according to one student of the era, provided the unions at Bethlehem with "the unencumbered right to organize" (Conner 1983:123). Since they could run candidates for the committees and mediation board, and since impasses on these bodies could be settled in the last resort by an impartial referee, the award provided the unions with an effective method to achieve recognition and to bargain collectively.[1]

Along with an earlier award at General Electric, the Bethlehem solution stood as the model that the NWLB used to introduce "industrial democracy" at many companies during the war. The model was the result of a compromise between the patterns of relations sought by employers and unions. The unions much preferred bargaining in the context of the closed union shop. Employers preferred what they sometimes called the "open shop" but more accurately has been described as the "closed nonunion shop"—a company or plant in which the employees were not permitted to be members of an "outside union," although they might be able to participate in a company-sponsored employee representation plan.

During the world war period the government of Woodrow Wilson sought a national consensus. Toward that end, it adopted the policy that it would back neither the closed union shop nor the closed nonunion shop, but it insisted that employers must agree to cooperate with employee representatives in order to avoid conflict and maximize production for the war effort. The Bethlehem Steel award was the model that put substance into the policy.

Note that the NWLB did not conduct an election at Bethlehem to determine whether or not the employees wanted collective representation. It was obvious to all involved that the problem was the absence of effective participative mechanisms, not the absence of a will to democratic participation. Indeed, the report of the National Commission on Industrial Relations, which appeared in 1915, had emphatically stated that American democracy was tainted by the persistence of industrial autocracy and called for the establishment of a labor policy that would result in democratic participation throughout industry

1. Unfortunately, the arrangement was not given a fair opportunity to succeed. Bethlehem's management temporized until the end of the war, when the labor board became ineffective and was disbanded. Absent government pressure, Bethlehem terminated the scheme imposed by the board.

(Graham Adams 1966; Conner 1983). In this call, the commission echoed a similar proposition made some twenty years earlier by the U.S. Industrial Commission.

When the World War I period dawned, a broad consensus had emerged that all employees should be able to participate in the making of the decisions under which they labored (Derber 1970). There was, however, no consensus on how that principle should be put into practice. The dominant position among employers was that there should be mechanisms composed entirely of representatives chosen by and from enterprise employees rather than from national unions. The justification was that "outside unions" had no interest in the welfare of the enterprise and thus were likely to have a disruptive effect on productivity and competitiveness. The solution offered by this group to the participation imperative was the establishment voluntarily by companies of employee representation plans.[2]

The compromise position worked out by the NWLB for the contrary stances of labor and management was acceptable to the American Federation of Labor. The AFL felt confident that under a "true open shop" system in which employees were free to join or not join but in which employers did not discriminate against those who became active in a union, the free and independent labor organizations would be able to convince the enfranchised employees to vote for union activists and, by demonstrating their ability, attract most employees to their ranks. Employers were not so confident of maintaining control of employment relations under such a system and thus shortly made new demands. At its conference in October 1918, the National Industrial Conference Board (NICB) stated that its members would tolerate what they called "cooperative representation" (rather than collective bargaining) only if the majority of employees entitled to vote requested such a system by voting in favor of it in an election held on company premises (Conner 1983:137). Since the NICB was the organization that nominated the management representatives to the NWLB, its views had considerable influence on that agency; and in the later months of its existence. it began to resort to representation elections (Taylor and Witney 1987:143). In the 1930s, when the first National Labor Board was established under the National Industrial Recovery Act, it drew upon this experience to hold elections when the majority status of a bargaining agent was in doubt (Taylor and Witney 1987:152). Later, the majority principle was embedded in the Wagner Act.

2. Although employee representation plans and company unions are often considered equivalent, it is better to treat them as separate phenomena. In many companies with employer-established representation schemes, independent unions competed with employer-sponsored company unions for seats on the council or committee. In the steel industry, for example, independent unions often were able to dominate the councils and thus use that means to take over the employee representation function from the company-favored internal union.

This story is instructive for at least a few reasons. First, the process of certification has been used in North America for so long now that it sometimes seems to be an immutable part of the institutional landscape. It should be viewed, however, as a choice to which there are alternatives. Certification is not the only method available for operationalizing the stated policy of the government to encourage the practice and procedure of collective bargaining. Second, the story illustrates several themes that were current earlier in the century not only in the United States but also in many of the other nations of the developing West. In all of the countries under popular control (those controlled by democratic rather than autocratic regimes) during the World War I period, governments pursued a policy of consensus, and within that context there was a general acceptance that working people should be recognized to be full citizens both in the political sphere (the adult franchise was made universal in several countries during this period) and in the industrial sphere. The United States was not an exception, but the specific means of operationalizing the principle was different in America from the methods adopted elsewhere. Only in the United States and later in Canada was certification used as a key element of policy implementation.

After a deep depression early in the 1920s, the thrust toward democratization waned as attention focused on economic problems, but it reappeared and gathered considerable momentum in several countries, including the United States, in the 1930s and 1940s. One result was the adoption in America of a policy intended to encourage the practice of collective bargaining and the passage of legislation designed to accomplish that end. Certification was a major instrument included as part of that legislation.

Today in the United States, certification is not a controversial issue. Trade unions would like to have easier access to unorganized employees, stronger guarantees of freedom of choice, and a speedier, less juridified process. But there is no call for doing away with certification altogether. Nor do organizations representing employer interests seek the repeal of certification. For the unions, certification results in compulsory collective bargaining, backed by a government agency with powers to compel an intransigent employer to enter into negotiations with a view toward signing a written collective agreement. Since achieving recognition for the purposes of collective bargaining is extremely difficult even with the aid of a government agency with substantial enforcement powers, without the aid of such an agency it would no doubt be much more difficult. Since certification leads to legal orders requiring reluctant employers to enter into negotiations, it is generally looked on as a pro-union policy invention. As noted above, however, it was first called for by employer spokespeople and for good reason. From the point of view of the nonunion employer seeking to maintain the status quo, certification has some outstanding positive traits.

First of all, American policy as it has evolved to the present permits the employer to contest employee representation campaigns.[3] Although the National Labor Relations Board when it was first created often certified unions on the basis of membership evidence or the signing of bargaining authorization cards, employers insisted that these methods were prone to abuse and that there should always be a vote (Millis and Brown 1950:133). During World War II votes were most often consent elections in which the employer did not actively oppose the establishment of collective bargaining (Millis and Brown 1950; Friedman and Prosten 1993). Commonly, the major purpose of the election was to establish which one of competing unions the employees wanted for their representative.

After the war, however, employers more often contested the elections. The Taft-Hartley Act gave them the explicit go-ahead to make use of their constitutional "right of free speech" to oppose unionization. Since they have had a great deal of power to affect the welfare of the employee for good or for ill, employers have had a major advantage in this contest; and over the years, as they have perfected their methods of opposing certification, they have become increasingly successful in winning elections (Goldfield 1987; Lawler 1990; Weiler 1990). Even though certification proceedings are only begun in situations in which there is considerable employee discontent with management policy and in situations in which the unions involved believe they have a very good chance of success, nevertheless, today in the United States, aggressive employers win most representation elections (Friedman and Prosten 1993).

A second major positive aspect of certification from the position of the nonunion employer is that it has entirely dissipated the pressure that existed during the first four decades of the twentieth century for the general enfranchisement of the industrial citizenry. As it has evolved in the United States, certification legitimizes industrial autocracy. Because employees have a means to establish collective bargaining through an electoral process, noncertified employers are considered entirely justified in refusing to recognize and deal with independent unions representing a minority of their employees. Minority unions may still attempt to convince the employer to deal with them and are permitted to make use of the strike toward that end, but because of the existence of certification, the labor movement has implicitly concluded that "a nonmajority union can serve no useful function" (Summers 1990b:155). Certification has taken from workers the moral authority to demand minority recognition. Neither the general public, nor workers, nor

3. Over time, as the practice of collective bargaining under the Wagner Act became more rigid and "juridified," it also gave employers increasing incentive to avoid unionization (Townley 1987). The growing spread between union and nonunion wages in the 1970s had the same effect (Freeman and Medoff 1984; Kochan, Katz, and McKersie 1986).

union leaders any longer consider the walkout to be the appropriate way to establish a bargaining relationship. Unions today do not generally make conscious, strategic use of the strike or strike threat toward that end. With some notable exceptions, they either put their efforts into certification or they defer to unilateral rule, even in those situations in which a substantial number of employees join the union. Their behavior has been molded by exigencies of the legislative framework.[4]

Not only are employers permitted to attempt to maintain unilateral control over the establishment of terms and conditions of employment, they are also forbidden from establishing employee representation plans voluntarily. Their alternative to collective bargaining with independent unions as a means of establishing industrial democracy has been outlawed. The unions successfully argued in the 1930s that such plans generally did not provide for genuine employee representation but instead were used by employers to avoid dealing with organizations freely chosen by the employees themselves. To remove that blockage on the road to real joint regulation of the conditions of work, the Wagner Act outlawed company unions (Taylor and Witney 1987). Because of this development, employers have been effectively relieved of the duty resting upon them earlier in the century to address the democratic void in industry positively.

The result of this evolution is that, in the United States today, only a small and diminishing part of the labor force has in place institutions that allow employees to influence the conditions under which they work. Four out of five American employees have their conditions of employment established within a system of industrial autocracy.[5] This system is supported by the arguments that employees have a choice to opt for collective bargaining if they want to do so and that they should have such a choice. The first proposition—that they have a choice—has been discredited by an enormous amount of research carried out over the past few decades that indicates that intimidation and fear of reprisal are rampant in the United States and that the true choice is between accepting the status quo or being victimized (Weiler 1990; Lawler 1990; Goldfield 1987). The second proposition—that employees should have a

4. A similar phenomenon is evident in Australia (and until recently New Zealand), where union behavior has been shaped by the existence of a legal framework that requires a specific kind of expertise for a trade union to make gains for its members through a government-administered arbitration system. Kevin Hince (1993) has gone as far as to argue that many "arbitration unions" have appeared for the sole reason of taking advantage of the provisions of the law. They were, in short, creatures of the law rather than the result of more fundamental socioeconomic forces acting on the working class. For a British analysis of how the NLRA remolded American union behavior, see Hart 1978.

5. Industrial autocrats are, of course, constrained by market forces and government regulations, but then so are political autocrats. For a comparison of industrial and political governance, see Adams 1988.

choice to opt for or out of employee representation—is rarely questioned but needs to be.

The certification election is justified as being similar to a political election campaign, and the association with democratic political institutions provides an ethical basis for it. Although this argument is convincing to many labor relations experts as well as members of the general public, it is, when closely examined, a specious analogy. The political election campaign is designed to pick leaders who will develop policy within the institutional framework of a democratic system. The certification election, by contrast, is more like a constitutional referendum. The choice is not between leaders within an established political system but rather between political systems. It is a choice between the perpetuation of industrial autocracy or the establishment of a form of industrial democracy. Within a democratic society, no such choice should ever be seriously entertained. Within a democratic society, the only legitimate discussion should be over the means for establishing industrial democracy and the types of plans that would qualify as democratic.

There are some who argue that collective bargaining under the Wagner Act is not a very robust form of democracy and that American policy makers should seek to establish a participatory framework truer to the democratic ideal (Klare 1978; Stone 1981). Although that argument is contentious, it is indisputably obvious that industrial autocracy does not qualify as a form of democracy. The implication of this argument is that the certification election has no legitimacy whatsoever because one of the choices available to the electors is to continue a system of organizational governance that is repugnant to democratic values. For those who cherish such values, and there are very few North Americans who do not, the labor law reform debate should focus on alternative means for the establishment of universal industrial democracy.[6] No consideration at all should be given to the continuation of an archaic industrial political system that has no place within a democratic society.

Alternatives to Certification

Swedish Solution

Just after the turn of the twentieth century, following a number of notable strikes and public demonstrations, unions representing blue-collar workers in Sweden were recognized by the Swedish Employers Federation (SAF). In the so-called December Compromise, the SAF agreed that its member associa-

---

6. An eloquent critique of the misfit of industrial autocracy in the midst of political democracy is provided by Charles Lindblom (1977).

tions and employers affiliated with them would no longer discriminate against trade unionists and would recognize the right of the unions to bargain on behalf of the employees within their claimed jurisdiction in return for recognition by the unions of the right of management to "hire, fire and direct work" (Johnston 1962). In short, management insisted on a "true open shop" in which employees could join or not join a union free from discrimination as well as union acceptance of what was in essence a management rights clause in return for general recognition. The unions accepted the deal, and collective bargaining, primarily of a multiemployer variety, over wages and hours spread rapidly.

There were no white-collar worker unions in the LO, the Swedish trade union confederation. In general, trade unionists considered white-collar workers to be close to or identical with management and thus made little effort to organize them (Adams 1975). During the World War I, however, several white-collar groups (e.g., bank workers, foremen) formed their own unions. For the most part, employers refused to deal with these organizations, saying (just like American employers) that unions of employees close to management were inappropriate. Despite this opposition, the white-collar organizations endured, and when a Social Democratic government was elected in the early 1930s, the organizations petitioned that government to compel the employers to negotiate. The result was a law very simple in form. It stated that employers were required to recognize and meet with any organization authorized by any relevant employees to negotiate on their behalf (Adlercreutz 1990). The government made it clear to employers that it had passed the law because it wanted to see the general establishment of bargaining procedures with the white-collar unions. There was an implicit threat that if satisfactory bargaining relationships were not quickly established, the government would return to the fray with additional legislation. Within a few years bargaining for white-collar workers was ubiquitous.

The strategy of the government in this case is exemplary of a general approach to labor policy that has been used by governments in Sweden throughout the twentieth century: Let the parties know what you want to see happen in general terms and let them work out the specifics. A key ingredient is that the government makes it clear that it will continue to monitor the situation until a satisfactory arrangement emerges and that it will not hesitate to pass legislation—that the parties might find to be onerous—if they are unable to arrive at their own solution.

From a North American perspective, one potential eventuality of the Swedish approach might be very disruptive. What if many small, minority unions all demanded recognition? How could the employer possibly deal with all of them? Because of rivalry between the AFL and the CIO in the 1930s, the

Wagner Act procedures were, in part, explicitly intended to deal with this issue.

Although the Swedish legislation required negotiations, it did not require employer agreement with union demands. Thus, Swedish employers could deal with the minority union problem by politely listening to minority representatives and then explaining to them that their requests could not be met because of agreements made with the more broadly representative union. That was precisely the tack taken by the associations affiliated with the SAF after the December Compromise when faced by demands from many unions. The refusal of the SAF to deal with multiple unions representing employees within a single industry put pressure on the LO to restructure. It was one of the factors that led to the reorganization of LO-affiliated unions into a small number of primarily industrial unions (Johnston 1962).

There is much more to the Swedish story, but what has been related is enough to illustrate the principles of an approach that is much different from certification. That approach has been enormously effective in Sweden. Today, nearly every employee is covered by a collective agreement (Hammarström 1993). In Sweden, the promise of industrial enfranchisement via collective bargaining is a reality.

German Solution

The reaction of German employers to the rise of the labor movement was much like that of American employers. As in the United States, a prevalent answer to the demand for industrial democracy was the voluntary establishment of employee representation schemes (Taft 1952; Havlovic 1990). Toward the end of World War I, however, the German monarchy collapsed and the country entered a period of near chaos. There was a good deal of radical activity and serious, practical fears that Germany was about to follow the road of Russia in establishing a totalitarian, communist state. It was within that milieu that the Social Democratic government that replaced the Kaiser pressured labor and management to come to a mutually acceptable cooperative arrangement. The result was the Legien-Stinnes Accord between the German Employers Federation and the German Workers Federation (Berghahn and Karsten 1987). The accord contained terms very similar to the Swedish December Compromise. Unions were recognized as the appropriate agents to negotiate on behalf of employees in their jurisdictions with employer associations to establish general terms and conditions of employment.

There was, however, one area in which agreement was very difficult. Reflecting back to their craft guild ancestors, German employers insisted on their right to total authority within the enterprise. This was not at all acceptable to the unions, which wanted to see the establishment of industrial democracy as a complement to political democracy. Under pressure, German employers were willing to concede (as had American employers) that perhaps employees should be accorded some say over conditions of employment at the level of the enterprise, but representation by "outside" unions was totally unacceptable. The reasons given for the employers' refusal to deal with unions at the plant level were identical to those given by employers in the United States. Outside unions had no commitment to the success of the enterprise and thus would not be sensitive to its unique needs.

The compromise was the establishment by legislation of works councils that had statutorily defined duties to represent employee interests with respect to a specified list of issues (such as training, discipline, and the establishment of piece rates) of unique concern at the enterprise and plant level. Employee representatives would be elected from among firm employees. The unions could, of course, run candidates. They did that, and as a result most councils were soon staffed by union activists.

At first, employers attempted to manipulate and control these new institutions, and throughout the 1920s they were often successful in doing so. After World War II, however, the councils were reinstituted and strengthened by revisions in the 1970s (Adams and Rummel 1977). Today the councils have "codetermination" authority with respect to several specified issues. If there is an impasse concerning any of these issues, it is settled by resort to what is in effect binding arbitration. The large majority of councillors throughout Germany are trade unionists with close ties to the national unions, which provide them with advice and training. The unions regard the councils as the instruments of the trade union movement within the enterprise.

The councils are not permitted by law to negotiate over wage issues. Those issues are the exclusive province of unions and collective bargaining. Theoretically, bargaining may take place at any level, but by mutual agreement most collective bargaining in Germany occurs at the multiemployer level.

The Germans, not only trade unionists, but also government, public, and perhaps surprisingly most employer representatives, are convinced that this system is to a large extent responsible for the economic success Germany has had during the past several decades (see, for example, Thelen 1991; Turner 1991; Jacobi, Keller, and Müller-Jentsch 1992). Industrial conflict is at a very low level, and a cooperative synergy produces very effective "productivity coalitions" at the level of the company (Windolf 1989). Even though the level of union density is not as high as it is in Sweden, the great majority of German workers are covered by a combination of collective agreements and works council agreements. In short, as in Sweden, the promise of universal industrial democracy has to a large extent been kept.

The logic of the German works councils system is that all working people have the right to be represented in the making of enterprise decisions that critically affect their interests. There is no choice between autocracy and democracy. The law simply specifies that councils must be established in all enterprises with more than five employees.[7] There is no technical reason a similar approach could not be used in North America. It is already in use with respect to public institutions such as school boards and city councils. In Canada, it has been used for the establishment of health and safety committees, and it has been recommended for use with a broader range of issues by several government-appointed inquiry commissions (Adams 1986). The major stumbling block would seem to be political opposition from defenders of the illegitimate, autocratic status quo.

British Solution

The British system of industrial relations is often referred to as voluntaristic. Compared with other advanced liberal democracies, there is very little labor legislation. During the nineteenth century and into the twentieth, a major political objective of the British unions was to minimize state intervention in industrial relations, a goal almost identical to the one pursued by the American Federation of Labor (Pelling 1971). The British unions, however, were more successful than those in the United States. They managed to get legislation passed in the first decade of the twentieth century that made them largely immune from intervention by the courts in their affairs—a deal the American unions would have gladly accepted (Hepple and Fredman 1986).

Although it passed little legislation regulating the conduct of collective bargaining, it would be wrong to conclude that the British government remained neutral or disinterested as an industrial relations actor. Indeed, it was the policy of the government from early in the twentieth century to encourage employers to recognize and negotiate with trade unions. During World War I, for example, it invited trade unionists to sit on various government boards concerned with managing the war effort, and it made it clear to employers that it expected them to recognize and cooperate with employee representatives. It appointed a commission (the Whitley Committee) to look into ways of securing a permanent improvement in the relations between labor and management. The commission concluded that "the popular demand for 'workers' control' might be met if [union-management] committees, constituted in each industry, both at the national level and at the local and even workshop level, were to discuss not only wages and conditions but also general problems of industrial efficiency and management" (Pelling 1971:160). The government accepted these recommendations and encouraged the development throughout the economy of collective bargaining and

---

7. Because of the less than perfect enforcement of this provision, there are many small companies in which no council has been set up. Skeptics sometimes point to this situation as a reason the German system should not be emulated. If perfect respect for its terms was the criterion for the establishment of any statute, however, there would be very few laws.

joint consultation. It also put the recommendations into effect in the public sector. Part of its rationale in doing so was to set an example of best practice for the private sector (Parris 1973). In addition, government officials became directly involved in several specific private-sector cases in which employers persisted in pursuing an intransigent strategy. The policy was, by North American standards, very successful. Either in the format recommended by the Whitley Committee or by more conventional means, by the end of the war, collective bargaining was widespread in Britain.

In the early 1930s, the British government again became concerned about its labor policy not only with respect to the United Kingdom but across its far-flung empire. Labor organizations were becoming restless everywhere, threatening to turn into revolutionary political organizations. To counter this threat, it became the policy of the government to encourage unionization and the orderly practice of collective bargaining throughout its colonies (Roberts 1964).

During World War II informal pressure was again applied to British employers to recognize and cooperate with unions during the war effort. Just after the war, a fair wages resolution was adopted by the House of Commons, which "in effect required government departments to include in their contracts with suppliers a clause which provided that 'the contractor shall recognize the freedom of his workpeople to be members of trade unions'" (Hepple and Fredman 1986:192). In staff handbooks all employees were explicitly encouraged to become union members in order better to facilitate collective bargaining. The statutes regulating nationalized corporations obliged the management of those corporations to recognize and negotiate with the unions.

During the 1970s a special agency was charged with promoting collective bargaining. Although it was no more successful than the NLRB in compelling employers determined to defy the letter and spirit of government policy, it nevertheless did help create a climate in which unionization and collective bargaining appeared to be "virtually inevitable" (Dickens and Bain 1986:93).

This policy of setting an example and imposing gentle but firm and continuous pressure on private-sector employers to conform to what was becoming a new and accepted "custom and practice" was followed by governments of both the right and the left and was very successful. By the mid-1970s approximately 75 percent of all British workers were covered by collective agreements—a rate lower than that achieved in Sweden but much higher than the peak achieved in the United States in the early 1950s (International Labour Office 1985:36). In 1979, however, Margaret Thatcher was elected prime minister and changed the policy radically. Her theory, unsupported by most academic research, was that unions and collective bargaining were responsible for many of Britain's economic ills (Edwards et al. 1992). She passed several laws that made it difficult for the unions to be effective and that encouraged employers to bypass or ignore the unions to introduce new technology and new human resources practices aimed at enhancing industrial competitiveness. To their credit, most employers did not take advantage of the situation to engage in the sort of overt union busting that occurred in the United States under the Reagan and Bush administrations. Nevertheless, union density and bargaining coverage did decrease markedly.

The positive British policy toward collective bargaining that existed up until 1979 certainly could be emulated with little technical difficulty in the United States. It would require that the federal government agree to bargain fully with its own employees rather than continue unilaterally to set such basic conditions of employment as pay and fringe benefits and that it encourage employees as a matter of policy to join the appropriate union. It would also require that it wholly support the development of bargaining on a universal basis in the private sector, that it back up that stance with a contract compliance policy, and that it refuse to accept as valid specious arguments about the lack of employee motivation for democratic participation as the reason for the absence of collective bargaining.

Conclusion

Because it legitimizes industrial autocracy, certification as it now exists in North America has no place in democratic society. There are other more effective ways to provide employees with a means to influence the rules under which they work, and the focus of labor law reform should be on developing a policy that effectively achieves full enfranchisement of all industrial citizens. None of the approaches reviewed here does that with perfect effectiveness, but all of the schemes worked out in the countries under review have performed better with respect to the achievement of that end than has the practice of certification. Although it may be difficult to import successfully legislation passed in other countries, the basic logic underlying labor policies is certainly transportable. The main reason for the absence of universal participation by working people in the making of the conditions under which they labor is the unwillingness of their governments to adopt policies appropriate for the achievement of that result. Arguments in favor of technical and motivational barriers to universal participation are entirely without merit.

19

On the Status of Workers' Rights to Organize in the United States and Canada

Peter G. Bruce

A climate of fear now stands in the way of a revival of American labor unionism. Recent polls have found that approximately 70 percent of Americans think that workers in general will be subject to economic coercion by their employers for attempting to unionize. And approximately 45 percent of workers fear that they themselves would be so treated for exercising collective bargaining rights they have had on paper for more than fifty years (Weiler 1990). These fears are grounded in the reality that today's U.S. workers are exceptionally likely to be subject to antiunion discrimination, both by historical standards and in comparison with workers in Canada, which enforces identical collective bargaining rights. Given this reality, I will argue that labor law reform is imperative to reverse the tide of union decline and will suggest some reforms to strengthen the best current proposal.

I will argue that employer unfair labor practices, and the weaknesses in the law that allow them, are perhaps the most important sources of labor union decline in the United States. I will do this by comparing this argument's explanatory power with its rivals'. I will then propose means of strengthening the administration of ULP cases, which I contend is the weakest link in Paul Weiler's generally adequate proposals for reforming collective bargaining policy, the best reform package currently on the table.

A near consensus of studies has found that weaknesses in collective bargaining law, and, derivatively, the exponential increase of employer ULPs since the 1950s, have been one of the most important factors accounting for the decline of the American labor movement. Indeed, after surveying most of the

I would like to thank NLRB former regional attorney Harold M. Kowal for several years of dialogue about ULP cases. That dialogue stimulated and assisted me in developing much of the analysis in this paper, especially regarding the NLRB's investigation process.

relevant studies, Richard Freeman and James Medoff concluded that between one-quarter and one-half of the decline in union membership in the private sector has been due to these factors.

The most common and destructive types of ULPs by employers have been Section 8(a)(3) and 8(a)(5) violations of the Wagner Act—that is, discriminatory discharge and related offenses and refusals by employers to bargain with unions, respectively. Although the destructive power of discriminatory discharges is obvious, that of refusals to bargain is more complex. It is often reinforced by the ability of employers permanently to replace, that is, effectively to fire, striking workers. The impact of this tactic was clearly illustrated in the Caterpillar strike of 1992, when that firm's management announced that it would hire workers from all over the nation to replace its UAW strikers. Although the workers had waged a strong strike for five months, their solidarity collapsed and the union declared an end to the strike in just over a week after the threat of such replacements had been raised (Saunders 1992).

The frequency of both of 8(a)(3) and 8(a)(5) ULPs has skyrocketed in recent decades. Section 8(a)(3) charges rose from 3,100 to more than 18,300 between 1955 and 1980, before dropping to 11,800 in 1985. Meanwhile, charges of violations of Section 8(a)(5) rose from 1,200 to nearly 10,000 in the same period (Weiler 1990).

Estimates of the frequency of ULPs in representation elections, the situation in which their impact is most likely to undermine attempts at unionization, are hotly contested, ranging from one-tenth to one-sixty-fourth of union supporters in such elections in some of the most influential studies (Weiler 1990; LaLonde and Meltzer 1991). But this debate generally seems to have lost sight of the fact that by comparative standards, any of these figures for the United States is exceptionally high. This is clear from a comparison with Canada.

Because the administration of the law (defining the same rights and ULPs) is more efficient in Canada, and perhaps because Canadian (national) employers tend to be less antiunion than their U.S. compeers (Bliss 1971), the frequency of ULPs north of the border has ranged from one-fourth to one-tenth of the U.S. rate per certification contest, even after one adjusts for differences in population. For instance, labor boards on both sides of the border specify a global category into which all ULPs are tabulated. Summing up these ULPs for all Canadian jurisdictions (collective bargaining policy falls under provincial jurisdiction), and then dividing this national total of ULPs by Canada's total number of certification cases to standardize for population differences in ways that allow comparison with the United States, one finds that the rate per certification election has ranged from approximately four to ten times higher in the United States than in Canada in the last two decades (see table 19.1). This appears to be true for discriminatory discharge violations per se, as well as for more general tabulations of antiunion discrimination. For instance, as Weiler (1983) has demonstrated for 1975 and 1980, discriminatory discharges were six to eight times more frequent in the United States than in Ontario, and seventeen to twenty-five times more frequent than in British Columbia per union certification campaign.

As Roy Adams (1989b) has asserted, differences in policy environments between the United States and Canada are probably the most important factor reducing employer ULPs and giving workers and unions more incentive to organize in Canada (see also Rose and Chaison 1988). Relatedly, differences in

Table 19.1. Ratio of ULP Cases in Canada and the United States to Certification Contests

Year	Canadian ULPs/ Contests	U.S. ULPs/ Contests	Ratio[a]	Adjustment[b]
1972	0.213	1.99	4.34	10.50
1973	0.228	1.85	8.11	9.00
1974	0.250	2.03	8.20	9.19
1975	0.269	2.37	8.81	10.17
1976	–	2.72	–	–
1977	0.637	2.75	4.31	4.84
1978	0.546	3.28	6.00	6.86
1979	0.629	3.60	5.72	6.59
1980	0.704	3.80	5.39	5.74
1981	0.796	2.79	3.51	3.94
1982	0.660	3.78	5.27	4.21
1983	0.604	3.87	6.41	5.18
1984	0.872	3.77	4.32	4.94
1985	0.799	3.12	3.90	4.65
1986	0.997	3.47	3.48	4.11
1987	0.856	3.48	4.07	4.88

Sources: For Canadian data except Quebec ULPs, Kumar, Coates, and Arrowsmith 1989:465–68 and 640; for Quebec ULPs, Bureau du commissaire general du travail 1989; for U.S. data, U.S. National Labor Relations Board annual reports 1972–1987.
[a] U.S. ratios divided by Canadian ratios.
[b] This column adjusts for the fact that ULPs in the English Canadian provinces include ULPs against unions as well as management. In recent years the former have constituted approximately 30 percent of all ULPs in British Columbia and Ontario, and it was assumed that this proportion held for the other English Canadian provinces as well. Interview with Wayne Mullins, assistant registrar, British Columbia Industrial Relations Council, Oct. 7, 1993, and with Ron Levi, solicitor, Ontario Labour Relations Board, Oct. 7, 1993. The adjustment thus reduced the number of all Canadian ULPs, except those from Quebec, by 30 percent before recalculating the national ratio.

national government structures and party systems account for the more frequent enactment of pro-union labor law reforms at lower levels of political pressure in Canada than in the United States (Bruce 1988).

Testing Rival Theories

Comparative analysis is extremely useful for testing the power of different theories explaining union membership decline in the United States. For instance, theories that attribute this decline to the decline of mass production and the rise of service industry (Bell 1973:129–42) are unable to explain why Canada's union density (approximately 36 percent) has remained relatively stable and is more than twice that (16 percent) of the United States, since similar structural changes have made its economy even more service and less manufacturing oriented than the U.S. economy (Lipset 1986:424–46). Likewise, arguments emphasizing the importance of Canada's larger public sector as the main cause of America's lower union density can explain no more than 7 percent of this difference (Riddell 1993).

Comparative political culture analyses provide a more plausible explanation. For instance, Lipset (1986) attributes the higher rate of unionization in Canada to its more statist and communitarian Tory value system. But like the sociological theories from which it derives, this theory is supra-historical (Barry 1978) and cannot explain why Canada's ostensibly greater collectivism has not led to more pro-union attitudes than in the United States (Lipset 1986). These relationships are simply assumed, as is also typical of sociological theories of "national character" (Lipset 1986). In fact, a deluge of subsequent studies have shown that public attitudes in Canada have been no more favorable toward unionism than those in the United States (Bruce 1988; Chaison and Rose 1991a; Bowden 1989; E. Robinson 1990; Riddell 1993) on questions measuring general approval of unions, the perceived power of unions, the threat of unions, and the esteem with which union leaders are viewed. As for the attitudes of workers themselves, nonunionized Canadian workers have indicated similar propensities to unionize as their U.S. counterparts in recent decades. That is, in surveys that have asked if such workers would choose to unionize if offered a formal choice to do so in the immediate future, 33 to 34 percent of U.S. workers and 31 to 39 percent of Canadians responded positively (Kochan 1979; Freeman 1988; Reid Associates 1989; and Canadian Federation of Labour 1990). Relatedly, although Canadian workers who want union representation generally obtain it, this is not true for a large proportion of U.S. workers (Riddell 1993).

Another theory contends that the divergence of U.S. and Canadian union density stems mostly from differences in the amount of effort and financial resources that unions have put into organizing the unorganized, since studies have found that Canadian unions have exerted several times more organizing effort than their American counterparts in recent decades (Chaison and Rose 1991a). This finding has been elaborated into a broad, single-factor theory by Edward Ian Robinson, who asserts that the divergence in American union density is "due to the failure of American unions to invest resources in organizing the unorganized, resulting in diminished momentum and economic power, and rising American employer resistance to union organizing efforts from the late 1950s" (Robinson 1990).

As the last phrase suggests, for Robinson, organizing performance and, relatedly, union militancy determine not only the frequency with which unions apply for certification but also the extent of employer ULPs. The more militant unions are, he contends, the less likely employers will be to engage in ULPs. Although his empirical description of the organizing efforts by the Canadians is convincing and important, the reductionism of Robinson's theory, with its echoes of Michels's "Iron Law of Oligarchy" and Lenin's critique of the "aristocracy of labor," obscures key relationships, especially the extent to which labor laws influence the frequency, intensity, and consequences of employer ULPs. Those consequences are not systematically analyzed, however, so that, by default, organizing performance is simply assumed to be the prime determinant of employer ULPs. This is a serious flaw, since virtually every study of the differences between U.S. and Canadian collective bargaining laws has demonstrated or argued that Canadian laws exert important effects in minimizing employer antiunion ULPs and facilitating union growth compared with the United States (Chaison and Rose 1991a; Weiler 1990; Bruce 1988).

Chaison and Rose (1991a) provide a more credible explanation for these nations' diverging union density rates in arguing that organizing effort is largely a function of the effectiveness of collective bargaining policies in regulating employer ULPs, an argument complementing the one in this paper. Put simply, more effective labor laws have helped Canada's unions win almost twice as large a proportion of their certification cases (approximately 70 percent versus 40 to 45 percent) as their U.S. counterparts, which gives the Canadians a much stronger incentive to organize, the ideological differences in these movements notwithstanding (Bruce 1988).

Michael Goldfield, writing from a perspective similar to Robinson's, claims that the passage of the Wagner Act was inessential to the tripling of American union density between 1935 and 1945, and he attributes this increase almost entirely to labor militancy (1990:1309). Actually, almost half of the workers (2.6 million) who became unionized between 1935 and 1940 required use of the NLRB's protections against employer coercion in ULP cases (U.S. NLRB annual reports 1935–40; Bain and Price 1980), and it was only after the

National Labor Relations Act was passed and ruled constitutional (1937) that many of the nations's largest and most antiunion employers began to recognize and bargain with unions (Gross 1982). Thus, as R. H. Tawney has argued, the rapidly growing American labor movement of this era was largely a "creation of the state" (1979:17).

These weaknesses in Robinson's and Goldfield's analyses show how reductionist organizing performance theories can mystify our understanding of union growth by devaluing the importance of the law. Conversely, they also suggest the need for labor law reform to revive unionism in the United States.

In *Governing the Workplace*, Paul Weiler presents what are probably the best-reasoned proposals in the current debate about how to strengthen union recognition rights. Apart from his visionary and probably politically unfeasible proposal for works councils, and his controversial proposal for amending Section 8(a)(2) of the Wagner Act, he proposes an agenda for labor law reform that appears nearly identical to that of the AFL-CIO, especially his "Reconstructive Model," which advocates "instant elections" to limit an employer's opportunities to engage in ULPs; a ban on employers permanently replacing striking workers; and changes in secondary boycott laws (1990:253–72). Even this reform package, though, ignores key problems that need to be remedied to make the existing law work—particularly the ease with which the NLRB can dismiss ULP cases. Weiler also proposes some inadequate remedies to reduce delay in litigated ULP cases, such as putting about five hundred ULP cases on a "fast track" and having the NLRB issue injunctions under Section 10(j) of the Wagner Act to make administrative law judge decisions semifinal (1990:246). (The problem with this approach is that ALJ decisions would still take too long to complete and would suffer from their legendary poor quality, and the thousands of cases outside of the fortunate five hundred would continue to languish in delay.) The remainder of this chapter analyzes these problems in the processing of ULP cases and proposes reforms to correct them.

Reforming this aspect of the NLRB's procedures is important, since even if the NLRB began certifying workers by instant elections or card checks, the more determined antiunion employers could counter the effectiveness of these procedures by bolstering their resources for surveilling workers and by taking coercive actions sooner. Thus, the delays and ease of dismissal of ULP charges in the NLRB's administrative process would still break many union drives. Understanding how ULP cases are processed in Canada provides useful insights for minimizing this sort of antiunion discrimination by employers in the United States. Since collective bargaining policy falls under provincial jurisdiction in Canada, I compare the administration of ULP cases at the NLRB with that at the Ontario Labour Relations Board, since Ontario is Canada's most populous and industrialized province and its labor relations board procedures are common to most other English Canadian jurisdictions (George Adams 1985).

Generally, the steps one must take to fight ULP cases alleging discriminatory discharges or related violations are similar in both nations. First, one files a complaint (or charge), and then officials seek to effect a settlement between the parties. Cases then go to a trial-type "hearing" if settlement fails. But, as the analysis below shows, qualification for a hearing at the OLRB is almost automatic, whereas at the NLRB, the charging parties must meet difficult criteria to qualify.

A second major difference is that in Canada cases are heard directly before a labor relations board, and that is also, almost always, the final stage. In the United States, cases are first heard by administrative law judges whose "recommended orders" can easily be appealed to NLRB headquarters, which may reverse the decision. From there, cases can then be easily appealed to the courts (Weiler 1983). So, basically, there are three stages in the U.S. process, versus one in most Canadian jurisdictions.

Promptness is crucial in the processing of discriminatory discharge cases because of the sorts of remedies they require, in particular, the reinstatement of discriminatorily fired worker(s) or the declaration of a "bargaining order." Also, the time it takes for ULP cases to go through a formal hearing and obtain a remedy is crucial to the outcomes of *all* ULP cases, even though only a small fraction of them (in both boards' processes) are litigated, since cases that are heard set the bargaining contexts for the large majority of cases resolved informally.

Differences in access to a hearing, and in the promptness of such hearings, lead to differences in the proportions of cases the labor boards dispose of as dismissals, withdrawals, or voluntary settlements. The OLRB has a more hearing-centered process. It heard approximately 15 to 20 percent of its ULP cases in the early 1980s, versus 3 percent at the NLRB. The OLRB also dismisses about one-tenth as many cases in the prehearing stage as the NLRB (3 percent versus 30 percent). A dismissed or withdrawn case cannot be won. Yet, at the NLRB, such "meritless" cases constituted two-thirds of all ULP cases, versus approximately 15 percent at the OLRB in the early 1980s (the only time-comparable, detailed data addressing these issues were available at these boards) (Bruce 1993). Thus, the NLRB, from the outset, precludes larger proportions of workers from winning ULP cases than the OLRB. Conversely, the OLRB effects approximately twice as large a proportion of settlements as the NLRB (70 percent versus 30 percent) (Bruce 1993).

The larger proportion of dismissed and withdrawn cases at the NLRB stems from the fact that it requires (1) a factual investigation and (2) an analysis of whether such facts as appear to be provable are "legally sufficient" so that the prosecutor should continue an effort to remedy the violation

(Miller 1980). The investigation is mandatory for all cases. As the NLRB's *Case-Handling Manual* asserts, "The investigation . . . must . . . reveal the 'entire picture' of the case" (U.S. National Labor Relations Board 1983), although the criteria for this are unclear and undefined by statutory standards (McClintock 1980). Clearly though, considerable evidence is required.

In Ontario, by contrast, cases are *automatically* scheduled for a hearing, and for the vast majority of cases there is no gate-keeping investigation at all. A screening panel attempts to weed out frivolous cases. But no effort is made to ascertain whether the main facts on which a case hinges are provable. In consequence, the OLRB is "very cautious in dismissing a complaint" and "will do so only when it considers the position of the applicant to be clearly untenable" (Bruce 1993). As such, qualification for a hearing is a right and is virtually automatic.

The NLRB's requirement that the investigation produce the *entire picture* of the case places a burden on the charging party absent at the OLRB. This burden is especially onerous, since jurisprudence at both labor boards has recognized "the practical reality that the employer is the party with the best access to proof of its motivation" in 8(a)(3) cases (*NLRB v. Wright-Line*, 251 N.L.R.B. 1083 (1980)) and that the key "facts lie peculiarly within the knowledge of one of the parties," that is, business (*National Automatic Vending*, 63 C.L.L.C. 1162 (1962)).

In NLRB investigations, the complainant is supposed to have legal weapons with which to offset the biases inherent in the access to information noted above—that is, the investigatory subpoena and rights to appeal dismissal decisions. But the use of the investigatory subpoena depends on the discretion of the general counsel, and its use has been granted only on "rare occasions" (Kammholz and Strauss 1980). Thus, investigations generally depend on employers voluntarily submitting evidence that could break their cases.

The NLRB's investigation process also lacks outside review. Neither the board in Washington nor the courts may hear appeals from cases dismissed in investigations. Such appeals are heard only by the general counsel's own staff. Thus, the general counsel's office has total control over the dismissal of NLRB cases; 94 percent of these appeals are rejected. This small rate of reversal is not surprising, since these procedures violate the principle that appeals should be heard by an institution other than that from which they originate (McClintock 1980).

Of course, if the charging parties (workers and unions) in 8(a)(3) cases agreed that their charges had "no merit" after receiving dismissal letters, one could assume that the NLRB's relatively high rates of dismissal and withdrawal simply eliminated cases that did not deserve a hearing. In recent decades, however, approximately half of all dismissed 8(a)(3) cases have been dismissed against the complainant's will (McClintock 1980). Contrary to the strictures of the NLRB's *Case-Handling Manual*, which state that dismissal letters must be written specifically enough so that workers know why their complaints were rejected and can easily appeal them, this appears to be done only rarely (Bruce 1988).

The OLRB is able to hear a larger proportion of its ULP cases and to dismiss smaller ones than the NLRB because (1) it covers a smaller population; (2) it has a smaller case load of ULPs because of better regulation; and (c) the charging parties, rather than the government, incur the responsibility and pay for their own prosecution.

Differences in Delays

In the mid-1980s, the NLRB took approximately four to five times as long to process ULP cases that went to a hearing as the OLRB—that is, approximately two years versus four to six months (Bruce 1993). Analyzing national time lapse differences by stage, one finds the biggest differences in the decision-writing period between the close of a hearing and the issuance of a decision and, at the NLRB, in the period in which appeals of the administrative law judge's decision are reviewed by NLRB headquarters in Washington. This latter process has no counterpart in Ontario and has added almost a year of extra delay to the NLRB's processing of ULP cases in recent years (NLRB annual reports 1980–86). Additionally, after the completion of this process, cases can easily by appealed to the courts, making the thousand-day ULP case a commonplace (Weiler 1983).

These time lapses reflect the more pervasive influence of courts and judicial review in the NLRB's process. The relatively great powers of U.S. courts have allowed them to disagree with the NLRB over which principles should decide 8(a)(3) cases (*NLRB v. Wright-Line* 1980); thus, court influence has also led to ambiguous criteria for determining violations. It has also led to more constraints on drawing inferences from records and to a greater emphasis on determining the employer's state of mind in NLRB than OLRB decisions (Bruce 1988).

These differences all tend to lead to more delays in decision-writing in the United States. Furthermore, the greater power of the courts in the U.S. constitutional system was responsible for the establishment of the NLRB's internal appeals stage to ensure the quality of ALJ decisions against judicial review (Bowman 1942). In Canadian legal and industrial relations circles, court influence is far more restricted. It is generally assumed that labor relations board officials are more expert than judges in industrial relations matters and that their decisions should be final and without appeal to the courts. Given these assumptions, most Canadian labor relations acts have banned appeals and strictly limited review of ULP decisions (George Adams 1985).

Proposals for Reform

Although the sorts of strict "privative clauses" that have limited judicial review and appeals in Canada would probably violate Article 3 of our Constitution, there nevertheless seem to be several reforms that together could lessen the power of the courts and perhaps make the NLRB as efficient as the OLRB in processing ULP cases.

First, make NLRB decisions self-enforcing, like those of the Federal Elections Commission, rather than requiring that they be enforced in the circuit courts.

Second, the NLRB should make its decisions by rule-making rather than by adjudication, in order to clarify its own rules, centralize the rules that the appeals courts apply to NLRB cases, and increase the board's protections against judicial review (Estreicher 1985; D. Shapiro 1965).

Third, to eliminate the necessity for the NLRB's internal stage of appeals, the use of ALJs should be abolished and tripartite board members, on the Canadian model, should adjudicate and provide final decisions on ULP cases. Each region should have its own tripartite board representatives.

Fourth, to simplify tests of witness credibility, a reverse onus should be instituted in ULP hearings in which employers are the respondent party, so that they would go first in ULP hearings and bear the primary burden for the production of evidence, which is mostly in their possession. This would speed, as well as simplify, such tests, especially if prosecuting lawyers played a more aggressive role in demanding employer records and in cutting past the "truth in faces" means of determining witness credibility.

As an earlier section of this chapter has demonstrated, problems with the NLRB's investigation process, as well as with the delay of litigation, has biased the administration of ULP cases in favor of employers. To help the NLRB approximate the fairness and efficiency of the OLRB in its investigation stage, I believe the following reforms should be considered: (1) allow the automatic use of the investigatory subpoena to overcome employers' advantages in access to information, and allow regional branches of the NLRB to grant the subpoena, to limit delays; (2) build pressure (academic and union) to force the NLRB to follow its own rules in writing dismissal letters; (3) subject appeals of dismissals to review by a new agency, independent of the general counsel, which would be more specialized in its functions and faster than the courts; (4) perhaps reduce the NLRB's cost pressures, which create enormous incentives for dismissals, by having union lawyers, rather than the NLRB, prosecute ULP cases.

PART VI
FRAMEWORKS FOR CHANGE

20

Making Postindustrial Unionism Possible

Dorothy Sue Cobble

The transition to a postindustrial future requires a sea change in labor-management culture and institutional practice and a radical revision in relevant public policy. As Secretary of Labor Robert Reich has emphasized, our current labor relations system was designed for a mass-production industrial workplace. It is no longer appropriate in a service-dominated, computer-based global economy in which success comes as much from quality, innovation, and the maximization of employee expertise as from quantity, standardization, and the efficient use of semiskilled labor.

Industrial relations scholars have delineated the problems embedded in the so-called New Deal industrial model and its inadequacies in the face of changing technology, workforce diversification, and economic restructuring (for example, Kochan, Katz, and McKersie 1986; Heckscher 1988; Kochan 1993a). This chapter will reinforce and extend these critiques by focusing on the specific ways in which the New Deal framework fails to address the representational needs of the new service workforce and, in so doing, fails to meet the needs of the majority of women workers. Some 84 percent of wage-earning women work in the expanding service economy (Sullivan 1989:405). Without a representational system designed with their realities in full view, the gender gap in employee representation that historically has existed between

Special thanks go to Michael Merrill for his many wise and encouraging words. The author would also like to thank Adrienne Eaton, Diane Faulkner, Jeffrey Keefe, Karl Klare, Donna Sockell, Howard Wial, the editors of this volume, and the anonymous ILR Press reviewers for their helpful suggestions and clarifications. Bridget Gilhool provided invaluable research assistance, particularly in preparing table 20.1. This work was supported by a grant from the Women's Bureau, U.S. Department of Labor.

men and women will continue.[1] A representational system that fails to incorporate women also will perpetuate gender inequality and underutilize the creative energies of close to half of the U.S. workforce.

Gender Biases of a Worksite-Based Taylorist System

The labor relations framework that rose to dominance in the 1930s and 1940s has two glaring assumptions embedded within it that make it increasingly inappropriate for today's work world, and in particular the work world of women: its worksite orientation and its adherence to Taylorist practices.[2] The new unionism of the 1930s was fundamentally different from the unionism that preceded it, in that it was worksite rather than occupationally based (Cobble 1991a; 1991b). Union benefits, both in economic returns and "voice," were tied to the individual employer. Recognitional processes and bargaining structures assumed a long-term, continuous, on-site, and full-time commitment to a single employer, in part because the New Deal system took the male-dominated, blue-collar industrial plant as the norm.

This worksite orientation is inadequate for the new contingent workforce, many of whom are highly mobile and only tenuously attached to a single employer. The contingent or "nonstandard" workforce—part-time, temporary, leased, on-call, subcontracted workers—is estimated to make up 25 percent of the workforce, and continued expansion is projected (Belous 1989).[3] A disproportionate number of these workers are female (Pearce 1987; Carré 1992).[4]

In addition, firm-based bargaining is not an effective approach for small employers with limited resources or for a workforce governed primarily by the exigencies of an external labor market. In contrast to manufacturing, the service sector (with the exception of government services) is often character-

1. Until the last decade, men consistently enjoyed unionization rates more than double those of women. In the 1980s, the gender gap in union membership lessened but did not close. By 1990, unions represented 21 percent of men and 14 percent of women (Cobble 1993:6).
2. Taylorist refers to the managerial philosophy of Frederick Winslow Taylor. Much of his advice for managing workers and for organizing production, laid out in his influential *Principles of Scientific Management* (1911), had been adopted by American manufacturers by World War I.
3. Indeed, the former general counsel to the National Staff Leasing Association predicted recently that the increasing use of staffing services will "culminate sometime in the next 10 or 50 years at a point when no one will ever again be employed by the people for whom they perform services" (*Daily Labor Report*, Aug. 12, 1993).
4. Diana Pearce, for example, estimated that in 1985, 52 percent of women, but only 33 percent of men, worked part time or part year. Carré notes that women accounted for 64.2 percent of temporary help services.

ized by small firms operating in local competitive markets.[5] In the private sector, women are much more likely than men to work for small firms and at worksites with fewer people (Brown, Hamilton, and Medoff 1990:1–15).

Moreover, many women's jobs in the service sector and throughout the economy are occupationally based, not worksite-based, functioning more in an external than an internal labor market. Women move from employer to employer and from industry to industry more frequently than do men.[6] But low job tenure is often combined with relatively high occupational tenure. Waitresses, nurses, and clerical workers, for example, move across industries and firms but stay within the same occupation (Cobble 1991a; Leigh and Hills 1987).

Women also rely less frequently than do men on training and opportunities for promotions within a firm-based internal labor market. Training for female occupations is usually external to the employer and less firm-specific. Opportunities for promotions are limited but linked to firm rather than job mobility; that is, one finds a better firm or a better employer rather than a better job within the same firm. A collective bargaining system that weds higher wages, benefits, skill upgrading, and employee voice to a specific firm will deny these basic employment enhancements to many women and will perpetuate the new forms of labor segmentation developing in the external labor markets that characterize service economies (Christopherson 1991).

In addition to its worksite orientation, certain Taylorist notions of work organization and management guided the formulation and subsequent evolution of the New Deal model. The most efficient organization of production would be achieved through a hierarchically structured, micro-managed workplace with narrow job titles, detailed work rules, and strict separation of managerial and worker functions. In this context, unions were adversaries, not partners with management. The typical grievance process, for example, fixed the union role as the reactor or objector to management actions rather than as the cocreator. In a classic division of labor, management retained authority over the design and organization of work; the union declined (and in some cases was denied) responsibility for supervisory functions, efficiency, and productivity.[7]

5. According to Wial's (1993) calculations, the average service-producing establishment has about thirteen workers; the average manufacturing about fifty-one.

6. As Hartmann (1993) and others have noted, job tenure, or the number of years spent at any one particular job or job site, is lower for women than for men.

7. It is important to note, however, that the Wagner Act of 1935 did not enshrine adversarialism or create the rigid demarcations between employer and employee that were later to evolve. Before the Taft-Hartley Act of 1947, for example, supervisors organized extensively in the printing trades, in retail grocery stores, in maritime, and in other sectors. The Supreme Court upheld their rights to organize under the National Labor Relations Act in early 1947,

As manufacturing has shifted toward "batch production,"[8] team work, and computer-based technologies, Taylorist management practices have become increasingly suspect (Piore and Sabel 1984; Zuboff 1988; Voos, Eaton, and Belman 1993). Yet these practices have always been ill suited to the realities of the service and white-collar work world with its heightened personalism and the blurring of employer and employee roles. Service and white-collar workers, for example, tend to be found not only in smaller establishments (restaurants, dental offices, retail shops) but in situations of close personal contact with their immediate boss (for example, clerical work). The line between employee and employer is more indistinct than in the traditional blue-collar, mass-production factory. Employee-employer relations may be personal and collaborative, rather than adversarial, formalized, and highly bureaucratic.

In addition, in the direct service environment, management efforts to deskill or to exclude employees from decisions affecting the quality and delivery of the service product have never been as successful or as widespread as in mass-production manufacturing. At times, management as well as labor realized that friendly service and attentive caring were not best extracted through authoritarian, top-down supervision; nor could creativity and problem-solving in white-collar employees be "mandated" from above. Hence, many nonfactory workers, professional and nonprofessional alike, have always engaged in certain "managerial" functions, such as planning, organization, and quality control. They work more autonomously or in self-managing teams (what I've termed peer management), where the senior member takes responsibility for organizing the flow of work, supervising less skilled coworkers, and maintaining work quality (Cobble 1991a; Benson 1986).

Given these divergent realities, it should come as no surprise that the traditional modes of organizing and representation that evolved within the New Deal and post–New Deal framework never appeared to work well in many service and white-collar workplaces. A labor relations system that allowed workers to exercise some managerial prerogatives, such as control over quality, work organization, and standards for worker competency, would be a better match with the ongoing practices of service and white-collar workplaces. Moreover, organizing and representational processes that empha-

noting that no basis existed in law for their elimination despite their "dual status" as agents of the employer and as employees (Leiter 1949:312). See Barenberg 1993 for an argument that the Wagner Act scheme was profoundly cooperationist, not adversarial.

8. In "batch production," as opposed to mass production, a smaller number of items are produced in any one production run. The technology is flexible and can be reconfigured quickly to produce numerous batches of slightly different products rather than a quantity of homogeneous items.

size greater participation, less adversarial proceedings, and more consensus-style "win-win" bargaining would be more appropriate.[9]

Lastly, in large part because of the worksite and Taylorist biases of the New Deal and post–New Deal framework, some 20 million women, or 38 percent of the female workforce, are now explicitly exempted from exercising their rights to collective bargaining under the National Labor Relations Act (see table 20.1). If one excludes public-sector workers, a good proportion of whom have some degree of bargaining rights under other enabling legislation, a fourth of the private-sector female workforce is excluded.[10] In large part, these workers are not defined as "employees," because they do not resemble blue-collar industrial workers: Their work world is not "industrial" (but domestic and agricultural); nor are they behind the Tayloristic curtain, removed from all "managerial" knowledge and responsibility.[11]

Moreover, although not legally excluded from coverage under the law, another large sector of the female workforce—perhaps as much as 25 percent—are "effectively barred" from collective representation. Almost insurmountable barriers exist to the organization of these nonstandard employees—a disproportionate number of whom are female. The low percentage of organized part-timers (8 percent) as opposed to organized full-timers (20 percent) and the virtual nonexistent unionization of at-home, temporary, and subcontracted employees (with the exception of janitorial) are suggestive of the difficulties in organizing nonstandard workers (U.S. Department of Labor 1992). Short-term contract workers, from musicians to data processors, may have dozens of different employers in a year's time. For them, the long, drawn-out NLRB election procedure is unworkable. Moreover, many part-timers,

9. Marion Crain (1991, 1992a, 1992b) and other feminist legal theorists reach conclusions similar to mine but for different reasons. Relying on the work of Carol Gilligan (1982), they argue that because women as a group value connection and shared decision-making, they are more comfortable with participatory, less adversarial forms of problem-solving. I would argue that these identifiable differences are as much the product of occupation as of gender. See also the account by Richard Hurd (1993) of the experience of Harvard clerical workers and Patricia A. Gwartney-Gibbs and Denise H. Lach's (1993) study of gender differences in grievance processing.

10. These high figures should come as no surprise since earlier estimates of the percentage of the total workforce not covered by the act have ranged from 50 to 63 percent (Rosenthal 1951; Sockell 1991:137n). I would argue, in fact, that my estimates are quite conservative. For example, in calculating the number of supervisory employees, I included only those occupational groupings specifically categorized as supervisory by the Census Bureau. Workers in many other occupational categories have also been found to exercise supervisory duties and are hence excluded from NLRA protection.

11. Some are exempted by statute, others by NLRB and court rulings. *NLRB v. Bell Aerospace Co.*, 416 U.S. 267, 274–75 (1974), excluded managerial employees. *NLRB v. Yeshiva Univ.*, 444 U.S. 672, 103 L.R.R.M. 2526 (1980), found faculty professionals to be managerial employees and hence ineligible.

Table 20.1.   Estimates of Numbers of Workers Excluded from NLRA Coverage, 1990 (in thousands)

	Total no. of workers	Total excluded	Total no. of women	Total no. of women excluded
Domestic workers	1,012	1,012	896	896
Agricultural workers[a]	2,861	2,861	554	554
Supervisors[b]	7,614	7,614	2,279	2,279
Managers	14,619	14,619	6,171	6,171
Self-employed workers (nonagricultural)	8,927	8,927	3,166	3,166
Professional employees[c]	16,648	2,945	8,941	722
Confidential employees[d]	250	250	175	175
Others[e]	335	335	92	92
Public-sector workers[f] (not elsewhere included)	12,019	12,019	6,441	6,441
Total excluded		50,582		20,496
Total employed		116,983		53,270
Percent of total excluded		43		38
Total private-sector excluded[g]		32,643		10,859
Total private-sector employment		99,044		43,633
Percent of private sector excluded		33		25

Sources: Domestic and agricultural workers: U.S. Department of Labor 1991, table A-24; supervisors, managers, self-employed workers, and confidential employees; U.S. Census Bureau 1992, table 2; others: U.S. Census Bureau 1991, table 860-1; public-sector workers, total employed, and total private-sector employment: U.S. Department of Labor 1991, table A-24.
[a] Includes wage and salary workers and self-employed workers in agriculture.
[b] Estimate based on totaling all occupational categories specified as supervisory except those included in other exempt categories.
[c] Estimate based on totaling figures for those professional occupations facing possible exclusion (postsecondary teachers, physicians, dentists, computer scientists, and others). The figure was then reduced by half.
[d] Based on the number of employees in personnel and labor relations managers category, plus estimates of confidential secretaries and assistants to persons with managerial functions in the field of labor relations.
[e] Based on estimates of employees in businesses with receipts below board requirement and number of employees in noncommercial, nonprofit religious operations.
[f] There were 17,939 government employees in 1990. The proportion of public-sector workers in the categories above were estimated and that number was subtracted from the total number of public-sector workers.
[g] The total number excluded (50,582) minus the total number of public-sector workers (17,939).

temporaries, and other casuals without likelihood of continued or regular employment are often exempted prior to NLRB elections because their inclusion is contested by the union or by management (Bronfenbrenner 1988c). In the case of leased and subcontracted employees, unless the business that hires the subcontractor is seen as a "joint employer," organizing is usually futile because the unionized contractor will simply be replaced and the bargaining unit lost (Bronfenbrenner 1988c; Howley 1990).

In short, then, by my estimates, the current legal and institutional framework of the NLRA disenfranchises more than half of the current female workforce. And, although a smaller proportion of women than men are legally excluded from coverage, because of their concentration in nonstandard employment, women may have even less opportunity than men to realize their desire for collective representation in the workplace.[12] Unless public policy shifts, access to collective bargaining for both men and women will become even more limited, since many of the exempted and barred categories—managers, supervisors, professionals, independent contractors, at-home and other nonstandard workers—are among the most rapidly growing sectors of the economy.[13]

Why Unionism Is Still Necessary

Yet despite the problems with the New Deal and mass-production model, there are tenets of the system that should be preserved. As with any realistic proposal for reform, elements of the old must be joined to the new. Let me specify three.

First, the old system rightly recognized that collective power for employees was essential for the existence of a genuinely collaborative relationship between labor and management. The most productive partnerships are between those relatively equal in power in which both parties have some degree of autonomy and security (Eaton and Voos 1992; Cornfield 1987:387). Yet the historic inequities of power between individual employees and their employers have widened not lessened since the 1930s. Employee representational schemes that fail to ensure autonomous, independent mechanisms for collective employee participation or that create joint committes in which management retains ultimate decision-making authority are in fact *out of touch* with the realities of today's workplace. The extension and stabilization of unionism and collective bargaining, albeit as transformed institutions, should remain at the heart of labor policy. As Karl Klare has argued; "Power-sharing is and should be on the agenda in the era of postindustrial transition" (1988:41).

Second, the need for both adversarial as well as cooperative encounters between employers and employees was acknowledged within the New Deal framework (Barenberg 1993). That need still exists. The interests of employers and employees overlap as well as diverge. Setting up a system that provides no way of expressing conflict and exerting pressures for its resolution will be a system that denies the fundamental realities of our economic system.

12. See Freeman and Rogers 1993b for a discussion of worker desire for collective representation. Research has consistently shown that women are more desirous of collective representation than men, and, in fact, when elections are held in their workplaces, they now vote for unions more frequently than do men (Kochan 1979; Bronfenbrenner 1990). Women are less organized than men in large part because they have less opportunity to participate in choosing a union.

13. See, for example, table 11, Bureau of Labor Statistics (1993) for the managerial and professional categories and duRivage (1992b) for the contingent work force.

The issue is not how to do away with "adversarialism" but how to minimize unhealthy and unnecessary adversarialism. Unions must be encouraged to accept more responsibility for the overall health and well-being of the enterprises with which they are linked, whether they be schools, hospitals, or auto factories. Yet the destructive adversarialism that has thrived in the last twenty years has been fueled not just by a limited unionism but by an American management culture deeply skeptical of the benefits of power-sharing and democracy at the workplace. American management's penchant for unilateral control, as Sanford Jacoby (1991) has argued, is the true American exceptionalism. Public policy must dampen the current adversarial culture by ensuring the institutional security of unions. Introducing "employee participation committees" or plant-level works councils might help close the "representation gap" for those 85 percent of the workforce without union representation.[14] But the widening "union gap" between the United States and other industrialized countries must also be closed if these committees are to function effectively and if a genuine realignment of power and decision-making is to occur.

Third, strong, autonomous unions act to counter gender, class, and racial divisions in our society and to further economic justice. Unionization raises the wages of women and minorities more than those of white men, especially in the public sector and in white-collar settings, where women have achieved the most power within their unions (Freeman and Leonard 1987). Unions with large female constituencies have also pushed for pay equity, family and medical leave, and other advantageous policies for women (Cobble 1993). Unions are rapidly feminizing. These transformed and feminized unions could be quite effective as vehicles for advancing the needs of women in the future. Yet without a shift in public policy supportive of collective bargaining, their potential will be thwarted.

Historical and Contemporary Alternatives

Much of the current critique of the New Deal system falsely equates all unionism with the form of unionism that became dominant by the 1940s. Thus, the argument goes, if industrial unionism is obsolete, so is unionism per se. This historical amnesia hampers attempts to create new forms of collective representation. Postindustrial unionism does not need to be invented out of whole cloth: It can be reassembled, reshaped, and extended from elements of past and current institutional practice. The institutional practices of what I

14. Freeman and Rogers (1993b) argue that a "representation gap" exists because a large majority of workers desire some form of representation yet only 15 percent are unionized. They conclude, therefore, that alternative forms of representation are needed to close this gap.

have termed "occupational unions" and the nontraditional approaches to representation taken by female-dominated professional and semiprofessional groups such as teachers, nurses, and clericals offer the best guide to the formulation of a postindustrial unionism.

Occupational unionism, the primary model of unionism before the New Deal, was neither Taylorist nor worksite-based (Cobble 1991a, 1991b). Although not every trade adopted "occupational unionism" in toto, before the New Deal the majority of organized trades and virtually every single trade that successfully organized mobile workers relied on some elements of occupational unionism. Occupational unions recruited and gained recognition on an occupational or local market basis rather than by industry or individual job site. Their representational systems emphasized occupationally based rights, benefits, and identity rather than worksite-based protections. Longshoremen, janitors, agricultural laborers, food servers, and garment workers, as well as such classic craft unionists as printers, building tradesmen, and performing artists, strove for control over hiring through closed-shop language and through union-run employment exchanges, rosters, and hiring halls; stressed employment security rather than "job rights" at individual worksites; offered portable benefits and privileges; and took responsibility for monitoring workplace performance.[15]

Occupational unionism flourished because it met the needs of workers and employers outside of mass-production settings. In local labor markets populated with numerous small employers, the unionization of garment workers, restaurant employees, teamsters, and others brought stability and predictability, inhibiting cutthroat competition. Employers gained a steady supply of skilled, responsible labor and an outside agency (the union) that ensured the competence and job performance of its members. In many cases, the union took responsibility for expanding the customer base for unionized enterprises. A floor for minimum wage and working conditions was established. Workers did not gain long-term job tenure but the opportunity to invest in their own "human capital" through training and experience at a variety of worksites. As long as the unionized sector remained competitive—a goal to which both labor and management were committed—unionized workers also gained real employment security, in that the union helped make them more employable individually and helped ensure there would be a supply of high-wage, "good" jobs. This unionism, then, in contrast to industrial unionism, never developed rigid seniority rules at individual worksites; it was committed to maintaining employee productivity, high-quality service and production, and to ensuring the viability of unionized firms. In short, it was flexible, cooperative as well as

15. The line between employee and employer was blurred as well. Not only did unions take responsibility for personnel decisions but many organizations (teamsters, musicians, retail workers, for example) included supervisors and small employers (Christensen 1933).

adversarial, and dedicated to skill enhancement and to the creation of a high-performance workplace (for examples, see Christensen 1933; Millis 1942; Slichter 1941; Cobble 1991a).

Occupational unionism declined dramatically in the postwar era, in part because of shifts in union institutional practice, as I have detailed extensively for the hotel and restaurant industry (Cobble 1991a). Legislative and legal decisions also severely hampered the ability of occupational unions to exert control over their members, to pressure employers for recognition, and to provide services to members and employers. Closed-shop, top-down organizing, secondary boycotts, the removal of members from the job for noncompliance with union bylaws and work rules, and union membership for supervisors all became illegal. Unions lost their ability to organize new shops, to maintain multiemployer bargaining structures, to set entrance requirements for the trade, to oversee job performance, and to punish recalcitrant members (Cobble 1991a; Millis and Brown 1950:636–42; Levinson 1980:135–37).

By the 1960s, occupational unionism was but a mere shadow of its former robust self. Only the building and construction trades (which obtained special legislative language exempting them from some of the new postwar legal restrictions on unions) and certain highly specialized professional groups (such as the performing arts occupations) retained some degree of power and influence (Kleingartner and Paul 1992; Mills 1980). Yet by the 1960s other alternatives to mass-production unionism were emerging. The professional and semiprofessional employee organizations built primarily by women, for example, initially focused less on extracting economic concessions from individual enterprises and more on the well-being of their industry or sector and on responding to the "professional" interests of their members. As state bargaining laws and other forces moved them toward more traditional "bargaining" relations with employers, they shed some of their occupational and associational orientation. Yet, as Charles Taylor Kerchner and Douglas E. Mitchell (1988) have argued for teacher unions, many are now moving toward a third stage of labor relations, in which they are as concerned with the welfare of the overall educational system and with meeting the needs of their clients as with protecting their own interests as employees. It is these alternative models of unionism that hold promise for the future.

Encouraging Postindustrial Alternatives

Fully integrating the realities of women's work—its mobility, its external and local market context, the personalized aspect of its work relations—into labor relations theory and policy would cause a reevalution of the most fundamental assumptions on which our labor law and institutional practice rely. I cannot undertake that project in a comprehensive fashion here. Nevertheless, I can point to the kind of transformations that should occur and suggest a number of concrete steps that would help crack the industrial union mold.

Let me make it clear that I am not arguing that the industrial model should be abandoned *wholesale*. Manufacturing itself is not going to disappear, and some of the practices of industrial unionism may continue to be appealing and advantageous to a wide variety of workers. Nonetheless, just as industrial unionism superseded craft unionism as technological change and economic restructuring transformed the workplace, so too must industrial unionism give way to other alternatives. We must now begin to think *once more* in terms of multiple and competing forms of unionism. A single model of labor relations cannot meet the needs of all workers. Multiple models must be allowed to thrive. In other words, we must make possible not just postindustrial unionism but postindustrial unionism*s*.

Toward that end, I have twelve recommendations to offer. My emphasis here is on creating structures that facilitate self-governance and mutual problem-solving in the work world as alternatives to regulatory intervention and unilateral decision-making.

1. *Expand the definition of "employee" under the NLRA to include those currently excluded either by statute or by case law.*

Some 50 million workers (43 percent of the workforce) are now explicitly exempted from exercising their rights to collective bargaining under the act. Of the private-sector workforce, a third (or some 32 million workers) are without access (See Table 20.1). The law must not discriminate against those such as domestic and agricultural workers whose worksites are still linked to the household economy. Nor should categories of workers be excluded simply because these workers exercise certain "managerial" or "supervisory" responsibilities and authority. In a post-Taylorist workplace, virtually every employee will participate in decisions once thought to be managerial prerogatives.

2. *The law must ensure that bargaining relations are structured to promote meaningful and maximum exchange. Where subcontracting and leasing arrangements exist, a narrow approach to determining joint employer status should be reconsidered. Also, part-time, temporary, and short-term hires should be included in bargaining units.*

Without such reforms, the growing ranks of the contingent workforce will be disenfranchised. In contrast with the expansive interpretations of joint liability taken by courts in considering Fair Labor Standard Act or Title VII cases, under the NLRA, as presently interpreted, host employers bear "little responsibility for the economic conditions of their contractors' employees" (Hiatt and Rhinehart 1993:20). Yet the client or host employer decides whether or not there will be jobs for those "employed" by the subcontractor. It is this ultimate power to give or withhold employment that makes the contractor the relevant bargaining party and a codeterminer of "the essential terms and conditions of employment." The "right to control" and the degree of supervision is no longer an appropriate determinate of employer status in a post-Taylorist work environment.[16]

The exclusion of nonstandard workers from bargaining units diminishes access for that one-fourth of working women who are so categorized. As the work world continues to shift toward nonstandard employment contracts, increasing numbers of both men and women will lose access to collective representation. If workplace democracy is to be retained as employers and employees move away from standard contractural arrangements, public policy should not penalize those who work off site, on other than full time schedules, or whose tenure is undefined. As Virginia duRivage (1992b: 116–21) argues, part-time, temporary, and short-term hires should be included in bargaining units based on "the content of their work rather than the classification of their employment."[17]

3. *For effective bargaining to exist in a service economy of numerous small employers, mechanisms are needed that facilitiate the extension of collective bargaining to other relevant employers in the service or labor market. Marketwide, multiemployer bargaining is necessary for stable, effective collective bargaining relationships.*

Decentralized, firm-based bargaining is increasingly unworkable. It heightens the economic burdens on unionized employers and fuels employer resistance to unionization. It is also simply too labor-intensive to bargain individual contracts with hundreds of small employers. The Hotel Employees and Restaurant Employees International Union, for example, cannot bargain individually with the thousands of independent and family-owned eating establishments that exist in even one major metropolitan area.

The law should facilitate the establishment of bargaining relationships that act as "patterns" or as "master contracts" with other employers. Marketwide, multiemployer bargaining could also be encouraged by certifying multiemployer bargaining units, by penalizing employers that withdraw from voluntarily

16. Rep. William Clay recently introduced a bill that would redefine "single employer" in the construction industry to include "any two or more business entities with substantial common ownership, management, or control" and would require such an employer to bargain collectively with the union. This bill should be expanded beyond the construction and building trades (*Daily Labor Report*, Dec. 11, 1993).

17. If "employee participation committees" are mandated, as Weiler (1993) and others propose, mechanisms for the participation of non-standard, high-turnover workers must be devised.

constituted multiemployer agreements, and by implementing "sectoral bargaining" legislation. Sectoral bargaining, as it exists and is being proposed in Canada, mandates that the minimum standards of an agreement be extended to other employers on an industry, occupational, or geographical basis (see Eaton 1993 for further elaboration).

Multiemployer bargaining could also be facilitated by removing the restrictions on the economic tools allowed labor organizations (See recommendation 4). Increasing the power of labor historically has often meant that employers— especially small employers in highly competitive markets—voluntarily sought multiemployer bargaining (for example, see Feinsinger 1949). This alternative approach would lessen rather than increase government regulation.

4. *The legal restrictions on prehire agreements, recognitional picketing, secondary boycotts and other "secondary activities," such as so-called hot cargo agreements, need to be removed when the object is securing or helping to secure recognition.*

Numerous commentators have made excellent proposals aimed at improving recognitional procedures (for example, Weiler 1990). Reforms such as increased penalties for employers that fire union activists, expedited election procedures, enhanced worksite access for union organizers, card check recognition, and first-contract arbitration would "level the playing field" and do much to facilitate the establishment of bargaining relationships. Yet with the dramatic decline in the willingness of employers to recognize unions voluntarily or to agree to "consent elections," unions must be allowed to exert heightened economic pressure on employers to secure recognition (Friedman and Prosten 1993). Increased government regulation and litigation are not the solution.

In particular, if a mobile, decentralized service workforce is to have representational rights, unions must once again have the ability to organize "top down" and to exert many of the economic pressures on employers that were once legal. Historically, the millions of nonfactory workers—teamsters, longshoremen, waitresses, cooks, musicians, and others—who successfully organized between the 1930s and the 1950s relied on prehire agreements, recognitional picketing, secondary boycotts, limitations on nonunion or substandard subcontractors, restrictions on the handling or transporting of non-union goods, and other approaches to secure bargaining rights (for example, Cobble 1991a; Slichter 1941). Making these approaches legal once again would make possible the organizing of workers from home-based legal transcribers and domestic cleaners to the millions of newly mobile professional consultants and managers. Only when representatives of the occupation can negotiate wages and working conditions for *future* as well as current employees will meaningful bargaining relationships be possible.[18]

Unions organizing mobile workers need to be able to conclude a contract without having first to demonstrate majority status through elaborate and cumbersome election proceedings. Election procedures, if requested by the employer, could be conducted subsequent to recognition. The presumption should be that majority status exists and that bargaining in good faith is required *unless* lack of majority status is demonstrated. Indeed, as we move toward occupationally based employee institutions rather than worksite-based, democracy will best be protected by ensuring democratic governance at the level of the association or union level, not the workplace.

5. *The notion of what is "protected economic activity" should be broadened. Not only should certain "secondary activities" be legal, but employees who honor concerted actions against employers other than their own should be fully protected.*

Many of these restrictions assume that "employers" are distinct entities, easily defined and delineated, and that they occupy distinct and immobile worksites. The lines between primary and secondary employers and hence between "primary and secondary economic activity" are no longer clear. Rigid distinctions between primary and secondary are particularly problematic for unions attempting to organize and bargain in industries and sectors with high degrees of transience and subcontracting.

6. *Promote the formation of employee-run or state-run employment bureaus, exchanges, and hiring halls as key institutions that can structure external labor markets, prevent "casualization" and disorder, and serve the needs of a mobile workforce.*

Worker-run or state-run employment agencies would appeal to today's mobile workforce just as they did in the past. Historically, these institutions—especially where they were worker run and linked to unionization—were critical in decasualizing the workforce. Operating among waitresses, agricultural workers, garment workers, performing artists, janitors, teamsters, longshoremen, and many other groups, they raised wages in the local labor market, offered portable, high-quality benefits that did not penalize intermittent workforce participation, and provided workers with control over their hours and work schedules without jeopardizing their employment security (Cobble 1991a). Increasingly, many workers desire mobility between employers and flexibility in their work lives. In particular, those balancing work and family are concerned with flexible scheduling and shortened work time. Nonprofit

18. The case of musicians offers a concrete example of the necessity for reform. The American Federation of Musicians has recommended that the prehire exemption allowed for the building and construction trades be extended to musicians and that the definitions of "employee" and "employer" be amended to once again allow for meaningful bargaining (Massagli 1993).

agencies could provide such variety and flexibility, and presumably they could offer higher wages than agencies run for profit.

Employee-run or state-run agencies would need to be subject to strict antidiscriminatory procedures that would guarantee the rights of minorities. Groups of workers or so-called neutral agencies can discriminate in hiring just as do employers. It is important to recognize, however, that hiring halls have not been solely the creature of the building trades and other male-dominated occupations. Historically, they served the interests of women and minorities in a wide range of industries, including garment, agricultural, and food service.

Although some employers might rely on such agencies voluntarily, most would seek cheaper labor if it were available. Hence, for these mechanisms to flourish, the union must be able either to exert control over the labor supply within a local labor market or to pressure employers through recognitional picketing, secondary and customer boycotts, and prehire and preferential hiring agreements (see recommendation 4).

7. *Promote institutions and practices that support higher probabilities of employment and income security as well as those that promote job security with an individual enterprise.*

The historic commitment of the occupational unions to providing employment and income security rather than merely guaranteeing job security at an individual worksite should be revived. Occupational unions fostered employment and income security by taking responsibility for employee competence and productivity and by promoting the health and viability of unionized employers. These practices helped preserve high-wage union jobs by creating an incentive among employers to be unionized.

The crisis in job growth and the decline in real earnings should be as serious an issue for those concerned about employee security as amending the "employment-at-will" doctrine and extending "just-cause" provisions to unorganized workplaces. Indeed, in some sectors of the economy, making a commitment to creating high-wage jobs, retraining workers, and providing income guarantees is more rational than tying the fates of individual employees to sinking enterprises. In the postindustrial future, employees who are mobile may in fact have greater long-term security (Hallett 1986).

8. *Promote statutes that raise wages and secure benefits for employees on a marketwide rather than an enterprise basis. Specifically, prevailing wage legislation (such as the Davis-Bacon Act or the Service Contracts Act) should be strengthened and extended to sectors of the economy in which subcontracting is proliferating. Benefit portability should also be guaranteed.*

The Davis-Bacon Act requires that employees working on federally financed construction projects be paid wages and offered fringe benefits at a rate equal to that prevailing in the area. The Service Contracts Act has a similar mandate for employees under service contracts with government agencies. Numerous states and municipalities also have prevailing wage legislation that protects employees working under state-financed contracts. Similar legislation should be extended to the private sector in those arenas in which subcontracting predominates.

Prevailing wage legislation promotes wage stability and establishes a floor below which wages and benefits cannot fall. It prevents the downward spiral of wages and hinders the reliance on wage cutting as the prime competitive strategy. It also provides institutional stabilization for unions by lowering employer resistance to unionization.

9. *Restore to unions the right to participate jointly in decisions concerning hiring, discipline, discharge, and training. Legal restrictions in these areas are numerous, but first steps should include repealing the prohibitions on closed shops and ending the restrictions on the ability of employee associations to recommend discipline and discharge actions.*

Historically, occupational unions, like professional associations, set standards for admission to the occupation, oversaw training and upgrading programs, and took responsibility for disciplining incompetent work performance. Members might lose their certification, their membership in the association, or in some cases be removed from the job (Cobble 1991a; Slichter 1941:9–52). Postindustrial unions could help promote a high-performance and humane workplace by once again taking on these "management" responsibilities. And, as Arthur Stinchcombe and others have argued, the substitution of craft and professional administration for bureaucratic managerial supervision is a more economically viable, efficient, and rational approach in the many sectors of the economy that require flexibility (Piore and Sabel 1984; Stinchcombe 1959; Block 1990).

Of equal importance, placing more responsibility in the hands of marketwide employee associations rather than individual enterprise-based work teams is crucial to the advancement and equity of those in external labor markets. Most proposals for enhancing joint decision-making recommend giving increased responsibilities for hiring, discipline, and training to employee teams at individual worksites. These proposals do little for employees at small worksites where training and promotion occur through the external market or for employees who move from employer to employer and hence are excluded from site-based training opportunities.

10. *Unions must help enhance the "human capital" resources of individual employees and address issues of promotion, career advancement, and opportunity. In some cases,*

unions should consider supporting individualized, performance-based compensation and recognition policies as well as continuing their support for more merit-blind mechanisms, such as seniority systems and across-the-board wage increases.

The union movement must reclaim the emphasis among occupational and associational unions on representing the individual as well as the collective interests of employees. In addition to offering training and other skill-enhancing services, occupational unions rewarded individual initiative and performance by devising pay schedules that combined seniority-based scales with wages pegged to skill. The performing arts unions still negotiate a collective contract that sets minimum standards while allowing individuals to bargain supplemental enhancements.

Taking more responsibility for compensation criteria can be difficult, but as Albert Shanker has argued in explaining the American Federation of Teachers' consistent support of a peer-determined merit pay system: "We will never convince the public that we are professionals unless we are prepared honestly to decide what constitutes competence in our profession and what constitutes incompetence and apply those definitions to ourselves and our colleagues" (1985:46–48).

It is critical that the labor movement rethink its institutional practices in light of survey data that repeatedly show that although the majority of workers want collective representation, they are not satisfied with the way in which most unions respond to the need for opportunitites for promotions and their desire for recognition of individual effort and achievement (Freeman and Rogers 1993b).

11. *Collective bargaining practices and procedures must be redesigned to enhance employee participation and to broaden the band of communication between employee and employer.*

The efforts of Harvard University and the Harvard Union of Technical and Clerical Workers (HUTCW) are perhaps the most instructive. Their agreement was primarily a statement of "value and principles, not an elaboration of rules and procedures" (Hoerr 1993:68). The interpretation of these principles was then left in the hands of groups of employees. Rigid, detailed work rules became less important in an environment in which decision-making and problem-solving had been shifted downward and in which trust and good relationships between parties was deemed of value. In addition, Harvard employees relied on large bargaining teams during contract negotiations and set up a system of joint problem-solving teams and councils that have involved hundreds of workers (Crain 1992a; Hoerr 1993). These new cooperative, participatory representation mechanisms were effective in large part because the local union vigorously maintained ties with its own members and relied on well-organized and traditional economic pressures when necessary.

HUTCW skillfully combined cooperative and adversarial strategies (Hurd 1993).[19]

12. *Restructure labor organizations to promote greater membership participation and intraunion bargaining. The leadership and participation of minorities and women can best be encouraged through redesigned union structures rather than by repealing the "exclusivity doctrine."*[20]

The protection of minority rights is critical to employee participation and productivity. The repeal of the "exclusivity doctrine," however, and its replacement with a system of "coordinated diversity" and "multilateral bargaining" will not necessarily safeguard minority interests.[21] In fact, such a system might result in less participation by minority groups because their interests would no longer be protected through legally guaranteed union democratic procedures and formal, intraunion bargaining structures. They would be competing in an unstructured, open arena with every other interest group. Structurelessness tends to perpetuate existing power relations rather than help dismantle them.

Union structures, however, need to be redesigned to facilitate participation better and to protect the rights of minorities. Setting up small, occupationally or other interest-based units within the large, heterogeneous general unions— many of which are products of the current merger wave—would help reduce bureaucracy, provide a sense of community, enhance union democracy, and protect the rights of minorities. Effective multilateral bargaining has and does occur *within* union institutions. Historically, it has often relied on the institutionalization of diverse interests, sometimes in small locals or caucuses organized along gender, ethnic, or occupational lines. These smaller units were then *each* guaranteed representation on joint boards or councils that functioned institutionally both to represent and reconcile competing interests (Cobble 1991a).[22] In contrast to the repeal of the exclusivity doctrine, the promotion of such formalized intraunion bargaining structures would ensure that the class needs of employees are met along with the needs that flow from their different racial, ethnic, and gender identities.

19. The Saturn-UAW case is another example of how extensive employee participation is compatible with collective bargaining (Rubinstein, Bennett, and Kochan 1993).

20. Once a union is secured as the majority union for a group of employees, it becomes the exclusive representative of all workers, as defined in Section 9 of the NLRA. Employers are not permitted to bargain with groups of workers other than those designated as union representatives.

21. See Crain 1992b and Heckscher 1988 for the contrasting viewpoint.

22. Representation was often some combination of interest and proportional, not unlike the representational system operating in the House of Representatives (proportional) and the Senate (interest).

21

New Bargaining Structures for New Forms of Business Organization

Howard Wial

This chapter addresses an issue that is likely to be of great importance to the future of collective bargaining in the United States but that has received virtually no attention in the current debate about labor law reform: the relationship between the structure of collective bargaining and the structure of American business. During the past decade, American businesses have implemented major structural changes. These changes have important consequences for the viability of existing collective bargaining relationships and for the extension of collective bargaining into heretofore unorganized sectors of the economy. Yet these changes have been largely unacknowledged in American labor law. Our legal rules and presumptions regarding appropriate bargaining units, the formation and dissolution of negotiating relationships, and restrictions on secondary pressures reflect the business structures of the earlier post–World War II period rather than those that have emerged in recent years. In important respects, these rules inhibit unions and employers from creating bargaining structures that are appropriate to today's business environment.

Consequences of Changing Business Structures for Collective Bargaining

The recent changes in business structure may be understood as departures from an organizational model that, until quite recently, was shared by academic observers of and unionists and managers in the mass-production core of

The analysis and conclusions presented in this chapter are solely those of the author and do not necessarily reflect the positions or views of his employer, the U.S. Department of Labor, or the U.S. government.

the U.S. economy during the post–World War II period. In that model, the basic unit of business organization was a highly vertically integrated, hierarchical firm whose relationships with other firms were carried out via arm's-length market transactions (Piore 1989). Both production workers and managers typically held long-term jobs within the firm (Osterman 1988). It was, therefore, relatively easy to determine which workers and managers were "inside" the firm and which were "outside" it and to conceive of collective bargaining as negotiation between "inside" management and a (local) labor union that represented the "inside" workers.

Recent changes in business structure have involved the breakdown of all of the major elements of this model: vertical integration, arm's-length contracting as the major form of relationship between firms, and long-term jobs within the organization. A wide variety of activities that were once performed within the vertically integrated organization, from the provision of food services to the manufacture of automotive components, are now performed by specialized subcontractors (Kanter 1989; Helper 1990). Even some activities that are not contracted out may be treated as quasi-independent businesses whose workers and managers must compete with "outsiders" (Kanter 1989). At the same time, firms that formerly dealt with one another at arm's length have formed cooperative relationships, such as joint ventures, consortia, and long-term alliances, with suppliers, customers, or distributors (Kanter 1989; Helper 1991). These relationships may give one firm (e.g., an automobile manufacturer) direct influence over the production methods used by another (e.g., an automobile parts supplier) or may require close cooperation among workers who are employed by different firms. Finally, the incidence of long-term job holding within individual firms appears to have declined somewhat during the 1980s (Swinnerton and Wial 1993). In sum, the boundary between the people and activities that are inside the firm and those that are outside has become much less sharp than in the model of the independent, vertically integrated firm.

These changes create a number of important problems that could potentially be resolved, at least in part, through collective bargaining. Subcontracting and other forms of vertical disaggregation raise problems concerning the equitable allocation of work. They may increase wage competition between workers and enable firms to compete on the basis of wage levels rather than product quality. They also have the potential to increase wage inequality; wages that were formerly influenced by the customary norms of individual firms (whether union or nonunion) are detached from those firms and removed from the equalizing influence of their wage norms.[1]

1. In post–World War II Japan, the desire of large firms, both union and nonunion, to escape the constraints imposed by these wage norms was an important reason for the development of the Japanese automobile industry's extensive subcontracting system (Smitka 1991).

Cooperative ties between firms may give workers employed by one firm an interest in the business practices of allied firms. Such ties may enable the management of one firm to have a substantial influence over wages, working conditions, and employment opportunities within an allied firm. If, in addition, these ties require close cooperation between workers employed by separate firms, then harmonization of wages and working conditions between workers who perform the same type of work for different firms may be a prerequisite to the success of the cooperative venture. The decreasing willingness or ability of individual firms to offer long-term jobs creates a need for alternative, multiemployer institutions to provide workers with training, employment continuity, and income security; these institutions can be established through collective bargaining.

Multiemployer bargaining structures could contribute to the resolution of the industrial relations problems that the new business structures have created. Yet the recent evolution of bargaining structures in the United States and other advanced industrial countries has proceeded in the opposite direction, toward decentralization of collective bargaining to the level of the individual firm or establishment (Katz 1993). The reasons for this trend are not yet well understood, but at a minimum the new business structures create a need to supplement decentralized bargaining over local workplace issues with broader bargaining structures.

What form should these broader structures take? Some might argue that all that is needed is a return to the industrywide pattern bargaining (Katz 1985) that characterized American mass-production industries during the earlier postwar period. The problem with this approach is that the new business structures may blur industrial boundaries. When, for example, janitors can be shifted across industrial boundaries depending on whether they work for cleaning contractors or for building owners, or when a joint venture brings the employees of a manufacturer into close cooperation with those of a distributor, it is unclear what "industry" is relevant for bargaining purposes.

Others might argue that the new business structures result solely from successful managerial attempts to compete on the basis of low wages and, therefore, should be resisted rather than accommodated. But although subcontracting and other forms of vertical business disaggregation can be motivated by low-wage strategies, there can also be legitimate business reasons for these practices. For example, an outside supplier may have special technical expertise or may be better able to pay attention to the details of product or service quality than a single, integrated firm (Helper 1990). For this reason, it is preferable to structure collective bargaining in ways that simultaneously limit wage competition and accommodate the new forms of business organization than to induce businesses to revert to earlier organizational forms.

For bargaining purposes, a useful way of understanding the new business structures is to view the locus of business decision-making as a network of loosely linked business units (Storper and Harrison 1991) rather than as an individual firm. From this view, collective bargaining is a part of the relationship between a network-based union(s)[2] and the management(s) that coordinate(s) or control(s) the business decisions of the network as a whole. Some networks, such as the construction contractors in a metropolitan area or the computer-related firms in Silicon Valley, are geographically concentrated groups of small firms with no central controller or coordinator. They are characterized by both interfirm product market competition and interfirm sharing or interchange of workers or new technology. In these networks, where the key business decisions that affect workers are dispersed throughout the network, collective bargaining could occur (as it does in the construction industry) between local network-based unions and an employer association that represents all the firms in the network.

Other networks, such as groups consisting of automobile manufacturers and the auto parts suppliers with which they have cooperative relationships, have firms (e.g., the auto manufacturers) that coordinate or control the entire network, which may be geographically concentrated or dispersed. The dominant firm(s) in the network may occupy their dominant positions because they own or participate financially in other network firms, because they exercise market power over the other firms, or because interfirm cooperative agreements give them influence over managerial decisions of the other firms. Because the decisions of the dominant firm(s) can affect the employment situations of all workers in the network, collective bargaining on a networkwide basis should enable network-based unions to bargain with the dominant firm(s) (U.S. Congress, Office of Technology Assessment 1992:46). This bargaining could occur, as in the previous case, between the union(s) and an employer association that includes all network firms. Alternatively, the network-based union could bargain with the dominant firm(s) on networkwide issues and leave "local" issues to be resolved within individual firms or smaller groups of firms in the network.

Forerunners of Network-Based Bargaining

Although network forms of business organization are new to much of the U.S. economy and to many American unions, they are not without historical

---

2. Whether the workers in a network should be represented by a single "industrial model" union or by a set of occupationally specific "craft model" unions is a question whose answer may vary across networks and across occupations. Network-based bargaining should be flexible enough to accommodate both representational forms. Moreover, network-based bargaining need not preclude bargaining on an even broader sectoral basis with respect to issues that are of concern to workers throughout an economic sector.

precedent. Some sectors, such as garment production, that were never part of the mass-production core of the postwar economy have long been characterized by geographically concentrated networks of small firms. In these sectors, unions developed effective bargaining structures before passage of the Wagner Act. More recently, there is some evidence that the enterprise-based United Automobile Workers local at General Motors' Saturn Corporation may be moving toward a network structure.

Bargaining Structures in the U.S. Garment Industry

Since the end of the nineteenth century, garment production has been organized through geographically concentrated networks of manufacturers (which design and market clothing and may perform some direct production), contractors (which specialize in direct production), and jobbers (which specialize in design and marketing).[3] Contractors produce for jobbers and manufacturers. In the early twentieth century, the two major garment workers' unions, the Amalgamated Clothing Workers and the ILGWU, developed areawide multiemployer bargaining as a response to this system of production. All manufacturers, contractors, and jobbers in an area bargained jointly and signed a common agreement with the relevant union. This agreement typically provided for a uniform wage scale that applied to all workers, regardless of employer.

Two features of this bargaining structure are instructive for the formation of new network-based bargaining structures. First, union organizing, collective bargaining, and contract enforcement were structurally separated. Organizing was extremely flexible and could proceed on the basis of employer, occupation, ethnicity, and/or gender. In the ILGWU, any group of at least seven workers within the union's geographical and industrial jurisdiction could form a local. Union rules required all of the locals in a given geographical area to form a joint board, which was responsible for bargaining with the relevant firms. Grievances under the collective agreement were handled by union representatives at the level of the individual business establishment. This example shows that highly decentralized organizing and enforcement can be compatible with more centralized, networkwide bargaining.

The second instructive feature of the garment union experience is the use of secondary economic pressure—that is, economic pressure applied against a firm other than one with which a union has a direct dispute. Firms that were parties to the union contract agreed not to subcontract work to nonunion firms, and the unions enforced this contract provision by striking against violators.

The Taft-Hartley Act forbids secondary picketing. The Landrum-Griffin Act prohibits union-management agreements to cease doing business with

3. This section is based on Lorwin 1924, Myers and Bloch 1942, and Robinson 1949.

other firms but exempts unions in the garment industry from this prohibition as well as from the ban on secondary picketing.[4] In the congressional debates over Landrum-Griffin, both Democratic and Republican legislators from garment-producing states argued that secondary pressures were instrumental in the elimination of garment sweatshops and necessary to prevent their return (U.S. Congress 1959, 2:1195, 1829). This argument may apply to networks outside the garment industry, especially those that consist of numerous small firms. In such networks, secondary economic pressure may play a role in reducing intra-network wage competition and in preventing firms that compete on the basis of low wages from joining the network.

Nascent Network Bargaining at Saturn Corporation

General Motors' Saturn Corporation and its UAW local have pioneered new forms of establishment-level union-management cooperation that include substantial union involvement in both production management and broader strategic management decisions. These developments have led some observers (e.g., Bluestone and Bluestone 1992) to view Saturn as a model for a new form of enterprise-based unionism.

There are, however, features of Saturn's industrial relations system that point in the direction of network-based bargaining. Saturn occupies a dominant position in a network that includes multiple suppliers and service providers. Local union and management representatives jointly choose Saturn's suppliers, subject to the approval of both the UAW International and Saturn management (Rubinstein, Bennett, and Kochan 1993). This form of union participation in supplier selection may have the same effects as the type of agreement prohibited by law, although its legality has not been challenged and its effects alone do not render it illegal. Like the prohibited type of agreement, it has the potential to keep out of Saturn's supplier network firms that compete on the basis of low wages rather than product quality.

The local union is also expanding to include employees of firms that have close business relationships with Saturn. The local already includes employees of Saturn's on-site food-service contractor and employees of a firm that provides a variety of other services at the Saturn plant. Employees of a trucking firm that serves Saturn will soon be included in the local as well (Rubinstein, Bennett, and Kochan 1993). Although the bargaining structure that will emerge from this broadening of the local's membership has not yet been determined, the potential exists for including all of the local's members under a single contract.

4. This statutory provision also exempts unions in the construction industry from the prohibition on agreements to cease doing business with others, but not from the ban on secondary picketing.

The Saturn case suggests that it may be possible for network-based bargaining to emerge from a single-employer union-management relationship in a firm that occupies a dominant position in a network. It is unlikely, however, that network-based bargaining will spread throughout the U.S. economy in this manner. Because some networks have no dominant firm, the Saturn case does not provide a model for broad-based bargaining in those networks. Even in networks that have dominant firms, it is uncertain whether unions that are based in the dominant firms will want to bargain jointly with all other network firms and workers, since such joint bargaining could redistribute wages and profits from the workers and shareholders of the dominant firm to other firms in the network.[5]

Legal Disincentives to Network-Based Bargaining

There is nothing in current American labor law that prohibits unions and firms from bargaining on a networkwide basis. The basic policies of the National Labor Relations Act, as amended, however, and the doctrines of the NLRB create disincentives to network-based bargaining. These disincentives are of two types: (1) rules that encourage unions to conduct both organizing and bargaining within the same narrowly defined units and (2) inappropriate restrictions on secondary pressures.

The NLRB defines "appropriate bargaining units" on the basis of whether workers share a "community of interest." The indicia of "community of interest" include a variety of factors that are under the control of individual employers (Rogers 1990; Wial 1993). In applying its "community of interest" test, the NLRB presumes the appropriateness of units that do not extend beyond the boundaries of individual firms or, in multiestablishment firms, individual worksites. It approves multiestablishment or multiemployer units only when an employer has a history of multiestablishment or multiemployer bargaining and intends to continue bargaining on such a broad basis (Rogers 1990; Wial 1993).

Strictly speaking, an "appropriate bargaining unit" is merely the unit within which a union certification election occurs. There is no requirement that bargaining be limited to the confines of this unit. However, the law

5. A similar concern about the distributional consequences of the scope of collective bargaining existed among members of the NLRB in the 1930s, who debated the scope of appropriate bargaining units. One board member favored establishmentwide units on the ground that such units would enable unskilled workers to benefit from the bargaining power of skilled craft workers in the same establishment (*Allis-Chalmers Manufacturing Co.*, 4 N.L.R.B. 159, 176 (1937) (board member Edwin Smith, dissenting); *American Can Co.*, 13 N.L.R.B. 1252, 1258 (1939) (board member Edwin Smith, concurring). Likewise, networkwide bargaining would diffuse throughout the network the benefits of union bargaining power in dominant firms.

inhibits the expansion of the scope of bargaining beyond the certified unit (Wial 1993). Where the certified unit is restricted to a single employer (or subdivision thereof), both the initial establishment of multiemployer bargaining and its continuation from one contract to the next are subject to the mutual agreement of the union and each separate employer. Although there are legal restrictions on the ability of any union or employer to withdraw from multiemployer negotiations once they are under way, any party may withdraw before the beginning of a new round of negotiations. Moreover, a union may not strike to compel multiemployer bargaining; nor may a union and an employer agree to impose their contract on other employers that are not parties to the contract.

Thus, the law creates incentives for both organizing and bargaining to occur within the same employer- or establishment-specific units unless there is a strong tradition of more broadly based bargaining. Because the network form of business organization has only recently begun to spread throughout the U.S. economy, a tradition of multiemployer bargaining along network lines does not exist for most workers and employers.[6] The current law of bargaining unit determination makes it unlikely that such a tradition will ever develop.

For network bargaining, the basic problem with the law of unit determination is that it conflates organizing structures with bargaining structures. In a system that has come to rely heavily on elections to establish the legal legitimacy of union representation, it is often sensible for unions to organize relatively small groups of workers. Indeed, this is the rationale that the NLRB has given for its presumptions that narrow bargaining units are appropriate (*Sav-On Drugs, Inc.*, 138 N.L.R.B. 1032 (1962)). But the appropriateness of narrow units for organizing purposes does not imply the appropriateness of such units for bargaining. Moreover, the historical example of the garment workers' unions shows that there is no practical bar to organizing and bargaining in different units. If network bargaining is to become widespread, some means by which organizing units may be amalgamated for bargaining purposes is essential.

The legal restrictions on secondary pressures are the second major disincentive to network-based bargaining. The statutory prohibitions were described above. The doctrinal justification for these restrictions is that a "neutral" employer ought to be free from economic pressure in a labor dispute in which it is not directly involved (*Frito-Lay, Inc. v. Retail Clerks Union Local No. 7*, 629 F.2d 653, 659 (8th Cir. 1980)). Even if this doctrinal principle is accepted, it does not follow that it should automatically apply to separate

6. Indeed, multiemployer bargaining of all types has become increasingly rare in the United States (Katz 1993).

firms in the same network. The existence of network ties among firms implies that at least some industrial relations issues cannot be confined to individual employers but involve other firms in the network. For example, an automobile manufacturer may exert a powerful influence over wages, working conditions, and production methods in an allied supplier. To prohibit a union from making an agreement with the manufacturer regarding the conditions under which the manufacturer will ally itself with suppliers is to deny the interdependence among firms in the manufacturer-supplier network.

There are limited legal exceptions to the prohibitions on secondary pressures. Sometimes two firms are deemed "joint employers," so that pressures against either are not considered secondary. Joint employer status may be based either on a common right of control over industrial relations and employment conditions or on a commonality of operations, management, and financial control (Wial 1993). These criteria are not broad enough to cover the variety of interfirm alliances that exist today, since those alliances need not involve common management or ownership and may give one firm actual control (but not the legal right to exercise direct control) over labor conditions in another firm. A second exception to the secondary-pressure restrictions is the "ally" doctrine, which permits secondary picketing when a struck employer farms out work to another firm (*NLRB v. Business Machine and Office Mechanics Conference Board, Local 459, IUE*, 228 F.2d. 553 (2nd Cir. 1955), *cert. denied*, 351 U.S. 962 (1956)). This doctrine recognizes workers' interest in the preservation of work within the struck firm but does not recognize other legitimate worker interests in influencing the policies of allied firms.

Both of the legal disincentives to network bargaining discussed here reflect the belief that the individual firm is a free-standing unit within whose confines most industrial relations problems can be solved. Because this model of the firm is increasingly inappropriate, the legal provisions that are based on it require reevaluation.

Options for Labor Law Reform

Within the current framework of American labor law, there are several alternative ways of breaking the link between organizing and bargaining. One option is to retain the current system of unit determination for the purpose of certifying a union as a bargaining representative but to empower the NLRB to aggregate those units for negotiating purposes (Wial 1993). Local unions that have organized separate units could be required to form joint councils to negotiate on behalf of all the workers in those units. Likewise, employers could be required to form bargaining associations that would represent all their members. The NLRB could either act on its own in requiring such aggregations or else act only in response to petitions filed by unions or employers.

The major problem with this system is the determination of the basis on which units are to be aggregated. To promote network-based bargaining, it would be desirable to aggregate units within a network. Because it is difficult to specify all of the forms that network ties between firms may take in the future, the determination of which units belong to the same network is inevitably fact-specific. Networks that have dominant firms could be defined in terms of the "dominant influence" that those firms exercise over other firms.[7] Criteria for defining networks that lack dominant firms might include geographical proximity, the interchange of workers or new technologies between firms, and the presence of joint ventures, consortia, or long-term contracts between firms.

It is possible that any individual unit within which a union is certified may belong to more than one network. In particular, a unit might simultaneously belong to a geographically concentrated network of firms that produce similar products and to a geographically far-flung network that is controlled or coordinated by a multinational corporation. This situation presents the possibility of disputes between unions (or between firms) that might seek to amalgamate units on different bases. If bargaining structures are to be subject to NLRB regulation, then the NLRB will have to develop criteria for resolving these disputes, just as it had to do when similar disputes arose between AFL and CIO unions earlier in this century.

There are alternatives to direct NLRB regulation of bargaining structures. One of these is for the NLRB to use negotiated rule-making to determine which units will be combined for bargaining purposes. With this procedure, representatives of the NLRB and of unions and firms that could be affected by the outcome of the decision would engage in multilateral negotiation about which units are to be aggregated for purposes of collective bargaining, and the NLRB would issue a rule that reflected the agreement of the parties. Alternatively, negotiated rule-making could be used to determine a general set of criteria for unit aggregation rather than to decide which units should be aggregated in a particular case. Another option is to allow unions and firms to bargain directly about which (if any) units should be aggregated for purposes of collective bargaining and to permit the use of economic pressure by both sides if no agreement can otherwise be reached. A final possibility is to allow

7. The July 1993 version of a proposed European Community council directive on labor-management consultation in multinational groups of allied enterprises adopts this formulation (European Commission 1993). It includes ownership and financial participation as examples of means by which a "dominant influence" may be exercised but does not restrict "dominant influence" to such cases. The proposed directive would give the employees of all firms that are subject to the "dominant influence" of another firm the right to consult with the management of the dominant firm.

units to be aggregated for negotiating purposes if a majority of workers in each unit votes for aggregation.

A similar range of options is available concerning the permissible extent of secondary pressures. One option is to allow secondary pressures only within NLRB-defined networks. This option raises all the problems of network definition and overlap that were mentioned above. A second option is to make the permissible extent of secondary pressure the subject of negotiated rule-making. A third possibility is to repeal all legal prohibitions on secondary pressures.

Finally, network-based bargaining might be encouraged if the United States had a legal procedure for multiemployer labor-management consultation and information-sharing on a networkwide basis. Such consultation could be made available to workers even in the absence of collective bargaining. It could serve as a precursor to bargaining or as an adjunct to an established bargaining relationship[8] and could be valuable even to workers who do not desire collective bargaining.

Space limitations preclude a discussion of the relative merits of the reform options outlined here. Because the issues raised in this chapter have not yet entered the public debate about industrial relations and labor law reform, a comprehensive discussion of reform options may be premature. The aim of this chapter has been to introduce new issues into the debate rather than to resolve it.

---

8. Network-based, multiemployer union-management consultation currently exists in the U.S. motion picture industry, where it coexists with collective bargaining (Counter 1992). For a proposed European system of networkwide consultation in networks with dominant firms, see European Commission 1993. Wial 1993 discusses procedural options for a possible U.S. system of multiemployer consultation.

22

Representing the Part-Time and Contingent Workforce: Challenges for Unions and Public Policy

Françoise J. Carré, Virginia duRivage, and Chris Tilly

The traditional employment model has begun to splinter in the United States. Long-term, full-time, direct employment with a single employer is eroding; temporary, part-time, and contracted or leased employment are growing in its stead. To respond to these changes, the labor movement must experiment with new forms of representation and venture onto unfamiliar bargaining terrain. Further, new public policies are needed: innovations in labor law to create the basis for union representation for these newly growing categories of workers and expanded employment law to guarantee them basic rights and benefits.

Part-time and contingent workers currently account for about one-quarter of the workforce (duRivage 1992a). This is a heterogeneous group; in addition to part-timers, it includes temporary help supply industry (THS) employees, direct short-term hires, leased workers, individual contractors working for single corporate clients, and workers in contracted-out business functions. These groups stand outside the standard employment relationship on which the framework of employment and labor law was built and thus lack basic protections.

Growth in these nonstandard forms of employment has outpaced the expansion of the full-time, permanent workforce since the 1970s. Some parts of the contingent workforce have literally exploded; for example, THS employment ballooned by 250 percent between 1982 and 1992, making Manpower, Inc., the nation's largest private employer (Castro 1993). Employer demand, not worker preferences, appears to be driving the surge in "temps" (Lapidus 1989; Golden and Appelbaum 1992), as well as the more gradual growth in part-time employment (Tilly 1992).

Compared with other workers, the part-time and contingent workforce faces a formidable array of problems, including low wages and little access to benefits; reduced employment security and significant barriers to advancement; low productivity, traceable in part to employers' and employees' low commitment to each other; and being trapped in these arrangements with few prospects for advancement (see Carré, duRivage, and Tilly 1994).[1] This workforce also has levels of union representation far below that of the rest of the workforce.

The expansion of part-time and contingent work poses a growing challenge for U.S. unions, employers, and policy makers. The remainder of this chapter examines how labor organizations and federal and state governments have responded to date and what a more systematic and complete response might look like. The next section offers a simple taxonomy of collective bargaining and policy approaches. This is followed by a review of the shortcomings of current labor law with respect to nonstandard workers. Finally, we outline needed changes in labor law and public policy.

Bargaining, Policy, and Representation Today

In dealing with part-time and contingent employment in the United States, collective bargaining and public policy have pursued four general approaches: to *limit* or prevent the growth of part-time and contingent work; to *control* compensation and working conditions; to *exploit* new possibilities for flexibility; and to *supplement* employer benefits with public or universal protections. We discuss each briefly.

Historically, many unions have attempted to *limit* the growth of nonstandard forms of work through collective bargaining. For example, a wide variety of unions in manufacturing, food processing, transportation, and the public sector have negotiated full-time percentages. Federal, state, and local governments, however, have made few efforts to help unions contain the growth of casual employment. In fact, one of the few restrictions in place, the ban on industrial home work effective since 1942, was lifted by the U.S. Department of Labor in 1984 (duRivage and Jacobs 1989). Some innovative strategies have enabled unions to make headway toward prevention; for example, the state of Connecticut recently enacted a law permitting competing building contractors to sue a contractor that has won a contract award by misclassifying employees as independent self-employed workers in order to reduce labor costs—a common practice in construction.

For unions representing a workforce with substantial numbers of part-timers or others with nonstandard work arrangements, *controlling* the employ-

---

1. Conversely, and ironically, some workers are employed full time involuntarily and are unable to work shorter and more flexible hours without forgoing significant benefits.

ment conditions of these workers has become a central goal. This requires
including part-time and contingent workers in the bargaining unit and
bargaining for parity in wages and benefits. For example, the United Food and
Commercial Workers union has targeted equal wages and prorated benefits
for part-time workers, with some success. In addition, some contracts mandate upgrading part-time or contingent workers to permanent status
(Bronfenbrenner 1988a).

The only significant government policy extending benefits for contingent
workers is the Tax Equity and Fiscal Responsibility Act of 1982 (TEFRA),
which mandates the extension of pension coverage to leased and temporary
help service employees working for a user firm providing a pension plan who
have completed twelve months of substantially full-time service (1,500 hours
yearly). TEFRA was amended in 1986 to extend coverage further by requiring
companies in which 20 percent of the workers are leased to cover these
workers in their pension plans. The Clinton administration's universal health-
care proposal—just unveiled at the time of our writing—would take a major
step forward, mandating prorated employer contributions to health coverage
for part-timers working ten or more hours a week.

Though unions have typically opposed part-time and contingent employment, a growing group of unions has concluded that flexibility is a *benefit* for
part of their workforce and, accordingly, have bargained to *exploit* that flexibility, making part-time or job sharing available to those desiring them. In
this way, unions adopt a responsive stance toward workforce needs for schedule flexibility while maintaining worker protections. The federal and some
state governments have adopted policies to make improved part-time employment available to their own employees.

A final approach is to *supplement* employer-provided benefits. Although
unions historically have sought to obtain benefits from individual employers,
they have begun to explore offering benefits such as mortgage or auto loan
programs and special insurance rates themselves. These benefits are particularly important for workers who move frequently from job to job, shift in and
out of the labor force, and/or are employed in nonstandard work arrangements. The main federal and state programs designed to supplement employer-
provided benefits—Social Security, unemployment insurance, and Medicare—
have glaring gaps of coverage where nonstandard workers are concerned.

Limitations of Current Labor Law

The National Labor Relations Act is designed to protect the rights of a
worker who is fast disappearing. The rights and remedies under the law work
best for workers employed permanently by one employer in a fixed location.
Exceptions have been made to accommodate organizational structures in

existence prior to the NLRA, such as those in the construction or garment industries (see chap. 21). Both sectors have complex employment structures, short work tenures, and unstable working conditions. With the restructuring of employer-employee relationships from a fixed to a more "flexible" system, however, labor law protections elude millions of workers today.

Depressed levels of unionization result. In 1990, 7 percent of part-timers were union members, compared with 19 percent of full-time workers (U.S. Department of Labor 1991). Even after controlling for gender, race, age, and education, more than two-thirds of the gap in union membership rates between part-time and full-time workers remains. And in 1988, only 7 percent of workers in the personnel supply service industry (which includes temporary help services) were unionized, compared with 17 percent of workers in other industries (Tilly 1991).

Indeed, in some cases, employers have expanded flexible forms of employment to undercut union organizing drives or to exact concessions during contract negotiations (Carré, duRivage, and Tilly 1994). In the construction industry, an increasingly common practice is to hire workers as self-employed contractors to avoid hiring through the union. No legislation prohibits the hiring of THS workers as strikebreakers. Numerous employers have resorted to this strategy, a practice outlawed in several Western European countries.

Here we highlight three deficient areas of labor law: bargaining unit determination, contracting out in the public sector, and the determination of joint employer status.

Inappropriate *bargaining unit determination* by the National Labor Relations Board often creates an obstacle to organizing part-time and contingent workers. Using "community of interest criteria," the NLRB has issued inconsistent rulings as to whether part-time and contingent workers hired directly by a firm should be covered by the same contract as regular employees (Bronfenbrenner 1988b). In some cases, the board has found that short-term hires may be part of a bargaining unit if no certain date has been set for their termination. Seasonal employees may be included in the unit if they have a reasonable expectation of reemployment. Factors that help determine the "community of interest" include performing similar kinds of work, working in the same location, and sharing common supervision and schedules (Service Employees' International Union 1993). Under the original Wagner Act, employees' preexisting patterns of preferences, as evidenced by the "extent of organizing," were often decisive in determining bargaining units. Since the passage of the Taft-Hartley Act, however, it is illegal for the "extent of organizing" to be the controlling factor in bargaining unit determination.

In the case of workforces where there is an intermediary employer, such as contracted, leased, or temporary employees, in addition to a finding of community of interest between the regular and contingent employees, there must also be a finding of joint employer status between the client firm (user) and the subcontractor (Service Employees International Union 1993).

When *public-sector work is contracted out to the private sector*, not only do workers lose union protection (Dantico 1987), but their contracted status makes them neither public nor private employees, leaving them covered by neither the NLRA nor state public-sector collective bargaining laws. An example documents the illogic of labor law regarding this workforce. In Michigan, fifteen thousand group home workers perform essential services for the state, working under a variety of private employers funded by the state treasury. When the American Federation of State, County and Municipal Employees tried to organize these workers, the NLRB denied representation on the grounds that they were state employees who were not covered by the NLRA. But when the union approached the state of Michigan Employment Relations Commission, the state successfully argued that the workers were private employees, and the commission denied AFSCME representation on this basis. Such seesawing is common in the public sector.

The issue of *joint employer status* arises because contract, THS, and leased employees have more than one employer. Two parties—the client company and the subcontractor or agency—are involved in controlling working conditions and wages. But the NLRB, drawing on outdated notions of a fixed worker-employer relationship, rarely finds a joint employer relationship.

The example of contracting out at the low-wage end of the service sector illustrates how this hobbles unions. The subcontracting agencies that have burgeoned over the past decade—particularly in building, food, and health services—lack the economic power to bargain with service-sector unions. That power rests in the pockets of the client companies, which also hold the ability to terminate a service contract (often without notice). Thus, a union can win recognition by a subcontracting agency only to find that the latter literally has no margin of capital with which to bargain.

Under current labor law, the NLRB uses a narrow "right-to-control" test to determine joint employer status. This test ignores the underlying economic realities of the client-contractor relationship, focusing instead on whether employers "share or codetermine those matters governing the essential terms and conditions of employment" (Hiatt and Rhinehart 1993:21). But even in cases in which the client is extensively involved in work assignments and supervision, the board has failed to recognize joint employer liability. (Sometimes, regional NLRBs use another test of "joint operations and management." Boards have shown little consistent patterns as to which of these two tests they use.)

As a result, remedies for unfair labor practices by client firms under the NLRA are not available. For example, owners of buildings can legally terminate a building service contract in retaliation for union activities—even though such an action ordinarily violates Section 7 of the NLRA. And no NLRA provision requires a successor contractor to hire the previous employer's workers, or to accept the collective bargaining contract (Hiatt and Rhinehart 1993).

Furthermore, despite the client company's economic control over contract workers' wages and working conditions, the company is protected from economic retaliation under current labor law. Taft-Hartley regards the client as a "neutral secondary employer," insulated from collective economic actions such as picketing or striking in the event of a labor dispute.

The obstacles to organizing contingent workers imposed by the NLRA appear so overwhelming that unions have in some cases bypassed this legal framework altogether. For example, the SEIU has given up trying to gain union recognition for contract janitors through the NLRB. Instead, their Justice for Janitors campaign uses economic boycotts and lawsuits for other violations to pressure building owners in a geographical area to recognize the union voluntarily (interview with John Hiatt, SEIU legal counsel, Sept. 14, 1993).

New Solutions

A comprehensive approach to improving terms of employment for workers in contingent employment must work on two fronts. First, we must facilitate representation of this workforce in unions and other organizations. Second, we need to provide a bottom line of employment protection and benefits through policy action.

Labor Law and Models of Representation

Labor laws must be refashioned to recognize the new employer-worker relationships. For example, to remove barriers to the inclusion of nonstandard workers within bargaining units, renewed attention should be given to employee preferences in unit determination.

To pull public-sector contract workers out of limbo, one strategy is to extend NLRA coverage to public employees in those states that do not have a public-sector bargaining law. Currently, only twenty-three states have comprehensive, NLRA-like laws regulating public-sector collective bargaining, and a number of states, including Virginia, Texas, and Missouri, outlaw public-sector unions. Additionally, contract workers providing essential services to a state should be classified as state employees. The administration of collective bargaining laws, whether public or private, should be coordinated so that no worker falls in between public and private representation.

Similarly, employees deliberately misclassified as independent contractors by their employers should be brought under NLRA coverage. Tax reformers as well as unions have begun to tackle this issue; the Internal Revenue Service, which has a more stringent definition of independent contractors than the NLRA, estimates that 38 percent of employers dodge payroll taxes by misclassifying employees in this way (U.S. General Accounting Office 1989). One solution may be to adopt a standardized, stricter definition of independent contractor across federal employment laws. As we clarify what constitutes an employer in labor law, we also need to focus on who is and is not an employee.

Guaranteeing contingent workers involved with an intermediary firm the right to organize also requires revising the NLRA's approach to joint employment. Other employment laws, such as the Fair Labor Standards Act and the Migrant and Seasonal Agricultural Workers Protection Act, draw less rigid distinctions between clients and contractors in finding joint liability for wage and hour violations.

Adopting universal prehire agreements, today permitted only in construction, would be a useful tool for ensuring that clients hire union contractors. And the Davis-Bacon Act, which requires contractors on public worksites to pay the prevailing wage rate, could be extended to contract workers beyond construction as well.

More broadly, as the Justice for Janitors example suggests, labor laws must support continued union exploration of new models of worker organization particularly suited to workers who move from employer to employer. For insights on such new forms of organization, we must look to the models being advocated for low-wage, low-skill, service-sector workforces. Firms in the low-wage service sector have unstable corporate structures and little control over market conditions. Thus, organizing structures in these settings must act as ways to build union from fragmentation and to enhance worker productivity and skill levels so that wages can rise. Without these structures, low-wage workforces will not benefit from alternative, nonunion, worksite-based representation systems (such as works councils) (Weiler 1990).

The models we consider are occupational unionism (Cobble 1991b), geographical/occupational unionism (Wial 1993), and associational unionism (Heckscher 1988). *Occupational unionism,* a model based on research on waitress unions from the turn of the century to the 1960s, rests on the following elements: a strong occupational (skill-based) identity; control by the union over the labor supply in the industry; multiemployer bargaining; a definition of rights and benefits as functions of occupational membership rather than of worksite affiliation; peer control over occupational performance standards; and an emphasis on employment security rather than "job rights."

This model could apply to contingent workers who shift among job sites. It depends, however, on skill homogeneity and union control over labor supply. Temporary and contracted workforces, while heterogeneous in their skills, could build an identity based on their distinctive experiences in the workplace and the labor market.

Wial (1993) spells out in greater detail the institutional changes required to implement the multiemployer bargaining structures inherent in establishing occupational unionism. Generalized from the Justice for Janitors strategy, the *geographical/occupational* union structures he proposes entail a uniform wage and benefit structure covering loosely defined occupational groups within a localized geographical area. Unlike the previous model, geographical unionism does not require strong occupational identity, union enforcement of job performance standards, or union control over the labor supply. Thus, this model departs from traditional skill-based forms of organization.

The prospect of areawide collective bargaining agreements, as envisioned in geographical/occupational unionism, encourages prebargaining associations between union and community groups that can turn into union locals. In this respect, that model meets *associational unionism* (Heckscher 1988), which advocates the formation of prebargaining associations on *any* basis, ranging from occupational identity, to shared industrial experience, to gender, race, or ethnicity.

The geographical union model requires portability of benefits to facilitate worker mobility across jobs. Unions do not control labor supply but do refer workers to jobs within the unions' jurisdiction. Because this is a multiemployer structure, the union can compel employers to invest in training.

The arts and entertainment unions, which represent workers with short-term, project-based jobs, incorporate many of the elements of both Cobble's and Wial's models. These unions provide services to ease job transitions, including referral and placement and transitional loan funds. They have bargained for pension portability and for health coverage that can be self-paid during spells of unemployment. The arts and entertainment unions are also directly involved in several areas traditionally left to management, such as hiring and the administration of compensation. Archie Kleingartner and Alan Paul (1992:3) note that "unions in arts and entertainment are effective, relevant, and valued by workers in the industry without being powerful in the sense of being able to impose their will on employers through strikes."

Both the occupational and geographical models posit multiemployer bargaining. This would require administrative reforms to the current legal framework, which favors smaller units (Wial 1993). Under both models, the

NLRB would determine the boundaries of the relevant labor market. An alternative, less regulatory approach would allow the parties to bargain over labor market boundaries.

Policy and Regulatory Approaches

By far the most effective short-term policy approach—but perhaps also the one most difficult to achieve in the United States—is to mandate wage and benefit parity between all part-time and contingent employees and the full-time, permanent workforce (in comparable positions) of the firm where they work. This provides nonstandard workers with significant benefits and simultaneously reduces the cost incentives to firms of substituting part-time or contingent workers for regular employees—combining goals of control and limitation.

A number of other short-term control measures would be effective. They include prohibiting the use of temporaries and short-term hires for strike replacement, monitoring by regulatory agencies of the THS and leasing industries and providing incentives for the establishment of industrywide insurance funds.

Ensuring that a wide range of jobs allow flexibility in response to changing worker preferences is the other side of the coin from making sure that flexible jobs bring decent wages, benefits, and security. Measures along these lines include parental leave, flextime, and the right to move between full-time and part-time status.

Finally, key benefits should be socially guaranteed. Universal health coverage is the single most important piece of this package. A logical next step would be a portable pension system with a guaranteed minimum. Part-time and contingent workers would also benefit from revised eligibility standards for unemployment insurance and workers' compensation, since they currently are often excluded by regulations.

Importance of a Twofold Approach

Both regulation and representation are needed to head off the problems of part-time and contingent workers. Indeed, the two complement each other. On the one hand, even if government regulations mandating wage and benefits parity are adopted, unions will play a crucial role in monitoring and enforcing these regulations—just as they do for current wage and hour laws, which in principle apply to all (nonexempt) workers. On the other hand, union organizing efforts can be greatly assisted by government requirements that build up security and stability for nonstandard workers.

Representing the interests of part-time and contingent workers requires that labor and government let go of outdated definitions of workplace and worker protection in favor of reforms that will ensure that flexibility benefits workers as well as employers. With a combination of government action and union organizing, part-time and contingent workers can start to keep pace with the rapid transformation of the American workplace.

References

Adams, George W. 1985. *Canadian Labour Law: A Comprehensive Text.* Aurora, Ont.: Canada Law Book.

———. 1993. *Canadian Labour Law.* 2d ed. Aurora, Ont.: Canada Law Book.

Adams, Graham, Jr. 1966. *The Age of Industrial Violence, 1910–1915: The Activities and Findings of the United States Commission on Industrial Relations.* New York: Columbia University Press.

Adams, Roy J. 1975. *The Growth of White-Collar Unionism in Britain and Sweden.* Madison: Industrial Relations Research Institute, University of Wisconsin.

———. 1986. "Two Policy Approaches to Labour-Management Decision Making at the Level of the Enterprise." In *Labour-Management Cooperation in Canada,* edited by Craig Riddell, 87–108. Toronto: University of Toronto Press.

———. 1988. "The Role of Management in a Political Conception of the Employment Relationship." In *Management under Differing Labour Market and Employment Systems,* edited by G. Dlugos, W. Dorow, and K. Weiermair, 177–91. Berlin: de Gruyter.

———. 1989a. "Industrial Relations Systems in Comparative Perspective." In *Union-Management Relations in Canada,* 2d ed., edited by John C. Anderson, Morley Gunderson, and Alan Ponak, 437–67. Don Mills, Ont.: Addison Wesley.

———. 1989b. "North American Industrial Relations: Divergent Trends in Canada and the United States." *International Labour Review* 128: 47–64.

Adams, Roy J., and C. H. Rummel. 1977. "Workers' Participation in Management in West Germany: Impact on the Worker, the Enterprise, and the Trade Union." *Industrial Relations Journal* 8 (1): 4–22.

Adlercreutz, Axel. 1990. *International Encyclopedia of Labour Law and Industrial Relations.* Vol. 11, *Sweden,* edited by Roger Blanpain. Deventer, the Netherlands: Kluwer.

AFL-CIO. 1984. Statistical and Tactical Information Report no. 18. Washington, D.C.

———. 1985. *The Changing Situation of Workers and Their Unions: Report of the Committee on the Evolution of Work.* Washington, D.C.

———. 1989. *AFL-CIO Organizing Survey: 1986–1987 NLRB Elections.* Washington, D.C.

AFL-CIO. Industrial Union Department. 1994. *Democracy on the Job: America's Path to a Just, High Skill, High Wage Economy.* Washington, D.C.

Albelda, Randy. 1993. "Engendering Unions: America's Northern Neighbor Leads the Way for Women." *Dollars and Sense* 189 (Sept./Oct.).

American Law Institute. 1984. "Principles of Corporate Governance: Analysis and Recommendations." Draft no. 2. Chicago.

Apcar, Leonard M. 1984. "Kirkland's Call to Void Labor Laws Ignites a Growing National Debate." *Wall Street Journal*, Nov. 6.

Atleson, James B. 1983. *Values and Assumptions in Labor Law.* Amherst: University of Massachusetts Press.

Auerbach, Jerold S. 1966. *Labor and Liberty: The LaFollette Committee and the New Deal.* Indianapolis: Bobbs-Merrill.

Avery, Dianne. 1989. "Federal Labor Rights and Access to Private Property: The NLRB and the Right to Exclude." *Industrial Relations Law Journal* 11: 145–227.

Axelrod, Jonathan G. 1986. "The Dotson Board, Good Faith Bargaining, and the Duty to Substantiate One's Bargaining Position." *Labor Lawyer* 2 (4): 751–69.

Baigent, John, Vince Ready, and Tom Roper. 1992. *Recommendations for Labour Law Reform.* British Columbia: Ministry of Labour.

Bain, George Sayers, and Robert A. Price. 1980. *Profiles of Union Growth.* Oxford: Basil Blackwell.

Barenberg, Mark. 1993. "The Political Economy of the Wagner Act: Power, Symbol, and Workplace Cooperation." *Harvard Law Review* 106: 1379–1496.

Barry, Brian. 1978. *Sociologists, Economists, and Democracy.* Chicago: University of Chicago Press.

Batten, Fred W. 1986. "Recent Decisions of the Reagan Board: A Management Perspective." *Labor Lawyer* 2 (1): 33–46.

"BC Moves to New Labour Bill." 1992. *Lancaster Labour Law Report* (legislative update), Dec.

Bell, Daniel. 1973. *The Coming of Post-Industrial Society.* New York: Basic Books.

Belman, D. 1989. "Unions, the Quality of Labor Relations and Firm Performance." Economic Policy Institute, Washington, D.C. Mimeo.

Belous, Richard. 1989. *The Contingent Economy: The Growth of the Temporary, Part-Time, and Subcontracted Work Force.* Washington, D.C.: National Planning Association.

Benson, Susan Porter. 1986. *Counter Cultures: Saleswomen, Managers, and Customers in American Department Stores, 1890–1940.* Urbana: University of Illinois Press.

Berghahn, Volker R., and Detlev Karsten. 1987. *Industrial Relations in West Germany.* Oxford: Berg.

Bernstein, Irving. 1950. *The New Deal Collective Bargaining Policy.* Berkeley: University of California Press.

———. 1970. *The Turbulent Years: A History of the American Worker, 1933–41.* Boston: Houghton Mifflin.

Best, Michael. 1990. *The New Competition: Institutions of Industrial Restructuring.* Cambridge: Harvard University Press.

Blanchflower, Daniel, and Richard B. Freeman. 1992. "Unionism in the United States and Other Advanced OECD Countries." In *Labor Market Institutions and the Future Role of Unions,* edited by Mario F. Bognanno and Morris M. Kleiner, 56–79. Oxford: Blackwell.

Blau, Francine, and Lawrence M. Kahn. 1993. "International Differences in Male Wage Inequality: Institutions versus Market Forces." Working Paper. University of Illinois.

Bliss, Michael. 1971. *A Living Profit*. Toronto: University of Toronto Press.

Block, Fred. 1990. *Postindustrial Possibilities*. Berkeley: University of California Press.

Block, Richard N., and Benjamin W. Wolkinson. 1986. "Delay in the Union Election Campaign Revisited: A Theoretical and Empirical Analysis." *Advances in Industrial and Labor Relations* 3:43–82. Greenwich, Conn.: JAI Press.

Block, Richard N., Benjamin W. Wolkinson, and James Kuhn. 1988. "Some Are More Equal Than Others: The Relative Status of Employers, Unions, and Employees in the Law of Union Organizing." *Industrial Relations Law Journal* 10: 220–40.

Bluestone, Barry, and Irving Bluestone. 1992. *Negotiating the Future*. New York: Basic Books.

Boltuch, Burton F. 1991. "Workplace Closures and Company Reorganizations: Enforcing NLRB, Contract and Noncontract Claims and Obligations." *Labor Lawyer* 7 (1): 53–109.

Boudin, Leonard. 1941. "The Right of Strikers." *Illinois Law Review* 35 (4): 817–39.

Bowden, Gary. 1989. "Labor Unions in the Public Mind: The Canadian Case." *Canadian Review of Sociology and Anthropology* 26: 723–42.

Bowers, John W. 1992. "Section 8(a)(2) and Participative Management: An Argument for Judicial and Legislative Change in a Modern Workplace." *Valparaiso University Law Review* 26: 525.

Bowman, D. O. 1942. *Public Control of Labor Relations: A Study of the National Labor Relations Board*. New York: Macmillan.

Braverman, Harry. 1974. *Labor and Monopoly Capital*. New York: Monthly Review Press.

Bredhoff, Elliot. 1987. "The NLRA: What Needs to Be Done?" In *American Labor Policy*, edited by Charles J. Morris, 47–56. Washington, D.C.: Bureau of National Affairs.

British Columbia Industrial Relations Council. 1980–91. *Annual Reports*.

British Columbia Ministry of Labour and Consumer Services and Ministry Responsible for Constitutional Affairs. 1992. *Bill 84: Labour Relations Code*. Victoria: Province of British Columbia.

Brody, David. 1965. *Labor in Crisis: The Steel Strike of 1919*. Philadelphia: Lippincott.

———. 1993. "Workplace Contractualism in Comparative Perspective." In *Industrial Democracy in America: The Ambiguous Promise*, edited by Nelson Lichtenstein and Howell John Harris, 176–205. New York: Cambridge University Press.

———. 1994 "The Future of the Labor Movement in Historical Perspective." *Dissent* (Winter): 57–66.

Bronfenbrenner, Kate. 1988a. "Bargaining for Part-Time and Temporary Workers." *Labor Notes* (Aug.): 11–12.

———. 1988b. "Legal Status of Contingency Workers." New York State School of Industrial and Labor Relations, Cornell University. Typescript.

———. 1988c. "Organizing and Representing the Contingent Work Force." Paper presented at the AFL-CIO Organizing Department, Sept.

————. 1993. "Seeds of Resurgence: Successful Union Strategies for Winning Certification Elections and First Contracts in the 1980's and Beyond." Ph.D. diss., Cornell University.

————. 1990. "Successful Union Strategies for Winning Certification Elections and First Contracts. Report to Union Participants. Pt. 1: Organizing Results Survey." Typescript.

Bronfenbrenner, Kate L., and Tom Juravich. 1994. "The Current Status of Union Organizing in the Public Sector." Report prepared for the AFL-CIO, Public Employee Department.

Brown, Charles, James Hamilton, and James Medoff. 1990. *Employers Large and Small*. Cambridge: Harvard University Press.

Bruce, Peter G. 1988. "Political Parties and the Evolution of Labor Law in Canada and the United States." Ph.D. diss., MIT.

————. 1989. "Political Parties and Labor Legislation in Canada and the U.S." *Industrial Relations* 28 (Spring): 115–41.

————. 1990. "The Processing of Unfair Labor Practice Cases in the United States and Canada." *Relations Industrielles/Industrial Relations* 45: 481–511.

————. 1993. "State Structures and Processing of Unfair Labor Practice Cases in the United States and Canada." In *The Challenge of Restructuring: North American Labor Movements Respond*, edited by Jane Jenson and Rianne Mahon, 180–206. Philadelphia: Temple University Press.

Cabot, Stephen J. 1993. "Scary New Union Activism . . . How to Fight It and Win." *Boardroom Reports* 22: 5–6.

Canada Labour Relations Board. 1980–81 to 1990–91. *Annual Reports*.

Canadian Federation of Labour. 1990. "Assessment of General Public and Membership Attitudes toward Labour Unions, the Canadian Federation of Labour and Related Issues." Report.

Carp, Robert A., and Ronald Stidham. 1985. *The Federal Courts*. Washington, D.C.: Congressional Quarterly Press.

Carré, Françoise J. 1992. "Temporary Employment in the Eighties." In *New Policies for the Part-Time and Contingent Workforce*, edited by Virginia duRivage, 45–87. Armonk, N.Y.: M. E. Sharpe.

Carré, Françoise J., Virginia duRivage, and Chris Tilly. 1994. "Piecing Together the Fragmented Workplace: Unions and Public Policy on Flexible Employment." In *Unions and Public Policy*, edited by Lawrence G. Flood. Westport, Conn.: Greenwood Press.

Carron, Reed, and Kathlyn E. Noecker. 1992. "The Employer's Duty to Supply Financial Information to the Union: When Has the Employer Asserted an Inability to Pay?—or—(The Boss Says Times Are Tough: How *Truitt* Is)." *Labor Lawyer* 8 (4): 815–30.

Carrothers, A.W.R., E. E. Palmer, and W. B. Raynor. 1986. *Collective Bargaining Law in Canada*. 2d ed. Toronto and Vancouver: Butterworths.

Carter, Donald D., and Thomas McIntosh. 1991. "Collective Bargaining and the Charter: Assessing the Impact of American Judicial Doctrines." *Relations Industrielles/Industrial Relations* 46: 722–50.

Casebeer, Kenneth. 1989. "Drafting Wagner's Act: Leon Keyserling and the Precommittee Drafts of the Labor Disputes Act and the National Labor Relations Act." *Industrial Relations Law Journal* 11: 73–131.

Castro, Janice. 1993. "Disposable Workers." *Time*, March 29, 43–47.

Chaison, Gary N., and Joseph B. Rose. 1991a. "Continental Divide: The Direction and Fate of North American Unions." In *Advances in Industrial and Labor Relations*, edited by Donna Sockell, David Lewin, and David B. Lipsky, 169–205. Greenwich, Conn.: JAI Press.

—————. 1991b. "The Macrodeterminants of Union Growth and Decline." In *The State of the Unions*, edited by George B. Strauss, Daniel G. Gallagher, and Jack Fiorito, 1–47. Industrial Relations Research Association Series. Madison, Wisc.: Industrial Relations Research Association.

Chaykowski, Richard P., and Anil Verma. 1992. "Adjustment and Restructuring in Canadian Industrial Relations: Challenges to the Traditional System." In *Industrial Relations in Canadian Industry*, edited by Richard P. Chaykowski and Anil Verma, 1–38. Toronto: Holt, Rinehart and Winston.

Chicoine, Jeffrey P. 1992. "The Business Necessity Defense to Unilateral Changes in Working Conditions under the Duty to Bargain in Good Faith." *Labor Lawyer* 8 (2): 297–312.

Christensen, C. Lawrence. 1933. *Collective Bargaining in Chicago*. Chicago: University of Chicago Press.

Christopherson, Susan. 1991. "Patterns of Transformation, Patterns of Persistence: Women's Employment in Services in OECD Countries." Working Paper in Planning no. 92. Cornell University Department of City and Regional Planning.

Clarke, Shaun G. 1987. "Rethinking the Adversarial Model in Labor Relations: An Argument for Repeal of Section 8(a)(2)." *Yale Law Journal* 96: 2021–50.

Coates, Mary Lou. 1991. *Industrial Relations in 1990: Trends and Emerging Issues*. Kingston, Ont.: Industrial Relations Center, Queen's University.

Cobble, Dorothy Sue. 1990. "Union Strategies for Organizing and Representing the New Service Workforce." Paper presented at the Forty-Third Annual Conference of the Industrial Relations Research Association, Washington, D.C., Dec. 28.

—————. 1991a. *Dishing It Out: Waitresses and Their Unions in the Twentieth Century*. Urbana: University of Illinois Press.

—————. 1991b. "Organizing the Postindustrial Work Force: Lessons from the History of Waitress Unionism." *Industrial and Labor Relations Review* 44 (April): 419–36.

—————. 1993. "Introduction: Remaking Unions for the New Majority." In *Women and Unions: Forging a Partnership*, edited by Dorothy Sue Cobble, 3–23. Ithaca, N.Y.: ILR Press.

Cohen, Joshua, and Joel Rogers. 1992. "Secondary Associations and Democratic Governance." *Politics and Society* 20 (Dec.): 393–472.

—————. 1993. "Associations and Democracy." *Social Philosophy and Policy* 10 (Summer): 282–312.

—————. Forthcoming. *Beyond Faction: Secondary Associations and Democratic Governance*. New York: Cambridge University Press.

Cohen, Leonard E. 1985. "The Duty To Bargain over Plant Relocation and Other Company Changes—*Otis Elevator v. NLRB*." *Labor Lawyer* 1 (3): 525–32.

"Collective Bargaining as an Industrial System: An Argument against Judicial Revision of Section 8(a)(2) of the National Labor Relations Act." 1983. *Harvard Law Review* 96: 1662–82.

Committee of Special Advisors. 1992. *Recommendations for Reform of the B.C. Industrial Relations Act*. Victoria: Province of British Columbia.

Conner, Valerie Jean. 1983. *The National War Labor Board: Stability, Social Justice, and the Voluntary State in World War I*. Chapel Hill: University of North Carolina Press.

Connor, Mairead E. 1992. "The *Dubuque Packing* Decision: New Test for Bargaining over Decision to Relocate." *Labor Lawyer* 3 (2): 289–95.

Cooke, William N. 1985. *Union Organizing and Public Policy Failure to Secure First Contracts*. Kalamazoo, Mich.: W. E. Upjohn Institute for Employment Research.

Cordova, Efren. 1986. "From Full-Time Wage Employment to Atypical Employment: A Major Shift in the Evolution of Labor Relations?" *International Labour Review* 125: 641–57.

Cornfield, Daniel. 1987. "Labor-Management Cooperation or Managerial Control: Emerging Patterns of Labor Relations in the U.S." In *Workers, Managers, and Technological Change*, edited by Daniel Cornfield, 331–54. New York: Plenum.

Costello, Joseph J., and Stacy K. Weinberg. 1993. "*Toledo Blade* and *Colorado Ute*: When Is Bargaining to Impasse Not Enough?" *Labor Lawyer* 9 (2): 127–35.

Counter, J. Nicholas, III. 1992. "New Collective Bargaining Strategies for the 1990s: Lessons from the Motion Picture Industry." In *Proceedings of the Forty-Fourth Annual Meeting of the Industrial Relations Research Association*, edited by John F. Burton, Jr., 32–38. Madison, Wisc.: Industrial Relations Research Association.

Cox, Archibald. 1947–48. "Some Aspects of the Labor Management Relations Act, 1947." *Harvard Law Review* 61: 1–49, 274–315.

Cox, Archibald, et al. 1991. *Labor Law Cases and Materials*. 11th ed. Westbury, N.Y.: Foundation Press.

Crain, Marion. 1991. "Feminizing Unions: Challenging the Gendered Structure of Wage Labor." *Michigan Law Review* 89: 1155–1221.

———. 1992a. "Feminism, Labor, and Power." *Southern California Law Review* 65: 1819–86.

———. 1992b. "Images of Power in Labor Law: A Feminist Deconstruction." *Boston College Law Review* 33: 481–537.

Craypo, Charles, and Bruce Nissen, eds. 1993. *Grand Designs: The Impact of Corporate Strategies on Workers, Unions, and Communities*. Ithaca, N.Y.: ILR Press.

Dallas, Lynne. 1988. "Two Models of Corporate Governance: Beyond Berle and Means." *University of Michigan Journal of Law Reform* 22: 19–116.

Daniel, Cletus E. 1980. *The ACLU and the Wagner Act*. Ithaca, N.Y.: ILR Press.

Dantico, Marilyn. 1987. "The Impact of Contracting Out on Women and Minorities." In *When Public Services Go Private*, prepared by the AFSCME Research Department. Washington, D.C.: AFSCME Research Department.

Dennis, Patricia Diaz. 1985. "A Principled Approach to NLRB Decisionmaking." *Labor Lawyer* 1 (3): 483–97.

Derber, Milton. 1970. *The American Idea of Industrial Democracy, 1865–1965*. Urbana: University of Illinois Press.

Dickens, Linda, and George Sayers Bain. 1986. "A Duty to Bargain? Union Recognition and Information Disclosure." In *Labour Law in Britain*, edited by Roy Lewis, 80–108. Oxford: Basil Blackwell.

Dickens, William. 1983. "The Effect of Company Campaigns on Certification Elections: Law and Reality Once Again." *Industrial and Labor Relations Review* 36 (July): 560–75.

Di Giovanni, Nicholas, Jr. 1986. "Surface v. Hard Bargaining: Tilting toward Nonintervention." *Labor Lawyer* 2 (4): 771–99.

"DOL Favors Changes to Strengthen WARN Act." 1993. *Labor Relations Week*, Sept. 15, 881.

Dotson, Donald. 1983. Speech to the Maryland Chapter Industrial Relations Research Association. September 28.

"Dotson's Exit: A Lot More Than Politics." 1987. *Business Week*, Nov. 9, 114.

duRivage, Virginia L. 1992a. "New Policies for the Part-Time and Contingent Workforce." In *New Policies for the Part-Time and Contingent Workforce*, edited by Virginia duRivage, 89–121. Armonk, N.Y.: M. E. Sharpe.

———, ed. 1992b. *New Policies for the Part-Time and Contingent Workforce*. Armonk, N.Y.: M. E. Sharpe.

duRivage, Virginia, and David Jacobs. 1989. "Home-Based Work: Labor's Choices." In *Homework: Historical and Comparative Perspectives on Paid Labor at Home*, edited by Eileen Boris and Cynthia R. Daniels, 258–71. Champaign-Urbana: University of Illinois Press.

Eaton, Adrienne, and Paula Voos. 1992. "Unions and Contemporary Innovations in Work Organization, Compensation, and Employee Participation." In *Unions and Economic Competitiveness*, edited by Lawrence Mishel and Paula Voos, 173–215. Armonk, N.Y.: M. E. Sharpe.

Eaton, Susan C. 1992. *Women Workers, Unions and Industrial Sectors in North America*. Geneva: International Labour Office.

———. 1993. "Women and Labor-Management Relations: Lessons from Canada." Research report prepared for the Women's Bureau, U.S. Department of Labor.

Economic Report of the President. 1984. Washington, D.C.: GPO.

Edwards, Paul, et al. 1992. "Great Britain: Still Muddling Through." In *Industrial Relations in the New Europe*, edited by Anthony Ferner and Richard Hyman, 1–69. Oxford: Basil Blackwell.

Elliott, Ralph, and James Huffman. 1984. "The Impact of Right-to-Work Laws on Employer Unfair Labor Practice Charges." *Journal of Labor Research* 5 (2): 165–76.

Erlich, Mark. 1990. *Labor at the Ballot Box*. Philadelphia: Temple University Press.

Estreicher, Samuel. 1985. "Policy Oscillation at the Labor Board: A Plea for Rulemaking." *Administrative Law Review* 37 (Spring): 163–81.

———. 1987. "Strikers and Replacements." *Labor Lawyer* 3 (4): 897–909.

European Commission. 1993. "Draft Council Directive on the Establishment of European Works Councils or Procedures in Community-Scale Undertakings and Community-Scale Groups of Undertakings for the Purposes of Informing and Consulting Employees." Brussels.

Farber, Henry S., and Alan Krueger. 1992. "Union Membership in the United States: The Decline Continues." Working Paper no. 4216. National Bureau of Economic Research, Washington, D.C.

Feinsinger, Nathan. 1949. *Collective Bargaining in the Trucking Industry*. Philadelphia: University of Pennsylvania Press.

Fine, Sidney. 1963. *The Automobile under the Blue Eagle*. Ann Arbor: University of Michigan Press.

Flanagan, Robert. 1989. "Compliance and Enforcement Decisions under the National Labor Relations Act." *Journal of Labor Economics* 7 (3): 257–80.

Freeman, Richard B. 1986. "The Effect of the Union Wage Differential on Management Opposition and Union Organizing Success." *AEA Papers and Proceedings* 76 (2): 92–96.

————. 1987. "Can American Unions Rebound?" *Wall Street Journal*, Dec. 8, 36.

————. 1988. "Contraction and Expansion: The Divergence of Private Sector and Public Sector Unionism in the United States." *Journal of Economic Perspectives* 2 (Spring): 63–88.

————. 1989a. "On the Divergence in Unionism among Developed Countries." National Bureau of Economic Research Working Paper no. 2817. National Bureau of Economic Research, Cambridge.

————. 1989b. "What Does the Future Hold for U.S. Unionism?" *Relations Industrielles/Industrial Relations* 44: 25–46.

————. 1990. *De-unionization of the United States: Good, Bad, or Irrelevant?* Washington, D.C.: Economic Policy Institute.

————. 1993. "How Much Has De-unionization Contributed to the Rise in Male Earnings Inequality?" In *Uneven Tides: Rising Inequality in America*, edited by Sheldon Danziger and Peter Gottschalk, 133–63. New York: Russell Sage Foundation.

Freeman, Richard B., and Morris Kleiner. 1990. "Employer Behavior in the Face of Union Organizing Drives." *Industrial and Labor Relations Review* 43 (April): 351–65.

Freeman, Richard B., and Jonathan S. Leonard. 1987. "Union Maids: Unions and the Female Work Force." In *Gender in the Workplace*, edited by Clair Brown and Joseph Pechman, 189–212. Washington, D.C.: Brookings Institution.

Freeman, Richard B., and James Medoff. 1984. *What Do Unions Do?* New York: Basic Books.

Freeman, Richard B., and Joel Rogers. 1993a. "A New Deal For Labor," *New York Times*, March 10, 19.

————. 1993b. "Who Speaks for Us? Employee Representation in a Non-Union Labor Market." In *Employee Representation: Alternatives and Future Directions*, edited by Bruce E. Kaufman and Morris M. Kleiner, 13–79. Madison, Wisc.: Industrial Relations Research Association.

————. 1993c. "Labor Relations: Let's Move into the 21st Century." Typescript.

————. 1993d. "What Workplace Representation and Participation Do American Workers Want?" Typescript.

————. Forthcoming. *Working Better: Reforming U.S. Labor Relations*. New York: Free Press.

Fried, Charles. 1985. "Individual and Collective Rights in Work Relations: Reflections on the Current State of Labor Law and Its Prospects." In *Labor Law and the Employment Market*, edited by Richard A. Epstein and Jeffrey Paul, 68–96. New Brunswick. N.J.: Transaction Books.

Friedman, Sheldon, and Richard Prosten. 1993. "How Come One Team *Still* Has to Play with Its Shoelaces Tied Together?" *Labor Law Journal* 44 (Aug.): 477–85.

Fudge, Judy. 1993. "Labour Needs Sectoral Bargaining Now." *Canadian Dimension* (March-April): 33–37.

Garson, Barbara. 1988. *The Electronic Sweatshop.* New York: Simon & Schuster.

Geoghegan, Thomas. 1991. *Which Side Are You On?* New York: Farrar, Straus & Giroux.

Getman, Julius G., and F. Ray Marshall. 1993. "Industrial Relations in Transition: The Paper Industry Example." *Yale Law Journal* 102: 1803–95.

Gifford, Courtney D. 1992. *Directory of U.S. Labor Organizations.* Washington, D.C.: Bureau of National Affairs.

Gilligan, Carol. 1982. *In a Different Voice.* Cambridge: Harvard University Press.

Gillispie, Hal K. 1972. "The *Mackay* Doctrine and the Myth of Business Necessity." *Texas Law Review* 50 (4): 782–97.

Gilpin, Toni. 1992. "Left by Themselves: A History of the United Farm Equipment and Metal Workers Union." Ph.D. diss., Yale University.

Gitelman, Howard M. 1988. *Legacy of the Ludlow Massacre: A Chapter in American Labor Relations.* Philadelphia: Temple University Press.

Gitlow, Howard, and Shelley Gitlow. 1987. *The Deming Guide to Quality and Competitive Position.* Englewood Cliffs, N.J.: Prentice-Hall.

Gold, Michael. 1989. *An Introduction to Labor Law.* Ithaca, N.Y.: ILR Press.

Golden, Lonnie, and Eileen Appelbaum. 1992. "What Is Driving the Boom in Temporary Employment?" *American Journal of Economics and Sociology* 51 (Oct.): 473–92.

Goldfield, Michael. 1987. *The Decline of Organized Labor in the United States.* Chicago: University of Chicago Press.

Gould, John P., and George Bittlingmayer. 1980. *The Economics of the Davis-Bacon Act: An Analysis of Prevailing Wage Laws.* New York: American Enterprise Institute.

Gould, William. 1982. *A Primer on American Labor Law.* Cambridge: MIT Press.

———. 1993. *Agenda for Reform: The Future of Employment Relationships and the Law.* Cambridge: MIT Press.

Green, Sara McL. 1986. "Plant Relocation after *Milwaukee Spring II* and *Otis Elevator*: The Battleground Shifts to Arbitration." *Labor Lawyer* 2 (2): 183–96.

Greenfield, Patricia, and Robert Pleasure. 1993. "Representatives of Their Own Choosing: Finding Workers' Voice in the Legitimacy and Power of their Unions." In *Employee Representation: Alternatives and Future Directions*, edited by Bruce E. Kaufman and Morris M. Kleiner, 169–96. Madison, Wisc.: Industrial Relations Research Association.

Gross, James A. 1974. *The Making of the National Labor Relations Board: A Study in Economics, Politics, and the Law.* Albany: State University of New York Press.

———. 1982. *The Reshaping of the National Labor Relations Board: National Labor Policy in Transition, 1937–1947.* Albany: State University of New York Press.

Gunderson, Morley, John Kervin, and Frank Reid. 1989. "The Effect of Labour Relations Legislation on Strike Incidence," *Canadian Journal of Economics* 22 (4): 779–95.

Gunderson, Morley, and Angelo Melino. 1990. "The Effects of Public Policy on Strike Duration." *Journal of Labor Economics* 8, (July): 295–316.

Gwartney-Gibbs, Patricia A., and Denise H. Lach. 1993. "Gender Differences in Grievance Processing and the Implications for Rethinking Shopfloor Practices."

In *Women and Unions: Forging a Partnership*, edited by Dorothy Sue Cobble, 299–315. Ithaca, N.Y.: ILR Press.

Hallett, Jeffrey J. 1986. "Unions in Our Future?" *Personnel Administrator* 31 (April): 40–44.

Hamper, Ben. 1991. *Rivethead: Tales from the Assembly Line*. New York: Warner Books.

Hammarström, Olle. 1993. "Industrial Relations in Sweden." In *International and Comparative Industrial Relations*, 2d ed., edited by Greg Bamber and Russell Lansbury, 197–219. St. Leonards, Australia: Allen and Unwin.

Hardin, Patrick, ed. 1992. *The Developing Labor Law: The Board, the Courts, and the National Labor Relations Act*. 3rd ed. Washington, D.C.: Bureau of National Affairs.

Hart, Moira. 1978. "Union Recognition in America: The Legislative Snare." *Industrial Law Journal* 7 (Dec): 201–15.

Havlovic, Stephen J. 1990. "German Works Councils: A Highly Evolved Institution of Industrial Democracy." *Labor Studies Journal* 15 (2): 62–71.

Haywood, Len. 1992. *Replacement of Striking Workers during Work Stoppages in 1991*. Toronto: Ontario Ministry of Labour.

Heckscher, Charles. 1988. *The New Unionism: Employee Involvement in the Changing Corporation*. New York: Basic Books.

Helper, Susan. 1990. "Subcontracting: Innovative Labor Strategies." *Labor Research Review* 15 (Spring): 89–99.

———. 1991. "Strategy and Irreversibility in Supplier Relations: The Case of the U.S. Automobile Industry." *Business History Review* 65 (Winter): 781–824.

Hepple, Bob, and Sandra Fredman. 1986. *Labour Law and Industrial Relations in Great Britain*. Deventer, The Netherlands: Kluwer.

Herrnstadt, Owen E. 1992. "Why Some Unions Hesitate to Participate in Labor-Management Cooperation Programs." *Labor Law Journal* 8: 71–79.

Hexter, Christopher T. 1992. "Duty to Supply Information—*Nielson Lithographing Company* Revisited: The Board's Retreat from Collective Bargaining as a Rational Process Leading to Agreement." *Labor Lawyer* 3 (4): 831–48.

Hiatt, Jonathon P., and Lynn Rhinehart. 1993. "The Growing Contingent Workforce: A Challenge for the Future." Paper presented to the American Bar Association Section on Employment and Labor Law, Aug. 10.

Hills, Stephen M. 1985. "The Attitudes of Union and Nonunion Male Workers toward Union Representation." *Industrial and Labor Relations Review* 36 (Jan.): 179–94.

Hince, Kevin. 1993. "Is Euro-American Union Theory Universally Applicable? An Australasian Perspective." In *Industrial Relations Theory: Its Nature, Scope and Pedagogy*, edited by Roy J. Adams and Noah M. Meltz, 81–102. Metuchen, N.J.: Scarecrow.

Hirsch, Barry T. 1991. *Labor Unions and the Economic Performance of Firms*. Kalamazoo, Mich.: W. E. Upjohn Institute for Employment Research.

Hirsch, Peter N. 1970. "*Laidlaw*—The *Mackay* Legacy." *Georgia Law Review* 4: 808–29.

Hoerr, John. 1988. *And the Wolf Finally Came: The Decline of the American Steel Industry*. Pittsburgh: University of Pittsburgh Press.

———. 1993. "Solidaritas at Harvard." *American Prospect* 14 (Summer): 67–82.

Hogler, Raymond L. 1989. "Worker Participation, Employer Anti-Unionism, and Labor Law: The Case of the Steel Industry, 1918–1937." *Hofstra Labor Journal* 7: 1–69.

Hogler, Raymond L., and Guillermo J. Grenier. 1992. *Employee Participation and Labor Law in the American Workplace*. Westport, Conn.: Quorum Books.

Horwitz, Morton J. 1992. *The Transformation of American Law, 1870–1960*. New York: Oxford University Press.

Howard, Robert. 1985. *Brave New Workplace*. New York: Viking Press.

Howley, John. 1990. "Justice for Janitors: The Challenge of Organizing in Contract Services." *Labor Relations Review* 15 (Spring): 61–72.

Hurd, Richard. 1993. "Organizing and Representing Clerical Workers: The Harvard Model." In *Women and Unions: Forging a Partnership*, edited by Dorothy Sue Cobble, 316–36. Ithaca, N.Y.: ILR Press.

Hutson, Melvin. 1992. "*Electromation*: Employee Involvement or Employer Domination?" *Labor Lawyer* 8: 389–404.

Hyde, Alan. 1993. "Employee Caucuses: A Key Institution in the Emerging System of Employment Law." *Chicago-Kent Law Review* 69: 149–93.

Ichniowski, Casey, John Delaney, and David Lewin. 1989. "The New Resource Management in U.S. Workplaces." *Relations Industrielles/Industrial Relations* 44: 97–119.

Institute for Women's Policy Research. 1989. *Low Wage Jobs and Workers: Trends and Options for Change*. Research report prepared for the Employment and Training Administration, U.S. Department of Labor. Washington, D.C.: Institute for Women's Policy Research.

International Labour Office. 1985. *World Labour Report 2*. Geneva.

Irving, John. 1993. "Union Plans to Amend the Labor Laws." Typescript.

Jacobi, Otto, Berndt Keller, and Walther Müller-Jentsch. 1992. "Germany: Codetermining the Future." In *Industrial Relations in the New Europe*, edited by Anthony Ferner and Richard Hyman, 218–69. Oxford: Basil Blackwell.

Jacoby, Sanford M. 1989. "Reckoning with Company Unions: The Case of Thompson Products, 1934–64." *Industrial and Labor Relations Review* 43 (Oct.): 19–40.

———. 1991. "American Exceptionalism Revisited: The Importance of Management." In *Masters to Managers: Historical and Comparative Perspectives on American Employers*, edited by Sanford M. Jacoby, 173–200. New York: Columbia University Press.

Jaikumur, Ramchandran. 1986. "Postindustrial Manufacturing." *Harvard Business Review* 64 (Nov.-Dec.): 69–76.

Janes, Brandon C. 1975. "The Illusion of Permanency for *Mackay* Doctrine Replacement Workers." *Texas Law Review* 54: 126–50.

Johnston, T. L. 1962. *Collective Bargaining in Sweden*. Cambridge: Harvard University Press.

Jones, S., and C. Stebbings. 1987. *A Dictionary of Legal Quotations*. New York: Macmillan.

Kamiat, Walter. 1992. "The Model Employment Termination Act." Typescript.

Kammholz, Theophil C., and Stanley R. Strauss. 1980. *Practice and Procedure before the National Labor Relations Board*. Philadelphia: American Law Institute–American Bar Association.

Kanter, Rosabeth Moss. 1989. *When Giants Learn to Dance*. New York: Simon & Schuster.

Karasek, Robert, and Tores Theorell. 1990. *Healthy Work: Stress, Productivity and the Reconstruction of Working Life.* New York: Basic Books.

Katz, Harry C. 1985. *Shifting Gears.* Cambridge: MIT Press.

————. 1993. "The Decentralization of Collective Bargaining: A Literature Review and Comparative Analysis." *Industrial and Labor Relations Review* 47 (Oct.): 3–22.

Kerchner, Charles Taylor, and Douglas E. Mitchell. 1988. *The Changing Idea of a Teachers' Union.* New York: Falmer Press.

Klare, Karl. 1978. "Judicial Deradicalization of the Wagner Act and the Origins of Modern Legal Consciousness, 1937–41." *Minnesota Law Review* 62: 265–339.

————. 1988. "Workplace Democracy and Market Reconstruction: An Agenda for Legal Reform." *Catholic University Law Review* 38: 1–68.

Kleiner, Morris M. 1984. "Unionism and Employer Discrimination: Analysis of 8(a)(3) Violations." *Industrial Relations* 23: 234–43.

Kleiner, Morris M., Robert McLean, and George Dreher. 1987. *Labor Markets and Human Resource Management.* Glenview, Ill.: Scott, Foresman.

Kleiner, Morris M., and Melanie Schliebs. 1991. "Regulatory Power and Good Faith Collective Bargaining: The Decision to Comply." In *Public Policy and Economic Institutions,* edited by Melvin Dubnick and Alan Gitelson, 10:131–45.

Kleingartner, Archie, and Alan Paul. 1992. "Member Attachment and Union Effectiveness in Arts and Entertainment." Paper presented at the Forty-Fourth Annual Meeting of the Industrial Relations Research Association, New Orleans, Jan. 3.

Kochan, Thomas A. 1979. "How American Workers View Labor Unions." *Monthly Labor Review* 102 (April): 23–31.

————. 1993a. "Trade Unionism and Industrial Relations." *Dialogues* 1 (May): 1–2.

————. 1993b. "Trade Unionism and Industrial Relations: Notes on Theory and Practice for the 1990s." In *Proceedings of the Forty-Fifth Annual Meeting of the Industrial Relations Research Association,* 185–95. Madison, Wisc.: Industrial Relations Research Association.

Kochan, Thomas A., Harry C. Katz, and Robert B. McKersie. 1986. *The Transformation of American Industrial Relations.* New York: Basic Books; Ithaca, N.Y.: ILR Press, 1994.

Koeller, Timothy. 1992. "Employer Unfair Labor Practices and Union Organizing Activity: A Simultaneous Equation Model." *Journal of Labor Research* 13 (2): 173–87.

Kohler, Thomas C. 1986. "Models of Worker Participation: The Uncertain Significance of Section 8(a)(2)." *Boston College Law Review* 27: 499–551.

Kolick, Joseph E., Jr., and Merle M. DeLancey, Jr. 1993. "Can One Unilaterally Gain the Right to Make Unilateral Changes in Working Conditions?" *Labor Lawyer* 9 (2): 137–48.

Kumar, Pradeep, Mary Lou Coates, and David Arrowsmith. 1989. *The Current Industrial Relations Scene in Canada. 1988.* Kingston, Ont.: Industrial Relations Centre, Queen's University.

Labour Canada. 1970–85. *Strikes and Lockouts in Canada.* Ottawa: Labour Canada.

————. 1993. *Industrial Relations Legislation in Canada, 1993–94.* Ottawa: Canada Communications Group.

LaLonde, Robert J., and Bernard D. Meltzer. 1991. "Hard Times for Unions: Another Look at the Significance of Employer Illegalities." *University of Chicago Law Review* 58: 953–1014.

Lapidus, June. 1989. "The Temporary Help Industry and the Operation of the Labor Market." Ph.D. diss., University of Massachusetts, Amherst.

Lawler, John J. 1990. *Unionization and Deunionization.* Columbia: University of South Carolina Press.

Leigh, Duane, and Stephen Hills. 1987. "Male-Female Differences in the Potential for Union Growth outside Traditionally Unionized Industries." *Journal of Labor Research* 8 (2): 131–42.

Leiter, Robert. 1949. "Supervisory Employees and the Taft-Hartley Law." *Southern Economic Journal* 15 (Jan.): 311–20.

Levinson, Harold M. 1980. "Trucking." In *Collective Bargaining: Contemporary American Experience,* edited by Gerald G. Somers, 99–149. Madison, Wisc.: Industrial Relations Research Association.

Lichtenstein, Nelson, and Howell John Harris, eds. 1993. *Industrial Democracy in America: The Ambiguous Promise.* New York: Cambridge University Press.

Lindblom, Charles. 1977. *Politics and Markets.* New York: Basic Books.

Lipset, Seymour Martin. 1986. "North American Labor Movements: A Comparative Perspective." In *Unions in Transition: Entering the Second Century,* edited by Seymour M. Lipset, 421–51. San Francisco: Institute for Contemporary Studies.

————. 1989. *Continental Divide: The Values and Institutions of the United States and Canada.* Toronto and Washington, D.C.: D. C. Howe Institute and National Planning Association.

Lorwin, Louis. 1924. *The Women's Garment Workers.* New York: B. W. Huebsch.

Luria, Daniel, and Joel Rogers. 1993. "Get Up and Dance! Strategies for High Wage Metropolitan Economic Development." Typescript.

Lyon, Leverett S. 1935. *The National Recovery Administration: An Analysis and Appraisal.* Washington, D.C.: Brookings Institution.

McClintock, Michael. 1980. *NLRB General Counsel: Unreviewable Power to Refuse to Issue an Unfair Labor Practice Complaint.* Arlington, Va.: Carrollton Press.

McHugh, Richard W. 1993. "Fair Warning or Foul? An Analysis of the Worker Adjustment and Retraining Notification (WARN) Act in Practice." *Berkeley Journal of Employment and Labor Law* 14: 1–71.

McLeod, Wilson. 1990. "Labor-Management Cooperation: Competing Visions and Labor's Challenge." *Industrial Relations Law Journal* 12: 233–91.

Massagli, Mark Tully. 1993. Statement of Mark Tully Massagli, President of the American Federation of Musicians of the U.S. and Canada, AFL-CIO-CLC, before the Subcommittee on Labor-Management Relations of the House Committee on Education and Labor in Support of the Live Performing Arts Labor Relations Amendments, H.R. 226., Washington, D.C., July 21.

Meltz, Noah. 1989. "Interstate v. Interprovincial Differences in Union Density." *Industrial Relations* 28 (Spring): 42–58.

————. 1990. "Unionism in Canada, U.S.: On Parallel Treadmills." *Forum for Applied Research and Public Policy* 15 (Winter): 46–52.

Miller, Edward. 1980. *An Administrative Appraisal of the NLRB.* Rev. ed. Philadelphia: University of Pennsylvania.

Millis, Harry A. 1942. *How Collective Bargaining Works*. New York: Twentieth Century Fund Labor Committee.

Millis, Harry A., and Emily Clark Brown. 1950. *From the Wagner Act to Taft-Hartley*. Chicago: University of Chicago Press.

Mills, D. Quinn. 1980. "Construction." In *Collective Bargaining: Contemporary American Experience*, edited by Gerald G. Somers, 49–98. Madison, Wisc.: Industrial Relations Research Association.

Mishel, Lawrence, and Jared Bernstein. 1993. *The State of Working America, 1992–93*. Washington, D.C.: Economic Policy Institute.

Mishel, Lawrence, and David M. Frankel. 1991. *The State of Working America, 1990–1991*. Armonk, N.Y.: M. E. Sharpe.

Moberly, Robert. 1985. "New Directions in Collective Bargaining." *West Virginia Law Review* 87: 765–87.

———. 1988. "Toward Labor-Management Cooperation in Government." *Ohio State Journal of Dispute Resolution* 4: 29–46.

Morris, Charles J. 1992. "National Labor Policy: Worker Participation and the Role of the NLRB." Paper presented at the Southern California Labor and Employment Law Symposium, Feb. 6. Reprinted in *Daily Labor Report*, March 4, 1992, E-1.

———, ed. 1983. *The Developing Labor Law: The Board, the Courts, and the National Labor Relations Act*. 2d ed. Washington, D.C.: Bureau of National Affairs.

Myers, Robert J., and Joseph W. Bloch. 1942. "Men's Clothing." In *How Collective Bargaining Works*, edited by Harry A. Millis, 381–449. New York: Twentieth Century Fund.

National Conference of Commissioners on Uniform State Laws. 1991. *Uniform Laws Annotated*. Vol. 7A, *Model Employment Termination Act*. St. Paul: West Publishing.

National Labor Relations Board. [1959] 1985. *Legislative History of the National Labor Relations Act, 1935*. Reprint. 2 vols. Washington, D.C.: GPO.

———. Fiscal 1976 to 1991. *Annual Reports*.

Nelson, Daniel. 1982. "The Company Union Movement: A Reexamination." *Business History Review* 56 (Autumn): 335–57.

Noble, Barbara Presley. 1993. "Worker Participation Programs Are Found Illegal." *New York Times*, June 8, A22.

Noble, David. 1984. *Forces of Production: A Social History of Industrial Automation*. New York: Oxford University Press.

O'Connor, Marleen A. 1993. "The Human Capital Era: Reconceptualizing Corporate Law to Facilitate Labor-Management Cooperation." *Cornell Law Review* 78: 899–965.

Ontario Labour Relations Board. 1980–81 to 1991–92. *Annual Reports*.

Ontario Ministry of Labour. 1991. "Proposed Reform of the Ontario Labour Relations Act: A Discussion Paper from the Minister of Labour." Toronto.

———. 1992a. *Bill 40*. Toronto: Queen's Printer for Ontario.

———. 1992b. "Ontario's Labour Reforms Get Final Approval." News release. Nov. 5.

Osterman, Paul. 1988. *Employment Futures*. New York: Oxford University Press.

Parker, Michael, and Jane Slaughter. 1988. *Choosing Sides: Unions and the Team Concept*. Boston: South End Press.

Parris, H. 1973. *Staff Relations in the Civil Service.* London: Her Majesty's Stationery Office.

"Participatory Management under Sections 2(5) and 8(a)(2) of the National Labor Relations Act." 1985. *Michigan Law Review* 83: 1736–69.

Pearce, Diana. 1987. "On the Edge: Marginal Women Workers and Employment Policy." In *Ingredients for Women's Employment Policy,* edited by Christine Bose and Glenna Spitze, 197–210. Albany: State University of New York Press.

Pelling, Henry. 1971. *A History of British Trade Unionism.* 2d ed. Hammondsworth, Middlesex: Penguin.

Perl, Arnold E. 1993. "Employee Involvement Groups: The Outcry over the NLRB's *Electromation* Decision." *Labor Law Journal* 44 (April): 195–207.

Perry, Charles R., Andrew M. Kramer, and Thomas J. Schneider. 1982. *Operating during Strikes.* Labor Relations and Public Policy Series 23. Philadelphia: Industrial Research Unit, Wharton School, University of Pennsylvania.

Phalen, Thomas F., Jr. 1986. "The Destabilization of Federal Labor Policy under the Reagan Board." *Labor Lawyer* 2 (1): 1–31.

Piore, Michael J. 1989. "Corporate Reform in American Manufacturing and the Challenge to Economic Theory." MIT Department of Economics Working Paper no. 533.

Piore, Michael J., and Charles Sabel. 1984. *The Second Industrial Divide: Possibilities for Prosperity.* New York: Basic Books.

Prosten, Richard. 1978. "The Longest Season: Union Organizing in the Last Decade, a/k/a How Come One Team Has to Play with Its Shoelaces Tied Together?" In *Proceedings of the Thirty-First Annual Meeting of the Industrial Relations Research Association,* 240–49. Madison, Wisc.: Industrial Relations Research Association.

"Quality Circle Busters." 1993. *Wall Street Journal,* June 9, A12.

Rathke, Wade, and Joel Rogers. 1993. "Labor Strategies." Typescript.

Reid Associates. 1989. "Canadian Public Opinion regarding the Organized Labour Movement: A Tracking Feature." *Reid Report* 4.

Richardson, Charles. 1993a. "Technology and Control in the Workplace." In *Technology for the Common Good,* edited by Michael Shuman and Julia Sweig. Washington, D.C.: Institute for Policy Studies.

———. 1993b. "When Only One Player Has to Follow the Rules: The Technological Assault on Collective Bargaining." *Workplace Topics* 3 (1): 33–54.

Riddell, W. Craig. 1993. "Unionization in Canada and the United States: A Tale of Two Countries." In *Small Differences That Matter: Labor Markets and Income Maintenance in Canada and the United States,* edited by David Card and Richard B. Freeman, 109–47. Chicago: University of Chicago Press.

Roberts, B. C. 1964. *Labour in the Tropical Territories of the Commonwealth.* London: Bell.

Robinson, Dwight. 1949. *Collective Bargaining and Market Control in the New York Coat and Suit Industry.* New York: Columbia University Press.

Robinson, Edward Ian. 1990. "Organizing Labour: Explaining Canada-U.S. Union Density Divergence in the Post-War Period." Ph.D. diss., Yale University.

Rogers, Joel. 1990. "Divide and Conquer: Further 'Reflections on the Distinctive Character of American Labor Laws.'" *Wisconsin Law Review* 1 (1): 1–147.

Rogers, Joel, and Charles Sabel. 1993. "Imagining Unions." *Boston Review* 18 (Oct./Nov.): 10–12.

Rogers, Joel, and Wolfgang Streeck. 1994a. "Producing Solidarity." In *Reinventing the Left,* edited by David Miliband. London: Polity Press.

———. 1994b. "Workplace Representation Overseas: The Works Councils Story." In *Working under Different Rules,* edited by Richard B. Freeman. New York: Russell Sage Foundation.

———. 1994c. *Works Councils: Consultation, Representation, Cooperation.* Chicago: University of Chicago Press and National Bureau of Economic Research.

Roomkin, Myron. 1981. "A Quantitative Study of Unfair Labor Practice Cases." *Industrial and Labor Relations Review* 34: 245–56.

Roomkin, Myron, and Dawn Harris. 1984. "Interindustry Patterns in Unfair Labor Practice Cases." *Journal of Labor Research* 5 (2): 113–26.

Rose, Joseph B., and Gary N. Chaison. 1985. "The State of the Unions: United States and Canada." *Journal of Labor Research* 6 (1): 97–111.

———. 1988. "The State of the Unions Revisited: The United States and Canada." In *Proceedings of the Twenty-Fourth Annual Meeting of the Canadian Industrial Relations Research Association,* 576–94. Hamilton: Canadian Industrial Relations Association.

———. 1990. "New Measures of Union Organizing Effectiveness." *Industrial Relations* 29 (Fall): 457–68.

Rosenthal, Robert. 1951. "Exclusions of Employees under the Taft-Hartley Act." *Industrial and Labor Relations Review* 4 (July): 556–70.

Ross, Philip. 1965. *The Government as a Source of Union Power: The Role of Public Policy in Collective Bargaining.* Providence: Brown University Press.

Rothstein, Richard. 1993. "New Bargain or No Bargain?" *American Prospect* 14 (Summer): 32–47.

Rubinstein, Saul, Michael Bennett, and Thomas Kochan. 1993. "The Saturn Partnership: Co-management and the Reinvention of the Local Union." In *Employee Representation: Alternatives and Future Directions,* edited by Bruce E. Kaufman and Morris M. Kleiner, 339–70. Madison, Wisc.: Industrial Relations Research Association.

St. Antoine, Theodore. 1980. "National Labor Policy: Reflections and Distortions of Social Justice." *Catholic University Law Review* 29: 535–56.

———. 1992. "Supreme Court Philosophy on Labor and Employment Issues." In *Proceedings of the Forty-Fourth Annual Meeting of the Industrial Relations Research Association,* 278–85. Madison, Wisc.: Industrial Relations Research Association.

Sales, Joseph E. 1984. "Replacing *Mackay:* Strikebreaking Acts and Other Assaults on the Permanent Replacement Doctrine." *Rutgers Law Review* 36: 861–86.

Saunders, John. 1992. "Bulldozing a Union." *Globe and Mail,* April 18, B1.

Schatzki, George. 1969. "Some Observations and Suggestions Concerning a Misnomer—'Protected' Concerted Activities." *Texas Law Review* 47: 378–403.

Schwartz, Ronald E. 1988. "Federal Chartering Revisited." *Michigan Journal of Law Reform* 22:7–18.

"Senate Vote Kills Bill to Restrict Use of Permanent Striker Replacements." 1992. *Employee Relations Weekly,* June 22, 647.

Service Employees International Union. Research Department. 1993. *Part-Time, Temporary and Contracted Work: Coping with the Growing Contingent Workforce.* Washington, D.C.

Sexton, Jean. 1991. "First Contract Arbitration: A Canadian Invention." In *Labour Arbitration Yearbook*, edited by William Kaplan, Jeffrey Sack, and Morley Gunderson, 231–40. Toronto: Butterworths and Lancaster House.

Shaiken, Harley. 1984. *Work Transformed: Automation and Labor in the Computer Age.* New York: Holt, Rinehart and Winston.

Shanker, Albert. 1985. *The Making of a Profession.* Washington, D.C.: American Federation of Teachers.

Shapiro, Barbara. 1980. "Sir Francis Bacon and the Mid-Seventeenth Century Movement for Law Reform." *American Journal of Legal History* 24: 331–62.

Shapiro, David L. 1965. "The Choice of Rulemaking or Adjudication in the Development of Administrative Policy." *Harvard Law Review* 78: 921–72.

Slichter, Sumner. 1941. *Union Policies and Industrial Management.* Washington, D.C.: Brookings Institution.

Smitka, Michael. 1991. *Competitive Ties.* New York: Columbia University Press.

Sockell, Donna. 1986. "The Scope of Mandatory Bargaining: A Critique and a Proposal." *Industrial and Labor Relations Review* 40 (Oct.): 19–34.

———. 1989. "The Future of Labor Law: A Mismatch between Statutory Interpretation and Industrial Reality?" *Boston College Law Review* 30: 987–1026.

———. 1991. "Research on Labor Law in the 1990s: The Challenge of Defining a Representational Form." In *The Future of Industrial Relations: Proceedings of the Second Bargaining Group Conference*, edited by Harry C. Katz, 120–38. Ithaca, N.Y.: Institute of Collective Bargaining, New York State School of Industrial Relations, Cornell University.

Spalter-Roth, Roberta M., and Heidi I. Hartmann. 1992. *Women in Telecommunications: Exception to the Rule of Low Pay for Women's Work.* Washington, D.C.: Institute for Women's Policy Research.

Spalter-Roth, Roberta, Heidi Hartmann, and Nancy Collins. 1994. *What Do Unions Do for Women?* Final report prepared for the Women's Bureau, U.S. Department of Labor. Washington, D.C.: Institute for Women's Policy Research.

State and Local Labor-Management Committee. 1993. *Labor-Management Cooperation in Today's Workplace.*

"Statement of Gary N. Chaison and Joseph B. Rose before the Subcommittee on Employment and Productivity of the Senate Committee on Labor and Human Resources, December 9, 1992." 1992. *Daily Labor Report*, Dec. 10, E1-E2.

Stinchcombe, Arthur L. 1959. "Bureaucratic and Craft Administration of Production." *Administrative Science Quarterly* 4 (Sept.): 168–87.

Stone, Katherine van Wezel. 1981. "The Post-War Paradigm in American Labor Law." *Yale Law Journal* 90: 1510–80.

Storper, Michael, and Bennett Harrison. 1991. "Flexibility, Hierarchy, and Regional Development: The Changing Structure of Industrial Production Systems and Their Forms of Governance in the 1990s." *Research Policy* 20 (Oct.): 407–22.

Sullivan, Teresa. 1989. "Women and Minorities in the New Economy: Optimistic, Pessimistic, and Mixed Scenarios." *Work and Occupations* 16 (Nov.): 393–415.

Summers, Clyde W. 1979. "Industrial Democracy: America's Unfulfilled Promise." *Cleveland State Law Review* 28: 29–49.

————. 1980. "Worker Participation in the U.S. and West Germany: A Comparative Study from an American Perspective." *American Journal of Comparative Law* 28: 367–92.

————. 1982. "Co-determination in the United States: A Projection of Problems and Potentials." *Journal of Comparative Corporate Law and Securities Regulation* 4: 155–91.

————. 1987. "An American Perspective of the German Model of Worker Participation." *Comparative Labor Law Journal* 8: 333–55.

————. 1990a. "Unions without a Majority." *Chicago-Kent Law Review* 66: 531–47.

————. 1990b. "Unions without Majorities: The Potentials of the NLRA." In *Proceedings of the Annual Meeting of the Industrial Relations Research Association,* 154–62. Madison, Wisc.: Industrial Relations Research Association.

Suskind, Ronald. 1992. "Threat of Cheap Labor Abroad Complicates Decisions to Unionize." *Wall Street Journal,* July 28, 1.

Swinnerton, Kenneth, and Howard Wial. 1993. "Is Job Stability Declining in the U.S. Economy?" Economic Discussion Paper no. 42. Bureau of International Labor Affairs, U.S. Department of Labor.

Taft, Philip. 1952. "Germany." In *Comparative Labor Movements,* edited by Walter Galenson, 243–312. New York: Prentice-Hall.

Tawney, R. H. 1979. *The American Labour Movement and Other Essays,* edited by J. M. Winter. New York: St. Martin's Press.

Taylor, Benjamin J. 1975. *Labor Relations Law.* Englewood Cliffs, N.J.: Prentice-Hall.

Taylor, Benjamin J., and Fred Witney. 1987. *Labor Relations Law.* Englewood Cliffs, N.J.: Prentice-Hall.

Taylor, Frederick. 1911. *Principles of Scientific Management.* New York: Harper and Brothers.

————. 1972. "Shop Management." In *Scientific Management, Comprising Shop Management, the Principles of Scientific Management, and Testimony before the Special House Committee.* Westport, Conn.: Greenwood Press.

Taylor, George W. 1948. *Government Regulation of Industrial Relations.* New York: Prentice-Hall.

Thieblot, Armand J., Jr. 1986. *Prevailing Wage Legislation, the Davis-Bacon Act, State "Little Davis-Bacon" Acts, the Walsh-Healey Act, and the Service Contract Act.* Philadelphia: Wharton School, Industrial Research Unit, University of Pennsylvania.

The Termination Report of the National War Labor Board: Industrial Disputes and Wage Stabilization in Wartime, January 12, 1942–December 31, 1945. 1947. Vols. 1–3. Washington D.C.: GPO.

Thelen, Kathleen A. 1991. *Union of Parts: Labor Politics in Postwar Germany.* Ithaca, N.Y.: Cornell University Press.

Thomason, Terry. 1993. "Managerial Opposition to Union Certification in Quebec and Ontario." Faculty of Management, McGill University. Typescript.

————. 1994. "Accelerated Certification Procedures and Their Effect on Union Organizing Success in Ontario." *Industrial and Labor Relations Review* 47 (Jan.): 207–26.

Tilly, Chris. 1991. Testimony on part-time and temporary work. Arbitration proceedings, U.S. Postal Service, National Association of Letter Carriers, and American Postal Workers Union, Washington, D.C., May 7.

———. 1992. "Short Hours, Short Shrift: Causes and Consequences of Part-Time Work." In *New Policies for the Part-Time and Contingent Workforce*, edited by Virginia duRivage, 15–44. Armonk, N.Y.: M. E. Sharpe.

Townley, Barbara. 1987. "Union Recognition: A Comparative Analysis of the Pros and Cons of a Legal Procedure." *British Journal of Industrial Relations* 15 (2): 177–99.

Troy, Leo. 1961. "Local Independent Unions and the American Labor Movement." *Industrial and Labor Relations Review* 14 (April): 331–49.

———. 1992. "Convergence in International Unionism: The Case of Canada and the USA." *British Journal of Industrial Relations* 30 (March): 1–43.

———. 1993. "Can Canada's Labor Policies Be a Model for the U.S.?" In *Proceedings of the Twenty-Eighth Conference of the Canadian Industrial Relations Association*, edited by Donald D. Carter, 59–64. Kingston: Canadian Industrial Relations Association.

Trevor-Roper, Hugh. 1967. "Three Foreigners: The Philosophy of the Puritan Revolution." In *Religion, the Reformation and Social Change, and Other Essays*, 244–45. London: Macmillan.

Turner, Lowell. 1991. *Democracy at Work: Changing World Markets and the Future of Labor Unions*. Ithaca, N.Y.: Cornell University Press.

Twining, William. 1985. *Karl Llewellyn and the Realist Movement*. Norman: University of Oklahoma Press.

"Union Membership Unchanged at 16.1 Percent of Employment." 1992. *Daily Labor Report*, Feb. 11, B1-B5.

U.S. Bureau of the Census. 1970. *Census of Population*.

———. 1987. *Census of Construction*.

———. 1989–91. *Current Population Survey*.

———. 1991. *Statistical Abstract of the United States*.

———. 1992. *1990 Census of Population: Equal Employment Opportunity Supplementary Report*.

U.S. Congress. 1959. *Legislative History of the Labor-Management Reporting and Disclosure Act of 1959*. 2 vols.

U.S. Congress. House. 1927. *Hours of Labor and Wages on Public Works*. Hearings before the Committee on Labor. 69th Cong., 2d sess., H.R. 17069.

U.S. Congress. House. Committee on Government Operations. 1984. *Has Labor Law Failed?* Pt. 2.

U.S. Congress. Joint Economic Committee. 1992. Families on a Treadmill. 1992.

U.S. Congress. Office of Technology Assessment. 1992. *U.S.-Mexico Trade: Pulling Together or Pulling Apart?*

U.S. Congress. Senate. Subcommittee of the Committee on Education and Labor. 1937. *Violations of Free Speech and Rights of Labor*. 75th Cong., 1st sess., pt. 17.

U.S. Department of Labor. Bureau of Labor Statistics. 1980. *Directory of National Unions and Employee Associations, 1979*.

———. 1989. *Employment and Earnings*.

———. 1991. *Employment and Earnings*.

———. 1992. *Employment and Earnings*.

———. 1993a. *A Briefing for the Commission on the Future of Worker-Management Relations*.

————. 1993b. *Employment and Earnings.*

U.S. General Accounting Office. 1982. *Concerns regarding the Impact of Employee Charges against Employers for Unfair Labor Practices.*

————. 1989. *Tax Administration Information Returns Can Be Used to Identify Employers Who Misclassify Employees.* Report to Congress.

U.S. Congress. House. 1927. *Hours of Labor and Wages on Public Works. Hearings before the Committee on Labor.* 69th Cong., 2d sess., H.R. 17069.

U.S. Congress. Senate. Subcommittee of the Committee on Education and Labor. 1937. *Violations of Free Speech and Rights of Labor.* 75th Cong., 1st sess., pt. 17.

U.S. National Labor Relations Board. 1983. *Case-Handling Manual.* Vol. 1, *Unfair Labor Practices.*

Voos, Paula, Adrienne Eaton, and Dale Belman. 1993. "Reforming Labor Law to Remove Barriers to High-Performance Work Organization." *Labor Law Journal* 44 (Aug.): 469–76.

Walker, Julian. 1987. *First Agreement Disputes and Public Policy in Canada.* Kingston, Ont.: Industrial Relations Center, Queen's University.

Weil, David. 1991. "Enforcing OSHA: The Role of Labor Unions." *Industrial Relations* 30: 20–36.

Weiler, Paul C. 1980. *Reconcilable Differences: New Directions in Canadian Labour Law.* Toronto: Carswell.

————. 1983. "Promises to Keep: Securing Workers' Rights to Self-Organization under the NLRA." *Harvard Law Review* 96: 1769–1827.

————. 1984. "Striking a New Balance: Freedom of Contract and the Prospects for Union Representation." *Harvard Law Review* 98: 351–420.

————. 1985. "Milestone or Millstone: The Wagner Act at Fifty." In *Arbitration 1985: Law and Practice,* edited by Walter J. Gershenfeld. Washington, D.C.: Bureau of National Affairs.

————. 1986. "Milestone or Tombstone: The Wagner Act at Fifty." *Harvard Journal on Legislation* 23 (1): 1–31.

————. 1990. *Governing the Workplace: The Future of Labor and Employment Law.* Cambridge: Harvard University Press.

————. 1993. "Governing the Workplace: Employee Representation in the Eyes of the Law." In *Employee Representation: Alternatives and Future Directions,* edited by Bruce E. Kaufman and Morris M. Kleiner, 81–104. Madison, Wisc.: Industrial Relations Research Association.

Weiler, Paul, and Guy Mundlak. 1993. "New Directions for the Law of the Workplace." *Yale Law Journal* 102: 1907–25.

Westfall, David. 1991. "Striker Replacement and Employee Freedom of Choice." *Labor Lawyer* 7 (1): 137–58.

Wheeler, Raymond L., and Patricia Murray. 1991. "Mergers, Acquisitions, and Takeovers: Labor Relations Consequences of Corporate Transactions." *Labor Lawyer* 7 (1): 111–35.

Wheeler, Russell R., and Howard R. Whitcomb, eds. 1977. *Judicial Administration: Text and Readings.* Englewood Cliffs, N.J.: Prentice-Hall.

Wial, Howard. 1993. "The Emerging Organizational Structure of Unionism in Low-Wage Services." *Rutgers Law Review* 45 (Spring): 671–738.

Winbury, Rex. 1975. *New Technology and the Press: A Study of Experience in the United States.* London: HMSO.

Windolf, Paul. 1989. "Productivity Coalitions and the Future of Corporatism." *Industrial Relations* 28 (Winter): 1–20.

Witte, Edwin E. 1946. "Wartime Handling of Labor Disputes." *Harvard Business Review* 25: 169–89.

Womack, James, Daniel Jones, and Daniel Roos. 1991. *The Machine That Changed the World.* New York: HarperCollins.

Woods, H. D. 1973. *Labour Policy in Canada.* 2d ed. Toronto: Macmillan.

Woods, H. D., et al. 1969. *Task Force on Labour Relations.* Ottawa: Information Canada.

Zimmerman, Don A. 1985. "Restoring Stability in the Implementation of the NLRA." *Labor Lawyer* 1 (1): 1–18.

Zuboff, Shoshanna. 1988. *In the Age of the Smart Machine.* New York: Basic Books.

Zurofsky, Bennet D. 1987. "Repudiation of Collective Bargaining Agreements in Bankruptcy: A Practical History and Guide for Union Representatives." *Labor Lawyer* 3 (4): 809–18.

———. 1992. "Everything Old Is New Again: Company Unions in the Era of Employee Involvement Programs." *Labor Lawyer* 8: 381–404.

About the Contributors

Roy J. Adams is a professor of industrial relations at McMaster University and an associate member of the Centre for Industrial Relations at the University of Toronto. He has been published in many industrial relations journals and is the editor of two books, *Comparative Industrial Relations: Contemporary Research and Theory* and, with Noah Meltz, *Industrial Relations Theory: Its Nature, Scope and Pedagogy.* He is also a consultant to various Canadian government and quasi-government agencies and is the editor of the *Comparative Industrial Relations Newsletter.*

Hamid Azari-Rad is a doctoral student in the Department of Economics at the University of Utah. In his work for the Labor Resource Center at the University of Utah, Azari-Rad is developing a database on union wages and benefits in construction since the late 1960s. His dissertation consists of three essays that relate macroeconomic instability to the behavior of firms, with a focus on construction labor markets.

Richard N. Block is a professor in the School of Labor and Industrial Relations at Michigan State University and an active arbitrator. He has written extensively on union administration, industrial relations and structural economic change, labor arbitration, employee privacy, and government-sponsored employee training. Block is also on the executive committee of the Industrial Relations Council on GOALS, a partnership of corporations, unions, and universities dedicated to recruiting minority members into industrial relations.

David Brody is a professor emeritus at the University of California at Davis and is also associated with the Institute of Industrial Relations at the University of California at Berkeley and with the George Meany Center. The author of dozens of articles and books on labor history, including *Workers in Industrial America: Essays on the Twentieth Century Struggle,* he has most recently written *In Labor's Cause: Main Themes on the History of the American Worker.*

Kate L. Bronfenbrenner is a senior extension associate at the New York State School of Industrial and Labor Relations at Cornell University, where she works with national unions in the areas of organizing, contract campaigns, contract administration, and leadership development. Before coming to Cornell, she was a labor education coordinator at Penn State University and an organizer and business agent with the United Woodcutters Association and with the SEIU. Recently, she and Tom Juravich completed a nationwide project, sponsored by the Public Employee Department of the AFL-CIO, on organizing in the public sector.

Peter G. Bruce is an assistant professor of political science at the College of the Holy Cross. Bruce has written on parties, state structures, and labor law in North America and is the author of the often-cited "Political Parties and Labor Legislation in Canada and the United States," published in *Industrial Relations*. His most recent article is "State Structures and the Processing of Unfair Labor Practice Cases in the United States and Canada" in *The Challenge of Re-Structuring: North American Labor Movements Respond*.

Françoise J. Carré is a research associate at the Center for Labor Research and the Mauricio Gaston Institute at the University of Massachusetts at Boston. Her research focuses on employer strategies and government policy with regard to temporary and short-term clerical employment in the United States and France. She is the author of several articles on temporary and short-term employment as well as of a commissioned paper for the Department of Labor's Women's Bureau Symposium on Women and Labor Law Reform.

Gary N. Chaison is a professor of industrial relations at the Graduate School of Management at Clark University, where he has been a faculty member since 1981. Before joining the faculty of Clark, Chaison taught for eight years at the University of New Brunswick. The author of *When Unions Merge*, Chaison has recently been conducting a comparative analysis of the state of North American labor movements, the development of the concept of union legitimacy, and a survey of union mergers in several countries.

Dorothy Sue Cobble is the director of the Center for Women and Work at Rutgers University. She is also an associate professor at the Institute of Management and Labor Relations, where she teaches industrial relations, history, and women's studies. The author of *Dishing It Out: Waitresses and Their Unions in the Twentieth Century*, winner of the 1992 Herbert A. Gutman Award, and the editor of *Women and Unions: Forging a Partnership*, she is especially interested in labor-management relations in the service sector and in the impact on women of the transition to a postindustrial economy.

Nancy Collins is a mathematical statistician in the Statistics of Income (SOI) Division of the Internal Revenue Service, where she measures the effect of nonsampling error on SOI estimates. Her interests and expertise are in the area of quality control and the various social and economic issues that affect women's lives. She also serves as a consultant to the Institute for Women's Policy Research.

Phil Comstock is the director of polling and demographic analysis for the United Food and Commercial Workers International Union and executive director of the Wilson Center for Public Research. He has written on a wide range of labor-related topics, including how professional workers view unions, employee stock ownership plans, and immigration policy, for a variety of publications, such as *Interface* and the *Journal of the Institute for Socioeconomic Studies*.

Virginia duRivage is a research fellow at the Institute for the Study of Labor Organizations at the George Meany Center and in the doctoral program in the Department of Sociology at Johns Hopkins University. She is the editor of the Economic Policy Institute volume *New Policies for the Part-Time and Contingent Workforce* and a member of the institute's research council.

Maier B. Fox is associate director for analysis at the Wilson Center for Public Research. He is the author of *United We Stand: The United Mine Workers of America, 1890–1990*, as well as the coauthor of articles on coal mining, including "Fatality Rates and Regulatory Policies in Bituminous Coal Mining, 1959–1981," published in the *American Journal of Public Health*, and "Reckless Deregulation in the Coal Mines," in *Business and Society Review*.

Sheldon Friedman is an economist in the Department of Economic Research of the AFL-CIO, where he has been since 1991. Before that, Friedman was research director for the United Auto Workers in Detroit. He has also served on the national executive board of the Industrial Relations Research Assocation.

Patricia A. Greenfield is director of the Labor Relations and Research Center at the University of Massachusetts at Amherst. She holds a Ph.D. from the New York State School of Industrial and Labor Relations at Cornell University and a J.D. from the Washington University School of Law. Recent publications include "Representatives of Their Own Choosing: Finding Workers' Voice in the Legitimacy and Power of Unions," with Robert Pleasure, in the 1993 IRRA annual research volume; and "How Do Arbitrators Treat External Law?" in *Industrial and Labor Relations Review*.

James A. Gross is a professor in the School of Industrial Relations at Cornell University. The author of *The Making of the National Labor Relations Board* and *The Reshaping of the National Labor Relations Board*, he is completing the third and final book in the series. The author of many articles on labor law and labor arbitration, he is also a member of the National Academy of Arbitrators and of the labor arbitration panels of the American Arbitration Association, the Federal Mediation and Conciliation Service, and the Public Employment Relations Board.

Gladys W. Gruenberg, a professor emeritus of economics and industrial relations at Saint Louis University, is a full-time labor arbitrator. While at Saint Louis University, she was co-director of the Personnel and Industrial Relations Program in the School of Business and Administration. She has served as regional chair and governor of the

National Academy of Arbitrators and editor of its annual proceedings and has also edited and authored several books and articles in the fields of human resources and labor economics.

Heidi Hartmann is director of the Washington-based Institute for Women's Policy Research. Trained as an economist, Hartmann also lectures widely to women's organizations, labor unions, community and business groups, and universities on public policy, feminist theory, and the political economy of gender. She is widely published in the United States and abroad on employment and other economic issues affecting women.

Richard W. Hurd is a professor and director of the labor studies program at the New York State School of Industrial and Labor Relations at Cornell University. He has published numerous articles on union political and organizing strategies, including "Organizing and Representing Clerical Workers: The Harvard Model," in *Women and Unions*; "Organizing Clerical Workers: Determinants of Success," with Adrienne McElwain, in *Industrial and Labor Relations Review*; and "Strategic Diversity in Labor PAC Contribution Patterns," with Jeffrey Sohl, in *Social Science Journal*.

Morris M. Kleiner is a professor of public affairs and industrial relations at the University of Minnesota. He has been on the faculty of the University of Kansas, a staff associate in employment policy at the Brookings Institution, and a member of the Labor Studies Program at the National Bureau of Economic Research. He is the coauthor or coeditor of *Labor Markets and Human Resource Management*, *Human Resources and the Performance of the Firm*, *Labor Market Institutions and the Future Role of Unions*, and *Employee Representation: Alternatives and Future Directions*.

Robert B. Moberly is a professor of law at the University of Florida College of Law. He is the author of two books and more than twenty-five articles on labor relations and dispute resolution. Much of his recent work, some of it funded by the U.S. Department of Labor, has focused on worker participation and labor-management cooperation.

Rudolph A. Oswald is the director of economic research for the AFL-CIO. Oswald is on various government advisory bodies, including the Advisory Committee on Trade Negotiations, the Panel of Economic Advisers to the Congressional Budget Office, and the Labor Advisory Committee to the Bureau of Labor Statistics, and is on the boards of the National Bureau of Economic Research, the National Planning Association, and the Joint Council on Economic Education.

Gordon R. Pavy is an associate coordinator for the Industrial Union Department of the AFL-CIO. He has also worked for the United Automobile Workers and the International Brotherhood of Teamsters.

Peter Philips is a professor of economics at the University of Utah. Philips has coedited, with Garth Mangum, *The Three Worlds of Labor Economics* and, with Martin

Brown, has written extensively on the U.S. canning industry, including "Industrialization, Unionization and the Labor Market Structure in the California Canneries," in the *Industrial and Labor Relations Review*, and "Mechanization, Unionization and the Decline of the Piece Rate System in the California Canneries" in *Industrial Relations*. Philips also writes on labor market discrimination.

Robert J. Pleasure is executive director of the George Meany Center and chair of labor studies in the McGregor School at Antioch University. His recent publications include "Representatives of Their Own Choosing: Finding Workers' Voice in the Legitimacy and Power of Unions," with Patricia Greenfield, in the 1993 annual research volume of the Industrial Relations Research Association, and *Construction Organizing*.

Charley Richardson is the director of the Technology and Work Program at the University of Massachusetts at Lowell, which provides training, technical support, and strategic planning assistance to unions and workers dealing with technological change, work reorganization, and quality and involvement initiatives. It also conducts research into and plays an active role in policy discussions on the impact of new technologies on the workplace. Richardson has also worked as a shipfitter in three different shipyards and served as a union shop steward.

Joseph B. Rose is a professor of industrial relations at the DeGroote School of Business at McMaster University. His research interests include trade unions, labor policy, construction labor relations, and dispute settlement. He is the author of *Public Policy, Bargaining Structure and the Construction Industry* and has been published widely in academic journals, including *Industrial Relations, Industrial and Labor Relations Review*, and *Relations Industrielles*. He also serves as an arbitrator in labor-management disputes.

James R. Rundle is the central New York labor education coordinator for the Division of Extension and Public Service in the New York State School of Industrial and Labor Relations at Cornell University. He has taught courses on contemporary labor issues, labor law, and labor history for Cornell's Labor Studies Program and has led workshops and seminars for union members on a variety of topics, including unions and employee involvement, building solidarity in the local union, contract campaigns, and civil rights in the workplace. He has also worked as an activist in union organizing campaigns.

Joel Rogers is a professor of law, political science, and sociology at the University of Wisconsin at Madison, where he directs the Center on Wisconsin Strategy. He has written widely on democratic theory and American politics and public policy, including, with Thomas Ferguson, *Right Turn: The Decline of the Democrats*, and, with Joshua Cohen, *The Future of American Politics*. Rogers's research includes studies of intercorporate litigation in the United States and alternative systems of labor representation. Rogers also serves as a consultant to the Labor and Human Resources Committee of the U.S. Senate.

Ronald L. Seeber is a professor and associate dean of the New York State School of Industrial and Labor Relations at Cornell University. Seeber's research activities have covered a wide range of topics, including the impact of technological change on labor relations in arts and entertainment, drug testing in the workplace, and union organizing strategies. The author or coauthor of three books, he has also been published extensively in scholarly academic journals and in the proceedings of the Industrial Relations Research Association.

Roberta Spalter-Roth is director of research at the Institute for Women's Policy Research and an assistant professor in the Department of Sociology at the American University. She has written extensively and delivered congressional testimony and participated in staff briefings on employment equity, family and work policies, and welfare reform.

Chris Tilly is an assistant professor of policy and planning at the University of Massachusetts at Lowell. He has written extensively on part-time work, low-wage service work, earnings inequality, and poverty and serves on the editorial board of *Dollars and Sense* magazine. He is co-principal investigator of the Greater Boston Social Survey of the Multi-City Study of Urban Inequality.

Joseph B. Uehlein is the executive assistant to the president of the Industrial Union Department of the AFL-CIO. He first came to the department in 1975 as an intern and has served in many capacities since then. In addition to his duties with the IUD, Uehlein serves as secretary to the North American Coordinating Committee of the International Federation of Chemical, Energy, and General Workers Unions and as president of the Labor Heritage Foundation, an organization dedicated to promoting the use of art and music as organizational tools in the labor movement.

Howard Wial is currently with the U.S. Department of Labor. He is the author of "The Emerging Organizational Structure of Unionism in Low-Wage Services" in *Rutgers Law Review* and of other articles on labor markets and industrial relations.

Anne Yeagle is a doctoral student in the Department of Economics at the University of Utah. As a member of the Labor Resource Center at the University of Utah, she has researched various local labor market issues. Yeagle's dissertation is an economic history of the passage, administration, and repeal of Utah's prevailing wage law.

Index

Action committees: as worker participation program, 150–55. See also employee participation committees
actual liberty of contract. See liberty of contract
administrative occupations: emphasis on in training programs, 216–17; unionized women in, 198–99; women's reduced wages in, 201–2. See also management; occupations
advertising: as antiunion tactic, 83, 87. See also union avoidance campaign
Aero Metal Forms, union avoidance campaign at, 62–63
affirmative action: negotiations for by unionized women, 206. See also minorities; women
African-Americans: civil rights protection for, 5; impact on of employer pressure, 101. See also civil rights; minorities
Aiello Dairy Farms, 179
air traffic controllers, 90, 119. See also replacement workers
Akron (Ohio), organizing campaign in, 36
Amalgamated Association of Iron, Steel and Tin Workers, 228
Amalgamated Clothing and Textile Workers Union (ACTWU): multiemployer bargaining procedures of, 307–8; organizing efforts by, 63, 64–65, 67
American Civil Liberties Union (ACLU), Wagner Act and, 33
American Federation of Labor (AFL), acceptance of NWLB policies by, 262
American Federation of Labor-Congress of Industrial Organizations (AFL-CIO): Committee on the Evolution of Work, 111; Department of Economic Research, 4; Industrial Union Department (IUD) survey, 6, 7, 61–74, 110; involvement of with labor law reform, 54–55; prevailing wage law campaign of, 207–8; publication of The Changing Situation of Workers and Their Unions, 243; relationship of to Democratic party, 52;

resistance of employers to, 76–89; wrongful-discharge proposals of, 128–29. See also labor movement; labor organizations; unions
American Federation of State, County and Municipal Employees (AFSCME): organizing campaign by, 65–66, 318. See also public employees
American Law Institute (ALI), 133–35
Andrew Jergens Co., 182
antiunion activity: as basis for automatic certification, 244–45; bribes as, 83, 84, 88; codification of in Wagner Act, 33; comparisons of, in U.S. and Canada, 10–11; by consultants and lawyers, 6–7, 62, 65–66, 70, 80–81, 84, 91, 111, 115–16; effect of on unions' decline, 16; effect of on worker interest in unionization, 7, 98–99, 273; labor law violations and, 66–69; legal delays as, 64–69, 86, 281–82; legal incentives for, 254–55; managerial commitment to, 4, 6, 61–74, 139–40, 165; Section 8(a)(2) violations as, 4–5, 8–9. See also unfair labor practices; union avoidance campaigns
antiunion committees: use of as antiunion tactic, 7, 80, 82, 88. See also employee participation committees
apprenticeship training: effect on of prevailing wage, 9–10; effect on of prevailing wage repeal, 212–17; nonunion programs for, 217–18; in union/nonunion environment, 217–20. See also education; skills; training
arbitrary treatment: requirements for protection against, 55–56, 57. See also civil rights; discrimination; social justice
arbitration: compulsory conciliation and, 242; as contribution of collective bargaining, 55; for expediting labor-management agreement, 19, 185–86; government guarantees required for, 56, 87, 258–59; NLRB deferral to, 186–87, 188; requirements for in Canadian policy, 242–43, 245–46

of at Saturn, 307, 308–9; organizing
efforts by, 69
United Food and Commercial Workers (UFCW),
organizing efforts by, 62–63, 70–71
United Mine Workers of America (UMWA),
organizing efforts by, 67, 71
United Paperworkers International Union
(UPIU), organizing efforts by, 70
United States: blacklisting in for union organizers, 140; economic interest of served by labor
framework, 3; effect on of prevailing wage law
repeal, 214; labor policy of, compared to
Canada, 241–42; law reform tradition of,
126; New Deal fiscal/monetary policy of, 17;
requirements for promotion of collective
bargaining in, 4; union membership in,
compared to Canada, 250; union membership
in, compared to Europe, 193; workers' rights
for organizing in, compared to Canada, 273–
82. *See also* government; society; state
United States Steel Corp., 34–35
United Steel Workers of America (USWA),
organizing efforts by, 65
United Technologies, 186
U.S. Commission on Industrial Relations, 32
Utah: prevailing wage law repeal in, 9–10,
207–22. *See also* prevailing wages

violence: effect on of replacement workers, 247–
48. *See also* replacement workers; strikes
vocational programs: effect on of prevailing wage
repeal, 215–17. *See also* skills upgrading;
training
voice. *See* worker voice

wage increases: collective action for producing,
15–16; as employer antiunion tactic, 7, 76,
80, 82, 86; employer reporting requirements
for, 182, 184; equivalency of to employer
penalties, 140–42; probability of affecting
union elections, 144; relationship of to
democratic productivism, 24; social benefits
of, under New Deal system, 17, 180; social
benefits of, under unionism, 193; as spur to
dynamic efficiencies, 21
wages: comparison of, for union/nonunion
workers, 90; distinguishing from social benefit
minima, 21; effect on of computerization, 228;
effect on of technological change, 227; effect
on of union membership, 195; erosion of in
present economy, 20, 96; male-female
disparity of, 9; merit pay, 301; nonunion
workers' dissatisfaction with, 94, 95–96; for
part-time workers, 316; prevailing wages,
144, 145; prevailing wages, referendum campaign against, 176; provisions for under
Section 7(a), 37; regulatory mechanisms for,
18; "social wages," 5–6, 21; stabilization of
under union contracts, 193–94, 292; uniformity of enhancing career security, 25, 26;
for women, 200–203; for younger workers,
97. *See also* prevailing wages

Wagner Act: actual language of, 3; collective
bargaining provisions of, 178–80; effect of on
union density rates, 277–78; history of, 31–
44; inappropriateness of to "new economic
realities," 15; intention of for industrial peace,
158; majority status requirements of, 262;
prohibition of employer-dominated labor
organizations under, 6, 148; relationship of to
Norris-La Guardia Act, 32; Section 8(a)(2)
and origins of, 39–42; Section 8(a)(2)
violations of in company-dominated unions,
4, 8–9; social justice premises of, 55. *See also*
National Labor Relations Act; Taft-Hartley
Act; specific Sections of Act
West Coast Industrial Relations Association
(WCIRA), management use of in union-
avoidance campaigns, 66
white-collar unions: evolution of in Sweden,
267; expanding role of, 194, 197; organizing
difficulties in, 288. *See also* unions
white male workers: effect on of employer
pressure, 101; declining role for in unionism,
194; trade unionism representation benefits
for, 11. *See also* men; women; workers
Whitin Machine Works, 184
Wilson Center: nonunion worker interviews by,
7; preorganizing-early organizing questionnaire of, 103–9; workplace organization
studies of, 91–96
women: benefits to from unions, 11, 193–206,
291–302; in blue-collar workforce, 199;
education level of, compared to men, 198–
200; effect of unionization on wages of, 9,
200–205; effect on of employer pressure, 101;
equal rights protection for, 5; exclusion of
from NLRA protection, 289–90; expanding
role for in unionism, 194, 197, 302; interest
of in unionization, 7, 9, 95; negotiations of for
affirmative action, 206; percentage of as union
workers, 194–95, 196–97; service industries
employment of, 199, 285–87; training
program emphasis for, 216–17; union
membership of affecting job security, 203–5;
union membership distribution table for, 198.
See also gender biases
Worker Adjustment and Retraining Notification
(WARN) Act, 131
worker committee. *See* employee participation
committee
worker participation committee. *See* employee
participation committee
workers: autonomy for in workplace governance,
18, 263; decrease of demands for unions by, 3;
as distinct from management under Wagner
Act, 16; effect on of employer pressure, 4, 19,
101; empowerment of for career security, 25,
26–27; European, 20; expanded range of
influence for, 23, 130–31, 147; expansion for
definition of under NLRA, 294; high-wage,
job security gains for, 203–4; high-wage,
unionization rates for, 197; involvement of in
new-model union, 27; low-wage, job security

ADF 0206   5/21/96

KF
3389
A2
R47
1994